Retirement Without Borders

How to Retire Abroad

in Mexico, France, Italy, Spain, Costa Rica, Panama,

and Other Sunny Foreign Places

(And the Secret to Making It Happen Without Stress)

BARRY GOLSON

WITH THIA GOLSON AND EXPERT EXPATS

SCRIBNER

New York   London   Toronto   Sydney

SCRIBNER
A Division of Simon & Schuster, Inc.
1230 Avenue of the Americas
New York, NY 10020

First Scribner trade paperback edition December 2008

SCRIBNER and design are registered trademarks of
The Gale Group, Inc., used under license
by Simon & Schuster, Inc., the publisher of this work.

For information about special discounts for bulk purchases,
please contact Simon & Schuster Special Sales:
1-800-456-6798 or business@simonandschuster.com.

Designed by Kyoko Watanabe
Text set in Minion

Manufactured in the United States of America

1   3   5   7   9   10   8   6   4   2

Library of Congress Control Number: 2008025968

ISBN-13: 978-0-7432-9701-1
ISBN-10: 0-7432-9701-6

Disclaimer

This publication contains the opinions and ideas of its authors. It is intended to provide helpful and informative material on the subjects addressed in the publication. It is sold with the understanding that the author and publisher are not engaged in rendering legal, finacial, insurance, health, or any other kind of personal professional services in the book. The reader should consult his or her legal, financial, insurance, health, or other competent professional before adopting any of the suggestions in this book or drawing inferences from it.

Although every attempt was made to ensure the accuracy of information contained in the publication, the author and publisher cannot accept responsibility for any outdated or inaccurate information, or for the content of any third-party websites referenced herein.

No warranty is made with respect to the accuracy or completeness of the information contained herein, and the authors and publisher specifically disclaim all responsibility for any liability, loss, or risk, personal or otherwise, which is incurred as a consequence, directly or indirectly, of the use and application of any of the contents of this book.

Think out of the box—
or outside your borders

- You've always dreamed of a tropical garden, and you figure that if you retire to Arizona, you'll finally be able to grow vegetables in the winter months.

    _Or_ you could move to Panama, near the rain forest, and grow orchids while you work at saving the timberland by the canal.

- You're retiring in North Carolina, and you love traveling in Europe, so you set enough money aside to plan a ten-day package tour to Italy or Spain.

    _Or_ you could live in an old farmhouse in Provence, where you'll plan long, adventurous road trips to out-of-the-way regions of Italy and Spain.

- You're retiring to a condo in Tampa, where you'll join the local beautification committee and attend your bridge club several times a week.

    _Or_ you could move to Nicaragua and live in a lovely, affordable house by the beach, where you'll tutor the neighborhood's neediest kids several times a week.

Contents

Country by Country
Prepare to Submerge

Retirement Without Borders

PROLOGUE

Ever since we, your authors and guides, passed a certain age, we've been stumbling over retirement books. Retire-on-less books, retire-in-sunny-places books, retire-and-rejoice books, retire-and-do-work-that-you-love books, retire-in-quaint-places books, retire-overseas books. The business is booming.

Why not? It's one thing we can absolutely count on. In some form, whether we keep working at something or kick back, we will eventually "retire" to another phase of our life. It's a growth industry. As the man in *The Graduate* might say today, "I've got one word for you, Benjamin: retirement." We are all on the same campus together, and we'll begin graduating with the class of 2010, when seventy-six million baby boomers start turning sixty-five. A new adventure begins.

This book is about retiring beyond U.S. (and Canadian) borders. It is also about retiring beyond the borders of your own experience, to explore how moving to a different culture in your later years can revitalize, enhance, and extend your life. It will examine the fantasy so many of us may have shared: moving to an exotic new locale; creating new interests, new friendships, and a new life; buying or building a house in a foreign land; living the romantic expatriate life. We're here to help you consider whether you want to take those first few steps. Here, amid the locations we've chosen for their potential to stir your inner Huckleberry Finn, you may find a way to light out for a new territory of your own. Not to mention your Ernest Hemingway, sipping his Pernod in a Paris café.

As our baby-boom generation begins to trade in what we've *had* to do for what we *want* to do, we are asking ourselves questions that will affect the rest of our lives:

- How do we want to live the time we have left—which may be as much as a third of our life span?
- Will we have the funds to live, if not lavishly, at least close to the level to which we've been accustomed?

1

- Do we want to continue living where, and how, we always have—or seek out something fresh, something challenging, something unlike what's come before?
- If we're looking for warmer nests, as so many of us do at a certain age, are we fated to become snowbirds shuttling back and forth on delayed, overbooked flights to Florida and Arizona?
- Will we ever have a chance to follow the dream many of us have harbored to explore other countries, experience other customs, immerse ourselves in other cultures?
- And for some of us, can we find places to live where we can express a new part of ourselves, contribute, or help change lives where the need is greatest?

We say: try living abroad, grasshoppers.

We did it ourselves. We bought a piece of land in Mexico on the strength—truth be told, on the *impulse*—of a couple of visits. In the first year we lived there, we built a beautiful home just off the beach. We are famously proud of it. One of us even wrote a book—*Gringos in Paradise*—about our first twelve months in *Sayulita,* on Mexico's Pacific coast. We worked mano a mano with our Mexican construction chief, building in the manner of a small Mexican village. Which could mean that while husband was bringing back a pile of bank pesos for our builder in an empty Cheetos bag (the economy in that part of the country runs strictly on cash), wife was in **Puerto Vallarta**, chasing down toilet seats. It was exhilarating, thrilling, challenging, fun.

But we wouldn't do it again. Not that way.

We've been part-time and full-time expatriates; we love the life, we love our friends and our Mexican home. But here's a hard truth: during the year that we spent building our house, we *didn't have one stress-free day.* Nor did most people we knew who built or—often—who bought. It was fine for writing the book. We had a saying: bad for life, good for book. In the retelling, our adventure was both funny and fulfilling. Loved it, got through it, whew! But in life, the toll on our nerves was high.

The dream of moving to an exotic, foreign land is equal parts fantasy and fear.

Here are the fantasies:
- You're lying on the beach in front of the whitewashed, thatch-roofed house you built near **Puerto Vallarta**, sipping a coconut

drink, and when the fishing ketch pulls up, you stroll over and buy the fresh red snapper you'll eat tonight . . .
- You're on the roof of the villa you rented for the first year in *Tuscany,* seeing the sun set over the red-tiled roofs of the hill town, listening to the sounds of an Italian mandolin serenade . . .
- You're on the porch of your spanking-new bed-and-breakfast in a mountain town of Panama, watching the hummingbirds hover over the hyacinth, awaiting this weekend's guests . . .

Here are the fears:
- Where do you go?
- How do you choose?
- Did you do enough research?
- Do you trust the research you did?
- You've sold your stuff and moved to an unfamiliar place!
- You don't know the language!
- You don't know the customs!
- You don't know what will happen if you get sick!
- You miss your family and friends!
- You can't buy the stuff you know and love!
- You want to buy a house but don't have any idea if it's priced right.
- You don't understand how mortgages work here!
- You're sinking a big part of your nest egg into this property!
- You don't know which way real estate prices will go!
- You don't know who's taking advantage of you!
- The people aren't as friendly as you'd hoped!
- You don't know whom to turn to for help!
- You've started to build but have no control over the final costs!
- You don't know if you have clear title!
- You don't know if you got the right permits!
- Can the government take it away from you?
- The currency might be devalued!
- Will you be able to sell easily if you change your mind?
- Will you owe capital gains?
- You've put your savings at risk!
- You're stuck there!
- You've burned your bridges!

- You're thousands of miles away and just made the biggest mistake of your life!
- In short, *you don't know the drill*!

Now, here's a fact: You *can* live the fantasy without the fear. There's a formula, a strategy that will make this possible. It will free you to consider more places than you thought possible. If it's right for you, that is. Because, honestly, it's not for everyone.

The goal of this book is fourfold:
- To consider the dream
- To explore the dream
- To show you the dream in selected countries
- To tell you honestly what the pitfalls are

We *don't* try to do it all. We won't be giving you all the gritty details of tax codes, or the step-by-steps of relocation. (Just some.) The more specific a printed book gets, the more likely it is that it will be obsolete, and that comes with this territory. Although there are lots of how-to books and informational websites out there, our main purpose is to get you thinking, to *start* the conversation.

There are wonderful, life-enhancing reasons to consider retiring abroad, and we'll share those with you. But there's also a lot of disinformation out there, and the internet has multiplied it exponentially. If some of you decide after reading this that life abroad is *not* for you, we'll be doing our job. Not just for you, but for expatriates already in place. We've often heard old hands lamenting the waves of eager, naive Americans who arrive with stars in their eyes. They believe they can live abroad like aristocrats on just their Social Security; they believe they can transplant their lives intact to foreign soil; they believe they can throw their often-hefty American weight around to change how things are done; they cannot wait to be serviced cheaply by a maid, a cook, a gardener. And so on. They end up disappointed, get hustled, complain a lot, give Americans a bad name, and often end up returning to the United States or Canada, leaving a bad taste in everyone's mouths.

We'll talk about this, consider all the pros and cons, and give you the general information you need to make a decision right for you. We'll offer you that "secret" formula we think can make all the difference. This book will look at the overall considerations of moving abroad, what countries might be a good fit for you, and what steps you can take to begin the journey.

We have chosen ten countries to cover in depth. Here, we *do* offer detail with the proviso that you know—and we know—that by the time you read this, some of the particulars will be out of date. Our purpose is to give you an immersive picture of retired life in each country, including prices current in 2008. But we need to say it again: you'll need to update much of it on the ground and online.

Your options are, of course, not limited to these countries; they are merely a range of venues amenable to North American retirees. Though we've spent much of our lives abroad, we haven't lived in all of these countries. So for these in-depth chapters, we recruited experienced writers who have lived in, and reported extensively on, each country. Old hands on the ground are *always* the best sources of information—better than official sources, better than tourist organizations, better than commercial enterprises—for the "unofficial" version of retired life in their adopted countries. (Caveat: when the "unofficial" advice you get is in *any* way about major financial or legal steps, the very next piece of advice to seek is, who's a reliable lawyer around here?)

We've also talked or corresponded with hundreds of expatriates, interviewing them about their lives, asking them to share their experiences. Scores of them have done just that in the pages following each of our country reports. And beyond these ten countries, we offer a few observations of other foreign venues you might also consider.

Finally, we have a strong sense that many, if not most, in our privileged generation want to do more than sit in the sun or relax on the porch. We're looking for ways to give back, to contribute, especially where it can make a tangible difference. From our earliest days in Mexico, the expats to whom we gravitated, who seemed the happiest, were those active in the lives of their local community—sometimes in an organized way, with charities and fund-raising; sometimes in more direct ways, such as volunteering to teach, organizing trash pickups, or distributing clothing to the destitute. Repeatedly, expats told us that in volunteering, they got back far more than they gave. That's the opportunity: live well, do good. In the spirit of volunteering "without borders," we've listed some of the local and global resources on volunteering practically anywhere your restless feet might take you.

So, classmates, meditate here on your future. And consider *all* points of the compass.

DAYDREAMS

- ✦ *Adventure*
- ✦ *Cost of living*
- ✦ *Pace*
- ✦ *Climate*
- ✦ *Freedom*
- ✦ *Benefits*

Chapter 1

TEN REASONS TO CONSIDER MOVING ABROAD

Retirement is a troublesome word to baby boomers, not just because many of us resist the idea of getting old, and not just because many of us have no intention of ceasing meaningful work. It is above all troublesome because so many of us, as our high-paying years begin to fade, will face one of two scenarios:

- We won't be able to afford the lives we've led until now.
- Even with adequate finances, we haven't lived out some of our dreams.

Surveys have shown that as many as four out of five baby boomers have not saved enough for a comfortable U.S. retirement, and the latest figures indicate a national savings rate approaching zero. (In Japan, it is 20 percent.) To those of us who were banking on our house values to see us through, our parents could have told us: what goes up also comes down. For many of us, this will mean continuing to work, even if work is no longer meaningful, in an attempt to keep the income flowing. For others, it will mean downsizing and downscaling, often to locations not intrinsically interesting to us. Baby boomers always did rebel against their parents, and although many of us will do the usual thing of moving to Florida and Arizona, many more will wonder if that's all there is.

Even when finances are not the prime consideration, it is natural that many of us will look forward to something *different*. After a lifetime of work that has given us little spare time, skimpy vacations, and the unrelenting pressures of job security, child rearing, and getting ahead, many of us may dream about a more fulfilling, culturally richer life that we may have glimpsed only on holidays, or in our reading, or in movies, or on postcards.

You may recall the feeling: You're leafing through a magazine with alluring photographs of someone's villa in Spain, and you lean back and begin to daydream. Or you've spent a couple of weeks at a resort in Costa Rica, and you and your spouse decide to check out the local real estate listings just out of curiosity. Or you're winding up a sunny tour in Europe, and one of you turns to the other and says, "Why do we have to fly back next Sunday? Wouldn't it be wonderful if we could just *live* here full time?"

That's how the thought creeps in.

Then you put down the magazine, or you fly back to your workaday lives, and the reality and familiarity kick back in. Change is scary, what's known is comforting, and that's why eight out of ten Americans say they want to retire where they presently live. Americans have a tendency toward insularity. More than other nationalities, we value convenience, we do not speak other languages (we insist others speak ours), we're bad at geography and history, we tend to draw conclusions from the anecdotal, and—especially compared to Europeans, who move seamlessly across each others' borders—we don't have that much experience with other cultures. We've strayed far from our immigrant roots. We travel, but mostly here at home.

But not all of us.

There are no hard figures on how many Americans live abroad, but estimates range from four million to six million, military excluded. Expats are advised to check in with their consulates when they first arrive; it's anyone's guess how many do. We didn't. Americans wary of being tracked by our government certainly don't. And no one tracks part-time residents who move around. As to how many of these Yanks abroad are retirees, we have an idea how many Social Security checks are sent abroad (about a half million), but that doesn't tell us much; most expats keep U.S. bank accounts. We do.

One thing is certain: the number is growing. If you're thinking about a move, you will feel less and less alone. In Mexico alone, some 20,000 American immigrants a month, in a reversal of the usual story, cross the border on their way down the coasts to buy, rent, or otherwise establish homes to the south. The word is getting out, just as work is letting out for the boomer generation. For some, it makes a lot of sense.

Here are ten reasons:

1. **A sense of adventure.** You've had a good working life, you may have launched your kids, you've lived in one place for quite a while. There are new things you'd like to do, passions you haven't yet tapped, a yearning for change. To reinvent yourself. One study shows that the

number one reason expats move abroad is *not* costs or climate but to experience a new chapter in their lives. Change can be the grit that keeps things interesting in your retirement years.

2. **A desire to travel, to get away.** Sure, you can quench your travel while living in the States, but how much easier would it be to get to know Latin America if you lived in Mexico or Panama? To travel around western and eastern Europe if your staging area were **Barcelona,** Spain? To experience Asia and Southeast Asia if you were living in **Chiang Mai,** Thailand? And to be able to spend *real* time in a new location, even put down a few roots, not just pass through. Moreover, some of you may feel a desire—a need—to experience a different political climate.

3. **Lower cost of living.** Boomers have saved an average of $50,000 for retirement, pensions are scarcer than ever, Social Security won't easily cover American-sized costs. Prospective retirees looking at twenty-five years on a fixed income may see a train wreck ahead, as housing, insurance, and medical costs keep going off the rails.

   As far as Latin America is concerned, then, the prospects are enticing: depending on what you choose, you can live on a fraction of your U.S. costs. In a passage much quoted on the expat online message boards, Walter Russell Mead, of the Council on Foreign Relations, wrote a couple of years ago, "An income that can barely cover a double-wide in Florida can swing a condo south of the border. For the price of a condo in Phoenix, you can often have a villa in Mexico." Well, he probably hasn't checked the price of Mexican villas lately, but we take his point: instead of downscaling, you can upscale.

   In Europe, even where it's more costly to live (for most of this 2K decade, that's been a *wide* swath of Europe), the expenses you *don't* have can make the difference. The affordable, or free, medical care you get from state-supported systems; the tax exemptions reserved especially for expats; the far cheaper insurance—these can make Europe, still, an attractive financial choice. One U.S. retiree in France, while acknowledging the effect of the falling dollar against the rising euro, told us, "There are ways of living here nicely. You can still find a house for twenty percent of the price of houses in the expensive parts of the U.S.—New York and Connecticut. Did you know the prices of baguettes and coffee are fixed? And the quality of life here is so much better!" We take her point: instead of living frugally in place, you can live frugally in style. Even if costs are similar, or higher than in the U.S., the allure of Europe's deeply rich culture and its "quality of life," as residents call it, balance out the costs for most. In some locations in Europe, stalled or falling house prices have mirrored those in the U.S. and may present an opportune moment to find good value.

4. **A slower pace.** Much of the world sees Americans as hurried, harried, driven, impatient. If we're honest, we probably see ourselves this way as well. Whether it's our overscheduled childhoods, our frenzied school years, our single-minded careers, our fifty-week work years, our fast-food meals, and our rush to get to the next place, fast, our counterparts in other parts of the world often think us mad.

  As you'll find in our Latin American chapters, expats there unanimously cite a more tranquil, slower-paced lifestyle as one of the chief pleasures of their new lives. While it's true that the relaxed sense of time in Latin countries can drive ex-corporate warriors around the bend, successful settlers adopt it as their own. They come to appreciate mañana as a way to slow down life's urgencies; they understand the word not so much as a specific promise as a good intention. They stretch out their days. They learn to stroll, not jog; to chat, not chatter; to relax, not relapse.

  In southern Europe as well, despite some acceleration from keeping pace with America (and Asia) in a competitive world, life for expats is a more tranquil affair. Among those who have made their homes among the natives of *Languedoc,* France, or *Umbria,* Italy, there is always time to linger over a market, a meal, an errand. Even in the big southern European cities, expats report that long, languid lunches and late, meandering dinners have not yet disappeared. The café life is alive and well.

5. **Climate.** It's not that America doesn't have a rich variety of climates. It's just that, given a preference for sunnier skies, and the high cost of living on almost any stretch of U.S. beach or coastline, the view from abroad offers a *world* of good weather to choose from. In dozens of countries, homes can be found in lovely, sunlit locations that would have been bought and flipped twice in the United States. Though we don't wish to be overly harsh about Florida's steaming summer days or Arizona's scorching afternoons, it's nice to contemplate year-round balmy temperatures in **Cuernavaca,** Mexico, spring breezes in **Aix-en-Provence,** France, or even the warm autumn drizzle of **Verona,** Italy. Furthermore, where costs are reasonable, it's more affordable for retirees to follow their own weather, shifting headquarters inland when the coasts become too hot or heading for the hills when their city streets simmer.

6. **Previous experience.** For some, retiring abroad is an opportunity to go back in time. Expats who once worked abroad and liked it may find that retirement is a chance to more fully live an experience that enriched them. Those who served in the military, who had memorable R & R experiences, are returning—to Southeast Asia or the Philippines or Panama—anywhere this country's troops have gone to capture hearts and minds. There is also a growing movement in heritage retirement, to return with an American savings account to settle in one's country of origin. This can mean a first-generation American immigrant return- ing to childhood friends and family or a third-generation citizen intrigued by his ethnic heritage.

7. **Greater freedom.** A common refrain among expats is that they feel freer abroad than they do in the U.S. It's odd at first to hear this in Latin Amer- ican countries where the bill of rights is less than robust, or in Euro- pean countries whose governments watch over its citizens protectively. Some of it undoubtedly is caused by nearly a decade of increased gov- ernment monitoring after 9/11, and some of it has to do with the sense that the U.S. is hemmed in by legal constraints; no nation has anywhere as many lawyers per capita. Daily life is a lawsuit waiting to happen.

   Abroad, people don't fear being sued for picking up and hugging someone else's child; they open a B and B with a certain amount of red tape, but without doubling their costs with liability insurance; they can carve out a private life high on a mountainside without fear that the "revenooers" are coming after them. We hear it often, and not just from older, political types. A young Mexican-American waitress of about eighteen was serving us in our village, working hard; she told us she'd lived in the States for several years but chose to return to Mexico. We asked her why. "To be more free," she said.

8. **Taxes.** Again, expats probably count a higher proportion of libertari- ans than the average U.S. population. They don't like government monitoring, and they especially don't like taxes. Volumes have been written on tax avoidance in overseas havens—the Caymans, anyone? In some of Europe and all of Latin America, property taxes are far lower than in the United States. One irritant is that the U.S. is among those countries that tax its citizens' income worldwide. But there's a big ben- efit for the ordinary middle-income retiree: you have an exemption of $85,700 on any income earned while living abroad. That said, other taxes, such as sales and capital gains—particularly in Europe—are another topic altogether, and not nearly as happy.

9. **Health care.** This deserves its own chapter, and gets it, but suffice it to say for now that this cardinal fear of Americans abroad—inadequate medical care—is, in many locations, and in many ways, a bad rap. In both Europe and, perhaps surprisingly, Latin America, health insurance, medical care, medical procedures, hospital facilities—even nursing-home care—is both more affordable and a lot better than Americans believe.

10. **Senior and retiree benefits.** In much of Latin America, *pensionados* have privileges ranging from special residence visas to deep discounts on taxes, lodging, and transportation. In 2008 Panama was offering pensionados an absolutely unbeatable array of benefits—from airline and hotel discounts to generous tax abatements—aggressively bidding for the retiree business.

    You won't find similar blandishments in European locales, other than benefits offered to *all* senior citizens. But we've heard from expats everywhere that older people receive genuine respect abroad. Family ties are close, parents and grandparents stay at home, and society—government, media, church—supports and nurtures the elder folk. In America, many of the aged find that they are tolerated, but not always esteemed, by family and society at large. Many look to a future in elderly enclaves or absurdly expensive nursing homes. So the prospect of feeling valuable again is no small benefit to gray-haired boomers looking overseas.

REALITY CHECK

- ✦ *Separation*
- ✦ *Culture shock*
- ✦ *Language*
- ✦ *Crime, corruption*
- ✦ *Legalities*

Chapter 2

UH-OH: SEVEN REASONS
NOT TO RETIRE ABROAD
(And a Few Rebuttals for Your Consideration)

1. **Separation from family.** This is far and away (to be literal about it) the number one regret of expats we've known and interviewed. To separate oneself from children, siblings, or growing grandchildren is to stint on one of life's most cherished experiences. So there's no getting around it: it can be a *real* sacrifice, especially as the geographic distance from home and hearth increases. For many it's a deal breaker. For others who've moved anyway, it's a reason to give it up and return.

   We've also observed the following: (a) In the age of email, instant messaging, and free Skype-like videophone calls, some of the pain of separation is mitigated. (b) With the proliferation of air routes worldwide, it is no longer so difficult to make frequent trips home to dandle one's grandchildren. (How far as the crow flies is less important than how long it takes <u>you</u> to fly, which is why your distance from an airport and the state of local transportation is something to think about.) (c) Living in an exotic locale can be catnip to a young family, especially its kids and teenagers. Coming to visit Grandmother and Grandfather in their beach house in Mexico or a cool walled city in Spain is probably a better motivator than getting them down for a visit to some conventional retirement community.

2. **Culture shock.** The thousand and one cultural differences expats encounter when they move overseas can be reasons for delight or dissatisfaction. For the dissatisfied, by far the biggest irritant we've found among our expat friends is inefficiency, in all its myriad flavors. We, along with the Germans, the Swiss, and the Japanese, live in highly effi-

cient societies. You may not realize it until you spend time abroad, but things at home run smoothly, promptness is rewarded, and most things tend to happen on time (motor vehicle departments and air departures strongly excepted).

Abroad, by comparison, especially in many fair-weather retirement locales, the red tape, bureaucratic tangles, hoop jumping, and casual appointment making can drive Americans to drink. (By the way, there *are* AA groups in nearly every town and village in which North Americans retire.) As one friend in **Ajijic**, Mexico, near **Guadalajara**, put it, "The very things you found so adorable at first—the slow pace, the casual hours, the easy come and go—are the very things that can drive you crazy a few years later." This applies both to famously time-flexible Latin American countries and to more developed countries; the hurdles in Spain or even France for those awaiting visa extensions, work permits, or car registration are daunting. We tried for months to pin down the precise residence requirements of Italy. You'll see what our expat reporter found, but trust us, even that's iffy.

Yes, it's true. Papers, papers, papers, said a correspondent in Spain. All we can tell you is that you get used to it—we did—and it can turn you into a calmer, less frenetic person. If you can put aside your impatience, your irritation, even your sputtering rage at the serpentine ways of bureaucracy, if you learn to shrug at the latest broken appointment and to take things in their stride, you'll come to understand something: Yeah, things happened more smoothly back home, but were you happier for it? Did saving that time enrich your life in some other way? And did waiting for your tardy plumber here in Costa Rica, sitting in your tropical garden, sipping pomegranate juice, really subtract anything valuable from your life?

3. **Language.** You don't know a word of the foreign language. You're too damn old to start learning now; everyone knows languages are best learned at a young age. It's going to affect everything you do: chatting with people on an afternoon walk, figuring out what the landlady is saying about the steam pipes, asking about the best key maker in town. It will mean you'll have no chance of a deep friendship with a local. You'll miss every nuance of every conversation, except with your fellow expats. You're living a half-understood life.

No question that you'll have a far richer experience if you try to learn the local language; even a smattering is usually appreciated (though in France you should expect to have your pronunciation corrected). But consider, <u>si'l vous plaît,</u> the following:

a. *Despite fulminations about the encroachment of American culture everywhere, English is the language of science, international business, diplomacy, air travel, and entertainment. If you must be stuck with one language abroad, you're stuck with the right one. English is now the default second language taught in virtually every country. The odds that absolutely no one within a radius of fifty kilometers will be able to understand you are increasingly rare. (OK, you may have to double that radius in very poor and undereducated countries such as Nicaragua or in slightly more exotic locales such as Croatia.)*

b. *We found our contractors and lawyers in Mexico to be excellent sign-language artists, adept at interpreting gringo nattering. Like virtually all our friends who were brave enough to build their own houses, we can't think of a time when anyone's poor Spanish resulted in a major catastrophe.*

c. *There are, in fact, new techniques—with CD sets like the excellent Pimsleur series and Rosetta Stone—to teach even the most stubbornly monolingual enough to get along. And again, the invigorating discipline of learning a new language at your age can keep your brain cells doing a healthy boogie.*

d. *As more and more expats choose to live in gated communities among U.S. expat colonies, they find they hardly need the local language at all. That's not our cup of coffee. They won't get bouquets from those of us who believe in living a more authentic experience. But they'll be able to bitch about the problems in _____ to their neighbors in English.*

4. **Crime and corruption.** Far less a problem in Europe than in Latin America, but it can be scary out there. You're leaving behind the norms of American life. In the U.S., at least you know how to dial 911. In the U.S., the cops will likely show up, the judge will likely be evenhanded and fair. At home, you know what neighborhoods to stay out of. We, too, heard the headlines before we moved to Mexico; a drug shoot-out, a home invasion, a kidnapping, an armed stickup. In Latin countries even poorer than Mexico, we assumed, it must be even worse. Who wants to live with broken glass on top of a walled compound, suspecting the locals, certain that every policeman is corrupt?

As for Italy and other European locales, where crime is lower than the U.S., the question is, What about corruption? In most places, it's accepted that local bureaucracies run on grease and that petty officials need to be offered incentives. How can you, a foreigner, find your way through the tangles of gratuities and jurisprudence, and learn who is to be avoided and who is to be stroked? And what about crime in the immigrant neighborhoods? Or the gypsies? Then there's the Mafia! Alice, did you see this village is called Corleone? Let's get back to Passaic!

First, the numbers. By every measure, the United States has more serious crime than most of the countries we've covered. The murder rate and crimes of violence in European countries are a small fraction of what they are in the United States. In Latin America it gets more complicated. (See appendix 1 for crime statistics.)

Latin American crime rates as measured by UN surveys are far lower than in the United States, though distrust of police means the numbers are underreported, probably drastically. But even if you <u>triple</u> or <u>quadruple</u> the Latin American stats, U.S. figures remain high or higher. Nobody knows for sure; the rap on Latin American crime is anecdotal. In Mexico, the estimated murder numbers are high, but the overwhelming proportion of violent crimes occur in **Mexico City** *and in the tough border cities. (Note: the closer to the U.S. border, the higher the crime rate.) However, crime is rising everywhere in Latin America, as drugs and drug battles become more prevalent. (Note: the drug trade is completely dependent on American demand.)*

And remember that guns are illegal in most places outside our borders; you don't have to worry that some irritated home owner will shoot you for accidentally trespassing. (Note: in America, there are enough guns in circulation for nine out of ten of our citizens.) Yes, as the National Rifle Association would say, it's the drug runners and organized criminals who have guns abroad. But by the numbers, the odds of a foreign resident getting caught in a drug shoot-out or a Mafia rubout are low indeed.

Petty thievery and house robbery are in fact common in Latin America and are becoming more so as rich foreigners settle next to poorer local neighbors. The ill-paid police in Mexico and Central America have a high degree of corruption, though new governments in Mexico, Nicaragua, and Panama are promising reform. But here's a point of view you hear a lot: How does the traffic cop looking for a small bribe, or a house-robbery detective who needs an incentive, compare with the grip of special interests on the governments of, well, more developed countries? As thoughtful expats often conclude, it's all relative.

Here's the wrap-up. Over and over, we hear the same story: no matter where expats wander, on a street outside **Lisbon**, *or in a village in Costa Rica, they claim to feel safe in their new countries. The vast majority of women say they stroll around at night unaccompanied, while the vast majority of men say they've encountered no crimes of violence and take petty thievery in their stride. They lock their doors, they don't leave* *valuables lying around, but—as we found in our own village—they do not live in fear.*

5. **Financial, legal worries.** The fear of ending up on the wrong side of a real estate investment, or of a devaluation, or of making a banking mistake are reasonable fears. A more generalized fear: insecurity about not knowing the local rule book. Residency requirements, and their attendant paperwork, are a major pain everywhere. (Note: nowhere are the immigration rules as stringent as in the U.S. post-9/11.) Can you be sure your papers are right? Is your car properly registered? Do you have the right documents? Are you properly insured? Buying property can be stressful in the best of times, traumatic the rest of the time. So, are you *sure* you own the property? Did you declare its true value? Have you paid proper taxes on it? Can they confiscate it?

   On the real estate front, there should be some comfort that some places abroad have become buyer's markets following the U.S. housing woes that began in 2008. But we'll have more to say on that in the following chapter. As to the fears of not knowing the rulebook, you can overcome these fears, but you have to work at it. Make at <u>least</u> one visit over there purely for investigative purposes (keep your bathing suit packed). Check with the locals and the expats about an honest lawyer. Consulates keep lists of lawyers with good reputations. Then ask around for a smart "facilitator." Anywhere there are expats, there are people who know their way around the bureaucracies, and for a fee, can legally get you the papers you need. Find out what paperwork has to be done ahead of time from home. (In many places, you can't apply for residency in-country; you have to get your papers done at one of their consulates in the U.S. before you arrive.) Nobody is saying this part is easy. We're saying that there are ways to beat down the major worries.

6. **I'll have to do without all my favorite stuff.** We North Americans live in a land of overwhelming abundance and choice. Sometimes we need to leave and return to be reminded of it. After our first year in our Mexican village, we came back to the States and were *dazzled* by the shops, malls, supermarkets, emporiums, boutiques, gourmet stores. We'd forgotten. At home in Mexico, we had three small grocery stores, a drugstore, and a few assorted clothes and sandal shops. We made do, happily. Back in New York, we suddenly remembered what we *should* have been unhappy about: all those personal preferences, things we *had* to have, like our favorite coffee, the shoe store with triple-wide, forty kinds of light fixtures . . .

Europe is more like America in its range of consumer choices, and in some places offers a richer cornucopia of goods. But it will still be *different*. You don't always find 1 percent milk in France. You may not easily find Snickers bars in Italy. You're going to miss *your stuff*. And are you willing to go on missing it for good, except for what you can bring in through customs every once in a while? Are you ready for a kind of scarcity in your life?

Take this one on faith. Living "a less materialistic life" is repeatedly mentioned as one of the chief satisfactions of the expat life—at least among the happier ones we've known. In Latin America, feeling less materialistic comes from less choice. In expensive Europe, it can happen by cutting back on expenses. Either way, you hear about people making do with less—and feeling more fulfilled. Or having less stuff and feeling freed by it.

But all of them miss their favorite snacks.

7. **Health care.** OK, this is the big one. It's all very well to say there's good health care overseas, but how can we know—

    We know you're worried. Just have a seat. The doctor will be with you shortly.

MEDICAL CHECKUP

- ✦ *Foreign health care*
- ✦ *Medicare*
- ✦ *Insurance*
- ✦ *Medical tourism*
- ✦ *Long-term care*

Chapter 3

HEALTH
The Big One

There are three looming concerns for retirees, something that binds them together no matter where they scatter: health, real estate, and money. And since, if you have your health, you have everything, let's give it the respect it deserves and start there. After all, if you're not feeling well, you're not going *anywhere.*

The quality of foreign medical care, its costs, insurance coverage, health facilities, and medical standards all are debated endlessly in cafés and online. It's very well to be ready to commit to a new country, but when it comes to all the ills that can befall an aging boomer, the what-ifs and oh-my-Gods suddenly stand out front and center.

In a developing country . . .
- How far below U.S. standards is medical care here?
- What if I go to a doctor and my symptoms are misdiagnosed?
- What if it turns out to be a serious illness requiring sophisticated care?
- What if the facilities are second rate?
- What if the drugs or medicine are untested or unapproved?
- What if I have a stroke or heart attack and need to get treatment fast?
- What if I can't be evacuated back to the States in time?

In a developed country . . .
- Are doctors here *really* up to U.S. standards?
- Am I covered by insurance here—my own or the national coverage?

- Will the doctors and nurses speak English?
- How long will I have to wait for an appointment?
- Are they using up-to-date medical treatment and drugs?
- How do I find out who the best doctors are? What are the best hospitals?

MEDICARE: FORGET IT

The first thing an over-sixty-five retiree should know is that Medicare will *not* cover you outside of the United States. This fact alone may cause a lot of you to stop reading right here. It's even a factor for those under sixty-five considering early retirement—do you want to settle in a place where you'll *never* be able to rely on Medicare?

Consider the implications.

The Medicare dilemma means aging expats must (a) find, and pay for, their own private insurance; (b) qualify for a national health service; (c) pay out of pocket for medical costs; or (d) get back to the U.S. in a timely fashion to make use of their Medicare.

Starting with the last, the problem in countries easily accessible to the U.S. is less urgent. In drive-in-and-out Mexico, or in Central American venues—Costa Rica, Panama, and so on—short flights to Miami offer reassurance. American expats regularly come back to the States for Medicare visits. But where the locations are more distant—living in isolated regions in Latin American countries, or a long, expensive flight away in European countries—the prospects can be troubling. Yes, an expat will have to rely on and pay for *local health care*!

U.S. VERSUS FOREIGN CARE

Americans (well-insured Americans, that is) still hold a near-legendary belief that the U.S. has the highest quality of medical care in the world. Now, the cost of doctors, health care, drugs, and hospitals may cause unending despair among the uninsured, and the unending battles with insurance companies demoralize everyone. But with all of that, Americans are suspicious of other varieties of medical care—whether "inferior" care in the third world or "socialized" care in Europe. (Canadians, with their universal health care system, have their own issues with medical delays in their home country but do not share the same suspicions of "socialized" health care systems. Indeed, Canadians driving through the U.S. to their retirement homes in Mexico worry more about falling ill or having an accident while they're in the *States;* they buy travel insurance for that purpose alone.)

Amend those legends. As Susan Michael, an expat living in **Lisbon**, says, "When I first moved to Europe, I believed that the U.S. medical system is first rate and could not be duplicated. I do not think this now. I think the general North American public is fed a bill of goods about the preeminence of U.S. medical care." A 2008 article in *Newsweek* referred to "best in the world" American health care as "misguided medical chauvinism." In category after category, from infant mortality rates, to cancer survival, to access to care, to longevity, the United States has seen its health care rankings slip further down the lists of international health organizations—to thirty-seventh in the World Health Organization's 2007 rankings (just above Slovenia). Of course, the U.S. still has some of the best medical facilities and the best-trained doctors in the world. Patients from all over the world come to the United States when the treatment is, you know, *complicated*. But even in these categories, it is no longer unchallenged; medical care in France is at least its equal. Certainly France's emphasis on preventive care leads the world. Other European countries rank highly as well.

In Latin America, facilities and technology are certainly not in the U.S. class, but the quality of care in urban locations can be good—and in many expats' opinions, more humane. When it comes to affordable access to care, and insurance coverage for both rich *and* poor, the United States is hardly on the charts, ranking below Honduras, Thailand, Romania, and the Dominican Republic. This issue of insurance coverage in the U. S. may change as the political picture changes, but the United States has a lot of catching up to do.

YIKES! FOREIGN TRAINED?

Think twice when you hear brokers and real estate developers abroad reassuring Americans because so many local doctors are "U.S. trained." You might just as well ask how many U.S. doctors *in the States* are "foreign trained." *The New England Journal of Medicine* says that 25 percent of U.S. doctors studied abroad and that 60 percent of those studied in developing countries. So if U.S. doctors are that good—and they are—but so many of them trained abroad, then . . . what's up, doc?

The majority of expats we canvassed in Europe and Latin America who settled near urban medical facilities say their care has been: pretty good, good, and excellent. Repeatedly, they report that physicians, nurses, and hospital personnel treat patients with more time and attention than they do in the United States. They get to know patients as well as diagnose them. (But as in Canada, there are plenty of complaints about the waiting times of national health systems almost everywhere.) More often, expats (1) sign up for the national service as a catastrophic backup, and (2) supplement it with private insurance or (3) pay out of pocket. *Anywhere* is less expensive out of pocket than the U.S.

A former D.C. accountant living in **Guadalajara** says, "Imagine, a doctor will actually take the time to talk to you! They make house calls! They give you their cell phone numbers!" A former Hollywood filmmaker in **Ajijic,** Mexico, says: "I had a quadruple bypass surgery last year, and I can swear that I have never in all my seventy-seven years had better treatment and medical care, and for exactly ten percent of what it would have been in Hollywood." In Italy, an expat talks about the national health service available to foreign residents. Office visits cost nothing, and three days of hospitalization for her husband's life-threatening illness cost $2,500. In France, Americans who qualify for national health coverage, with supplemental but inexpensive private coverage, can be scathing about the U.S. health care system they left behind. Throughout Europe, it is extraordinary to see Americans gather in a café in **Barcelona,** or a trattoria in **Modena,** Italy, to swap stories about their medical care—and to hear, for a change, happy stories, not horror stories.

The special European nit to pick, as always, is bureaucracy. Each EU country has different tests for foreigners to qualify. To be enrolled for "free" coverage in Italy, for instance, you must pay a fee of 7.5 percent of your income. For those in the lower income brackets, it's a great deal. For those in the higher brackets, private insurance is also available. But there's a catch-22: to qualify for residence, you must prove that you came into the country *with* health insurance (nope, Medicare doesn't count); only then do you qualify for residency, which in turn qualifies you for the national insurance system. It works out. Oh, and be prepared for local differences. "We're pleased with our doctor here," said one of our expats from **Umbria,** "but he smokes."

Our own experience in Mexico was good. We asked around town, and expats had good things to say about a family doctor in the next village. We drove over to meet him when I had a medical problem. At first we were nervous about his small, somewhat shabby office just one building away from a busy grocery store. But as we often found in Latin America, what's outside does not always match what's inside. Our doctor, a graduate of a **Mexico City** medical school, spoke English well, took down our histories without rushing us, diagnosed the problem, and prescribed treatment—all perfectly, as far we could tell. He didn't have a lot of modern equipment but assured us that if there was anything he couldn't handle, he would send us to one of several good hospitals in **Puerto Vallarta,** forty minutes away. He charged us $16 for the office visit. In point of fact, Mexico has an enlightened government policy when it comes to health, mandating clinics in the smallest villages, keeping medical costs down, requiring its graduating doctors to serve for a period in the hinterlands.

Why do many expats (such as our contributing writers) in Central American republics report that good care is available, when the World Health Organization ranks these nations low in health care? Because, sadly, medical care may indeed be inferior for the public at large in these nations. But unfairly or not, expats who can pay the affordable out-of-pocket costs can find good to excellent private care. Kind of like in the U.S., come to think of it.

THE JOYS OF PRIVATE CARE

By far, the most prevalent way an expat gets health coverage is through international medical insurance. (See our "Resources" section for recommended companies.) In Latin America, it's to ensure the highest standard of care; in Europe, it may be because proof of private coverage is required before residence may be applied for. Like any health insurance, you'll have to research its benefits and restrictions, with a few added questions for the expat life: Is preauthorization (calling your insurance company for permission to have a procedure) required? Will you be covered if you travel—either to other countries or back to the States for a visit? What kinds of procedures will be covered abroad—and which won't be? What will be covered in the case of evacuation, if you sign up for that?

In Latin America, evacuation is a very popular benefit. The image of a red-crossed helicopter swooping down to pick you up and rushing you to the safety of a U.S. hospital can be most reassuring. In practice, it is rarely used. We know of one twist on it: A year-round expat friend of ours in Mexico travels to the States fairly often on business. In case anything happens stateside, she has Mexican insurance that guarantees evacuation *back to Mexico.*

REALISTIC CONCERNS: PLENTY

We don't say that there aren't real and legitimate concerns. In Latin American countries, care can be antiquated, sloppy, sometimes unhygienic. If you choose to live in an isolated place on the beach or up a mountain, you take a major risk. Expats in these out-of-the way places are optimistic *and* fatalistic about their health prospects. An American living on an island off *Bocas del Toro,* in Panama, says, "You just have to think about it this way: when your number's up, it's up." Their confidence in their good health is in direct proportion to the distance they're willing to live from a good hospital. If you're in **Panama City** near one of its good hospitals, you're fine. If you're far away in the village of **Boquete,** currently hot with retirees, you have to trust that if you have a serious problem, it can wait for an hour's drive down the mountain, a ride to the airport, an hour's flight to **Panama City,** and a taxi the rest of the way.

The challenge in Latin America will be for its major hospitals to continue improving to the level at which they become accredited by the Joint Commission International, the agency whose standards are generally accepted as indicators of world-class care. So far, few Latin American hospitals have this accreditation, but it is expected to change. Especially as a new phenomenon arises: the rising tide of visitors who travel for one reason alone—to get medical treatment abroad.

MEDICAL TOURISM: GOING ABROAD TO GET WELL—CHEAP

Medical tourism to developing countries is one of the travel industry's fastest-growing categories; it is expected that, as 76 million American boomers pass the retirement tollgate, demanding higher standards, it will transform the medical infrastructure of Latin America. It's already more than a cottage industry: India's better hospitals are now a major medical destination. Among retiree destinations, say Milica and Karla Bookman, authors of *Medical Tourism in Developing Countries,* Costa Rica receives 150,000 medical tourists a year, Thailand 400,000.

Personally, we've recommended to friends that they come down on vacation to **Puerto Vallarta** or **Guadalajara** to take care of any serious dental problems while they're here. Since dental insurance is so limited in the States, it can be a tremendous bargain abroad; our experience has been uniformly good, our care professional and up-to-date. We had problems ranging from root canals to complex oral surgery, and the results were excellent, the costs about a quarter what they would have been in the States. For our friends, this more than made up for their travel costs, and they got a jaunt in the sun to boot.

The really big deal till now has been cosmetic surgery—yes, a $16,000 face-lift in the States can be performed for $4,000 in Costa Rica. But there's more: an uninsured double bypass surgery that could cost $100, 000 in the States can be obtained for $15,000 in an up-to-date **Buenos Aires,** Argentina, hospital. In **Guadalajara,** a woman who visited long enough to qualify for the national health service—for a yearly premium of $300— had "excellent" gallbladder surgery at no cost. She had to bring her own blankets and hire a nurse, though.

In developing countries, increased American demand for better quality will inevitably raise standards. The specter of health care as a reason for retirees to *fear* life abroad may turn into its opposite: the prospect of accessible, affordable medical care can become an *incentive* to live beyond America's borders.

There has been a movement among expats to lobby the U.S. Congress to make Medicare valid overseas. Council on Foreign Relations scholar Walter Russell Mead, quoted earlier, argues for changing the law to allow expats to use Medicare at approved clinics. Expats would be allowed to participate in a Medicare system (for which they paid taxes all those years) without making a costly journey home. It would cost Medicare far less to reimburse expats for lower medical costs than to wait for them to return and pay for U.S. costs. In other words, by living abroad and using Medicare, expats would save money for themselves *and* the U.S. taxpayer.

An idea ahead of its time? Does it have a chance of being passed?

Dream on. As realists point out, American authorities and businesses can't crack down on $4 pirated DVDs that show up a day or two after a movie's theatrical release. To assume that U.S. Medicare can enforce its regulations abroad seems, alas, wishful thinking for the near future.

NOW, POPS, ABOUT THAT NURSING HOME . . .

Old hands know that there's a phenomenon among retirees who've put in ten or twenty years abroad: many return, some reluctantly, to the States. Face it, those charming cobblestone streets you loved at first become nasty bumps now that your arthritic joints ache. Besides, you may appreciate the medical care you've received and its reasonable costs, but when it comes to the big-time diseases of the old and infirm, don't you *really* trust U.S. medicine more? And won't it be nice to live where you can use your Medicare, no fuss?

But the question for those aging folks who return to the States is, What then? You'll get older and frailer. You'll need more help. If you have family ready to take you in, or the funds for a superior assisted-living facility, fine. But American families are more fractured than ever; there are no guarantees anymore of being taken in by children or relatives. As for finances, a private room in a U.S. nursing home costs an average of $6,300 a month in 2008 dollars. Care in an assisted-living unit is $3,000 a month and climbing. And that Medicare you crossed back to get? It doesn't cover long-term care.

So something interesting has been happening. Around *Lake Chapala,* Mexico's largest retired gringo enclave, and in **San Miguel de Allende,** a

small industry has sprung up to provide affordable nursing-room care. So
far it's just a handful of facilities, some quite modest, without much oversight, but it's being talked about as the shape of things to come. In an article for *USA Today* in late 2007, Chris Hawley reported on new American
residents such as seventy-four-year-old Jean Douglas, from Oregon.
"Shocked" by the costs and impersonal care of assisted-living facilities in
the States, she researched **Chapala** online and made her move to Mexico.
There, in **Ajijic,** by a beautiful lake, Douglas pays $1,300 a month for "a
studio apartment, three meals a day, laundry and cleaning, and twenty-
four-hour care from an attentive staff, many of whom speak English." Elsewhere in **Chapala,** Hawley reported, three or four elderly American
residents chipped in on a cottage and now live independently with twenty-
four-hour nursing care for $550 a month, with free medical treatments and
prescriptions under their state-sponsored IMSS (Instituto Mexicano del
Seguro Social, Mexico's national health plan) coverage.

Some of these nursing homes have failed, and disgruntled gringo residents report a few bad experiences. But the economics—and the charac-
teristics of Latin American society—suggest that this will develop further,
probably in a big way. Dr. David Truly, an academic who has studied American migration into Mexico, predicts a flourishing business in Latin America in nursing-home care. "It's ironic," he says. "American families don't
take care of their own as they used to, so you have the nursing-home phenomenon. Mexicans, with their family tradition and respect for older people—they are *not* sent off to nursing homes—are uniquely qualified to care
for aging gringos in these new facilities. But as I say, it's ironic."

DO YOUR *HOME* WORK

- ✦ *Housing hype*
- ✦ *Price rises*
- ✦ *Property purchase*
- ✦ *The revelation!*
- ✦ *Roaming retirement*

Chapter 4

AT LAST: REAL ESTATE!

Our Secret Sauce

Along with health, the most obsessive concern of expat retirees is—get ready for it—real estate.

In our view, it may be the single most popular (or at least the most frequent) topic of expat conversations all over the world, whether over a bottle of Dos Equis or a glass of Beaujolais. And it doesn't stop when you've made the purchase—yes, it's just *that* fascinating. And worrisome. In our first year in Mexico, I'd guess we talked about something touching on real estate every day.

Such as: the costs, the rise in prices, the fall in prices, the great deals, the horror stories, the hot markets, the sneaky brokers, the weird financing, the honest lawyers, the dishonest lawyers, the notaries public, the tricky permits, the byzantine paperwork, the murky deeds, the best accountants, the bad contractors, the unexpected mishaps, the undelivered tiles, the size of the pool, the rickety plumbing, the undersized roof beams . . .

Outside the borders of this book is a world of practical advice and hard information about retiring abroad. Most of it is on the internet. You'll find thousands of websites, newsletters, online forums, seminar offers, travel sites, informational sites, bulletin boards, government sites, and more. (We'll list some of the better ones in our "Resources" chapter.)

Amid the shimmering-palm headlines, amid the photos of gorgeous condos with killer views and the fabulous rustic stone farmhouses, you quickly realize that all too many websites are doing one thing: selling real estate. Often you can't tell; there is genuinely useful advice being offered, with the soft sell between the lines. And there's plenty of hard sell.

The hard sellers will tell you about the beachfront house you can buy in Baja or Belize for a tiny fraction of what you'd pay in the States—*only you better hurry, these deals are going quick.* They'll tell you about the beachside lot you can buy in Nicaragua for peanuts, *but the lots are being picked off fast.* They'll tell you how comfortable life can be in a three-bedroom house in a gated community in Costa Rica, *but move now, because most of the units have already been sold.* Even in high-cost Europe, they'll tell you that you can still buy an inexpensive house in an out-of-the-way place, *but these bargains may not last,* so don't hesitate, *buy your dream house now, alors, vite!*

And why not? Americans see home ownership as a birthright. Our dream of retirement abroad is most often expressed as owning or building our dream house. It was for us. It will be for many.

But there is another way.

In the world of overseas retirement, you'll hear this a thousand times—indeed, you'll hear it repeatedly from the expats who figure in our in-depth chapters.

Rent before you buy.

It's the expat mantra. And a right good piece of advice it is. Even the websites selling real estate give it lip service: Don't make that down payment on the strength of a brochure. Resist the blandishments of that English-speaking broker. Don't get dazzled by the view. Don't get caught up in the fever of skyrocketing house prices. Get the lay of the land. Rent first.

We're going one better. Here's our simple formula.

> *Rent, <u>don't</u> buy.*

Simple, but it can change *everything.* It can not only transform the way you live in your country of choice, it may change what country you choose. Suddenly, as you'll see, what may have seemed out of reach, such as a higher-cost country, might seem possible, affordable. It can offer you a different dream.

BUY A DREAM LIFE,
RENT A DREAM HOME

Remember that list of I'm-terrified-of-retiring-abroad fears at the beginning of the book? Let's run the same list past you again. This time, please note the asterisks.

- Where do you go?
- How do you choose?
- Did you do enough research?*
- Do you trust the research you did?*
- You've sold your stuff and moved to an unfamiliar place!
- You don't know the language!*
- You don't know the customs!*
- You don't know what will happen if you get sick!
- You miss your family and friends!
- You can't buy the stuff you know and love!
- You want to buy a house, but don't have any idea if it's priced right.*
- You don't understand how mortgages work here!*
- You're sinking a big part of your nest egg into this property!*
- You don't know which way the real estate prices will go!*
- You don't know who's taking advantage of you!*
- The people aren't as friendly as you'd hoped!
- You don't know whom to turn to for help!*
- You've started to build but have no control over the final costs!*
- You don't know if you have clear title!*
- You don't know if you got the right permits!*
- Can the government take it away from you?*
- The currency might be devalued!*
- Will you be able to sell easily if you change your mind?*
- Will you owe capital gains?*
- You've put your savings at risk!*
- You're stuck there!*
- You've burned your bridges!*
- You're thousands of miles away and just made the biggest mistake of your life!*
- In short, *you don't know the drill!*

There's one leading player in all the asterisked fears.

Yes, *real estate.*

Take away the purchase of real estate, and each fear with an asterisk above—and countless more—disappears or recedes. So imagine for a moment that you're moving abroad, but that buying real estate isn't part of the equation. Instead you rent indefinitely. Now . . .

- As a renter, you no longer have to do all that research.
- You don't have to figure out if the price is right.
- You don't have to worry if real estate goes bust.
- You don't have to distrust everyone.
- You don't have to take a crash course in titles, deeds, permits, taxes—the whole twisty, unknowable, foreign, bureaucratic nine yards.
- You won't be responsible for floods, hurricanes, robbery, raging bulldozers, toppling trees, new boilers, and the rest. In fact, you won't care about any of it, other than getting out of the way of the flood and the hurricane.
- You won't have paranoid dreams about not having the right documents, leading to a knock on the door.
- You don't have to worry about property taxes.
- You won't have to worry about owner's insurance.
- You won't have to learn who are the best builders, masons, painters, carpenters in town—that's mostly up to your landlord.
- No big deal if you don't speak the language.
- You don't have to figure out how mortgages work.
- In many countries, if a dispute arises, the law favors the renter.
- You pay far less in fees to lawyers, brokers, accountants, local government.
- You don't—and this is a big one—put your savings at risk. No big down payment or all-cash purchase. You keep your principal.

Which will have these effects:
- The interest from the principal will boost your retirement income.
- You can have a higher standard of living.
- You can go out more.
- You can travel more.
- You can see your kids and family more often.
- You don't have to worry about currency fluctuations. You keep most of your principal in a U.S. bank.
- You've burned no bridges; all you have is a lease.
- You don't have to worry that it will be harder to sell than it was to buy.
- You can—and this is another big one—move on.

Which will have these effects:
- You'll have the time and freedom to see where the best rentals are.
- You can find out if the living is easier down the coast.
- You're not stuck forever with neighbors from hell.
- When you're gone, you won't have the house-sitting problems a landlord does.

Which will let you look at retirement abroad in a whole new way:
- You don't have the existential angst of thinking "I'm stuck! I've made the mistake of my life."
- You're not stuck anywhere. You can go back home.
- You can retire somewhere else altogether on short notice—you still have all that principal, no sale necessary.
- You can ignore all the advice intended to get you through the rigors of a "permanent" move (including quite a lot in this book!)

Against all that, the thrills of ownership?
- Possible appreciation. Or not.
- Rent can't be recouped.
- Possible rent increases (long-term leases are the way to go).
- Possible unavailability of cheap rentals (absolutely a consideration).
- Bragging rights.

There is a corollary to this, and it is:

Rent, don't build.

Sure, it can feel terrific to build your own dream house. There *are* compensations. We already admitted that building our own house in Mexico brought us a lot of joy, but that we wouldn't do it again. Not that way.

Just a few reasons, straight out of *Gringos in Paradise* (see page 2): sketchy surveys, unclear zoning, contractor's honesty, contractor's punctuality, enhanced language difficulties, permits, more permits, "social security" for laborers, all-cash advances, quality of materials; electrician no-show, carpenter no-go, air conditioner no-flow, plumber but no boiler; buy your own tiles, fixtures, appliances, doors, windows, toilets, toilet fixtures . . .

In Europe, construction is not much of an issue simply because construction is often not permitted—or it's severely limited. As we know from those moving-to Europe memoirs, reconstruction and rehabbing are most encouraged. Even there, however, since you must own what you rehab, a whole lot of reconstruction hilarity—and pain—ensues as well. As we used to say to ourselves, bad for life, good for book.

One other thing that renting indefinitely can do for you: you get to audition this stage of your life.

THE STAY AWHILE OPTION

Try it out. If you don't like it, take it on the road. Retirement doesn't have to mean a permanent move. You can just stay awhile: long enough to be more than a tourist—to experience the living, not the visiting—but stay loose, limber. You're a baby boomer, and boomers don't stand still. Retirement isn't a one-time-only event for our generation. Some of us will retire for a while, then go back to the U.S. or Canada to work for a while (we did and do), then re-retire.

In our Mexican village, the couple we feel has *the* best life is a celebrated artist and her husband. The couple spend four months in their terraced house above the beach in **Sayulita**; another four months in Santa Fe, New Mexico, at their desert home; and the remaining four months in Italy or the South of France, giving art lessons. If that isn't a way to live out your allotted time, what is?

YOUR LEASE ON LIFE

Not everyone is fortunate enough to have this splendid sort of rotational retirement, so like most of us, you'll probably look to putting down some roots—researching, choosing a place, preparing, and, if you've been paying attention, finding a good rental lease.

Most books tell you to make certain you see a real estate broker on that first trip. Nope. Make that a *rental* agent. Now, it's true that your renting plans can be stymied if long-term rentals aren't available, or available only at very high prices. So that's one of the first things you investigate during your first visit. Multiple listings are less common abroad, so looking for rentals is very much a matter of looking around in person. Often, the attractive rentals are not posted online; local paper classifieds can be useful, but not always. In Europe, it's always been more word of mouth. You need to check with more than one rental agent. You ask the expats sitting at the next table if they've heard of anything for rent; you take a walk through a neighborhood you like and stop to inquire. In some places in Europe, key money can be expensive, as can deposits. But the costs are still small when compared to purchase costs.

The other challenge is finding a suitable rental in high-priced tourist areas, with per-night rates of several hundred dollars. Still, our experience is that it's usually possible to find reasonable year-round rental rates: landlords often prefer a longer-term, lower-cost lease to avoid the hassles of short-term renting. A couple we know who kept their house on the Pacific coast decided to begin spending half the year in **San Miguel de Allende**. Few towns in Mexico have seen the explosion of prices that **San Miguel** has. But by hanging out at the main plaza (the Jardin) for a week or two, our friends heard about a rental available for two years. A lovely, spacious apartment that would have fetched $200 a night. They got it for $800 a month on a two-year lease—in one of Mexico's priciest towns.

So . . .

Does all this mean we're omitting the oh-so-lively topic of real estate purchases from this book? No. There's plenty. Many of our chapter writers are owners themselves, so we couldn't have stopped them from giving you the real estate lowdown. (They're even foolhardy enough to include current house prices—just to give you a snapshot in time of local costs—which should be accurate for, oh, six months.) We're realists. We've been around the plaza enough to know that people won't stop yearning for their *own* dream home. They'll want to do what we did. They'll want to get in on the home prices for the last, great, cheaper investment of their life.

It is also true that more conventional real estate purchase procedures in Europe, and the increasing availability of U.S.-financed developments in Latin America, can mitigate the stress factor. So can U.S.-backed mortgages and title companies, which are becoming more available in Latin America, particularly in *Baja California*.

So yes, we'll go along, telling you what prices are like in Panama (up and down!) and how much you pay for a cottage in *Tuscany*. (Lots!)

But trust us, you'll think back on this chapter.

DO THE MATH

- ✦ *Finances*
- ✦ *U.S. taxes*
- ✦ *The exemption*
- ✦ *Foreign taxes*
- ✦ *Capital gains*

Chapter 5

MONEY

OK, Maybe <u>This</u> Is the Big One

When old-hand expats in Latin America give advice, they warn against moving down *only* for financial reasons. Kelly Thomas, formerly of Massachusetts and New York, and who now owns a bookstore in Nicaragua, says, "People who move here solely because of the cost of living tend to be miserable here. You have to want to be a part of Nicaragua to enjoy it. Otherwise it will drive you nuts."

Which is demonstrably true everywhere. We've seen people of modest means who moved down for the cheaper prices, only to return in frustration to the States. They liked the costs, but weren't prepared for the cultural differences—and challenges—of a life abroad. On the other hand, we know plenty of rich expats in Latin America who clearly did not need to move down for the costs. They are there for the adventure of it. They're among the ones who are likely to be happy with their new lives. It's about attitude, not just means.

Of course, there *are* the rich who move down there to pump themselves up, to live even higher on the hog than they did in the States. They build their palaces, flaunt their wealth, do their ugly-American thing, treating others with disdain and arrogance—for a time. Expat communities are basically small towns, and in small towns, obnoxious town bullies usually get their comeuppance, either from fellow expats or locals.

We say "usually," because where rich bullies gather in a group, bad deeds sometimes go unpunished. You'll run into gated communities, condo complexes, and, occasionally, an entire neighborhood, where groups of rich, insufferable gringos reinforce one another's behavior and prejudices—

abusing the help, mocking the locals, complaining about everything, competing with one another on extravagance and bad taste. As we often say, not all expats are charming and intrepid.

In Europe, when old-hand expats give advice, they describe the charms of their host country, then wince as they describe the fall of the dollar. Clearly, the idea of moving to some of Europe's high-profile, high-priced locations for their cost of living is an oxymoron. North American retirees move to Western Europe because they dream of moving there, not to save money. Most can either afford it or are willingly seeking simpler lives—to find affordable European locations and cut down on expenses. Over and over, we heard from expats that living a less materialistic life, buying and owning fewer things, added to their state of satisfaction. So money is not the overwhelming consideration there, either.

But having said that, let's acknowledge that for many, if not most, the allure of life abroad is the prospect of living well on less. With Americans facing rising costs and their houses worth much less than they'd hoped, the timing may be right to "change the game"—the money game—by a move to Latin America or even Europe. Although real estate in some countries has held its value or continued to go up, in others there will be an opportunity, not seen in years, to buy or rent reasonably. For Americans who can no longer tap the equity in their U.S. homes, or who want to wait until the market comes back, moving abroad may become an even more appealing way to stretch their battered dollars.

Not that the money game will be a snap to play.

As with so much else, there are good and bad trade-offs.

Best: Cost of living aside, there are numerous financial advantages to living abroad, many of them revolving around taxes.

Worst: There are numerous—no, make that innumerable—hurdles in seeking out the financial advantages of living abroad, most revolving around learning the rules.

TAXES—THE GOOD PARTS

Although the U.S. will tax your worldwide income, you are exempt from U.S. taxes for the first $85,700 of what you earn per year while living abroad as a foreign resident. If your spouse works, he or she will also have an $85,700 exemption. Some foreign countries also tax your income, some don't; some are supposed to but don't get around to it. (Americans owe the IRS simply by being U.S. citizens, no matter where they move. Canadians can minimize Canadian taxes simply by moving away.)

TAXES—THE TICKLISH PARTS

The bit about the exemption can be confusing because of the definitions of *resident* and *income*.

Resident

You get the income exemption in one of two ways:

- You qualify under the "bona fide resident" test. This means that you were a legal resident of a country and remained there for an uninterrupted full tax year.
- You qualify under the "physical presence" test. This means that you resided abroad (not necessarily as an official resident) for 330 out of 365 days.

Income

The $85,700 that you can exempt from Uncle Sam is for what you earn— salaries, bonuses, commissions, royalties—but not for "passive income," such as pension payments, interest, dividends, or rents. You must earn it while living as a resident in a foreign country, though it doesn't matter where your earnings originate.

- *Example:* You get payments from a U.S. firm for consulting via the internet, or you get payment for your artwork from a U.S. patron, or you're resourceful enough to get a salaried job abroad. You owe no U.S. federal taxes on anything you earn up to $85,700. But you'll have to determine what you owe your host country, if anything. *Consult a tax expert.*
- *Example:* You receive income from your pension, or from the sale of stock, or a regular IRA payout, or the rental of a property you own in the U.S. or abroad. Yes, you do owe federal taxes on any and all of it, no exemption. As to state taxes, you may owe those too, but for very complicated reasons. Ditto on taxes owed to your host country. *Consult a tax expert.*
- *Example:* You don't stay in one place; you're practicing rotational retirement, moving here and there every few months a year. Your income exemption is still good because the IRS doesn't care where you live or for how long, as long as you stay the hell out of the U.S.

except for short periods. You still need to figure out what your "tax home" is, so: *consult a tax expert.*

TAXES—THE TOUGH PARTS

What if you earn your income abroad and deposit your funds in a foreign bank? Will the IRS know about it? Once upon a time, probably not. Today, probably yes. For one thing, the IRS has agents working abroad who are supposed to help expats with their tax questions, and, in fact, could be useful to you. But it also makes it easy for them to be snitches and keep an eye out for unreported expat income. For another, you're required to fill out a form when you file your U.S. taxes informing the IRS whether you have a foreign bank account or trust. If you check the yes box, they can find out what you have deposited abroad—there are treaties for such things. If you check the no box and keep more than $10,000 in the account, and the IRS finds out about it, *consult a tax expert*—this time on the finer points of fraud.

You need to file your U.S. tax forms every year, no matter what. Some expats figure that they're outside the States for good, and their income isn't over $85,700, so why bother filing? Because you won't get the exemption unless you do. Expats may tell you that you really don't have to—after all, the IRS estimates that two-thirds of Americans living abroad either file incorrectly or not at all. But there are all sorts of measures afoot (including linking your passport renewal to your tax returns) that strongly suggest you could be in trouble if you take that advice. Yes, it turns out that the only sure things are, indeed, death and taxes, at least if you're an American.

TAXES—THE FOREIGN PARTS

Paying income taxes to the foreign country in which you reside varies with the country. Many nations have treaties with the U.S. that keep you from being taxed twice—in other words, what you've paid in one country can be offset by what you owe the other. In some countries (notably in Europe), even if you think you'll owe nothing because you've paid Uncle Sam, you're still required to file your local taxes. In Latin America, where tax avoidance is more popular than soccer, many (most?) foreign residents don't file local taxes on their local income. For one thing, it's *hard* to pay them. Unaccountably, Latin American governments make signing up to pay taxes as complicated as getting a building permit. A friend who owns a B and B in Mexico spoke to his accountant about starting the paperwork, saying that he wanted to pay his taxes on a small bar he had opened. The accountant asked, *"Why?"*

On the other hand, things *are* changing in Latin America. Computers are mating with computers, and information is being exchanged. In some gringo areas in Mexico, for instance, especially where home owners advertise their house rentals online, officials are taking notes and starting to take action, locale by locale. Our advice to friends with rental units in Mexico is to go through the hassles now and pay Hacienda (the Mexican IRS) its taxes. They're really quite reasonable; as low as 5 percent of receipts, that you report yourself. If you ignore it, and Hacienda finally catches up in a year or three, it can impute what your rentals were for the last year or three and tack on a very large penalty as well.

Mexico aside, tax laws can be just as daunting elsewhere in the retirement universe, in Europe as in Latin America. In France, Spain, Portugal, and Italy, property taxes are just the start (though not if you rent!), and there will be all manner of other amusing concerns, from paying into your host country's health care and social security, to things you might never think of, such as death duties or inheritance laws. In some places, if you die, your spouse may not automatically inherit your property the way she would in North America.

TAXES—CAPITAL GAINS KIND

On both continents, in virtually every country, capital gains are—well, they're an unholy mess. They're confusing, cumbersome, changeable. They can make all the difference in your decision to buy a piece of property, even if the market is red hot. *You'll want a tax expert.* In our country-by-country chapters, you'll find more detail on this, and several books, including Tom Kelly's and Mitch Creekmore's *Cashing In on a Second Home in Mexico,* have long discussions about this. But as with the book you're holding in your hand, watch out for the twists and turns that can make even the best advice obsolete.

TAXES—AVOIDING THEM ALTOGETHER

As to offshore banking and the shielding of assets and income, that's beyond the scope of this book. There are endless sources of information about foreign tax havens and their benefits. Some people use these offshore locations as depositories; others choose to settle where they park their assets. That's not following a dream; it's following a bank account. If shielding your money from taxes is your chief goal in life, it's probably a smart thing to do. But it often means setting up elaborate schemes of residence, hopping around a lot, and joining a fraternity of shady people in sunny places. Good luck.

• • •

Our little mantra about consulting a tax expert means that you must do your due diligence before you make any sudden financial moves. For instance, you may think you're buying into a hot real estate market, calculate your gains, make a lunge for your checkbook—and find that transaction costs and capital gains taxes will cut your imagined profit down to a pittance. Or you may hear from the U.S. expat community that certain tax obligations are enforced, but others can be safely avoided—and find that they were right only in the "old days," as local laws and enforcement policies may have changed since they first settled there.

Scared you out of your dream? Tax dazed? Remind yourself of this: U.S. tax law *at home* is just as impenetrable, the red tape just as formidable, the penalties probably more severe. Unless your finances are pure and simple, you've probably had to pay someone to file your taxes or use increasingly sophisticated software. You can do the same overseas. Six million Americans have managed.

Useful source: *Tax Guide for U.S. Citizens and Resident Aliens Abroad,* publications 54, 515, 593, www.irs.gov/publications. There's even an international hotline: (215) 516-2000.

OTHER MONEY POINTS

• Most expats in Latin America keep their money in dollars, in U.S. banks, transferring funds in smaller amounts to their local banks. There is the ever-present possibility of devaluation or economic crisis, which seems to occur somewhere in Latin America every decade or so. (It happened in Mexico in 1994 and in Argentina more recently.) On the plus side, your dollars generally don't lose their value in Latin America. In Panama and Ecuador, the dollar *is* the currency.

  That's more than can be said about Europe, where the fast-rising euro gave the dollar a thumping not previously felt by Americans in our lifetime. There the smart expat converted as much as he could, as early as he could, into euro accounts.

• Place your financial affairs—and all else—online. Everything in your life that can be uploaded, should be. Bills, bank accounts, credit card payments, mortgages, your medical information, scans of your family deeds, certificates, and titles, the works. Every payment that can be automated should be.

  The internet is *the* transforming change for expats in the past ten years. It's given us a whole new way to stay connected to absent friends and family—the number one lament of expats everywhere. And it streamlines bureaucracy and makes a lot of paperwork unnecessary—the number one complaint of expats everywhere. (In our Mexican village, the first year we stood in line to pay our telephone bills; by the second, we could do it online.) The internet of course keeps expats informed, but often employed too, without running into local restrictions. The morning routine of sitting down at your computer to do your accounts, check stocks, and answer email is now as much a part of expat life as the morning swim and the freshly squeezed orange juice.

TEST YOURSELF

- ✦ *Checklist*

- ✦ *Country? City?*

- ✦ *Residency and work*

- ✦ *One key question*

- ✦ *Right about now . . .*

Chapter 6

CHECKLIST

What's Important to You (and Your Spouse)

We've lost count of the expat retirees we've met who've uttered some variation of this: "We came to _____ and we just *fell in love* with it." Or "I stepped into the garden and just felt we *belong* here." Romantic, but on short notice, not always the best way to choose a new country or a new home. Of course infatuation is part of it, but so is how you feel the day after—or week, or month, or year. Waking up to find you've made a fundamental mistake can sometimes turn on a simple thing: You *thought* you'd like to live in a town at the edge of a tropical jungle; it's every Tarzan movie you ever dreamed about. You arrive—me Jane!—and just adore the place. It's paradise, all right. But soon you find that nobody told you about the painful gnats in the hot season; the night critters in the bush keep you constantly rattled. Oh, and no internet yet. Disaster. But you're already there, you've made your move! Isn't it more sensible—hold the romance, please—to wake up to reality before you've made any sudden moves? While you're still thinking about it?

And if you're going to move *with* someone, double that.

You have to do your personal homework. You need first of all to ask yourself what you want.

Try this: If you've been daydreaming about a specific place—a mountain retreat in Costa Rica, a Parisian apartment with a view—put it out of your mind for now. Start fresh. Ask yourself these questions about your ideal location and try to assign the importance you attach to each:

- Do I want to live in a city? A small town? The countryside? The beach?

- Do I want to live here year-round or seasonally?
- Do I have someplace else to go for part of the year?
- How far will I be from the U.S. or Canada? How easy is it to return?
- How expensive is it to go back?
- Is English spoken? Do I need to learn a new language?
- Is it easy to get modern amenities (phones, TV, internet)?
- Do I want to live among locals or in a gated community?
- Do I mainly want to relax or have an active lifestyle?
- Can I play sports? Practice my hobbies?
- What about shopping? Local crafts? Big Boxes?
- Are there any American amenities? Imported foods?
- Will I need a car? Can I buy one at a reasonable price?
- Am I near an airport?
- Are there travel opportunities nearby, or is it splendid isolation?
- Do I want to be near a U.S. expat community?
- Do I want to be far away from a U.S. expat community?
- If I'm around expats, what kinds of expats?
  + Just retirees or all ages?
  + Couples or single friendly?
  + Liberal? Conservative? Libertarian?
  + Religious? Heathen?
  + Sophisticated travelers? Homespun?
  + Similar financials?
  + Welcoming to new expats?
  + U.S. lifestyle or local?
  + Ugly Americans or guests in another country?
- What about my church? AA?
- Will there be any kind of opportunity to work?
- Will there be an opportunity to volunteer?

Have your spouse or companion check these off. Compare and contrast. We often hear—and can testify ourselves—that embarking on a new life, sweating out a project in tandem in a strange new land, meeting the challenges and overcoming them, can bring a couple closer together than ever.

Or not.

The brochures won't tell you this, but there's a high divorce rate among expatriate retirees. It's absolutely essential that the two of you agree on just about everything before you make any moves. This is one corner of life where the goal isn't compromise; it needs to be unanimous. Often, you're making this decision at a time of tremendous changes in the rest of your life: an empty nest, a job ending. It's easy to think that a move overseas is a chance to take the marriage out for a stretch, get a fresh start.

But we've seen it happen: A couple "falls in love" with a place. A location in which English is not much spoken. Husband is a whiz at languages, wife is definitely not. They discuss; she's hesitant. He wins her over, convinces her language won't make a difference, they make the move. A year later, he's chattering with the locals. She hasn't had a decent conversation with anyone in twelve months. He's happier than he hoped; she's miserable. He stays, she leaves.

Or vice versa.

FIVE BASIC QUESTIONS
ABOUT RED TAPE, RESIDENCY, AND WORK
(AND SOME GENERAL ANSWERS)

1. *When I'm ready to seek residency abroad, what kind of red tape should I expect?*

First, you should know that in every country we've covered, many residents live under the radar; that is, they live on a tourist visa that they extend endlessly, or they simply live without extending it at all— on an expired tourist visa, in other words. You can do that and avoid all the hassles, at a cost to yourself: the stress of not knowing if you'll be found out. We're not going to spend much time on this. Not just because it may not be wise to live in this nerve-gnawing way, but because it's utterly unpredictable. In Mexico, for instance, where living without a residency visa is often thought to be a snap, a friend of ours had a residency visa—known as the FM3—for four years and neglected to have it renewed for several months. She was tracked down by a couple of *federales,* escorted to their jeep, and told she would be deported. She wasn't, but it took clout and cash to get her off. (For every story like that, a hundred gringos will saunter out of the shade and whisper that they've been on a tourist visa for two decades.) On the other hand, in France, where the law is the law, we were surprised to learn that a large number of expats live on nothing more than temporary tourist visas; their experience is that officials there don't care much about the legalities as long as expats pay their own way (and their taxes) and stay out of trouble. But what if trouble finds *you*?

If you want to become a legal resident, there are a number of ways to achieve this, the most common being: a retiree's visa, an investor's visa, or a work visa. In fact, some countries have dozens of visas, but you'll probably concern yourself most with these three, especially the first. Assuming that you're going after the retiree's visa, every foreign country, without exception, will require that you prove you have sufficient income. This is, of course, to make certain that you do not become a ward of the state, and, by implication, to discourage you from finding work that might eliminate jobs for locals.

The required income varies from as little as $500 a month in less developed countries in Latin America and Asia; to a more usual $1,000 to $2,000 in developing countries such as Mexico; to more substantial amounts of $3,000 to $4,000 in some developed countries of Europe; to prohibitive amounts in other parts of Europe, the Caribbean, and Australia and New Zealand. And the "substantial" financial requirements can be hard to pin down because they may change from year to year or vary within the countries themselves.

Income generally has to be verified with proof of a permanent pension or annuity, your U.S. Social Security being the obvious example. Our chapter writers list the requirements in the country-by-country section of this book, but you should look up the latest on a government website before you go. There are places where, in practice, you actually don't have to show any income proof at all. You can present bank account statements, and if you show enough assets—a couple hundred thousand dollars in your account usually suffices in Latin America—you're in. But you have to know that you can do this as a hard fact, not a rumor, or you may find yourself flying back home.

2. *What else, besides proof of income, will I have to produce?*

Just about everywhere, you have to prove that you're healthy (which can mean passing an AIDS test), and show that you do not have a police record. These are not always easy to get, either; U.S. medical and police institutions aren't used to producing documented proof of this kind, so you'll have to know exactly what you're looking for and spell it out to the docs and the cops.

Mostly, these documents need to be *exact* in how they record your data. For all the easy-come, easy-go attitudes of Latin America on some matters, officials can get very picky when they have documents in front of them that don't meet specified requirements to the letter. We've known of expats who got tangled in red tape because a middle initial was off. In Europe, they may give you a bit more leeway.

3. *What about an investor's visa?*

Less common, but generally it means that you're required to deposit a healthy sum in a local bank or a project approved by the government. Usually it means not less than $50,000, ranging to several hundred thousand dollars and up. It's most painless when they count your purchase of a home as the deposit, especially if you were already planning to pay cash for a house or condo. You get your money back later when and if you sell the property. But it can be more onerous than that: you're required to tie up a large amount of principal for a large amount of time, and get it back only if you leave, with a large amount of paperwork. Sometimes the investment is for a good cause—reforestation, for instance—and that can remove the sting for expats looking to do good while they live well.

4. *And work visas? I'd <u>really</u> like to work . . .*

The trickiest of the three, the hardest to generalize about. The easiest course is when a local or international company hires you for your skills and obtains the working visa for you. Honestly, this doesn't happen often to retirees, and if it does, be prepared for a much-reduced salary range, not stateside wages.

The hardest is when you want to find a job for pay that could be performed by a local. (That's why it's nearly impossible to practice a profession, such as doctor or lawyer.) Although working at a job is done everywhere—expats are waiters, barkeeps, shopgirls, and scuba instructors—it's also the most vulnerable to exposure. If a local knows you're working and wants to blow the whistle, you may get a knock at the door, resulting in fines, bribes, or even deportation.

Starting a business falls somewhere in between. You can start your own businesses, such as a B and B, or a restaurant, or a vacation rental, with varying degrees of paperwork, especially with a stipulation that it will mean jobs for locals. Given the importance of tourism in many of the retirement havens, there will always be a gringo market for food and lodging, so this can be an excellent way of securing income for yourself. It's not that it's easy to get a working visa or permit, but it's possible. Sometimes it can be surprisingly hassle-free, as reported by many expats in Latin America. But it also means getting involved in paying local taxes, and that—as we've seen—is never hassle-free.

In practice, pushing aside the red tape, entrepreneurship is often rewarded. If you think up a service—more likely an expat service—

that's not being provided, and you're willing to put in the investment and the hours, it can be a lucrative second career. One friend in Mexico saw how difficult it was for expats in a remote area to pick up groceries and mail, and made himself into his own kind of Fed Ex–type delivery guy. Another did it by going right at the red tape itself: seeing how flummoxed expats became over property paperwork or construction permits, he learned the ropes and became a red-tape Sherpa for the whole expat community, taking his payments in cash. Teaching English or English as a second language is a big favorite, and is often paid for under the table. The catch: it's hard to teach foreigners English if you don't speak their language as well. And the pay, as it is for many teachers, is low, very low.

5. *So if all of this is so complicated, are my options really so limited?*

No, not at all. As we've said, the internet changed everything, and that's where your opportunities lie. On the internet you can come up with any of a million income-producing ideas and try them out without fear or hassle. Online you are connected to the global economy, not the local, so you can charge what the global market will bear. And you can use the internet in limitless ways, to create, market, and sell your service or product. A couple in **Chapala** publishes books on demand for customers all over the world. An entrepreneur in Costa Rica creates an export-import business in native handicrafts on eBay. An expat in *Tuscany* finds exotic olive oil and establishes a niche in the culinary world online. A Canadian in Croatia grades papers for a university back in Montreal. As to money, simple: a wire transfer to your bank, a payment to your PayPal account.

Just as important as the income is the opportunity to *do* something. If you've been an achiever in your former life, the web gives you a chance to continue being an achiever, but in your flip-flops.

There's a caption from a *New Yorker* cartoon: "On the internet, no one knows you're a dog." To expats, the saying is: on the internet, no one knows—or cares—where the hell you are.

ONE FUNDAMENTAL QUESTION
IN CONSIDERING LATIN AMERICA

How do I feel about living in comfort amid poverty? How <u>should</u> I feel? Am I exploiting the local population when I pay for services far more cheaply than I'd pay in North America? Is this just a new kind of colonial mentality?

PERSONAL TESTIMONY FROM YOUR AUTHORS

Everyone who moves to Latin America has his or her own answer to this question. It's a fact that some expats settle in their adopted country with a sense of entitlement. For some of those who live at a remove, often isolated in gated communities, the local population is there to service them. The poverty around them gives them license not only to live at a higher standard but to look down from a higher perch than they could at home.

We didn't feel that way, and neither did the expats with whom we became friends. We arrived in Mexico determined to live as guests of our new country, with the obligations of a guest. For starters, we determined to do our business with local Mexicans, which doesn't just mean hiring a Mexican gardener or a maid. We worked with a Mexican lawyer, a Mexican architect, a Mexican contractor, a Mexican accountant, Mexican builders. This is not only the right thing to do, it is also smart. The Mexican community feels an investment in you.

One of the unfortunate facts about Latin America's growing professional class is that education does not necessarily mean more jobs—not right away, anyway. That's why so many seek to emigrate rather than to put their skills to work in their own countries. So it's at least a fortunate trend that as the number of expats grows in a Latin American country, there will be more and more demand for professional services. That in itself could be one modest answer to Latin America's traditional scourge of unemployment.

Our group of friends also joined in community volunteer efforts. One expat, described at length in *Gringos in Paradise,* spends every weekend driving his Jeep up into the mountains on missions of mercy. There he distributes food, clothing, and medicine to Indians—historically, and still, the most oppressed of Mexico's poor—living in wretchedness less than an hour away from the beach communities. He is an exemplar of the retired American who came down to live a more comfortable life but found his satisfaction in helping others to a better life. (More on this follows the reports on each country in this book, and in the chapter "Volunteering Without Borders.")

At the same time, we also found that even the most well-intentioned efforts can slip over the edge into patronization. Local people do not always appreciate efforts they have not asked for, and it is easy to believe you're being helpful when all you're doing is stoking resentment. You have to do your legwork on this, inquiring, checking first with the people who live there, stepping softly.

Finally, we did our damndest not to be Ugly Americans, a bracing idea not just in Latin America, but anywhere. We tried not to throw our weight around or lecture anyone on how things were done back home. We knew that our Mexican hosts dislike confrontation or saying no, so we tried not to be obnoxious. We refused the game of haggling—the unpretty gringo habit of gaining bragging rights by talking an old gentleman down a few pesos for a trinket on the street. Most of all, we looked for, and found, the things we admired in the culture around us. We came down to be a part of things, to learn something new—else, why move at all? As a Mexican friend said about Americans who constantly compare life in Mexico to life in the States, "What is difficult for us Mexicans to understand is, If there are so many things some Americans don't like about living here, why are they living here?"

TWELVE THINGS YOU SHOULD BE ASKING YOURSELF RIGHT ABOUT NOW

1. Am I ready for something different? How have I adjusted to major changes in lifestyle in the past? Have I enjoyed or struggled with change?

2. Why am I thinking about doing this? Expats say that moving abroad just because it's cheaper is never a good enough reason. Do I know my real motives?

3. Do I reflexively believe that America does, makes, runs things better than other countries? Or do I think it's likely that other societies, developed or developing, do things just as well in other ways?

4. What is my tolerance for inefficiency? Do I become irritated with long lines, broken appointments, unnecessary paperwork? Or do I let most things roll off my back?

5. Am I willing to live *without*? No matter how well I'll live, am I aware that many of the things I'm used to may be unavailable?

6. How do I feel about the prospect of psychological isolation? Without a familiar structure under me, living under someone else's laws, rights, appeal process?

7. Am I in complete harmony with my spouse or companion?

8. Am I willing to spend what it takes to visit a place repeatedly before deciding? To shell out for legal and tax consultation, here and in my destination?

9. Have I thought through the implications of living far from family? Have I realistically considered the costs of going back or having them visit me?

10. Do I have something to *do* where I'm going? Do I realize that just sitting in the sun, sipping a drink with an umbrella in it, is going to get old fast? Do I have a passion I've postponed and want to pursue? A desire to contribute?

11. Am I ready for the "small-town" life? Do I realize that wherever I move, I'll be a minority, and that we expats will reach out and bond as friends—but also gossip about one another, judge one another, wear on one another?

12. How's my humility? Am I a potential Ugly American—arrogant, superior? Would I recognize that in myself if it exists? How do I treat other nationalities on my home ground?

GET YOUR GRADES

- ✦ *Report card*
- ✦ *Latin American studies*
- ✦ *European studies*

Chapter 7

A REPORT CARD

You've considered the dream; you've awakened for a reality check; you've thought about health care; you've boned up on finances; you've ticked off a general checklist; you've considered a strategy to make a move practical and affordable. Now it's time to narrow down your choices. The *carne* and *pommes de terre* of this book will be the in-depth reporting on ten countries we've chosen to spotlight.

So at the outset, we offer a couple of cheat sheets: a report card and, in the next chapter, a kind of calculator.

REPORT CARD

These are grades we're giving ten countries in subjects that will be important to you in choosing a country. We've mashed together data from independent studies, government figures (yes, the CIA website can be helpful), other published sources, expat interviews, and our own experience. The grades may not correspond precisely to what our reporters write, or to individual lists and surveys, or to some of the testimony you'll read from expats later in this book. They are *our* best estimates, based on all of the above.

Here's how we define the categories we're grading:

- **Weather:** We're grading high on temperate or sunny weather, low on more than a few months of rain or cold. A mountainside village described as "eternal springtime" may have winds that blow your roof off.
- **Ease of residency:** Difficulty in getting the proper visas to stay more than the standard three months—red tape, costs, effort. (In some countries, you have to return to the U.S. before you can establish residency.)

- **Special retiree benefits:** Highest grades went to countries that have laws designed specifically to attract retirees. Others get pretty good grades because retirees get to share in the benefits of local residents of a similar age.
- **Affordability:** A very general estimate that cannot only vary dramatically within a country but is a moving target as prices rise. Includes real estate, rentals, food, utilities, domestic help, travel. (See next chapter.)
- **Health care:** We're talking about the availability, access, costs, and general quality of medical care available to retirees.
- **English sufficient:** High grades go to places where you'll be understood in your native tongue; lower grades go to places where you get an uncomprehending stare. But to repeat ourselves, learning the language greatly deepens your experience.
- **U.S. expat community:** You may or may not like it, but this measures the general pervasiveness of other North Americans. We assume retiring abroad can be made easier if there are others of your ilk who share your experience.
- **Property restrictions:** In some locations, buying or owning property can be restricted—like Mexico's coasts and border areas. In others, new construction may be discouraged or forbidden. In still others, the red tape may be a snarl.
- **Serious crime:** This is mainly crimes of violence or worse. In developed countries, the stats are thought to be accurate; in undeveloped countries, they are notoriously underreported. Our estimates in Latin American countries are just that—estimates. (See appendix 1 for various kinds of measures used.)
- **Petty crime:** We've distinguished between severity of crime because it's one thing to be in fear for your life or your person, another to encounter burglaries and robberies—which are more tolerable but definitely not confined to undeveloped or Latin American countries.
- **Corruption:** These stats are issued by Transparency International, the organization that tallies countries' official and petty corruption by research on a number of indicators. (See appendix 1.)
- **Culture:** A measure of the depth of a variety of cultural arts—not everywhere in a country, but available to those who want to find it.
- **Infrastructure:** The quality (or existence) of good roads, energy, water, television, internet.
- **Food variety:** In some countries, it's fish and chicken all year round, other places offer variety and abundance. Sure, generally

speaking, most urban areas have variety and isolated places do not; we're giving a rough sense of how retirees report it, because we heard about it so often either as a complaint or a source of joy.
- **Distance, access to the U.S. or Canada:** availability, distance, time, and cost.

So yes, this grading exercise is a highly subjective exercise—oh, let's admit it—it's a hoot. Grading an entire country! Just think of it as a way to orient yourself before drilling down into a part of the earth that interests you.
These are countries we think play well with others—you, that is.

LATIN AMERICA

Mexico

Weather (some hurricanes)	A− (coast summers, D)
Ease of residency	A
Special retiree benefits	B
Affordability (costs, housing)	B+ (chic places, C)
Health care (city)	B (A− in some cities; rural, C+)
English sufficient	B−
U.S. expat community	A
Property restrictions	B− (coasts and borders)
Serious crime (most places)	B+ (border cities, F)
Petty crime	C−
Corruption	C
Culture (some regions)	A−
Infrastructure (roads, TV, web)	B−
Food variety (cities, resorts)	A− (rural, C)
Distance, access to U.S.	A+

Belize (not technically Latin America)

Weather (hurricane belt)	B (hot summers, gnats, D)
Ease of residency	A−
Special retiree benefits	B+

Affordability (costs, housing)	B (real estate, C)
Health care	C (but Mexico nearby)
English sufficient	A+
U.S. expat community	B−
Property restrictions	B
Serious crime	B+ (city, C−)
Petty crime	C−
Corruption	C−
Culture	D
Infrastructure	D+
Food variety	D
Distance, access to U.S.	B+

Costa Rica

Weather (hurricane belt)	B− (hot, humid summers, D)
Ease of residency	B+
Special retiree benefits	B− (duties high)
Affordability (costs, housing)	B− (costs rising)
Health care (city)	B
English sufficient	B−
U.S. expat community	A
Property restrictions	A−
Serious crime	B
Petty crime	C−
Corruption	A
Culture	C (ecoculture, A+)
Infrastructure	C+
Food variety	C+
Distance, access to U.S.	B+

Nicaragua

Weather (hurricane belt)	B (hot, humid summers, D)
Ease of residency	A

Special retiree benefits	B
Affordability (costs, housing)	A
Health care (city)	C (rural, D)
English sufficient	D
U.S. expat community	C (small colony)
Property restrictions	B+ (troubles in past)
Serious crime	B
Petty crime	C
Corruption	D
Culture	C
Infrastructure	D-
Food variety	C
Distance, access to U.S.	B

Panama

Weather (no hurricanes)	B (humid summers, lots of rain)
Ease of residency	A−
Special retiree benefits	A+
Affordability	B− (rural, B+)
Health care (city)	B+ (rural, D)
English sufficient	B+
U.S. expat community	A−
Property restrictions	B+ (real estate hustles, D)
Serious crime	B+
Petty crime	C+
Corruption (judicial)	D
Culture	B− (rural, D)
Infrastructure	C+
Food variety	A− (rural, C)
Distance, access to U.S.	B+

EUROPE

France

Weather (in the south)	A− (north, C)
Ease of residency	B
Special retiree benefits	C
Affordability (cities, chic spots)	D (less traveled, rural, B)
Health care	A++
English sufficient	B+ (occasional attitude, B−)
U.S. expat community	A (not necessarily in groups)
Property restrictions (rent, buy)	B+
Serious crime	A
Petty crime	A−
Corruption	A
Culture	A++
Infrastructure	B+
Food variety	In a class of its own
Distance, access to U.S.	C+

Italy

Weather	A−
Ease of residency	B− (moving target)
Special retiree benefits	C
Affordability (cities, chic spots)	D (less traveled, rural, B)
Health care	A
English sufficient	B
U.S. expat community	A
Property restrictions (rent, buy)	A−
Serious crime	B−
Petty crime	B
Corruption	C
Culture	A++
Infrastructure	B−

Food variety	A++
Distance, access to U.S.	C+

Croatia

Weather	A
Ease of residency	B
Special retiree benefits	D
Affordability (coast, city)	C+ (inland, A−)
Health care	B
English sufficient	C−
U.S. expat community	D
Property restrictions	B−
Serious crime	A
Petty crime	A−
Corruption	B+
Culture	C+
Infrastructure	C
Food variety	B
Distance, access to U.S.	C−

Spain

Weather	A
Ease of residency	B+
Special retiree benefits	C
Affordability (costs, housing)	B (D in chic spots)
Health care	A−
English sufficient	A− (lots of Brits)
U.S. expat community	B+ (more European)
Property restrictions	B+
Serious crime	A−
Petty crime	B+
Corruption	A−
Culture	A

Infrastructure	A−
Food variety	A
Distance, access to U.S.	C+

Portugal

Weather	A
Ease of residency	B+
Special retiree benefits	B
Affordability	B+ (city, coasts, B−)
Health care	B
English sufficient	C−
U.S. expat community	C (nice but small)
Property restrictions	A
Serious crime	A
Petty crime	A−
Corruption	A
Culture	B
Infrastructure	B
Food variety	B
Distance, access to U.S.	B−

Chapter 8

ADD IT UP

How Much Will I Need to Live On?

Here, for the Big Ten Countries we cover in depth and our "Also Consider" list, are our estimates of what it costs in 2008–2009 to live a *comfortable life* for two people.

A comfortable life means available modern amenities, eating out, some travel, perhaps domestic help. It includes rental costs or upkeep for an owned property.

We also strongly suggest that you have some savings, either for a house purchase if that's your intention (mortgages are often expensive or unavailable), or because there are *always* unanticipated expenses not covered by income. A minimum of $100,000 in the bank is a good number to shoot for.

There are huge differences within countries among major cities, resort towns, inland towns, and modest villages (beach or rural). We've tried to indicate some of these differences, with a certain humble modesty that comes from knowing how wildly divergent costs can be.

Can you live on much less than we estimate in some of these areas?

Yes.

Will there be plenty of people who stand up and say, "I live well on just _____!"?

Yes.

But by far, the most disappointed retirees are those who arrive thinking they can live high on a small pension or Social Security. Living on Social Security might have been true a few years ago. And in some places, it is still true for those willing to live a frugal "local" life—tacos, not steak. But newer arrivals, seduced by website promotions and promises of a new life on $800 a month, are among the unhappiest of retirees, and they make older expats even less happy.

So we're probably erring on the high side. But you'll be happy we did.

Very Affordable
(Live on $12,000–$18,000 per Year)

Argentina (inland towns, villages)
Nicaragua
Ecuador
Philippines
Honduras
Thailand (inland, some resort towns)

Affordable:
(Live on $18,000–$35,000 per Year)

Belize
Argentina (big cities)
Panama (inland, some resort towns)
Costa Rica (inland, some resort towns)
Mexico (inland, some resort towns, villages)
Thailand (big city, some resort towns)
Croatia (inland, some beach towns, villages)
Portugal (inland, some beach towns, villages)

Moderate
(Live on $35,000–$50,000 per Year)

Panama (city, some resorts and inland towns)
Costa Rica (city, resorts)
Mexico (towns, inland gringo colonies, some resorts)
Caribbean (Dominican Republic, others)
Croatia (city, coastal)
Italy (rural, less traveled)
France (rural, less traveled)
Greece (inland, some islands)
Thailand (city, islands)
Portugal (some coastal)
Spain (inland, some coastal)

Expensive:
(Live on $50,000–$90,000 per Year)

France
Italy
Mexico (**Mexico City**, some inland towns, major resorts)
Greek Islands
Spain (big city, resort towns)
Portugal (some resorts)
Caribbean (Barbados, some islands)

Very Expensive:
(Sky's the Limit)

France (**Paris, Riviera**)
Italy (**Rome, Milan/lakes,** *Tuscany*)
Caribbean (**Bahamas, Bermuda, Virgin Islands**)
Australia and New Zealand (because of large investment required for
     residency)

CHOOSING A MAJOR

✦ Ten Major Countries in Depth

COUNTRY BY COUNTRY
Prepare to Submerge

And so we come to the reporting: the Big Ten. Our choices come from Latin America and Europe. (There are, of course, dozens of other destinations to consider, including Asia and the Caribbean—see "Also Consider.") Our constant is weather: with a few exceptions, such as **Paris,** we're covering just the warmer parts of the world. We assume the vast majority of you want to settle in balmy climes. Our Latin American choices begin at the Rio Grande and go south in a narrow line to the far edge of Central America. Our European choices form a sunny crescent along the Mediterranean and across the Adriatic Sea.

Our reporters were asked to describe their adopted country as if a reader were encountering it for the first time. This gives you a deep immersion in the pleasures and challenges of each country, from its security and history to some of the practical steps you'd have to take if you moved there. They include a quick snapshot in time of three sets of costs: an upscale location, a midpriced location, and a modest location. Our writers report their stories warts and all, but each has lived or is currently living in these countries, and the common reason is that they've followed their own dream. So, honestly, they *like* where they live.

Following each country you'll find a number of personal testimonies by expat residents from among the hundreds we've questioned ("My Mexico," "My Italy," and so on). Their points of view are theirs alone, some quite idiosyncratic, and we've chosen to let them say what they have to say without toning them down. A few may contradict what our writer has reported—there are as many opinions out there as there are expats—and a few are not as pleased with their move as we might expect. Most share their delight, without avoiding the drawbacks, at the way their lives have turned out.

LATIN AMERICA

MEXICO

We'll start closest to the U.S., giving a lot of space to our southern neighbor. Mexico is the most popular destination for American and Canadian retirees, whether full-time or part-time, by a long shot—perhaps twice all the other countries combined. It regularly heads the lists of desirable retirement destinations for North Americans.

But before we start . . .

Wait!

POP QUIZ!

Today, class, there will be a quiz to see whether you'd be a good candidate for retirement in Mexico. It will also reflect your aptitude for living in other Latin American countries. There will be no further quizzes on this part of the world.

LATIN AMERICAN STUDIES

SHOULD YOU RETIRE IN MEXICO?

Test Yourself, Amigo

1. **How familiar are you with Mexico?**
   a) I've visited more than once, traveled widely beyond the tourist areas, read history, cultural, and guidebooks, know or want to learn Spanish, saw *Y Tu Mamá También*.
   b) I've been to Mexican resorts several times, traveled a bit, read a guidebook, have Mexican friends, know a bit of Spanish, saw *Like Water for Chocolate*.
   c) I've crossed over the border for shopping, restaurants, and nightlife, which I enjoy. I've spent time with Mexican-Americans, I can speak some Spanish phrases, saw *Frida*.
   d) I went to **Cancún** once but can't remember it. I eat Mexican food, try to talk Spanish with the waiters; I read a used book called *Mexico on $400 a Month*, saw *The Treasure of the Sierra Madre* on TV.

2. **How would you characterize your main purpose in moving to Mexico, full- or part-time?**
   a) I want to find a mostly pleasant climate, change my life, live a bit more affordably, adapt to a new culture, and settle among both Mexicans and gringos.
   b) I want terrific weather, not too much change, am willing to get a taste of a new culture, to live well on a lot less, and to settle in a gated community with like-minded people.
   c) I want a fantastic year-round climate where I can live much more cheaply among fellow gringos, and have inexpensive Mexican maids and gardeners.
   d) I want to go where the weather's perfect, live like a prince on my Social Security check, and the fewer locals, the better.

3. **What are your greatest concerns about Mexico?**
   a) The usual suspects—crime, corruption—but I know it depends on where and how you choose to live in Mexico, as it does in the States. I choose to believe that people are honest and well intentioned unless they prove otherwise.
   b) Well, I'm certain I'll see my share of petty crime and corruption, but it's no big deal, I'm prepared for it, and I'm willing to roll with the punches.
   c) When I get asked for a payoff by a cop, I'll refuse and take him to traffic court. If I catch a burglar, I'll press charges. I don't bend the rules at home, I'm not bending them here.
   d) I have little or no confidence in the Mexican police, the courts, or public officials. I fully expect I'll have to bribe them all.

4. **A Mexican makes an appointment and shows up three hours late. You:**
   a) Shrug and get on with it.
   b) Ask him to be more punctual in the future.
   c) Tell him you're upset, and that he has no respect for your time.
   d) Bawl him out publicly and tell him you'll fire him next time.

5. **The waiter at an upscale restaurant pours you a glass of water with ice in it. You:**
   a) Drink it without concern, knowing ice is made from purified water by Mexican law.
   b) Drink it with some concern, and don't suck the ice.
   c) Send back the water and ice and ask for a sealed bottle of mineral water.
   d) Pour the ice into the potted palm and order a tequila.

6. **You are ready to consider buying real estate in Mexico. Your first steps are:**
   a) To resist buying at all. Rent a place, talk to people over time, get to know the lay of the land. Refuse to get caught up in real estate fever.

b) Wait till you get down there, rent for a while, but be ready to make a bid on a property before the price goes up.
c) Before you go, check out real estate on the internet; when you see photos you like, email the broker. When you get there, if it looks as good, contact a lawyer and offer a deposit.
d) Before you go, check out real estate on the internet; when you see photos you like, email the broker. He tells you properties are going fast; you wire-transfer payment to him.

7. **You come down with flulike symptoms. You:**
a) Ask friends about the best doctor in the area, Mexican or otherwise, and pay a visit.
b) Ask friends about any English-speaking doctors in the area and pay a visit.
c) Ask if there are any American doctors in the area and drive as far as it takes to be certain you're getting American medical care.
d) Call in the chopper and evacuate.

8. **Your attitude toward Mexicans can best be described as:**
a) A hard-working people with a rich culture and strong family ties living in a beautiful country with significant economic problems but a rising middle class. Luckily, they are more welcoming toward gringos in their country than we are toward them in ours.
b) A hard-working people with a rich culture and strong family ties living in a semidysfunctional society with widespread poverty. I like the Mexicans I've met, and I look forward to teaching them how we do things so they can improve their lot.
c) A hard-working people ready to flee north at the drop of a sombrero. Their economy is a mess, as is their government. I think Mexicans are all right, but I hope they'll be grateful for the money and employment we retirees will bring.
d) I like Mexico, except for the Mexicans.

KEY: *Give yourself 5 points for every "a" answer, 4 points for every "b," 3 points for every "c," and 0 points for every "d."*

35–40 points: *You're a thoughtful, open-minded, and promising candidate for moving to Mexico.*

25–35 points: *With a bit more study, visits, and on-the-ground experience, you may become a candidate for moving to Mexico.*

15–25 points: *You need to learn a lot more before you consider doing anything more permanent than visiting Mexico as a tourist.*

0–15 points: *Stay home.*

Chapter 9

MEXICO

The Primary Destination

By Eileen Pierce

Mexico, all 754,120 square miles of her, is as rich in culture as she is in natural beauty. She is bold, loud, excessive, generous, and as wily as she is naive. You can dally with Mexico. She likes a good time, doesn't go to bed early. But underneath the glitz of an $11 billion tourist economy, snug and safe beyond the bulldozers and cranes that are fashioning a glossy new Mexico, the old one, its cultural roots buried deep in its Indian past, survives.

Besides the fact that, in her tropics, butterflies flit in and out of the house like pets, bougainvillea grows like weeds, and splashy sunsets punctuate the end of most every day, Mexico also offers a panoply of pragmatic reasons to choose it as a great adventure of later life. It is welcoming, easily affordable, has a multitude of expatriate communities within a one-, two-, or three-day drive of the border, and offers the essentials of contemporary life. Unless you pitch a *palapa* on some remote beach, your retirement will be all-inclusive, with high-speed internet access, satellite TV, cell phone service, liberal immigration laws, friendly, polite, welcoming people, inexpensive health care (see "Health Care/Medical"), and a breathtaking variety of temperate and tropical climates.

Mexicans are unapologetically imperfect, among the hardest-working and the most fiesta-prone people, both embracing change and resistant to it. A blood-spattered history characterized by a corrupt ruling class, vast poverty, natural disasters, and an endless series of invasions has imbued the population with a sense of acceptance—except when they revolt. (See "History.") There will be catastrophes, people will die, babies will be born, miracles will happen. Mexico will endure.

UPSIDES

1. A sunny climate, no need for heat or air-conditioning (except coasts in the summer).
2. Lower cost of living in highest-standard-of-living nation in Latin America.
3. Well-established expat communities.
4. Can drive to Mexico, on an ever-improving highway system.
5. Time is not of the essence.

DOWNSIDES

1. Petty crime, particularly robbery, is common.
2. Drug use is still less per capita than in the U.S. but a growing problem.
3. Mexico's infrastructure can be erratic: electricity, water shortages.
4. Even with Wal-Mart, Home Depot, products with a plug not so good.
5. Time is not of the essence.

LOCATION

Mexico's northern border stretches in a series of descending steps, beginning just south of San Diego on the Pacific coast and ending 1,933 dry, dusty miles later at the Gulf of Mexico. Along the way, Mexico unveils six of its thirty-one states: *Baja California, Sonora, Chihuahua, Coahuila, Nuevo León,* and *Tamaulipas.* With 350 million people legally crossing it each year, it is the most frequently crossed international border in the world. To the south, the Mexican states of *Chiapas* and *Campeche* border on Guatemala, and *Quintana Roo* on Belize.

The remainder of Mexico is encircled by sea: the Gulf of Mexico and the Caribbean seas on the east, the Pacific Ocean and the Sea of Cortés on the west. For many North Americans, these 5,800 miles of Mexico's idyllic coastline represent the new retirement frontier.

CLIMATE

In terms of temperature, the Tropic of Cancer divides Mexico into two climatic zones. Retirees will find a delightful, generally temperate climate in

Guadalajara, *Lake Chapala,* San Miguel de Allende, Mexico City, and Cuernavaca. In San Miguel, the summers are temperate, while the winters can be chilly, even a bit raw and occasionally frosty. Drop a thousand feet to Guadalajara, *Lake Chapala,* and Cuernavaca (the Land of Eternal Spring) for a more temperate year-round climate.

The average North American resident revels in a winter climate where temperatures rarely drop below 55 or 60 in the evenings. From November through April, the air is temperate, with no humidity. Summers are hot and humid all over, but are particularly uncomfortable in Puerto Vallarta, the *Yucatán* and *Baja* Peninsulas.

The country as a whole has only two seasons: rainy (generally from May or June through September and October, with a shorter season of rains in the more temperate central and northern parts of the country) and dry (October or November through April or May).

PEOPLE

The largest Spanish-speaking country in the world, with an estimated population of 109,955,400 people in 2008, Mexico is the eleventh most populous country in the world. Its people are 60 percent Mestizo (Amerindian-Spanish), 30 percent Amerindian, 9 percent white, and 1 percent other. Eighty-nine percent are Catholic, though regular church attendance (except for major religious holidays) has decreased over the last decade.

Roughly one million North Americans have chosen to live in Mexico. More U.S. expatriates live in Mexico than in any other country in the world. With neither the U.S. nor Mexico focusing on counting the fluctuating expatriate community, much less those who are "retired," it is impossible to retrieve exact figures.

HISTORY

Beginning in 200 BC, preclassic indigenous groups—the Olmecs, Toltecs, Aztecs, and Mayans—were building large communities, pyramids, irrigation canals, and systems of writing, mathematics, and astronomy. When the Spanish conquistador Hernán Cortés conquered the Aztec capital, Tenochtitlán (now Mexico City), and its ruler, Montezuma, in 1519, he rechristened the country New Spain. By 1620 Mexico's population, impoverished, enslaved, and sickened by diseases imported by the conquistadores, was reduced to three million.

Mexico rebelled against Spain in the 1810 War of Independence, but with the notable exceptions of Benito Juárez and, later, Lázaro Cárdenas, rulers were inept, corrupt, despotic, and greedy. If Juárez, the only Indian ever elected, continues to be Mexico's most revered president, the dictator General Porfirio Díaz, who succeeded him in office, is the most infamous. His three decades of corruption ended in 1910 when Emiliano Zapata and Pancho Villa launched the Mexican Revolution. It wasn't until Vicente Fox was elected, in 2000, that Mexicans had a viable second political party, the National Action Party (PAN). Fox became the first truly democratically elected president in seven decades and paved the way for another PAN president, Felipe Calderón, elected in 2006.

GOVERNMENT

Mexico's constitution, written in 1917, calls for a government very much like that of the United States. A federation of thirty-one states, it has three branches: executive, legislative, and judicial (Supreme Court). Public officials on all three levels of government—federal, state, and municipal—are elected.

During President Vicente Fox's six-year term, he tried to make inroads against rampant government corruption, laying the groundwork for the modernization of Mexico's justice system, and moved the government toward more accountability and transparency. He did not, however, confront the heightened violence between warring drug cartels or immigration woes with Mexico's neighbors. By the end of his term, a frustrated lower class had organized into a vital third, left-leaning political party, the PRD. Its candidate, Andrés Manuel Lopéz Obrador, ran against Felipe Calderón, the conservative candidate backed by Fox's PAN party. When Lopéz Obrador lost the presidential election by less than 1 percent, he and his PRD followers took to **Mexico City**'s streets for several weeks.

President Calderón met the challenge by declaring war against the drug cartels and launching a number of economic and social reforms. Calderón, like Vicente Fox, has the daunting task of bringing Mexico's congressional factions into line behind him. Mexico's struggle for economic and social balance continues, and its people, patient and fatalistic, seem willing to give their new president a chance.

WHERE TO LIVE

The largest foreign communities are centered around the beach resorts of **Puerto Vallarta** and **Mazatlán** on the Pacific coast; the colonial cities and towns in Mexico's central highlands, such as **San Miguel de Allende;** the *Baja Peninsula* with its striking desert, mountain, and ocean villages; and

the stretch of white sand beach in the *Yucatán Peninsula,* which includes both the bustling resort of **Cancún** and dozy coastal villages down to the Belize border.

Central America and Colonial Highlands

Lifestyles vary as much as weather systems in Mexico, and for those who prefer a wardrobe with as many turtlenecks as bathing suits, the inland colonial highlands of central Mexico, the first region to experience a large influx of expatriates, continue to be very popular. The colonial destinations that are seeing the largest growth among retirees are **San Miguel de Allende, Cuernavaca, Mexico City, Guadalajara,** and its neighbors *Lake Chapala* and Ajijic. They share common traits: an excellent year-round climate, a sound communication infrastructure, striking colonial architecture, a lively cultural epicenter, educational opportunities (language, art, history, cooking, music), good, nearby health care, large well-integrated foreign communities, and an ambience wrapped in Mexican preclassic and colonial history.

San Miguel de Allende

San Miguel has one of the best locations in Mexico for retirees who don't want to be more than a day and a half's drive from the U.S. border. Its population is 140,000, with half living in the city, and the other half living in its environs. An estimated 12,000 to 14,000 foreigners live in San Miguel de Allende, 70 percent of them from the U.S., 20 percent from Canada, and 10 percent from thirty-one other countries.

If you have a dream of what a typical Mexican village looks like, and if that dream is full of flowers and walled courtyards, a vibrant, shaded central plaza with an astonishingly romantic Gothic church, a tumble of narrow cobbled streets, and if that town—all of it, every stone and balcony and wooden door in the whole place—was protected by the Mexican government as a National Historic Landmark, go directly to San Miguel de Allende.

On the other hand, if your dream requires immersing yourself in the daily life of Mexico, San Miguel has an overwhelming foreign presence that may seem a bit over the top. You may not be rubbing shoulders with the local indigenous population in the town's pricey restaurants and clubs, and you won't have to worry about speaking much Spanish or finding your favorite cereal in the two new super supermarkets next to the eight-screen cineplex theater.

San Miguel is drenched in Mexican history, and for the North Americans—mostly Texans—who discovered its charms in the late 1970s when land was cheap and plentiful—it was a perfect fit. Today, with the exception of the stylish parts of Mexico City, there is nowhere in the country quite as trendy as San Miguel, or for that matter, quite as expensive. It is claimed that some Americans live in or around San Miguel on their Social Security, but Caren Cross, a psychotherapist from Virginia who moved here with her husband and became a filmmaker, says, "The reality is you probably need sixty thousand dollars a year to live well, and that includes occasional trips." Cross filmed the journeys, real and psychological, of a number of San Miguel expats in her movie Lost and Found in Mexico.

In San Miguel, the "simple life" you may have wished for up north can be swallowed up by music, dance, theatrical events, fitness programs, cooking classes, Tibetan monk healing ceremonies, wine tastings, and 12-step recovery meetings. Add on the cocktail hours and miscellaneous fiestas, and before you know it, you'll be busier than you ever were back home. It's more crowded with cars and visitors than ever, and the strain on its roads and infrastructure shows. But all the while, Mexico is still in the background, in the freshly washed early morning cobblestone streets and in the mariachi singers strolling around the plaza in the cool evenings.

Guadalajara

Mexico's second-largest city, **Guadalajara,** has a population of 6.1 million. An estimated 50,000 retired Americans live in and around the city. The beating heart of **Guadalajara**'s twelve-block square city center is its massive sixteenth-century cathedral and the plazas, which adjoin one another like a series of tiled carpets rolled across seven blocks from the cathedral. Residents meander alongside tourists and expatriates, and sooner or later everyone finds a bench from which to watch the stream of life. **Guadalajara** has been called Mexico's most Mexican city, and is the birthplace of mariachi music, the Mexican hat dance, and tequila. The city has matchless murals by José Clemente Orozco and Diego Rivera, world-class restaurants, an excellent health care system, and an extensive foreign community. Unfortunately, like most of the world's large, industrial cities, **Guadalajara** suffers from traffic congestion and dangerous levels of air pollution. Its crime rate is also high, though expats report that relatively little serious has touched them.

Lake Chapala and Ajijic

The expatriate communities that rim *Lake Chapala,* the four-hundred-square-mile mountain lake thirty-five miles south of **Guadalajara,** include the two villages of **Ajijic** and **Chapala,** and are referred to as the Lakeside Communities. They have a combined population of 60,000 people, with an estimated 15,000 to 20,000 expatriates, half Canadian, half American. Together with the **Guadalajara** expats in the same general area, this is the biggest U.S. expat community anywhere.

American and Canadian residents intermingle through the auspices of a large number of organizations, including the VFW, the American Legion, and the Rotary club. There is a vast network of bingo, quilting, bridge, church, volunteer opportunities (see "Volunteering Without Borders" and "Volunteer Heaven" in chapter 21), theater, boating—the social calendar here is dizzying.

Large, comfortable houses, coupled with the area's temperate year-round climate, offer an alluring outdoor lifestyle to North Americans accustomed to holing up through the long winter season. Many "Lakesiders" enjoy frequent trips to **Guadalajara,** stopping at Costco, Wal-Mart, Home Depot, or Sam's Club to pick up stateside staples and luxuries.

But Lakeside's expatriates have enough going on to keep them quite happily anchored to home. They like the quiet of the lake and the view, though many lament the pollution that has made the lake unswimmable for years. They'd rather bird-watch or walk down a cobbled street than suffer the crowds and traffic of their big city neighbor **Guadalajara.** For them, Lakeside has more than enough cafés and restaurants, markets and stores, and companionship.

Tod Jonson is one such Lakeside expat. Formerly of Hollywood, California, the seventy-seven-year-old ex-actor and producer came to **Ajijic** twenty-four years ago. "I fell in love with the simpler way of life," he says. "It reminded me of my youth in Oklahoma. The weather is excellent to superb, the setting is gorgeous, and we get the Bolshoi Ballet every year."

Cuernavaca

Located fifty miles south of **Mexico City, Cuernavaca,** "The Land of Eternal Spring," is set in the center of some of Mexico's most beautiful countryside and is a favorite weekend getaway for people who live in **Mexico City** and its environs. With former residents such as Hernán Cortés, Montezuma, the Emperor Maximilian, Diego, and the exiled shah of Iran, **Cuernavaca** is a city of memories, of woodland picnics, boating parties, palaces, and tropic gardens hidden behind the high walls lining hilly, cobbled streets.

Today, wealthy Mexicans and foreigners continue to sequester themselves in guarded residential communities. But the addition of a vast industrial park, an ever-increasing onslaught of weekend tourists, and a population that is at the one million mark, has resulted in worsening smog, pollution, crime, and traffic congestion. Twenty-first century urbanization has left its mark on **Cuernavaca.** But with its perfect climate, volcanic vistas, and green university campuses, **Cuernavaca** has managed to retain more than a bit of charm. For expatriates the city is a perfect hub, well within a ninety-minute drive not only of the wealth of **Mexico City** attractions, but of dozens of the country's most interesting villages, ruins, and natural wonders.

The Pacific Coast

Mexico's long, lazy western coastline has two port cities of particular note for expatriates—**Mazatlán** and **Puerto Vallarta**—each within a seven-hour drive of each other. They both have large foreign communities, beautiful beaches, and a tourism-driven economy abetted by the regular arrival of cruise ships. A sprinkling of up-and-coming beach communities is growing north of Vallarta and offers, as well, a variety of retirement options. This area, the *Riviera Nayarit,* is seeing a great deal of development both by the government and foreign investors.

To the south on the Pacific coastline is the sprawling, rowdy city of **Acapulco,** once a playground for the rich from all over the world. **Acapulco** has its American residents but has become worn and seedy along its naturally beautiful coastline. The city only recently began to clean up and recapture its tourist trade. Drug gang activity and sordid crimes haven't helped its image.

Ixtapa and Zihuatanejo

No two sisters could be more different than the Mexican resorts of **Ixtapa** and **Zihuatanejo.** Linked by a four-lane, four-mile-long highway, they reflect Mexico's ancient past and its tourism-driven present.

Zihuatanejo, a city of 70,000 and a growing American and Canadian expatriate community, has preserved some of its heritage: Its streets are predictably cobbled, and if cruise ships insist on spilling their thousands of passengers onto the dock on a regular basis, the town's fishermen still support their families with the day's catch.

Ixtapa, the spawn of the same bankers and businessmen who created **Cancún** a year earlier in 1974, vibrates with condos, time shares, and four-star, high-rise hotels. With one tenth of the population of **Zihua, Ixta** has experienced a slower, greener, and gentler growth yet boasts golf courses and shopping malls. An international airport serves **Ixtapa-Zihuatanejo,** as well as smaller villages like **Troncones** and **Barra de Potosi,** where North Americans looking for less-crowded, less tourist-driven economies are settling.

Puerto Vallarta

Puerto Vallarta and environs have a population of more than 300,000 people, with approximately 20,000 American and Canadian expatriates. North of **Vallarta,** there are another estimated 5,000 expatriates living in small cities and towns. These coastal villages stretching up to forty miles north of **Vallarta** are experiencing tremendous growth.

Puerto Vallarta was a small, virtually inaccessible, and unknown fishing village until 1963 when director John Huston chose it over the booming Mexican resort of **Acapulco** for his film *The Night of the Iguana.* What the movie didn't do for **Vallarta,** star Richard Burton's frantic new romance with Liz Taylor did.

More sophisticated than **Mazatlán,** with a sway in her walk and a lot more cosmetic surgery under her belt, **Vallarta** has many suitors for her many charms. Her character, style, and substance all point to **Vallarta** being the real thing and not just a seven-day, fly-by-night chunk of beach with lots of high-rise megatels. Expatriates who settle here are lured by her barefoot-bar charm, her gourmet restaurants, her splashy nightlife, and her artists' and writers' colony.

The city, the mountains that shelter it, and the coast ten miles south are overpopulated, and the land that's still available to build on is being developed by high-rise hotels and condominiums. To the north, two expatriate and wealthy suburban communities in **Vallarta**'s environs have a fairly equal mix of wealthy Mexicans and foreigners, and offer a quieter alternative to retirees who don't want to live in a bawdy resort town. Both **Marina Vallarta,** the oldest, and just five miles distant from **Vallarta**'s boisterous so-called Romantic Zone, and **Nuevo Vallarta,** another five miles farther north, with its marinas, golf courses, hotels, and vacation-share resorts and condos, lure some residents and a lot of tourists.

The Riviera Nayarit

The border between the states of *Jalisco* (location of both **Guadalajara** and **Puerto Vallarta**) and *Nayarit* (the new *"Riviera"* of northern towns and villages) is where the time zone changes—it's one hour earlier in *Nayarit*— and even locals get confused by the time change. A few miles into the zone, **Bucerias** is a working man's town that supplies most of the area with its basic construction, service, and staffing needs. The beach here is long and pleasant with stunning views of **Vallarta,** but the town itself is dusty and hot, with rundown shops.

North of **Bucerias** is where the jungle gets serious, the highway enters the foothills of the *Sierra Madre,* and you see a Mexico of palm trees, thick vines, and bougainvillea the size of garages.

Sayulita
Retirees hungering for a lazy beach life with noisy nights and sunny days full of tacos and cerveza need drive only forty minutes or so north on the jungle road to **Sayulita** where the dining is casual, the bars are packed, and the excellent surf breathes fire into a booming tourist economy. (This is the village where the authors of this book settled, resulting in *Gringos in Paradise.*)

Sayulita is at heart a surfing town and has almost as many beach restaurants as bars. About as dusty as an oceanfront village can get, its central plaza is always abuzz, its many restaurants full in the high season. This village has a mix of Mexican families and cabbies and tourists and a rush of brown, well-toned bodies. There is an air about **Sayulita** that endears it to many tourists who drive into the village, park their rental cars, and walk into the nearest real estate office.

San Pancho

Just three miles farther north, **San Pancho** follows the same seasonal timeline as **Sayulita,** but its rough surf, strong riptides, and legends of drowned swimmers have kept the surfers and tourists away. But real estate values are high, and north of the town, villas precede one another down the terraced side of the mountain, conical palapas perch on their rooftops, and turquoise pools stretch toward the afternoon sun. Fortunately, the flavor of the town remains architecturally Mexican.

Punta de Mita

Between **Vallarta** and the northern villages is an outcropping of land known as **Punta de Mita.** There Americans live in a row of condominiums along the local village's narrow beachfront or in numerous well-guarded gated communities secluded in the surrounding countryside. With oceanfront property running as high as $1,000 a square meter, *Punta Mita* is where the wealthy have pitched their multimillion-dollar homes. In the planning stages are 11,000 hotel rooms, a 150-slip marina, three golf courses, a marine theme park, 34,000 homes and condos, and an airport.

For retirees looking for an expensive, more or less worry-free, not-very-Mexican retirement, *Punta Mita* holds a lot of promise.

Mazatlán

Meanwhile, the more traditional city of **Mazatlán** finds itself in a slower real estate market, a simple way of life, a significantly lower cost of living, and a reputation for marlin sport fishing and the sweet taste of fresh shrimp. In fact, long-term gringos who remember what brought them to Mexico in the first place point to **Mazatlán.** It was easy, they sigh, didn't take much work, and left you to your own devices most of the time.

Mazatlán has a population of 400,000, with an estimated 6,000 North Americans. The largest number of expatriates live in a number of neighborhoods, including some gated communities between the *Gold Zone* and *Playa Norte,* where real estate prices are relatively low, and there's proximity to the beach, golf courses, and the marina. Retirees looking for a middle-income sportsman's retirement will find **Mazatlán** similar to retirement in Florida, only a lot cheaper.

Mazatlán is unpretentious and has quieted down after a mad fling as a spring-break mecca. (College kids, always fickle, headed for other shores.) For retirees less concerned with chic and more about an affordable cost of living, this may become an ever more popular destination.

"Arizona South"

Puerto Peñasco (Rocky Point)

Just sixty miles south of Mexico's border with Arizona, **Puerto Peñasco** has long been a vacation destination for residents of Tucson and Phoenix desperate for an ocean view and a moonlit dip. Today millions of dollars are being pumped into the area where the market for condominiums and houses is increasing daily. More than a dozen planned subdivisions with hundreds of homes (and in some cases, thousands) have either been completed or are in process, and a $45 million international airport is planned.

Puerto Peñasco has been nicknamed **Rocky Point** by the thousands of gringos who visit and who've moved here. For retirees looking for a weekend or seasonal getaway, close to a lovely beach, just a short drive from their family, friends, and doctors back in the States, this big bite of back home is a reliable option.

San Carlos

Drive five hours south of **Nogales** to **San Carlos,** often called "Arizona South," and discover an extraordinary landscape as stark as a *Star Wars* set, with rocky cliffs plummeting into an azure sea. This small community of 5,000, primarily American second-home owners and retirees on the Gulf of California, was fashioned out of the parched desert of *Sonora* state.

A first visit to this unique landscape is quite literally breathtaking. In its first stages of development, **San Carlos** seemed the perfect compromise. It was close enough to Arizona to serve as a weekend getaway and yet more Mexican than any community in *Baja Norte*. But over time, **San Carlos** has become the town that Mexicans commute to rather than live in. Its restaurants, hotels, and shops are all geared to a North American community that can tend toward insularity and even claustrophobia.

San Carlos is clearly not the only town in Mexico overrun with gringos, but it is the only one built from scratch by them.

The Baja Peninsula

From the air, *Baja* looks like a spinal column, an eight-hundred-mile-long, mostly desert peninsula with a jagged row of mountains running down its center. Made of rock and cactus and the plain scrub born of arid soil, its character is formed by lying between the two seas that surround it: the Gulf of California (aka the Sea of Cortés) and the Pacific Ocean. Most expatriates have chosen to live along the *Baja*'s 2,000 miles of coastline in the northern state of *Baja California* (the towns of **Ensenada, Rosarito Beach,** and **San Felipe**), or the southern state, *Baja California Sur* (the towns of **La Paz, Loreto, Todos Santos,** and **the Cabos**). The farther south you go, the higher the real estate, the finer and whiter the beaches, the clearer the water.

Baja California Sur (South)

The Cabos

The Cabos are two resort towns located on capes that form the southernmost part of the *Baja Peninsula*. They are expensive—San Jose del Cabo—and very, very expensive—Cabo San Lucas. Connected by an eighteen-mile-long stretch of smooth road called the Corridor, the two **Cabos** are *Baja*'s richest gold mine.

Cabo San Lucas

Picture this: white sand beaches, seaside sunsets, a fistful of five-star resorts, sleek marinas, and golf courses growing like miracles in the parched desert floor. Now think about this: tourists as thick as flies, land so expensive it might as well be uranium, dinner for two costing as much as a weeklong vacation in the Poconos, and an oppressively loud, star-studded nightlife.

Cabo San Lucas is part of the new CEO culture, a big-money machine of a town where "millionaires only" need apply. Condos, gated communities, three English language newspapers, and a population that has more than doubled in the last decade have extracted much of the essence of this ravishingly beautiful equation of sun, sea, sand, and sky. If your major retirement priority is changing climates, not cultures, if you don't mind living in a town that barely closes its eyes, can afford at least $1 million for a new condominium or house, and have no abiding interest in learning Spanish, **Cabo San Lucas** may be for you.

San Jose del Cabo

The Corridor, or Transpeninsular Highway, which connects **Cabo San Lucas** and **San Jose del Cabo,** is lined with five spectacular resort communities: **Palmilla, Querencia, Cabo Real, Cabo del Sol, Punta Ballena.** Each features its own pools, championship golf course, beaches, hotels, and private residences. Unlike its ultrasleek neighbor **Cabo San Lucas,** Mexico still lurks in **San Jose del Cabo**'s narrow streets, its colonial plaza, and the mission cathedral that oversees its park benches and shade trees.

Like so many areas of Mexico where expatriates are settling, however, **San Jose** is feeling frisky, shaking off its colonial past and moving toward cafés and even art galleries. You can almost see the glint of gated communities in strangers' eyes and the pulse of the town quickening. It's still possible to find affordable apartments as well as rentals in **San Jose,** but land is going fast, and prices are some of the highest on the *Baja.*

La Paz

While **Cabo San Lucas** was becoming the priciest tourism and retirement destination in Mexico, most people used to whiz by **La Paz,** the capital of *Baja California Sur.* But in 2003, when *Money* magazine named it one of the best places in the world to retire, the unswerving headlights of the baby-boomer generation, hot on the trail of the next best retirement spot, swept over **La Paz**—and the prices have been rising ever since. A quarter million people live in this city on the Sea of Cortés; between 3,000 and 4,000 of them are North Americans. (It's hard to tell the difference between full-time residents, snowbirds, and owners of vacation homes.)

Founded by Cortés in 1535, modern **La Paz** is sophisticated: it has five universities, three museums, a theater that shows art films, a large city theater, and one of the highest standards of living in Mexico. Three islands off its coast offer great kayaking and diving; the deep-sea fishing is as fine as any along the *Baja Coast.* Life is good in **La Paz,** a city small enough to offer community but large enough to sustain a fine health care network. Gated communities on the city's outskirts will no doubt change **La Paz'**s ambience a bit, but for most of its residents, life will go on as usual.

Todos Santos

Todos Santos, just forty-five miles north of **Cabo San Lucas,** is an artists' colony, a little slice of bohemia. It's a village tucked just off the Pacific coast, thick with mango and papaya orchards. When a road was built between **Todos Santos** and **La Paz** in 1980, California's surfers discovered the village and its three neat surf breaks, and the mass of restless, southbound, bargain-seeking missiles known as boomers were just a few boogie boards behind them.

Colonial buildings have been turned into galleries, studios, restaurants, shops, and hotels. Developers have also moved in, tearing down existing structures and building an alarming number of retail plazas in this charming old town. Everywhere, land is being snatched up, reflecting the planned, mostly gated communities and resorts that developers believe are the wave of *Baja*'s gold rush of a future.

Loreto

Jacques Cousteau remarked that this particular mid-*Baja* area of the Sea of Cortés was the "world's aquarium," and **Loreto** offers some of the best diving, fishing, sailing, and kayaking in all of Mexico, plus a fine new boardwalk along the oceanfront. The first Spanish mission in Baja California, as well as its first capital, **Loreto** is a wobbly little Mexican town with a colorful history.

For the last three decades, Mexico's national tourist board has been actively trying to establish Loreto as the new **Cancún,** but with little success. Most North Americans who choose to live here settle south of the old town in the newly developing *Loreto Bay* and **Puerto Escondido** projects, gated communities with golf courses, marinas, and homes.

Baja California (North)

Rosarito Beach

Just across the border from San Diego with a population of 70,000, **Rosarito Beach**'s 25,000 or so North Americans, full- and part-timers, enjoy proximity to U.S. health care, shopping, great surf breaks, and Southern California weather. However, familiarity can breed contempt, and the town's accessibility hasn't always been its best feature. **Rosarito** was the first resort in *Baja* and became a raffish destination for movie stars getting away from the rigors of Hollywood. Today it's more about young Californians looking for cheap beer and all-night parties than it is about colonial architecture and cobblestone streets. Crime has also been climbing. Still, unlike sleazy **Tijuana** and **Mexicali** to its north, **Rosarito** offers shelter to retirees willing to overlook its rougher edges. They will find a lot of "back home" in **Rosarito,** with its significant social life, brisk rental and housing market, and nice beaches.

Ensenada

Located seventy miles south of the U.S. border, **Ensenada,** with 450,000 people, has a large foreign population, many of whom have settled in the city's north and south sides, far from the hustle and bustle of its port. Thirty percent of all cruise ship tourists sailing to Mexico visit **Ensenada,** and its weekends are frantic with Northerners heading south for sun, sand, and cerveza.

Retirees here are happy with their choice. They point to **Ensenada**'s proximity to the border, as well as its lower cost of living, more tranquil lifestyle, excellent health care (though many continue to go to the States for health care concerns), and dependable communications network. Housing costs vary here, tilting toward the expensive, but remain far less than in Southern California, where many of its residents lived prior to retiring in Mexico. In 2008, a series of kidnappings along the coast scared away tourists; the residents appeared to take it in stride.

Mexico City

Mexico City is a wonder of a city, ragged and mean in its surrounding slums, a historic and cultural jewel at its rich, well-packed center. Taxis dart through red lights, buses belch and brawl their way from stop to stop, and somehow, people—nearly 30 million of them—have found a tiny little piece of this brilliant beast of a city that they can call home. One of the most polluted cities in the world, it's trying to clean up with new regulations like the one that lets you drive only every other day on the city's streets.

This is very definitely a fasten-your-seat-belt urban adventure where the rich and poor coincide without benefit of municipal planning. With a corrupt and ineffectual bureaucracy and a magnetic presence that draws the hopeful from all over the country, this capital city is growing so fast, you can feel it moving under your feet. (Actually, it is, with some buildings sinking slowly into the city's original lake sediment.) Shockingly overpopulated, congested—and in many sections dangerous—**Mexico City** demands patience and a love for an upbeat, culturally rich, historically profound, exciting daily life that only a world-class city can offer.

Most gringo expatriates in **Mexico City** are thought to be there for business reasons, and many choose neighborhoods that are convenient to their workplace. Retiree numbers are hard to pin down. It is not generally thought of as a retirement destination in and of itself; that distinction goes to the surrounding towns such as **Cuernavaca** or even **San Miguel,** three hours north. But certainly there are **Mexico City** gringo retirees, especially those posted there on business, who loved the experience and knew the city well enough to settle there without feeling intimidated.

Below are a few of the many neighborhoods in **Mexico City** you might want to reconnoiter.

In *Bosques de las Lomas, Lomas de Bezares,* and *Vista Hermosa* security is high, with guards patrolling many of the streets. All three have been developed recently and offer a nice mix of residential and business areas. All grown up and very expensive, *Lomas de Chapultepec* is a suburban dream in the middle of the rushing tides that lap its safe and relatively serene shores. *Santa Fe* incorporates the biggest mall in all of Central America and South America, and is awash in gated communities.

Perhaps the best and safest place to live for devout urban cowboys is *Polanco,* where expats will find museums, theater, restaurants, parks, and superb shopping, as well as residential areas.

Once the belle of the ball before Polanco, the *Zona Rosa* has morphed into a more tawdry Times Square of an area with an escalating crime rate and the bull's-eye for political demonstrations.

For Frida Kahlo fans, *Coyoacán* is a good place to check out. Not only did she and Diego Rivera live here in their Blue House, but this artistic stronghold, with its striking colonial architecture, continues to offer a rich helping of cafés, bookstores, galleries, and boutiques.

The Yucatán

The *Yucatán* can be divided into three significant segments. The northern third, crowned the *Mayan Riviera,* packs a wallop with a coastline sliding south from **Cancún** to **Tulum,** running parallel to a four-lane freeway that was the government's first step in opening up the *Yucatán* to further tourism. The middle section, a government-protected biosphere, takes the next sweet bite of the peninsula and winds down to **Majahual,** where a second new highway has developers racing down to **Chetumal** and Mexico's border with Belize. Dubbed the *Costa Maya,* this sparsely populated area of the coast is still largely uncorrupted, and for the hardier of boomers, it may be the last chance to buy affordable oceanfront property in what many are calling the New Belize.

With its highway system connecting it from tip to toe, the *Yucatán Peninsula* has literally paved the way for tourism and residential development. The Mexican government says it is committed to safekeeping the rain forests, the coastline, the barrier reef, and the ragged reminders of the Mayans' spectacular civilization. Still, with 25,000 hotel rooms to the north, 20,000 more to the south, and still another 15,000 under construction, the *Yucatán Peninsula* is definitely on a roll—for tourists and a good number of full-time expats.

Cancún

In 1967 a group of bankers and businessmen began looking for the ideal location for Mexico's first major planned resort city, betting that the country's economic future lay in the bold new world of international travel. Their computers came up with the coordinates for the undeveloped, underpopulated, and virtually unknown knobby northeastern tip of the *Yucatán Peninsula.*

Once "discovered," **Cancún** and the *Yucatán*—with their powdery sugar beaches and turquoise seas, and their splendid climate from May to September—would become to tourism what gold had been to Cortés. When the group factored in the area's extraordinary assortment of major archaeological sites, they knew beyond doubt that this *must* be the place.

What was once a long, uninhabited stretch of beach has grown into Mexico's number one resort, and one of the world's most popular tourism destinations. Over 200,000 of **Cancún**'s 500,000 residents earn their living in a tourism industry that, with a 90 percent occupancy rate, makes the resort city Mexico's most cherished cash cow after oil.

When Hurricane Wilma howled across its fake Mayan facades in 2005, **Cancún**'s hotels were showing their age. Three years and thousands of tons of concrete later, **Cancún** has experienced an astonishing makeover. Sand was hauled in, palm trees planted, roads paved, and resort hotels became too expensive for college kids. **Cancún**'s scars are fading, and the storm's unexpected windfall has added a fistful of five-star hotels to her entourage. Nevertheless, tropical storms and hurricanes are the bane of residents in this part of the world, as was evidenced in the devastating floods in **Tampico,** southwest of *Yucatán,* in 2007.

Until recently, accommodations in downtown **Cancún** were mostly cheap ($400 to $500 month) unfurnished apartments. But with at least twenty new residential developments offering condos and private villas, retirees looking for bargains will have to ride farther south to find them.

Playa del Carmen

Dubbed the fastest-growing little fishing village in Latin America by the *Guinness Book of Records,* bustling *Playa del Carmen* has been experiencing a tremendous growth spurt. The beach, one of the most beautiful in the *Yucatán,* and the stunning reef offshore, make up the kind of paradise Nortes fantasize about in the dead middle of February when the Weather Channel has become their best and only friend. But the nightlife, the McDonald's and Burger Kings and souvenir and T-shirt shops, and the cruise ship tourists have had a serious impact on the village's languid, slumbering early days.

Playa del Carmen has 65,000 residents and counting, including 1,000 or so expatriates, most of whom are snowbirds who run north between May and October to escape the bugs, the heat, the rain, and the possibility of hurricanes. When Playa was still inhabited by a small I-just-want-to-fish-and-dive-in-peace crowd (seems like fifteen minutes ago), nobody could have predicted the tourist explosion. With a new hospital nearby and a slew of other health care options only thirty miles north in **Cancún, Playa del Carmen** will continue to grow and attract retirees.

Mérida/Costa Maya

Mérida, the graciously aging capital city of the state of *Yucatán,* is the largest city on the peninsula, with a population of 800,000 people. Its wide selection of restaurants and cultural activities are reminiscent of **Guadalajara.** Though plagued with traffic, **Mérida**'s ties to Mexico's vibrant past, as well as its architecture, plazas, churches, and cultural diversity, continue to make it a dominant player in Mexico's political, economic, and social life.

The University of Yucatán is one of the finest medical schools in Mexico, and people from all over the southeast section of the peninsula and from as far away as Belize come here for health and dental care. There is an international airport, and the surrounding towns and archaeological sites, the beach at *Progreso,* the exciting nightlife, the city's trove of museums, and the low cost of living all make **Mérida** an excellent choice for expats who want to smell the rich scent of a Mexico that still breathes fire into everyday living.

AMBIENCE

In Mexico, the palette of options is vast: design your own furniture, commission a wall mural, indulge yourself with watercolor lessons, improve your golf game, volunteer at the animal shelter, play polo, launch an online English newspaper, parasail at sunset, cradle an orphan.

Expatriates are a restless lot, traveling back and forth to the homeland to visit family and friends, or throwing an overnight bag in the trunk and heading off to explore some remote village or beach with a great surf break. They climb pyramids, visit museums, hike mountains, visit butterfly reserves, kayak, dive, sail, fish, discover. Many North Americans arrive in Mexico, settle in, make a few friends, and tap into the vast expatriate network, and before you know it, they're on the road again, searching for new adventures. Others sink into Mexico as if it's a mattress, slipping into a luscious routine of aimless days of delicious meals and the company of friends. One of the outdoor restaurants along the beach is perfect for lunch; at home the gardens look like an ad for Miracle-Gro. You talk to the gardener about planting a few fruit trees: lemon, grapefruit, orange. A Mexican orchard! "What do you think?" you ask him. "Is it possible?" He smiles. "In Mexico, Señora, all things are possible."

STANDARD OF LIVING

NAFTA, the North American Free Trade Agreement, which banished most protectionist trade barriers, is not popular in some American cities where jobs have shifted to Mexico. But in Mexico overall, the standard of living has improved greatly since NAFTA was passed in 1993. And with foreign investment increasing, the peso strong, inflation low, the economy more vibrant than ever, and the middle class expanding, Mexico is moving forward. However, a history of corruption, greed, and nepotism doesn't disappear overnight, and the majority of Mexicans live on an average income of $5 a day. In addition, the advent of NAFTA is a mixed blessing even for Mexico. For every dollar of big-time foreign investment, one more *mamá-y-papá* store is put out of business—the Wal-Mart effect. Mexico's casserole of layered classes remains more or less in place: its bottom layer is thinning, its center is thickening, but the top crust remains the same.

Mexico's expatriate community continues to be divided into the lower-, middle-, and upper-middle classes they left behind, but in Mexico their standard of living has been rising. Some live on fixed incomes and do not enjoy the services of a maid or gardener, can't afford a pool, and tough it out with ceiling fans. Others dine out more frequently, travel regularly, and have a small staff. For the wealthy, expatriate life in Mexico is limitless. With absurdly low property taxes, a sales tax widely ignored, and the ability to earn as much as $85,700 USD annually before worrying about the IRS, the standard of living in Mexico is much higher.

San Miguel de Allende, the Pacific coast, **Cuernavaca,** *Baja Sur,* and parts of the *Mayan Riviera* are more expensive than **Guadalajara,** *Lake Chapala,* **Mazatlán,** and the *Yucatán Peninsula.* As a general rule, aside from these high-end locales, $30,000 to $40,000 (in 2008 dollars) will buy you a comfortable lifestyle in the more affordable locations, with a couple of dinners out each week and a trip home to catch up with the grandkids. In the more expensive locales, you'd make out pretty well at $40,000 to $50,000 and up. There are always people who can live on less, even in the higher-end locales, but one thing is for sure: they've been there awhile and know where the bargains are to be found.

CULTURE

There are few countries in the world, and none in Latin America, with a more vibrant and sophisticated cultural life than Mexico. **Mexico City** and **Guadalajara** both offer an array of theater, concerts, dance, and enough art and history museums to rival some European countries. **San Miguel de Allende,** *Lake Chapala,* and **Puerto Vallarta** have active amateur theater groups, a staggering number of art galleries, and music series that go from mariachi to jazz to Beethoven. Out of 137 countries on UNESCO's World Heritage List, Mexico ranks first in the Americas and eighth in the world, with twenty-five historical, cultural, and natural landmarks.

Mexicans love fiestas and celebrations, and for the most part, they stretch from three days to two weeks. At the heart of every Mexican fiesta is food, and each All Saints' Day or Children's Day or Mother's Day is a culinary occasion. Many North Americans are pleasantly surprised to find that Mexican cuisine is far more than tacos, burritos, and quesadillas. Fresh grilled fish, giant butterfly shrimp, rich sauces, soups, stews, and fresh vegetables are all on the menu. With more and more international tourists and expatriates arriving in Mexico, restaurants have radically changed, and today most restaurants serve food that has been prepared in safe and sanitary conditions. Though tap water is still undrinkable, all but the most humble of establishments serve bottled water and purified ice cubes; reports of dysentery seem to come less frequently.

Mexico is a flamboyant country. It doesn't hide much of itself or its culture. It loves the fireworks that splash across the night sky at the mere hint of a special occasion. Plaza life is rich, bands play, people fall in love, the scent of onions and spices hover as the sunsets and folks stroll along the sea or settle on a park bench. You don't need a special password to discover Mexico or to know that its people like their music loud, their food hot, and their weekends long.

LEISURE

Mexico's official national sport is the rodeo, or *charrería*, but the one that closes the shops earlier than usual and sparks debate inside every restaurant's kitchen is soccer. Every town, city, and state has a soccer field and at least one team.

Mexicans love rodeos, bullfights, and cockfights, all accompanied with generous doses of cerveza. The country's most professional baseball league plays in the U.S., Japan, and Korea, as well as in a Caribbean Series—a sort of mini world series. It's not at all rare to see Mexicans walking around in Steelers, Cowboys, Dolphins, and Raiders hats. Closer to the Mexican heart, however, is its loud and loyal devotion to professional wrestling known as *lucha libre*.

Along Mexico's coastlines, deep-sea fishing, sailing, diving, snorkeling, kayaking, parasailing, jet skiing, and surfing are all popular. Faced with a vast array of locations, hikers, campers, and off-roaders will be hard pressed to choose the best spot. There are many RV parks and marinas, and no end of diving and surfing schools. For the outdoorsman, Mexico cannot be beat.

But you don't need to be interested or active in sports to enjoy yourself in Mexico, where the social life ranges from local book clubs to major art exhibit openings. Much of Mexico's cultural life is centered inland in the *colonial highlands*—the colorful, hilly city of **Guanajuato,** perpetual-spring **Cuernavaca,** artsy **San Miguel de Allende,** and lumbering, lively **Guadalajara.**

With its long relationship with the Catholic Church, it's surprising to note that **Mexico City** recently legalized abortion and gay civil unions. Indeed, it is the most gay-friendly country in Latin America, and gay colonies have sprouted up in many expatriate communities, most particularly in **Puerto Vallarta** and **San Miguel de Allende**.

SOCIAL CUSTOMS

Although illegal immigration has become a major political issue in the United States, Mexicans continue—for the most part—to welcome Americans to their country.

There is political tension over the xenophobic rants in the U.S. Congress, in particular calls for further construction of the wall at the border, but it doesn't seem to spill over into personal relations. As the expatriate community expands, and Mexicans see their job opportunities and income growing, social interaction is also increasing. This can be a double-edged sword. Many expatriates are working within their new communities to improve education, health care, and infrastructure, and for the most part, it is appreciated. But the economic differences, and the insensitivity of some North Americans can cause resentment. Unfortunately, the more expats, the more jerks. (See "Standard of Living.")

As in most Latin American countries, daily life here is relaxed, and Americans "dress up" for one another more than they do for their Mexican neighbors. Though "society" exists in many cities and towns, and men wear jackets while women slip into evening dresses, casual Mexico is far more predominant, and expatriates on the coasts are happy in their cutoffs, flip-flops, and open-necked shirts.

Though the Mexican culture still has a large share of chauvinism and machismo, many North American women find the country nonthreatening. Some widows who lost their husbands after moving to Mexico decided to remain in the country. They were comfortable here, felt safe, had an extensive network of friends, an active social life, and could continue to have a standard of living they would not be able to match in the States. Other women, single and divorced, are attracted by the sense that they can spread their wings and take advantage of an affordable environment where they can reinvent themselves. (See *Midlife Mavericks* in "Resources.") In some communities, like **Chapala**, U.S. and Canadian women outnumber men by a healthy margin.

If many North Americans feel that life has suddenly gone into slow motion when they first arrive in the land of mañana, they learn quickly enough that no matter how hard they try, they are not going to make a dent in Mexico's pace of life. Businesses will close, workers will fall asleep in a shady place. Back home, bosses may have stretched the workweek from forty to fifty hours, but in Mexico the siesta is part of the national DNA, and the smart expatriate will quickly learn to kick off his shoes, grab his hammock, and take a nap at noon along with everyone else.

HEALTH CARE/MEDICAL

Health care in Mexico runs the gamut from small, even inadequate, clinics to large hospitals with cutting-edge technology. The country also has no shortage of excellent physicians, specialists, surgeons, dentists, and nurses. Private physicians charge between $15 and $20 a visit, while those associated with hospitals can charge as much as $40. Doctors make house calls for slightly more; place significant emphasis on alternative, less radical therapies where appropriate; rarely keep patients waiting; and listen patiently.

Many drugs requiring prescriptions in the States and Canada (antidepressants, antibiotics, muscle relaxers) are available over the counter and are far less expensive. Chemotherapy is extraordinarily inexpensive; a six-month course of chemo for colon cancer costs $22,000 without insurance as compared to $320,000 for the same treatment in the United States. An open MRI runs $400; X-rays, $15 to $25. Facelifts begin at $2,500 and breast reductions at $3,000.

Most health insurance in the United States will not cover medical expenses in Mexico. However, you don't need to be a Mexican citizen to take advantage of its health care system, IMSS. Anyone living as a resident in Mexico is eligible to sign up for the national system. Because IMSS assigns patients to a specific clinic or hospital, and because the quality of its very basic care varies dramatically, most expatriates choose to buy policies from private insurers, which cost $1,000 to $1,200 annually but allow policy holders the freedom to choose their own health care providers. (Pre-existing conditions can make this difficult but not impossible.)

A large number of insurance companies sell health insurance policies online to expatriates (see "Resources").

Cele Hahn is a former state representative from Boston who moved with her husband, Curt, to **San Miguel de Allende** in 2000. "I have a trauma surgeon, nephrologist, rheumatologist, and gastroenterologist," she says. "I've had several surgeries and emergency visits in Mexico. My knee replacement was a fifth of what it would have been in the States."

In **Cuernavaca, Mexico City,** and **Guadalajara,** there are twelve highly ranked hospitals with bilingual medical staffs. **San Miguel**'s Hospital de la Fe has a staff of qualified physicians and specialists, many of them bilingual. **Cabo San Lucas, Puerto Vallarta,** and **Ajijic-Chapala** each have three highly respected hospitals. Balboa Hospital in **Mazatlán** is excellent, and the University of Yucatán in **Mérida** has a large number of its graduates on the staffs of the city's four major hospitals. Both the Hospital Americano in **Cancún**, and the Centro Médico Americano in **Progreso** are well-staffed, quality hospitals.

RESIDENCY AND RED TAPE

Getting residency in Mexico, though fraught with paperwork and the usual bureaucracy, is easier than in many other foreign countries.

FMT (tourist visa): A simple form to fill out, the FMT is available at all ports of entry and distributed on arrival. It allows foreigners to enter the country for a maximum of 180 days. Cost: $21. Yes, many Americans and Canadians live on perpetual tourist visas, since enforcement is spotty. But it's becoming less spotty as the computers catch up with people, and it's highly advisable, if you intend to settle here, to apply for:

FM3 (visitor, or nonimmigrant, visa): This temporary resident's permit is good for one year and is renewable each year thereafter. If you are buying property in Mexico, you will definitely need an FM3. If you don't have an FM3, and you own a car, you will have to cross the border every six months in order for you and your car to be legal in Mexico. You don't have to give up your American or Canadian citizenship to become a resident of Mexico, and should you want to work in Mexico, you won't need anything more than the FM3 to do so. The authorities have a pretty good handle on who has FM3s (unlike the more numerous, harder-to-track tourist-visa residents) and have become tough on those who let their FM3s expire.

There are more types of FM3s than there are states in Mexico, but if you are retiring to or buying a second home in Mexico, you will need only the following:

- A passport and photos.
- Statements from your bank, investment company, or Social Security proving that you have a monthly income of $1,000 minimum, and $500 for each dependent fifteen or under.
- A marriage certificate if your spouse wants an FM3.
- Proof of residency. If renting, a lease agreement will be sufficient. If you've purchased property, an electric bill in your name will do.
- Possibly, a letter from your home police department affirming that you're not a criminal—but we don't know anyone who was ever asked for this.

FM2 (immigrant visa): If you are contemplating living permanently in Mexico, you may want to consider an FM2, which will give you all the same rights as a Mexican citizen except for voting—including buying land in the "restricted zone" in your own name. (Foreigners cannot own land along Mexico's coasts and borders; they must lease it. See details in "Real Estate.") There are slightly different requirements, and you will need to show a monthly income of $1,500.

There are any number of companies and individuals (facilitators) who will assist in the application process, charging anywhere from $75 to $125 for their services.

Working

Foreign residents can and do make a living in Mexico. But it's a murky area. Mexico's work rules state that you cannot work if you take a job away from a Mexican. If you do find work that a Mexican can't do—teaching English, for instance—you have to apply for a work visa. Supposedly, breaking these rules puts you at risk of all kinds of awful things, including deportation. But it's a rule far, far more honored in the breach: tens of thousands of Americans and Canadians work in Mexico without work visas because, in general, the authorities don't care about it unless someone brings it forcefully to their attention.

Expats often opt to go into real estate and vacation-share sales, teaching, and tourism. They offer consulting services to Mexicans or other North Americans, open restaurants, boutiques, bookstores, small inns, surf shops, marinas, B and Bs, and art galleries. Contractors, developers, architects, landscapers, and interior decorators are finding Mexico a great place to set up shop. Other North Americans find employment with international corporations who have branches in Mexico, though the pay is far less than they might have expected. In a twist, Mexican companies who need English-speaking personnel or special skills will hire an American off the books, much as U.S. companies hire illegals in the States. With one difference: neither Mexico's congress nor law enforcement cares very much about expats working. The attitude is: these businesses give jobs to locals and contribute to the economy.

Americans are entitled to earn $85,700 free of federal taxes from earned income. If over 50 percent of their income is obtained from a source within the country, they will need to pay taxes to the Mexican government. Not many do, but in this sphere, the authorities *are* becoming more interested.

COST OF LIVING

If expatriates are looking for the bargain-basement Mexico of old, they won't find it in many of the retirement destinations described in this chapter. Though Mexico is still at least 25 percent to 35 percent less expensive than the United States and Canada, its emergence as a retirement destination has precipitated a sharp increase in prices, especially real estate. But Mexico is big enough and diverse enough that there are still many towns and cities where the cost of living is much cheaper. If real estate prices are factored out, costs can be cheaper still.

Domestic help is becoming more expensive—a good thing for locals, a damper on retirees who came down expecting maids and gardeners for pennies. As for live-in help, that's becoming less common, as expats discover how many legal responsibilities they take on with a Mexican employee under their roof. People with pools will see double the electric bill of their neighbors; electricity is as expensive in Mexico as it is in Canada and the United States. However, there are no furnaces in Mexico, and most people use air-conditioning only during the summer months. Restaurants can be as expensive as those in New York and San Francisco, yet many expatriates enjoy eating at small Mexican restaurants where breakfast and lunch are under $4 and dinner less than $10.

Monthly Cost of Living in San Miguel de Allende
Rent for a two-bedroom home, condo, or apartment: $500 and up, depending on location.
Taxes: $125 a year for a $250,000 house.
Groceries for two: $300.
Utilities: Water, $60; electricity, without air conditioner and pool, $200.
TV: Satellite TV, $30 to $65.
Internet: $40.
Telephone: Similar to States.
Transportation: Taxi, $2; car insurance $350 to $800 annually.
Maid service: Five days a week, three hours a day, $200.
Restaurants for two: $35 with drinks and tip.

Monthly Cost of Living along the Coast
Rent for a two-bedroom home, condo, or apartment: "Mexican-style" house, $600; "American style" house with up-to-date amenities, $1,000 and up.

Taxes: $25 a year for a $250,000 house.

Groceries for two: $300.

Utilities: Water, $50; electricity, without air conditioner and pool, $200.

TV: Satellite or cable TV, $30 to $65.

Internet: $40.

Telephone: Similar to States.

Transportation: Taxi prices are moderate but vary. City bus service in **Puerto Vallarta** and **Mazatlán** is cheap and reliable.

Maid service: Five days a week, three hours a day, $200.

Restaurants for two: $25 to $80 with tax and tip; taco stands, $6.

Monthly Cost of Living in Chapala, Cuernavaca, and Guadalajara

Rent for a two-bedroom home, condo, or apartment: $500 and up, most with American-style amenities.

Taxes: $100 a year for a $250,000 house.

Groceries for two: $350.

Utilities: Water, $50; electricity, without air conditioner and pool, $200.

TV: Satellite or cable TV, $30 to $65.

Internet: $40.

Telephone: Similar to States.

Transportation: Taxi prices are moderate but vary. Good cheap bus service in **Cuernavaca** and **Guadalajara**.

Maid service: Five days a week, three hours a day, $200.

Restaurants for two: $25 with tax and tip; taco stands $6.

REAL ESTATE

Because the Mexican constitution wanted to protect the country from foreign encroachment, it banned foreigners from purchasing property in its restricted zones: land within one hundred kilometers of its borders or fifty kilometers of its beaches. To get around those ownership restrictions, the Mexican government created a system of land trusts that allows foreigners to buy restricted land through a major Mexican bank, which will hold the deed in trust. As owners in all but name, foreigners don't need to be residents and are allowed to develop, rent, lease, or sell their property. It's nice, however, to get an FM3 visa.

Ejido land—property set aside for peasants and their communities after the end of the Mexican Revolution—is a special case. Purchasing it remains a difficult and complex process. Foreigners buying ejido or even former ejido property are strongly advised to hire an attorney who will make sure that the deed is "clean" and there are no liens against it. Indeed, avoiding ejido land altogether is probably the best advice.

Real estate brokerages from Century 21 and Coldwell Banker to small North American and Mexican brokerage firms are cashing in on Mexico's land rush—which has been slowed by its northern neighbor's housing problem. If you're determined to buy, take precautions in making your choice, and remember that even storefronts with names like Century 21 are small outpost franchises of their big daddies up North.

The purchase of any Mexican property will be directed by a *notario público*. Unlike the notary publics in the States, they are appointed by the governor of each state, hold law degrees, have three years' experience in a notary public's office, and have passed a stringent exam. Their role is to make certain that the transaction is proper and that the Mexican government is getting its rightful share.

Renting first is always the way to go, whether you do so on a temporary basis or permanently. Many retirees use their rental as a hub and explore various additional settlement options. Apartment availability varies according to location and season, with yearlong rentals in prime resort destinations hard to come by and very expensive during the high season. Reasonable long-term rentals aren't advertised; they are most often found by people who've spent some time there.

Others decide they want a free-standing house *right away*. Less daunting, and by far the most practical thing for them, is to buy into one of the scores of new gated communities, large developments, or condominium complexes, which didn't exist a few years ago.

Still others may choose to renovate or build from scratch, and may oversee the job themselves or hire a third party to act as a liaison for them. These buyer agents provide a broad spectrum of services to clients, everything from sending out bids to subcontractors, to translating conferences between owners and builders, to creating websites for people who want to watch the progress of their new house from the comfort of their old one.

The number of mortgage lenders is small but growing. Title insurance is also becoming more available.

The key tax issue faced by expatriates is a capital gains tax of up to 28 percent on the net profit made on the sale of Mexican real estate, or 25 percent of the sale price, depending on whether you're a resident or not. In theory, if you decide to sell your Mexican house and have lived in it for five years, you will be exempt from capital gains. You may also claim an exemption if you sell your house for less than $528,000 (2007 rates).

TRANSPORTATION

Mexico's local and international airports now blanket a large portion of the country, and more are being built every year. Many Canadians and Americans choose to drive their cars back and forth across the border, especially if they live in Mexico for six months or less, or have an FM3, which allows them to keep their car in the country indefinitely. Toll highways, though expensive compared to those up North, are well maintained and have frequent rest stops. Because Mexican drivers, including long-haulers, prefer taking the bumpy, potholed "free" roads, there is little traffic.

Off the toll and major highways, driving in Mexico can be hairy. The slow pace of Mexican life does not extend to the highway, where drivers pass on curves, ignore double lines, run lights, and generally drive much too fast. North Americans who live in the larger towns and cities often use municipal bus systems rather than try to find parking or fight through heavy urban traffic. "I take the local buses into **Guadalajara** to save on gas and unnecessary mileage," says a resident of **Chapala**. "The bus costs me four and a half pesos [about 40 cents]."

SECURITY

The Mexican government regularly issues statements that it is committed to struggle against corruption at all levels. But bribes are routinely expected, even requested, by the police or government officials and village, city, and state governments worry little about federal oversight. The Mexican people have learned through the centuries to work around "the law" and the powers that be, in what is called *la manera Mexicana*— the Mexican way.

Despite bad press in the States, serious crime is not prevalent in much of Mexico, with the notable exception of larger cities, including **Mexico City** and **Acapulco,** and especially along the border, where the country's two major drug cartels—armed with automatic weapons and arms bought and smuggled in from the States—have been in a territorial war the last few years. Still, tourists or U.S. residents are generally not targeted if they stay out of trouble themselves, and that would include purchasing drugs. (In 2007 and 2008, the strip along the west coast of *Baja* was seeing some serious crime against tourists. Indeed, visits to **Tijuana** dropped precipitously.)

Most small- to midsized cities and towns report petty crimes, particularly burglaries, which, with the increase in drugs, have become a more persistent problem. Most expatriates have a safe, lock their doors, and take care when in crowds. Mexicans and expatriates alike, wary of retribution, rarely identify the dealers, who are generally well known within the community. The police, often on the take, cannot be depended on as a general rule, though President Calderón has doubled the salaries of the country's drug officers and is reportedly addressing drug-related crimes.

COMMUNICATIONS AND MEDIA

The government telephone system, Telmex, is undependable, offers erratic customer support, and, depending on usage, can be as expensive or more expensive than those in the U.S. and Canada. Because calling internationally is expensive, an increasing number of expatriates have chosen to use computer systems like Vonage and Skype, which cost only about $20 a month and offer unlimited free calls within and outside of Mexico. Cell phones are inexpensive, but the minutes, which can be purchased as needed, are not cheap. Telmex is a monopoly owned by multibillionaire Carlos Sim, who recently nudged Bill Gates out of first place as the world's richest man. Like all monopolies, prices are high, and innovation low. However, in-home internet service is now available throughout Mexico.

Multiplex cinemas can be found in every resort and city in Mexico. For the most part, recent American and Canadian films are screened in English with Spanish subtitles.

UP-AND-COMING AREAS

Lo de Marcos, Nayarit State

There aren't many bargains left along the coast north of **Puerto Vallarta**, but there are several villages and towns where retirees can still find affordable land and a lower cost of living. **Lo de Marcos** is the nearest, with a couple of RV parks along the beach and relatively few expats living in the village during the winter. Though a pleasant town with a long beachfront, "Lo" doesn't have much of a tourist infrastructure and lacks restaurants, shops, and other expat-friendly amenities. Still, with the massive building planned for expensive *Punta Mita* down the coast, these northern villages are being talked about as bargains—for the moment.

Mineral de Pozos, Guanajuato State

Though only twenty-five miles from **San Miguel**, this small town of 5,000 might seem a bit isolated for retirees seeking reliable health care and a sophisticated communication network. Still, it clearly deserves the honor bestowed upon it by the Mexican government in 1982, when **Mineral de Pozos** was declared a National Historic Landmark. There isn't much of a foreign presence as yet—possibly a bit more than 100 people—but its proximity to **San Miguel** and low cost of living could make it the next high-desert town on the boomer horizon.

Huatulco, Oaxaca State

With nine bays and a population of less than 20,000, this small town created by Mexico's national tourist authority on the Pacific coast has some of the most extraordinarily beautiful scenery in Mexico. A former pirate refuge drenched in romantic history, **Huatulco** is undergoing huge development by the government; as in *Punta Mita* in *Nayarit*, it will include thousands of hotel rooms, condominiums, and residential homes. Though **Huatulco** has an airport, there are relatively few flights available on a regular basis, and much of the Mexico Tourism Authority's plans are still in the conceptual phase, stymied by environmentalists. At the time of this writing, there are an estimated 1,000 or so expatriates living in **Huatulco**.

Puerto Escondido, Oaxaca

Puerto Escondido is 230 miles south of **Acapulco** on the Pacific coast. It is very, very hot and rainy in the summer, when it gives new meaning to the word *deluge*.

In addition to being one of the world's best surfing destinations, **Puerto Escondido** is for many expats the kind of laid-back, low-cost beach town that any self-respecting ex-hippie would fit into like a second skin. The nearest airport is a three-hour drive away in **Huatulco**, but there's plenty of nightlife to keep the Nortes happy.

There are several condominium complexes, none as chic as those being constructed in other coastal areas, but they are moderately priced, and even budget housing is readily available. Retirees might want to consider their health before settling into a hammock slung between two palm trees in **Puerto Escondido,** however, as health care is rudimentary and runs to spiritual, new-age cures with lots of yoga and organic foodstuffs. If you're thinking early retirement, and don't mind being the only gringo on the beach in the summertime, you might at least want to check out **Puerto Escondido,** which sprung up all on its own.

Other small villages and secluded bays down this southern stretch of gorgeous coastline are showing signs of expat life, and they're worth exploring, too.

Chetumal, Costa Maya Region

Glorious beaches, great diving, archeological ruins, and one of the least-populated areas in Mexico make the city of **Chetumal** an interesting, if remote, retirement destination. With the nearest airport four hours distant in **Cancún,** getting to and from this small city straddling the line between Mexico and Belize is the greatest barrier to settling here. The area's infrastructure is weak, and if you're not willing to forgo Cheerios and Newman's Own, the *Costa Maya* is probably not for you. **Chetumal** is an exotic mix of Spanish and Caribbean cultures, but it is still a dusty, trafficked border town with no tourism infrastructure. This is off-the-beaten-path retirement, and not for those who want reliable medical care and a large expatriate community. Some expats find a creative home and their creative muse in isolated villages along the coast, or forty-five miles inland at **Bacalar,** a charming lakeside community of 10,000. The Laguna Bacalar, know as the Lake of Seven Colors, is clear and cold, a beautiful place to wash away the heat of a *Yucatán* day.

Mulege, Mid-Baja

Small, and one of mid-*Baja*'s secret little pleasures, **Mulege** doesn't offer much in the way of culture or society. A river, however, does run through it—the only real river in *Baja*—and like **Todos Santos,** it is refreshingly verdant. UNESCO has deemed the ancient cave paintings here a World Heritage site, and the beaches on its beautiful Bahía de Concepción are enticingly uncrowded. The nearest airport is eighty-five miles north in **Loreto,** which makes **Mulege** a bit difficult to get to, but it is definitely on the radar screen for North Americans looking for a quiet place to retire.

Pátzcuaro, Michoacán State

At seven thousand feet, the clarity of Pátzcuaro's light illuminates the tiniest detail. Pátzcuaro is attracting more and more Nortes who aren't interested in the sunny, laid-back lifestyle along Mexico's coasts. A major plus is that it's also not far from the bigger, so-called "aristo-cratic colonial city" of Morelia, which some expats in the busy Guadalajara area mention as the "next thing" for those seeking a qui-eter, more elegant urban setting.

Pátzcuaro's few expats find this town, with its industrious indige-nous population, cool and mysterious. They love shopping for dinner in the sprawling market, and exploring the surrounding countryside, poking through small villages like Tzintzuntzan, known for its straw handicrafts; Santa Clara del Cobre, famous for copper; and Tupataro and Cuanajo, renowned for hand-carved furniture. Health care is rough around the edges, but the low cost of living is as attractive as the small city's white stucco buildings with their wine-red borders. Unique and haunting, Pátzcuaro is quite simply one of the loveliest places in all of Mexico.

VOLUNTEERING WITHOUT BORDERS

Because the government doesn't have an abundance of social programs, with the exception of health care, Mexico offers many opportunities to expats who want to make a difference. The expat communities volunteer in groups whose missions range from spay-and-neuter clinics to preserv-ing the ecosystem.

- In San Miguel de Allende, Asilio de Ancianos (ALMA) provides the elderly with shelter, food, and medicine at little or no cost (www.almasma.org).
- Patronato por Niños provides free medical and dental care to low-income children in Guanajuato and San Miguel de Allende (www.patronatoporninos.org).
- Casa de Hogar runs an orphanage, which improves the living

conditions and promotes education for abandoned children in
Morelia and *Michoacán* (www.casadehogar.org).

- CASA (Citizens' Assessment of Structural Adjustment) is the
Mexican organization, part of a global network operating across
the country, that guides and supports scores of community
projects, with a special focus on women's and children's issues
(www.saprin.org.index).

- Children of the Dump helps poor children living in and around the
dump in **Puerto Vallarta**. Volunteers provide meals, education, and
run a day-care center for the children of working mothers
(www.childrenofthedumpvallarta.org).

- In the **Ajijic** area, the Lake Chapala Society is an umbrella
organization that coordinates groups whose missions range from
spay-and-neuter clinics to a shelter for abused and abandoned
children (www.lakechapalasociety.org).

Eileen Pierce is a travel writer, columnist, innkeeper, and co-owner of Build-Mexico, in San Pancho, Nayarit, which facilitates home building for other gringos.

MY MEXICO

A Professor Who Never Intended to Leave Oregon

Name, age, origin: Jane Saracen, fifty-six, Portland, Oregon.

Where I live: San Miguel de Allende.

Previous/present occupation: University professor.

Reasons for moving here: We loved living in Portland and had a lovely home on the Oregon coast and dear, dear friends as well. We have traveled extensively and lived in other parts of the world but *never* had any thoughts to leave Oregon. We had visited **San Miguel** five times, but just on vacation. One day we just started talking to each other about how it might be fun to have a little house here to visit every once in a while. That just morphed into moving here.

Finances: My husband and I are fortunate to be quite comfortable.

Costs: We rented while we built our house. Rent (including maid, gardener, phone) was $1,000 a month. Dinner for two at a midpriced restaurant is $20 to $30. Our utilities are comparable to the U.S.

My community: We have a midsized home here in the central part of town; our neighborhood is a mix of foreigners and Mexicans. We purposely did not choose to live in a gringo-only or gated community. Why live in Mexico if you aren't going to be around Mexicans? We designed our house and had it built, and that was a very fun, creative process.

Weather: Great, one of the big sellers on living here.

Leisure: Walking, hiking, studying Spanish, playing tennis, book club, gardening, yoga. We are both involved in community service and spend lots of time doing volunteer work. It's an excellent way to meet people and practice Spanish, but more important, it's the "right" thing to do to help out in the poor rural areas that surround our community.

Health care/medical: Very positive experiences. We have seen dental, dermatologic, and orthopedic specialists. The cost is very reasonable, and the treatment was professional and excellent.

Crime, corruption: We have not had any trouble of any kind.

Locals' attitudes toward gringos: A mix of attitudes. On the one hand, more people have jobs because the gringos are here, eating in restaurants, shopping in stores, taking taxis, hiring maids. But it also means that prices are higher for Mexicans as rents go up, and their town is not only theirs anymore. I personally have never had anything said or done to me as a result of being a gringa.

Main difference: Type A gringos don't really do well here. They usually either change or leave. Mexicans are mostly wonderful, but their government officials are corrupt and out of touch. Mexicans seem to make the best of it and don't seem to complain or become jealous. I've seen really poor Mexicans give pesos to strangers who appear to be even less fortunate—I've never seen that in the USA.

Common misperceptions: Though my friends and family from the USA are a sophisticated, well-traveled bunch, they all seem to think that all of Mexico is either a dangerous drug border zone or a hot, steamy beach. I'm amazed at how ignorant most gringos are about Mexico, our closest neighbor.

Best: Some of the best times I have had are showing friends from the U.S. my life here in Mexico. They are blown away by the beauty, the scenery, the myriad things to do, the culture, the friendly people. They suddenly "get" why we are here. It's happened with all fourteen of the visitors we had in the past year.

Pace of life, opportunity to experience new things and meet new people, the warmth and generosity of the Mexican people. The chances to stretch yourself in new ways and learn new things is very important.

What I miss most: My friends, Trader Joe's, Thai food.

MY MEXICO
A Gringa Who Went to a Cockfight

Name, age, origin: Regina Potenza, sixty, Sarasota, Florida.

Where I live: Ajijic, *Jalisco.*

Previous/present occupation: Personnel manager, high school English teacher.

Reasons for moving here: I came for the summer in 1986, spent six months here, returned to Florida to prepare to move, then came here permanently. At the time, I considered no other countries. This year I have visited Argentina, Guatemala, and Panama to consider another move to another foreign country.

Finances: I am comfortable on my savings but too young yet to receive Social Security.

Costs: Rent, $375 U.S.; dinner for two, $35.

My community: Small pueblo with as many as 3,000 foreigners living here, one hour from **Guadalajara**.

Leisure: Any activity imaginable: yoga, volleyball, bridge, golf, volunteer opportunities.

Culture: Traditional Mexican holiday celebrations, philharmonic, concerts, dance.

Health care/medical: I had a hysterectomy here and felt medical care was more personal and as competent as any in U.S. A friend recently had a prostatectomy.

Crime, corruption: I was once burglarized. I live alone but have no fear with reasonable caution.

Locals' attitudes toward gringos: Seem to accept us to a point. Some foreigners assimilate, others wish to adapt local customs to gringo ways—unsuccessfully.

Common misperceptions: That Mexican workers are lazy, politicians are on the take, shopkeepers are out to cheat the foreigner. Not true.

Best: Learning about Mexican history, culture, destinations for travel. Friends I have met here. Being the only gringa at a cockfight.

Worst: Burglary and a three-year lawsuit over severance pay. Too many gringos arriving just because it is cheap to live here. Many have no manners or class.

Happiest when: Reading a book in my hammock on a sunny day with no schedule.

MY MEXICO
A Hollywood Producer Who Came Early to Lake Chapala

Name, age, origin: Tod Jonson, seventy-seven, Hollywood, California.

Where I live: Ajijic, *Jalisco.*

Previous/present occupation: Motion picture producer of documentary films and actor in films.

Reasons for moving here: I came down to do a documentary on Diego Rivera and fell in love with the simpler way of life, reminding me of my youth in Oklahoma. I moved down within three months. I didn't consider anything else. **Paris** is my favorite city, but it's just too damn expensive to live there, so I visit a lot when I can.

Finances: Upper middle.

Costs: Own my home clear, two house assistants, taxes very cheap, dinner out can be from $10 to $15 in the finest restaurants, comparable to any I frequented in Hollywood, California.

My community: The setting is gorgeous, overlooking Mexico's largest natural lake. I find all the Mexican people, Americans, and Canadians delightful people. There is a bit too much gossiping, but usually the fire is right there after the smoke. Many, many, many activities, which are hard to keep up with, but I enjoy all of them. It is a cultural center with heart.

Weather: Excellent to absolutely superb.

Culture: A tremendous amount, if you look for it. We have the annual Bolshoi Ballet, and many celebrity performers (singer Glenn Yarbrough lives only a mile from us), a monthly music appreciation event, cultural events every week. We get first-rate movies at exactly the same time you get them in the U.S.

Health care/medical: IMSS and private, medical and dental, both above average in care and much lower in cost. I had a quadruple bypass surgery last year, and I can swear that I have never in all my seventy-seven years had better treatment and medical care and for exactly 10 percent of what it would have been in Hollywood.

Crime, corruption: We are heavily involved with the community, and since we respect and enjoy Mexican people, we see no crime whatsoever. I sure did in Hollywood in 1983 and 1984.

Locals' attitudes toward gringos: Little change in attitude toward the old-time gringos. But a more demanding bunch of people are coming here from the U.S. Gulf Coast areas; they treat Mexicans without respect or consideration.

Common misperceptions: PR in the USA claims it's cheap to live and buy real estate in Mexico, but here, that isn't true. Gringos have driven home prices *way, way* up.

Drawbacks: *Lakeside* is becoming overcrowded; there are so many activities offered, it can wear you down.

Best: Food, shopping, sightseeing are absolutely fabulous. Trips from here are great: for instance, we went to a five-star hotel/spa for Thanksgiving in **Puerto Vallarta,** all expenses paid, for $310.

Worst: Losing so many elderly friends to heaven.

What I miss most: Barnes & Noble, and seeing a relative once in a while. But most of them come down here to visit.

MY MEXICO

B-and-B Owners, Formerly High-tech Execs from Silicon Valley

Name, age, origin: Barbara and Bill Kirkwood, fifty-six and fifty-eight, San José, California.

Where we live: San Francisco, *Nayarit.* We live in a large home partially designated as a B and B on beach-facing property.

How long in Mexico: Five years. We live full-time in Mexico; we return to the States only for short summer visits when we run out of clothes or our favorite snacks (pretzels, red licorice). Other than that, you'll find us in Mexico full-time, all the time, having a good time. Time?? What's time?

Previous/present occupation: Barbara, sales executive in high-tech industry; Bill, operations executive, computer industry. Now we both run a B and B and also a small consultancy company called BuildMexico, designed to help other North Americans build their dream home in Mexico.

Reasons for moving here: Mostly we were afraid we would die at our desks because Silicon Valley was no longer affordable unless you were a two-income family. We couldn't see a way to ever retire. Since we didn't have children, it occurred to us (under the influence of tequila during a vacation in **Puerto Vallarta**), that we didn't have to wait for death, we could choose life—and we could choose it at age fifty, which we did!

Finances: Mostly stocks and other mysterious things where we gave some guy all our money, and he did something with it that made us more money. We had about a million in "stuff" after selling houses, buying stocks, saving our pennies.

My community: We live in a beautiful little beach town that is surrounded by the Sierra Madre mountain range and nestled into a fabulous *Colima* palm forest. The pueblo of **San Pancho** has about 2,000 full-time residents (only about 20 full-time gringos). The plaza here, like in all Mexican towns, is the heart and soul of the pueblo. During the high season, the other gringos come; mostly the expats are Americans, with a few Canadians, in their late fifties or older. We also have some European residents.

Weather: November through April, perfect. December and January can have me looking for a sweater at night, but everyone laughs at me. May through September, it is increasingly hot and humid; you could break a sweat if you get out of the pool too many times to get another beer. Fans feel like hair dryers. Dog hasn't moved in two weeks. Water well is low, so you wash in the pool, which feels like soup. October into November, relax, tell part-time expats about summer, and watch as they stare at you in disbelief. What rain? What bugs? What humidity? What water shortage?

Locals' attitudes toward gringos: I think the Mexicans like the expats. We've provided full-time employment and have, generally speaking, not tried to change the place (or the pace). A few times I've heard people lament that things cost more now (tacos, beer, and so forth) and they think that is because the gringos have driven up prices. But they understand that they now are employed, allowing them to pay the higher prices—so they shrug their shoulders and forget about it.

In **San Pancho,** mail service is Joaquina—a woman who brings your mail to your door for a tip. The electric bills are delivered to the taco stand. The phone bills get delivered and paid at the pharmacy.

Heath care/medical: I love my doctor; he speaks English, was trained in Mexico, and charges $18 for an office visit. He has referred me to many specialists, all of them great. A visit to the cardiologist, including an EKG, is $50. Open-heart surgery averages $3,800. Face-lifts? Under $4,000. Boob job? $2,500. (What are you waiting for, ladies?) Most of my doctors are Mexican educated, most speak English, and all are fabulously caring. They take the time you need and keep you involved.

I have an insurance policy with ING that has a deductible of $2,000. The premium is $1,000 a year. It's for catastrophe: cancer, surgery. The rest I just pay as I go. I have a friend who has $35,000 in the bank. They claim that if you can't cure it for $35K, you're dying anyway.

Residency and visas: Lots of gringos come in with a temporary visa stamped "good for ninety days" and stay longer. It doesn't seem to be a problem—unless you get into some kind of trouble and have to produce your expired temporary visa. But most people get the FM3 visa.

Crime, corruption: Nope, not here. This town polices itself. If there is a robbery (rare), it is almost always an outsider. Tipping police (some call it bribing) is common but, except for traffic tickets, I don't think you can bribe them to allow you to break the law. As to overall corruption, our new president is fabulous and working on the drug rings that are at the heart of the corruption in Mexico. It's going to take a long time, but I see Mexico as less corrupt than I did even five years ago.

Other expats: I have both gringo and Mexican friends. In the hot summers, I don't sit around waiting for the part-time gringos to reappear when the weather is good. Someone recently asked if I get sad in the summer because all the people are gone. My response was, "*All* the people aren't gone. My friends live here."

Wish we'd known before: That a Toyota was so hard to service where we live. I should have bought a GM or VW product.

Volunteering: You can start a project or join a project almost any day of the week here. My pet project is the spay-and-neutering clinics. I volunteer for several days every month, going from town to town helping volunteer vets care for sick animals while they also manage thirty to thirty-five spay/neuters per day. This has really cut down on unwanted street animals and brought new awareness to the Mexicans of their obligations to animals. I also work with a gringa who runs a free library and community services.

When we sell the B and B I think I'll be doing some kind of volunteering full-time.

Best: The natural beauty, the nice people, the pace. It's family first here. My house won't get cleaned if my cleaning woman's mother-in-law is sick—that's OK. Children are included in everything, and their needs are met before anyone else's. Everyone can discipline them, and everyone can love them. Babies are held until they can walk.

Worst: The mañana thing. You just can't muscle Mexico. Things get done when they get done, and your temper tantrum hurts more than helps. There's no one to complain to.

What we miss most: Snacks. Old friends. The radio (although now I have satellite radio). Blowout sales. I miss black people—their spirit, their style, their music.

Expected to miss but didn't: Working in a profession. And "things." In the States, I had more things and access to more things. Every whim, every desire could be satisfied. Here, I need (and therefore want) less.

MY MEXICO

A Former Therapist Turned Filmmaker in San Miguel de Allende

Name, origin: Caren Cross, Philadelphia and Virginia.

Where I live: San Miguel de Allende.

Previous/present occupation: Psychotherapist for twenty-seven years. After a one-week vacation to Mexico at age fifty-three, I went home to dismantle my practice, end relationships with clients, and prepare for a permanent move to Mexico. I am now a documentary filmmaker.

Reasons for moving here: I always thought I would work until I was eighty. I loved my profession; it was creative and challenging. But in the last years of work, the insurance issues around mental health became so intense, it was wiping me out emotionally.

My husband, on the other hand, had never found satisfaction in his work. He was trained as an engineer, but the work he did wasn't personally fulfilling. So he was always hoping that we could save enough money so that by fifty he could stop and find his "passion." So at fifty, Dave semiretired and was free to figure out what he wanted to do when he grows up.

He traveled the U.S. by car for long periods of time. He checked out all of those cities on the "Best Places to Live in the U.S." list. He called home every night to report in. "Oh, I'm in Santa Rosa, California, and you would love it because of the many bookstores. But I don't think this is the place." Or, from Bozeman, Montana: "Nice college town, lots of culture, but too cold for too long." Or, from Austin, Texas: "I don't know why this place is on all the lists."

Then by chance we went on a one-week vacation to **San Miguel de Allende**. We had heard about this town, and we knew that it had what we were looking for. We're not big beach people, so this time, instead of going to the Caribbean, we went to the mountains of central Mexico. That was it.

Finances: We've *always* lived below our means. Fancy cars, houses, and stuff didn't appeal to us; after saving for the kids' education and our old age, we still wonder what the "magic number" is that will mean we can stop worrying.

Costs: The myth is that you can live on Social Security rather easily. The reality is that here you probably need $60,000 a year to live *well*—and that includes occasional trips.

Rentals range from "student type" rentals starting at $450 to those costing several thousand dollars a month, with every luxury possible, including full staffs. Restaurants are probably comparable to the States. No sophisticated food here, however.

Our community: We're in the mountains of central Mexico, 6,200 feet high. Desert. Far from everything! Eight hours to the Texas border, eight hours to either coast, four hours to **Mexico City**. Beautiful old town, streets are walled, and the houses are behind them, so there is no "showing off." How you live is hidden.

There are about 10,000 expats in a town of 100,000 Mexican nationals. Great variety of people. People who play bridge or golf five days a week. People who dedicate their lives to charity. Writers, painters, recluses who hole up. People who do their work online. Older retired people doing exactly what they would have done at home in the States. People taking Spanish and art courses. People who own five houses around the world and are here only briefly. People who try to make ends meet on their Social Security checks.

Weather: Pretty perfect much of the time. If I wanted to be really picky, I'd say too hot in May and too cold in December and January.

Leisure: Tennis, golf, aerobics, bridge, hiking, swimming.

Culture: Theater, music, dance performances (most pretty amateurish). The annual chamber music concert series lasts two weeks and brings in top-notch talent.

Health care/medical: There *is* decent-to-good care in Mexico if you research. Here in **San Miguel,** Dave got kidney stones. After a saga involving antique X-ray machines, a hospital with locked doors, and a visit to a doctor's office that reminded me of bombed-out Beirut, Dave was finally treated at home. The doctor and nurse made house calls every three to four hours. The pain medicine the doctor administered worked better than an earlier kidney stone experience in the States.

But it can be scary some places in Mexico. You have to decide if the fear of having an accident, for which you'll want excellent emergency care, determines where you live. A bad accident in Mexico can mean death. But I don't live my life ruled by these fears.

Crime, corruption: No personal experiences with crime, except one (see below). Corruption is widespread but manageable. It might not be any worse than in the U.S.; for instance, if you know someone in the Housing and Permits Office, you are more likely to get what you want.

Once a friend applied for a Mexican driver's license. At the vision test, she said to the guy, "Gee, I can't see the letters on the chart because I left my glasses at home." He said, "Well, if you had your glasses *on,* would you be able to see these letters?" She got the license.

Common misperceptions: I had no idea that there were racist ideas inside me. It was shocking to be surprised by the work ethic of the average Mexican. Where did I get the idea that "Mexicans are lazy"? Nothing is further from the truth. And who taught me that Mexicans steal and can't be trusted? In nine years here, I can say this is just not true.

Volunteering: There are *thousands* of Americans in this town who dedicate anywhere from a few hours a week to their total lives in helping Mexicans. It is so impressive. There is no culture of philanthropy in Mexico as there is in the United States. And the Americans here really have it in their beings to share and help.

Best: Finding that at the age of fifty-three I could *start* to be freer, more open, more myself. No longer being part of either culture allowed me to just *be.* I was a successful psychotherapist who thought she knew herself. But here I realized that I had been living my life so that I fit in—success, hipness, clothes. After two or three years here, I realized that I was now more relaxed, less judgmental of myself and others, less rigid, more at peace.

This realization was so overwhelming that I thought, "You need to make a documentary film about this." So I did. Three and a half years later, the film, *Lost and Found in Mexico,* was completed. The process of making and marketing the film forced me to reveal my true self—overcoming my lifetime fear of public speaking, for instance. It was transformative, and I don't think I would have come this far without having gotten out of my culture.

Worst: Unbeknown to us, over time our first builder stole $30,000.

Happiest when: I'm walking through the streets, enveloped in colors and life.

What I miss most: Variety of foods. Especially Thai. And curling up with the newspaper on Sunday morning. News on the internet doesn't do it for me. Old habits die hard.

MY MEXICO

A Curmudgeon in Chapala

Name, age, origin: Bernie Gudaitis, sixty-four, Plano, Texas.

Where I live: San Juan Cosala, on *Lake Chapala.*

Previous/present occupation: Was a sales and marketing manager.

Reasons for moving here: I made six visits to Mexico, never considered any other countries. I'd say cost of living was the main reason.

Finances: Upper middle. I own my own home. Taxes are $43 a year.

My community: In a village that is part of the *Lake Chapala* area, there are 50 percent gringos and 50 percent Mexican. U.S. and Canadians are cutthroats, gossipers, and backstabbers.

Weather: Excellent all year round. Don't have to leave for the hot season, as with many places in Mexico.

Leisure: Tennis (racquet club), dining out, visiting **Guadalajara**. There are a lot more things to do in the USA. That is why we are considering moving to **Mazatlán,** a much bigger city.

Culture: Gringos here have *no* culture.

Health care/medical: I have both the national health service (IMSS) and private medical and dental plans. Both are above average in care and much lower in cost.

Crime, corruption: Break-ins and robberies are frustrating.

Locals' attitudes toward gringos: Changing. The Mexican lower class sees us as a paycheck, middle and upper classes are beginning to resent us.

Common misperceptions: Most common is that it is cheap to live here. Wrong. Second-most common is that gringos are all friendly. Wrong.

Wish I'd known before: No regrets. I did my homework and visited six times.

Volunteering: Charity here is nonsense. They're always asking for more; you can never give enough to these organizations.

Best: Weather, Mexican nationals, food, shopping, sightseeing, watching the infighting among the gringos.

Worst: *Lakeside* (**Chapala**) is overcrowded, with too many idiots living here. Most gringos are afraid of everything, and, seeing how easy it is to get someone to do things for them, they hire a service for everything.

Happiest when: Visiting **Guadalajara**.

What I miss most: Some U.S. goods. We make a restocking trip to the U.S. once a year.

Expected to miss but didn't: Newspaper.

MY MEXICO

Innkeepers in the Yucatán

Name, age, origin: Emily Navar and Alfred Rordame, forty-one and fifty-one, Seattle.

Where we live: Izamal, *Yucatán,* a small colonial city east of **Mérida**.

Previous/present occupations: Alfred was a web designer, I was a yoga teacher and massage therapist. We now own the Hotel Macan ché Bed and Breakfast, where we host yoga retreats.

Reasons for moving here: We were living in Seattle and were looking to make a change. We considered different countries such as New Zealand (too far) or Hawaii. But they were lateral economic moves. Our profit from the sale of our home would go much further in Mexico.

We came to this area once for three weeks in 2004; my husband became interested in its colonial architecture, the haciendas. Then we stumbled on **Izamal** and actually stayed at the hotel we now own. Later we saw that the hotel, Macan ché, was for sale, and a few months later, we sent our down payment. We moved in 2005.

Finances: We own our property, and it is the only property we own. We have no mortgage. Our business pays for our living expenses. We travel a few times a year. We are working gringos, we do not collect retirement funds, nor do we have big investments.

Costs: We live on the hotel property. It is approximately five acres of tropical gardens with bungalows scattered about. The hotel pays for most of our living expenses. Food costs are relatively cheap, but luxuries are expensive. We don't eat out unless we go to **Mérida,** and we can either spend $15 for two at a *cocina económica* or $40 to $80 for a nice lunch or dinner. A couple whose housing is taken care of can live well on $500 per month, but that's cooking the majority of your meals at home. Electricity is the biggest expense here for us. Our hotel racks up almost $2,000 for two months of electricity in the summer.

Our community: Izamal is one of the best-preserved colonial towns in Mexico. Most of the buildings are painted yellow, and horse-drawn carriages are still the local taxis. The locals are very proud and consider themselves Yucatecan first, Mexican second. In Mayan times, **Izamal** was an important religious center, and there are seven pyramid ruins right in our city.

There is a very small expat community here (you can count us on your hands), but we are connected to the larger expat community in **Mérida.** We are a forty-five-minute drive from **Mérida** and go there two, three times weekly for shopping and entertainment.

Culture: Living in Mexico is a cultural experience unto itself. If you are talking about fine arts, **Mérida** has beautiful museums and art galleries, a symphony orchestra, and visiting dance companies.

Health care/medical: It's very good here in **Mérida** and inexpensive. Dental care is also good.

Crime, corruption: Mexico gets such a bad rap in the U.S.! Sure, there are bad parts in Mexico—the border, **Mexico City,** for example, but there are dangerous places in the U.S. as well. The **Yucatán** is a very safe place and Yucatecans take great pride in this fact. *Muy tranquilo!* But I do think the government here is very corrupt.

Locals' attitudes toward gringos: We both feel accepted and yet a little like aliens. We try to participate as much as possible in the language and culture. I much prefer speaking in Spanish, and in **Izamal,** it is really the only option. Mayan is also spoken here (regrettably less than in the past). We know only a few words, but they open doors to the older generation and a wealth of history.

Common misperceptions: Not all Mexicans are poor, nor are they all trying to rip you off. There is a growing middle class. Another misperception is that Mexico is one big resort. There is an entire country that many U.S. citizens do not know exists. Yes, there are resort towns in the **Yucatán,** and nothing compares to that beautiful blue Caribbean water, but the country beyond is also quite varied in both culture and landscape.

Best: History, friendly people, the warmth, the rainy season (we like a little humidity, clean air, and green plants!), colonial buildings.

Worst: Flat landscape, super hot at times, government bureaucracy, occasional isolation because of the small expat community here—though we do have local friends. We don't love the local cuisine, but the fruit and avocados are abundant and delicious.

Happiest when: I'm busy but not too busy. Some days I love the B-and-B business, and sometimes I think it is not the best fit for me. That said, I have absolutely no regrets for doing this. To me life is a chain of experiences, and I love being able to have this one!

What we miss most: Cold-water fish like sushi, and a lot of Asian foods like Thai and Japanese. I miss friends. I miss some of the ease of consumerism in the U.S., but these are also things that can drive me crazy if I am in the U.S. for too long again.

Chapter 10

BELIZE

The English-spoken Enclave

By Lan Sluder

You wake up with the sun. You walk to the veranda and watch the waves breaking on the barrier reef. For breakfast you peel a banana—ten for a dollar at the market—and enjoy a mango from the tree in your yard. Then you go for a swim or perhaps try your luck again with the bonefish in the flats. After lunch you bicycle up to check out that new beach bar. Under a thatch palapa, you sip happy-hour rums and swap stories with fellow expats and friendly locals. You bump into an old diving buddy and make plans to go diving tomorrow at *Turneffe Atoll*. Before long, you're ready for dinner at your favorite seaside restaurant, where you order conch fritters, a lobster that was pulled out of the sea that morning, and a glass of lime juice. After dinner you stroll back to your house, check your email with your broadband connection, watch cable for a couple of hours, then doze off with the sounds of the sea lapping on the shore.

This is one of the scenarios drawing retirees to Belize, the little subtropical anomaly on the Caribbean coast of Central America. The Belize government welcomes retirees with a package of benefits and tax advantages, and Belizeans, although they may secretly harbor resentments against the foreigners buying up "the Jewel," are universally considered among the friendliest folks in the hemisphere. (See "Residency and Red Tape.")

Formerly little known except to a coterie of diving and fishing fanatics, or to adventurers seeking to spot a jaguar or explore lost Mayan ruins, Belize is fast becoming a mainstream vacation and retirement destination, attracting a quarter million international tourists a year, three quarters of a million cruise ship day-trippers annually, and, to date, some 5,000 Americans and Canadians looking to stretch their retirement dollars by the Caribbean Sea. (See "Standard of Living.")

Two islands in northern Belize—*Ambergris Caye* and *Caye Caulker*—along with the coastal area of the *Placencia Peninsula* in southern Belize, get the most attention from those looking for their own place near the water. **Corozal Town** in northern Belize, perched on the Bay of Chetumal, and *Cayo District,* Belize's Wild West, with cattle ranches, cowboys, and citrus groves nestled in the hills, also attract expats, especially those looking for less expensive real estate. *Toledo District* in the far south, getting over 150 inches of rain a year, is lush, green, and truly tropical. It is just now starting to attract retirement-bound expats.

UPSIDES

1. Land, homes, and rentals are affordable, even cheap, in most areas.
2. Year-round fishing, boating, diving, hiking, birding, gardening, and more.
3. No need to learn a foreign language, as English is the official language.
4. Friendly, multicultural society generally welcomes foreign retirees of all backgrounds.

DOWNSIDES

1. Crime, especially burglary and petty theft, is a fact of life.
2. Medical care, while inexpensive and getting better, still leaves much to be desired.
3. High import duties and taxes mean many items cost twice as much as back home.
4. Belize is in the hurricane belt.
5. Shopaholics need not apply, as the nearest mall is in Mexico.

LOCATION

On a map, Belize is that little splotch of land about the size of your thumb just south of Mexico and east of Guatemala. It is a narrow band of low mountains, savannah, and seafront, comprising about 8,800 square miles of land area, an area about the size of Massachusetts, sandwiched between Mexico's *Yucatán Peninsula* and Guatemala's *Peten* region on the Caribbean Sea. Belize has more than four hundred islands, the longest barrier reef in the Western and Northern hemispheres, almost two hundred miles of coastline on the mainland, and some of the best diving, snorkeling, fishing, and boating in the world. Surrounded by Latin neighbors, Belize has a laid-back Caribbean atmosphere. In a region where *Español* rules, the official language of Belize is English.

CLIMATE

The climate is similar to that of South Florida. It never snows or frosts in Belize, and when it gets down to the low 60s, or into the 50s in the Maya Mountains, long-time residents pull on sweaters and put a blanket on the bed. Belize is in the hurricane belt, but on average it gets only about one hurricane every four or five years. More than 80 percent of the hurricanes to hit Belize arrive in September and October. Hurricane Dean only sideswiped the northern tip of Belize, and Hurricane Felix missed to the south. Neither caused any deaths in Belize. There are no volcanoes, tornadoes, or serious earthquakes to worry about.

PEOPLE

About 300,000 people call Belize home. Belizeans are a peaceful gumbo of mestizos; Creoles of African heritage (who constitute about one-fourth of the population); and Garifuna (people of mixed African and Carib Indian heritage, originally from Saint Vincent in the Lesser Antilles) and Maya, each of whom makes up one-tenth of the population. East Indians, Chinese, and gringos round out the ethnic mix.

HISTORY

For more than four thousand years, Belize was at the heart of the Mayan world. At the height of the Mayan Classic Period, around AD 250 to AD 900, it's believed that Belize's population was well over one million. Columbus sailed by Belize in 1502 but did not land. The first Europeans—Spanish sailors—set foot in northern Belize in 1511. Most were immediately killed by the Maya or made slaves.

The British arrived in the late eighteenth century, establishing logging camps and pirate bases, and formally established the colony of British

Honduras in 1840. In 1973 the name was officially changed to Belize, and the country became independent in 1981.

GOVERNMENT

Today Belize is a stable and independent, if sometimes eccentric, parliamentary democracy. It is a member of the British Commonwealth, with a Westminster-style government consisting of an elected house of representatives, an appointed senate, and a prime minister chosen from the party winning the most house seats. In 2008, Dean Barrow, a U.S.- and Jamaican-educated lawyer, became prime minister. Belizeans take their democracy seriously—in important elections, usually more than 80 percent of those eligible turn out to vote—and their constitution guarantees freedom of speech, press, worship, movement, and association.

WHERE TO LIVE

For a small country, Belize has a surprising variety of options for living. You can live like a hermit "bak-a-bush" (remote jungle), get involved in a bustling resort town, raise cattle or grow oranges in a farming community, or escape from civilization in the mountains or on a small island.

Expats generally choose one of the following areas:

Ambergris Caye, an island in northern Belize, about one-half the size of Barbados, was once an extension of the *Yucatán Peninsula.* It's now separated from Mexico only by a narrow channel dredged by the ancient Maya. *Ambergris Caye,* or **San Pedro** as it's often called after the island's only town, is Belize's most popular destination for both tourists and expats. An estimated 2,500 to 3,000 Americans, Canadians, and Europeans—full-timers and snowbirds—rub shoulders with some 15,000 Belizeans. **San Pedro** has fancy restaurants and two wine stores, and it's the only place in Belize where you can get imported cheeses and foie gras. Hundreds of upscale condo units are now under construction, mostly on the north end of the island. *Ambergris Caye* enjoys cooling trade winds from the sea, making even hot, humid days more bearable.

Caye Caulker, about forty-five minutes by boat from **Belize City,** is *Ambergris Caye*'s sister island—smaller and a cheaper date. The caye's only village, **Caulker** village, has about 2,000 people, including several hundred foreign expats, some of whom just own property here and visit occasionally. Like **San Pedro, Caulker** benefits from prevailing sea breezes.

Corozal Town, in northern Belize, just nine miles from the Mexican border, has become popular with expats who like the low cost of housing, the pleasant setting on Corozal Bay, and its proximity to the movie theaters, malls, and medical doctors of **Chetumal,** Mexico. For gamblers, three casinos are open near Belize's duty-free zone at the border. *Corozal District* is the driest part of Belize, with only around fifty inches of rain a year, and a major hurricane hasn't hit the area since Janet in 1955. Several real estate developments targeting foreign buyers have opened recently in rural areas around **Corozal Town.** As many as a thousand Americans and Canadians live in the area, or at least own property here, and more are arriving every month.

The *Placencia Peninsula,* once a sleepy outpost on the southern coast, is in the midst of a real estate boom, with beachfront lot prices doubling every couple of years, but the condo market has softened—which could be an opportunity for new arrivals. The number of full-time foreign residents is still small, however; perhaps a few hundred. With the long-awaited paving of the Peninsula Road, the number of expats here should increase.

Cayo District in western Belize attracts those seeking affordable inland living, perhaps on a few acres of ranch land or citrus groves. Refugees from the snowy north like the hot, sunny days and cooler evenings, and the relative lack of mosquitoes. The twin towns of **San Ignacio** (also, somewhat confusedly, called **El Cayo**) and **Santa Elena** (together, population under 20,000), like ancient **Rome** built on seven hills, and Belize's tiny but now fast-growing capital of **Belmopan** (population 15,000) get the most expats.

Belize City (metro population about 80,000), Belize's commercial, transportation, media, and cultural hub, is *not* a location of choice for most expats, unless they have business reasons to stay in the city. **Belize City**'s reputation for serious crime problems—hardly a week goes by when there isn't a drive-by shooting or a series of murders—is the reason. (See "Real Estate.")

AMBIENCE

The pace of life in Belize is mercifully slow. The hot, humid weather assures that even Type As will slow down and take it easier in Belize. "Right now!" is a common expression among Belizeans, and in Belize it means just the opposite of what you think it does—as does mañana elsewhere in Latin America. If you ask a restaurant waitress to bring you a cup of coffee, she'll say "Right now!" This means she'll bring your coffee in ten or fifteen minutes, or when she gets around to it. But she'll bring it with a smile.

Although English is the official language of Belize, depending on what part of the country you're in, your neighbors may speak Kriol (a mixture of mostly English vocabulary and West African grammar, spoken with a drawl that is difficult for an outsider to understand) or Spanish, a Maya dialect, or Garifuna as a first language. Many of the 8,000 or so Mennonites in Belize speak a Low German.

If Belize is beginning to sound like your kind of place, slow down and consider these caveats: Crime, especially property crime, is a serious issue in Belize. Medical care isn't always up to snuff. The cost to duplicate a North American lifestyle, with air-conditioning (electricity is at least twice as costly as in the United States), an SUV in the driveway (gas is expensive), and imported vodka in the liquor cabinet (import duties range up to 80 percent), can be as high as some parts of North America. Island fever, or village fever, also strikes some expats, who find that endless days of nothing much to do can lead to bouts with a bottle.

The frustrations of daily life, from restaurants that take an hour to bring your fish platter, to absurd government red tape, to unpaved roads that beat your car to death, take a toll on expats. After all, little Belize has about the same financial and human resources as a small city in the U.S., yet it has to provide all the services that any country has to deliver: an army, embassies around the world, national health care and education systems, and so on. It's a wonder that anything ever gets done in Belize.

Many expats also are exasperated at the amount of corruption that exists in Belize. Corruption is minimal at the lower levels of government—most customs officers and police constables want your respect, not your money—but some in senior government positions are bleeding Belize to death. Many tens of millions of U.S. dollars have disappeared in recent years from Belize's meager coffers.

STANDARD OF LIVING

Even if you are living month to month on a Social Security check, Belizeans probably will consider you affluent. Per capita income in Belize is only $3,500 a year, less than one-tenth that in the U.S. Minimum wage is $1.50 an hour for most categories of workers. The salary of a skilled carpenter or mason might be only $125 a week. A housekeeper gets around $15 to $20 a day. Teachers with four-year college degrees make about $1,000 a month.

This is not to say that Belizeans are poverty stricken. Belize has the third-highest standard of living in Central America, after Costa Rica and Panama. In comparison with Guatemala or Honduras, many Belizeans are positively middle class. Their houses may look a little rundown, but in most cases they have running water, electric power, and maybe a cell phone. Medical care at government clinics is inexpensive or free. Buses are cheap. An expat with a late-model car, a well-built home, someone to help out part-time with house work and to tend the yard, however, looks wealthy to the average Belizean.

All in all, retirees and other expats in Belize don't seem to be into conspicuous consumption. With the exception of those who have invested in big beachfront homes or condos on *Ambergris Caye* and **Placencia,** most live in relatively modest surroundings, in small concrete block or wood houses on small lots. By and large, this is not a place for high-rolling bling. Belize is more like the conservative west coast of Florida, rather than the glamorous Gold Coast and hip Miami. Things may change in the future, however, as more upmarket gated developments open, some promising golf courses and marinas.

Belize's currency is the Belize dollar, which for many years has been pegged to the U.S. dollar at a rate of two Belize dollars to one U.S. dollar.

(All dollar amounts in this chapter are in American currency.) But U.S. dollars are accepted everywhere in Belize, and the greenback is in effect a parallel currency. The Belize dollar is difficult if not impossible to exchange anywhere outside of Belize.

CULTURE

Chances are, you wouldn't consider living in Belize if you needed frequent hits of culture. Belize has no symphony orchestra, no opera, no daily newspapers, and only a handful of art galleries. Live theater rarely rises above the community theater level. Bookshops are as rare as first editions. Those looking for the pleasures of urban life probably won't find them in Belize.

Belize does have an active popular music scene, with a vibrant community of Garifuna, mestizo, and Creole musicians. Hip-hop, soca, reggae, and other musical genres have their popularizers in Belize, too. For some unfathomable reason, karaoke is wildly popular. There's also a small but dynamic group of Belizean artists.

LEISURE

Most of Belize's leisure attractions are outdoors. For anglers, Belize has some of the best sports fishing in the Americas for permit, tarpon, snook, and bonefish, and you can also feed yourself and your family on the bounty of the sea: lobster, conch, and all types of eating fish. Belizeans themselves prize the barracuda above all others for eating.

Belize consistently ranks near the top in diving and snorkeling destinations, with almost two hundred miles of barrier reef plus three of the four true atolls outside the Pacific Ocean (the fourth is off the *Yucatán Coast* of Mexico). Boating and sailing also are excellent, though Belize's shallow waters and hidden coral heads can be tricky. Windsurfing, kitesurfing, waterskiing, and parasailing also are possible.

On the mainland, you have a wealth of outdoor sports activities: canoeing Belize's many gentle rivers, caving (some of the cave systems are still unexplored), horseback riding, mountain biking, and hiking.

SOCIAL CUSTOMS

In most cases, expat life in Belize revolves around personal pursuits, family, and a small group of friends. As there's not much in the way of organized community programs, you have to make your own entertainment.

Belizeans, by and large, are very welcoming to foreigners. In fact, if you live in a small village, you may find that your neighbors constantly drop by just to talk—or perhaps to cadge a small loan. Kids (almost two-thirds of Belizeans are under age twenty-two) are everywhere, and troops of them may stop by to use your computer or to watch TV.

Despite its multicultural diversity, Belize has its share of racial and ethnic prejudice, and yet most people seem to get along pretty well. One long-time expat in **San Pedro** puts it this way: "The San Pedranos dislike the Creoles. The Creoles think the Garifuna are horrible. The Garifuna scowl at the Chinese. The Chinese avoid the East Indians. The East Indians don't trust the Arabs. The Arabs think all the gringos have money. The gringos are equally divided about politics in the USA. And, of course, everybody ignores the Maya. However, I've not met one person (except for newly arrived gringos) who isn't related to most everyone else by marriage or adoption. Despite the voiced prejudice, there is amazing harmony and tolerance here. It never ceases to amaze me."

Belize generally takes a "don't ask, don't tell" approach to homosexuality. While Belizeans are fairly conservative about gay sexuality, overtly homophobic behavior is rare. As anywhere, there are gay and lesbian people in Belize, but no gay bars or clubs.

HEALTH CARE/MEDICAL

Preventively speaking, Belize could be good for your health. Here you tend to walk and exercise more, get more fresh air, and eat simpler, healthier meals of complex carbohydrates and fresh fruits. One expat in **Placencia**, Frank Da Silva, chef at Robert's Grove resort, recalls that after a year in Belize, he went for a health checkup. He found that his blood pressure was down fifteen points and his weight down fifteen pounds. "But what do you expect?" he asks. "I live on the beach, walk twenty-five feet to work, and eat almost nothing but fresh fish and fruit."

But as a developing country, Belize's medical resources are limited. If you are older and especially if you face chronic health problems, you will have to look closely at the health care trade-offs: a healthier way of living, lower medical costs, and more personalized care in Belize, versus the high-tech but high-cost health care and health insurance back home.

Belize has a mixed public and private health care system. The vast majority of Belizeans, and some expats, get medical care through government-run hospitals and clinics. Belize has a network of more than fifty public health clinics in many towns and villages around the country, providing primary medical and dental care. Volunteer physicians and nurses from Cuba and

Nigeria staff some of these. And there are two private hospitals in **San Ignacio**. In **Belize City** and in larger towns, physicians and dentists in private practice serve the Belize middle class and expats. Most trained in Guatemala, Mexico, or Cuba.

If you can accept long waits and less than state-of-the-art medical technology, you won't have to spend your entire pension to get care in Belize. "Medical, dental, and eye care are a fraction of the cost of the U.S.," says Diane Campbell, a Californian who now lives in **San Pedro** full-time. "I pay twenty dollars for an office visit to my physician, and medications are cheap." A root canal with crown might cost $250 to $500, and hospitalization usually runs under $100 per day. Prescription drug costs vary but are generally less expensive than in the U.S.

For more complex procedures, many expats in Belize go to **Chetumal**, Mexico, just across the northern border. Physicians and dentists there provide high-quality medical care at costs even lower than in Belize. A National Health Insurance scheme, proposed in the 1990s, is ever so slowly being put in place in Belize. It is being tested in **Belize City**, with medical care coverage through the Belize social security system. Under the plan, eventually all Belizeans and permanent residents will get medical care through a system somewhat similar to that in Britain.

RESIDENCY AND RED TAPE

You have three options for retiring or living in Belize.

Qualified Retired Persons Program

If you or your spouse are at least forty-five years old and can demonstrate that you have a retirement income of at least $2,000 a month per couple, you may be eligible for the Qualified Retired Persons program. This program, implemented in 2001, was developed by the Belize government in an effort to attract middle-class retirees. It offers a package of benefits, including the entry of household goods, a car, a boat, and even an airplane into Belize without paying any import duties. Red tape is minimal, and approval usually is quick—typically in a few weeks to a few months. Your income must be from a verifiable pension or Social Security or other guaranteed income, and you must agree to deposit it in a financial institution in Belize. This money *can* be used for your living expenses in Belize. The $2,000 a month is for either an individual or a couple.

However, the QRP program has drawbacks. Among these is the fact that you are getting in effect a renewable tourist visa rather than true permanent residency. Application fees and costs for the QRP program have increased and now total $2,100 for a couple. Also, many retirees don't like, or can't meet, the requirement of depositing $24,000 annually into a Belize bank. For these and other reasons, the QRP program has not been a big success, and to date only a few hundred retirees have taken advantage of the program. But for some retirees, it can be an attractive option.

Although under the QRP program you cannot work for pay in Belize, you can own investment or rental property, and you can own a business. To maintain your QRP status, you need stay in the country only for one month a year. As a QRP retiree in Belize, none of your investment or earned income outside Belize is taxed.

Tourist Card

If you're not quite ready to make the commitment to the Qualified Retired Persons program, you can opt for entry under a regular tourist card, renewable monthly. This is what most retirees and other expats do, at least initially. You can buy or rent property, but you cannot work for pay. In theory, when you renew your tourist card, you are supposed to be able to prove that you have sufficient resources, set at $60 a day, to stay in Belize, but this requirement is not usually enforced.

Permanent Residency

A third option for living in Belize is official permanent residency. This gives you almost all the benefits of citizenship, except voting. (If you are a citizen of a British Commonwealth country, you can vote in local, not national, elections in Belize without actually holding Belizean citizenship.) After five years of residency, you can apply for Belizean citizenship. As a permanent resident, you can work for pay in Belize, own or rent property, and otherwise conduct yourself as an official, guaranteed resident. To obtain this, though, you must live in Belize for a full year on a tourist card, without leaving the country for a total of more than two weeks.

Working

Unless you are a Belizean citizen or an official permanent resident, you cannot legally work in Belize without a work permit from the government. You also need a Belize social security card. Some foreigners without work permits have jobs and take under-the-table payments, but if you're caught working without a permit, you could be in trouble.

There are two types of work permits. One is a work permit that is obtained by an employer in Belize. The employer has to prove that he or she can't fill the job with a Belizean. The other type of work permit is the self-employment certificate. This category applies to those who are starting a business in Belize, where it is assumed that the venture will lead to the creation of jobs for Belizeans. The applicant has to show proof of adequate funds for the proposed venture. In opening a bed-and-breakfast, a reference from the Ministry of Tourism may be required.

COST OF LIVING

As in any country, the cost of living in Belize depends on where and how you live. *Ambergris Caye* and **Belize City** are the two most expensive places to live; **Corozal Town** and **San Ignacio** are the two least expensive towns.

Lifestyle is also a factor. If you try to duplicate an American lifestyle, with air-conditioning, a gas-guzzling auto, and imported food and drink, it will cost more to live in Belize than back home. If instead you choose to live like Belizeans do, eating beans and rice and other local food, taking the bus, and running a fan instead of the AC, you can live for a fraction of what it costs in the U.S.

Here's a sampler of costs for common items in Belize, as of 2008. All prices are shown here in U.S. dollars and include the 10 percent goods and services tax (GST).

Monthly Cost of Living on Ambergris Caye

Rent for a two-bedroom home, condo, or apartment: $900 to $1,800.

Taxes: 10 percent GST on food, drink. Property taxes are low; a decent-sized home would cost about $100 a year; a mansion, $300 plus.

Groceries for two: $150.

Utilities: Water, $100; electricity, $200 plus; butane, $50.

Cable TV: $30.

Internet: Basic connection, $50; fast, $200.

Transportation: Taxi, $5 to most destinations; water taxi to mainland, $15.

Maid service: $20 to $25 a day.

Restaurants for two: $50 in a midrange restaurant; $100 in a top restaurant.

Monthly Cost of Living in Corozal Town

Rent for two-bedroom home, condo, or apartment: $250 to $500.
Groceries for two: $150.
Utilities: Water, $15; electricity, $100; butane, $35.
Cable TV: $25.
Internet: Basic connection, $50; fast, $200.
Transportation: Taxi, $2 to $5 around town; bus to Belize City, $6.
Maid service: $15 a day.
Restaurants for two: $15 to $25 in a midrange restaurant.

Monthly Cost of Living in Rural Area of Cayo District

Rent for a two-bedroom home, condo, or apartment: $100 to $400.
Groceries for two: $100.
Utilities: Water, $10; electricity, $100; butane, $35.
Cable TV: $25 (not available in all rural areas).
Internet: Basic connection, $50; fast, $200 (not available in all rural areas).
Transportation: Intervillage taxi and group taxi, $2 to $10; bus to Belize City, $4.
Maid service: $12 to $15 a day.
Restaurants for two: $20 in a midrange restaurant.

REAL ESTATE

Affordable real estate, low real estate taxes, no restrictions on what or where you can buy, and familiar procedures for buying are among the reasons Americans and Canadians purchase property in Belize. Real estate transactions in Belize work about the same as in the U.S. However, there are a few wrinkles to buying property in Belize, and some pitfalls to be aware of.

For one thing, real estate brokers and salespeople in Belize are unregulated and unlicensed. Anybody with a business card and a cell phone can open a real estate office; a lot of bartenders and hotel owners in Belize moonlight peddling real estate.

Except in a few areas such as **San Pedro,** where a lot of activity is going on, most property for sale is not listed by real estate brokers. In fact, most property is not advertised for sale at all. To find out what's for sale, you have to ask around. Put the word out at local watering holes and shops, and soon owners will be bringing offers to you.

Don't pay too much attention to asking prices, especially on the internet. In Belize's small, inefficient marketplace, sellers often assign ridiculous prices to their properties, hoping some foolish gringo will come along and pay the price. Many properties (again, excepting prime beachfront property) may actually sell for one-third to one-half less than the original asking price.

Financing real estate in Belize can be a real problem. Most local banks are reluctant to offer mortgages to nonresidents, and even if you can get a mortgage, you'll pay through the nose. Mortgage rates in Belize generally are about twice as high as in the U.S. Expats who have financed with Belize banks often complain about hidden fees and inaccurate records.

So most buyers either pay cash or arrange financing through the seller. Most subdivisions and developments in Belize *do* offer financing of homes and lots, typically with 10 percent to 20 percent down. More recently, a few international banks, including Scotiabank, have begun offering reasonable mortgage financing.

Keep in mind that in Belize the pool of qualified buyers is quite small. Often, foreigners make up the majority of buyers. So it can be a tough sell when you decide to move on. Except perhaps for beachfront real estate, which tends to turn over more quickly, property in Belize is a highly illiquid investment. In fact, there are known to be parcels of land and hotels that were for sale fifteen years ago and are still for sale today!

The good news is that Belize has no capital gains tax, and real estate taxes are very low. Tax rates vary, but typically are about 1.5 percent of the value of the *improvements* on the property. However, even on a big new home, annual property taxes are rarely more than a couple hundred dollars.

Property Costs

All over the board. You can buy a small Belizean-style house in a rural area for under $25,000, or you can pay a half million U.S. or more for a beachfront home. Generally, except on the beach, you'll pay $80 to $150 per square foot for an existing concrete home, built to North American specs, depending on location and amenities. Thus, a 1,200-square-foot concrete house, a few years old, might cost $96,000 to $180,000.

Building lots also vary greatly in price. Small lots (approximately a quarter acre) with utilities and road access start at around $7,500 in **San Ignacio, Corozal Town,** and other small towns and villages. By contrast, buildable waterfront lots start at around $50,000 but can run $250,000 or more. Currently, asking prices for beachfront land on *Ambergris Caye* range from around $3,000 to more than $10,000 per front foot, and around $2,500 to $3,500 per foot in *Placencia.*

For the penny-pinching retiree with some construction skills, home building can be done very cheaply in Belize. One expat in **Corozal** put together his lagoonside home from scrap materials for $4,000. Another affordable option is Mennonite-built prefab houses. These wood cottages, complete with electrical and plumbing, can be set on stilts on your lot for $10,000 to $20,000, depending on size and finish.

Rentals

If you've read this far, you know the drill about renting before you buy. Here you have to take your time to look for that rental. Few homes or apartments are advertised for rent, and, again, word of mouth is your best bet. As in buying, rentals on or near the water are the most expensive. A two-bedroom condo on *Ambergris Caye* is likely to rent for at least $1,000 a month, whereas in **Corozal Town** or **San Ignacio,** even a newly built three-bedroom house won't be much more than $500 to $800 a month.

TRANSPORTATION

Belize City is a two-hour flight from Houston or Miami. During the winter, a weekly charter service flies from Toronto to **Belize City,** and with a runway extension completed at the international airport near **Belize City,** limited direct service from Europe was scheduled to begin in 2008.

Expats relocating to Belize may decide to drive through Mexico. From Brownsville, Texas, it's a 1,400-mile drive to the Belize border at **Chetumal,** Mexico. It can take three to four days and is an adventure in and of itself.

Although Belize is a small country, only about 200 miles from top to bottom as the toucan flies, getting from one place to another always seems to take twice as long as expected. Only four highways in the country are paved, and together they total just a little over 300 miles. Most other roads are unpaved, dusty in the dry season, and muddy and rutted in the rainy season. Liability insurance is mandatory in Belize—a good thing, too, as traffic accidents are the number one cause of premature death here.

Most Belizeans get around by bus, typically old Blue Bird school buses from the U.S. The country has more than fifty small bus lines that provide frequent service on the four main highways. Rates are low, and you can get from one end of the country to the other for about $20.

SECURITY

Petty theft, burglaries, and other property crimes are facts of life in Belize, but the most common story heard from expats is that, beyond taking ordinary precautions, they have few concerns about their personal safety. Police in Belize may try to do a professional job, but too often they are ill-trained, underpaid, and lack even basic equipment such as gasoline for their police cars. Among the strategies expats employ are: burglar bars on windows, a caretaker, or a dog. A dog is *the* most effective deterrent to break-ins in Belize. It doesn't have to be a vicious dog, but it should have a vicious bark.

Statistics on violent crime in Belize are unreliable, but the murder rate is considerably higher than in large urban areas of the United States. Typically, there are seventy to ninety murders a year in Belize, a murder rate three to four times higher than the average in the U.S. However, most of the murders are concentrated in **Belize City,** and much of the other violent crime involves someone getting drunk on Saturday night and knifing or machete chopping somebody in a "cool spot"—what Belizeans call a bar.

COMMUNICATIONS AND MEDIA

The coconut telegraph moves information and gossip around Belize at the speed of sound, but if you need more formal news coverage, Belize has eight or ten weekly newspapers. The reporting in Belize may not always be accurate, or even completely literate, but it's always entertaining, and it's definitely free. In most areas, cable TV is available, with around fifty channels, a mix of American and Mexican programming.

Belize has a reliable telephone system and cell phone service, and increasingly, the country is internet ready, though it's expensive: $50 to $200 a month. Internet cafés are common; the Belize postal service is, perhaps surprisingly, efficient, reliable, and inexpensive.

UP-AND-COMING AREAS

Rainy, beautiful, and remote, *Punta Gorda* in far southern Belize is the jumping-off point for unspoiled Mayan villages and for onward travel to Guatemala and Honduras. The area is expected to take off as the final few miles of the paving of the Southern Highway to *Punta Gorda* are completed and the road is extended into Guatemala. "PG," as it's known, has about 5,000 people, mostly Garifuna, Maya, and immigrants from Guatemala. Undeveloped land is inexpensive here, with acreage beginning at a couple hundred U.S. dollars an acre. A few North American–style homes are for sale, typically for under $100,000.

Hopkins, a small Garifuna village in Stann Creek District between *Dangriga* and **Placencia,** is getting the overflow from **Placencia.** Most of the beachfront lots here have been sold to North Americans, and several luxury condo developments have sprung up, but there are still affordable lots available with frontage on the Sittee River. Sandflies (tiny no-see-ums) here can be ferocious.

Another up-and-coming area is in the far northeastern part of the country, in *Corozal District* along the Bay of Chetumal. Several bayfront real estate developments have sprung up around *Cerros,* *Copper Bank,* and the charming but remote fishing village of **Sarteneja.** While many lots have been sold, mostly for future retirement living, few homes have been constructed at these developments.

VOLUNTEERING WITHOUT BORDERS

In Belize, there are numerous organizations involved mostly in social welfare, conservation, and reef-protection activities. Many U.S. evangelical religious groups send missions to Belize, building schools and churches. The country also gets many medical missions, with doctors, dentists, and nurses donating their services for periods of weeks to months.

Some examples:

- Plenty International is one of these medical missions (www.plenty.org).
- The Cornerstone Foundation is one of the best-known organizations in Belize. Its programs includes cultural and community service in the *Cayo District* (www.peacecorner.org).
- In **Benque Viejo del Carmen,** the Mount Carmel High School has an all-volunteer faculty (www.mchsbenque.org).
- The Belize Audubon Society, Green Reef, and the Belize Zoo also use volunteers (www.belizeaudubon.org, www.ambergriscaye.com, www.belizezoo.org).

Lan Sluder is the author of Living Abroad in Belize *and two more eBooks on living and retiring in Belize,* Easy Belize *and* Island Living in Belize, *both available through the Escape Artist website (www.escapeartist.com).*

MY BELIZE

A Former Attorney from St. Louis

Name, age, origin: Jane Jones (pseudonym), fifty, St. Louis.

Where I live: Placencia village in a beach apartment.

How long in Belize: Eight years.

Previous/present occupation: Was an attorney; now a travel agent and salt-water fly-fishing tour operator.

Reasons for moving here: Midlife crisis.

Finances: Savings, and not much.

Costs: I pay $600 a month for my beach apartment. The high cost of utilities makes my monthly housing costs about what they would be in the university neighborhood from which I moved in St. Louis. Groceries are about the same unless you eat only local foods; if you eat imported foods, grocery costs will be double or triple—if you can find anything. Dinner for two can be $60.

My community: I live on the beach in a small community of about 600 people—once a Creole fishing village, now a tourist destination. The building boom has brought in many people from other parts of the country, plus Guatemalans and Hondurans usually working here illegally. Maybe 150 expats. The peninsula attracts an unusual kind of expat: usually people out of the mainstream, often may not play well with others, very individualistic. A kind description would be *eccentric*. A less kind description would be *dysfunctional*. (I don't exclude myself from this description.) The relationship between the local population and expats is a love-hate one, as I expect it is in most places.

Health care/medical: Locally, we have a Cuban doctor. Care for routine medical matters is pretty good. For minor emergencies, you travel to **Belize City**. In life-threatening emergencies, the British Army can be called and will send a helicopter to get you to **Belize City,** and from there to somewhere else—if you live that long. I wouldn't spend a night in the local hospital if I could help it. So far, I have been able to help it. Stay healthy is the best advice.

Crime, corruption: Petty theft and burglary are the primary crime problems where I live. Crimes against persons (except domestic disputes) are still extremely uncommon. As for the government, I'd say it's stably corrupt.

Best: I enjoy my work more, the climate is better, I have more close friends here—and see them more—than in my former life. I laugh a lot more here.

Wish I'd known before: The many veils of Belize. On the surface, it looks a lot like home: British legal system, English as official language, dress. But it's not, not even close.

What I miss most: Old friends, spring and fall, restaurants, theaters, museums, and, sometimes, paved roads, variety and good quality of vegetables.

MY BELIZE

A British Couple in the Tropics

Name, age, origin: Ian and Kate Morton, fifty and forty, Devon, England.

Where we live: Punta Gorda, *Toledo District.*

How long in Belize: Three years.

Previous occupations: Social housing, marketing.

Reasons for moving here: We wanted to retire early. We vaguely researched Australia and New Zealand as alternatives, but immigration requirements were restrictive (age and skills), and we felt we'd be swapping one rat race for another. In 1996 we set out on a trip to *Yucatán* to make a loop from **Mérida** to **San Ignacio,** Guatemala's **Tikal** and **Antigua,** then **Punta Gorda,** and finally **Belize City.** This country drew us, and we looked at the practicalities: English speaking, actively encouraged immigration, land prices. We visited twice more to confirm our choice.

We then had a trial run of six months out here, went on an eight-week local building and electrical-wiring course and spent three months as caretaker-managers of a remote jungle lodge. We left because we were homesick, and at that stage viewed any move as permanent and irreversible.

The idea came to life again in 2002, when we felt we'd broadened our skills, had enough capital, and, most important, when we finally woke up to the fact that this *didn't* have to be for life. We could move on the basis of reviewing life every, say, five years and decide whether we were still enjoying things.

So in 2002 we visited Belize again and spent three weeks looking at land, touring all the hardware and building suppliers, as well as the other goods available there. We found our plot of land on our penultimate day, agreed on a price with the vendor, and arranged for a local friend to oversee the purchase process. Three months later, the sale was complete, and three months after that, we arrived in Belize—lock, stock, and three dogs!

Costs: You think that because it is a developing country, everything's going to be cheap. You *can* live relatively cheaply here (just as you can in the UK or the U.S.) but, let's face it, most of us like our luxuries to a lesser or greater extent! And they cost plenty, here as everywhere.

Common misperceptions: People fall in love with the country and its people, and expect their moving and adapting to be as rose tinted as their plans and dreams. Why *should* living here not be frustrating? It can be, and probably is, anywhere in the world! We found the residency application process extremely lengthy and frustrating, but I'm sure it's a darned sight easier than for those immigrating to the UK!

What we learned: consider health, communications, adaptability. Most of us tend to get more set in our ways as we grow older, and I think to be happy here demands patience, tolerance, flexibility, and to be as open-minded as possible.

Before considering retirement here, ask yourself:

- Do you think you may want to return "home" at any stage? If so, you must consider that you may not even get your real estate investment back, let alone a profit.
- Are you practical? Can you repair a water pump, can you make bread if you get sick of the bread sold here? Can you build or oversee a building or remodeling contract with confidence that the job is being done correctly? Are you prepared to try, learn, and adapt?
- Can you do without? We were used to having everything we wanted available in the UK supermarkets. Are you prepared to go without fresh artichokes and asparagus?
- How much will you miss your family if your opportunities to meet up with them are likely to be limited by finances?
- How do you cope with heat, humidity, bugs, and mold?

Best: Building our guesthouse—being able to dream, plan, and complete it, then sitting on the deck in the morning looking at our beautiful piece of land—and meeting great people, Belizeans, and tourists. Since we arrived, the country is much more developed. A wider range of goods, a more educated population, and improved infrastructure. At the risk of sounding materialistic, being able to go to *Punta Gorda* and get fresh milk or buy a printer cartridge or a bed or a fridge makes life so much easier. We don't subscribe to the "badge of honor brigade," where you earn points for just how many sacrifices you can make!

Worst: Losing our dog Charlie to a poison toad.

We're happiest when: We try to work with the systems and culture of the country, and not stress ourselves with how we think things ought to be done.

What we miss most: Without a doubt, family. Improved phone service and satellite internet/email go a long way to minimizing this, but . . . We also miss decent, unbiased TV reporting, books, and good tea, but those aren't deal breakers.

MY BELIZE

A Former School Administrator from Canada

Name, age, origin: Sarah James, sixty-two, Ontario, Canada.

Where I live: Placencia, in a rental apartment. It's a small village located at the tip of a peninsula bounded by the Caribbean Sea and a lagoon.

How long in Belize: Eight years.

Previous/present occupation: School administrator turned restaurant manager.

Reasons for moving here: Climate, seaside, desire to be part of another culture.

Finances: Three pensions totaling $50,000, but I live on what I earn here.

Costs: I live simply. My small apartment in the village rents for $200 a month. But I have to say, this would not have happened unless I'd been here for quite some time. Most rents are three times higher.

My community: Our population is about 800, mixed ethnically among Creole, Garifuna, Spanish, Maya, and expats. There are three groups of expats: one lives here pretty much as dropouts, with a minimalist lifestyle, and they tend to be drinkers and like to party. Another is the moneyed group with large houses, and they tend to stand off from locals, are patronizing, and socialize only with one another. The third are in business or work here, mainly connected to tourism.

Weather: Pleasant, sunny most of the year—but the books don't tell you that it's really hot and humid for four months a year, with lots of thunderstorms.

Leisure: Friends, books, swimming, snorkeling (very big here). We make our own entertainment, like board games on a rainy day or costume parties with themes like "tacky tourists."

Culture: Not much. An annual arts festival.

Crime, corruption: A problem with petty crime. Drugs—marijuana and crack—are a growing problem, which lead to thefts and burglary, mostly empty houses. I've never been a target so far (touch wood).

Locals' attitudes toward gringos: Locals are very friendly outwardly, but it is difficult to really integrate into the community. Some see gringos as a source of start-up funds for this or that project, and investment schemes often end badly. But there is no real animosity, and the longer you are here, the more accepted you are. I am an older woman, so I am treated with the utmost respect. Belizeans go out of their way to assist me if they can, including bureaucrats from Taxation and Social Security.

Volunteering: After Hurricane Iris, I started my own education foundation, which is a registered charity in Canada. We help local schools with books, building, and equipment.

Best: I enjoy being part of a small community. I live with less materially and enjoy that. The area is beautiful, and I have good friends, both local and expat. I feel more connected to people and less depersonalized.

Chapter 11

NICARAGUA

Coming Up on the Radar

By Tim Rogers

Twenty years ago, people would have looked at you like you were crazy if you mentioned the words *Nicaragua* and *retirement destination* in the same sentence. *That* Nicaragua, with its Sandinistas and its wars? Today most people will still look at you like you're crazy—and you just might be—but it's no longer a strict requirement for retiring here. Trying desperately to outgrow its old image, the Nicaragua of today is a more mature version of its former, revolutionary self. Foreigners who first came here with solidarity brigades in the 1980s now marvel at how much the country has changed when they return as tourists.

For those considering the move, it's a matter of risk versus opportunity. The threat of political or social volatility makes Nicaragua a dicier proposition than, say, a move to peaceful neighbor Costa Rica. But for those who aren't faint of heart, the opportunities in Nicaragua—for an affordable life, for the chance to give back where it's badly needed—are that much greater.

Today, SUVs fill parking lots at **Managua** shopping malls, neon lights flicker in the night to announce downtown casinos and bars, and attractive, smartly dressed Nicaraguan socialites fill outdoor patios of restaurants and trendy nightclubs, mixing with North Americans who wear shorts and flip-flops and look like they didn't get the memo about the dress code. At the beach, shirtless tourists walk with surfboards under their arms, paw through racks of designer bathing suits in clothing boutiques, and drink cold Toña beers while they watch the sun melt into the ocean.

Though the country is still very underdeveloped, many of the creature comforts that North Americans are accustomed to are available here. Even two-hundred-year-old colonial homes in **Granada** are now hooked up for wireless internet and satellite TV. Getting a cell phone takes ten minutes, even faster if you have exact change.

Nicaragua is a country of vibrant and colorful culture, a place where you argue politics at a baseball game and discuss baseball with politicians. Usually rum or beer is involved in both scenarios. The country's cultural and architectural uniqueness distinguishes it from neighboring Costa Rica.

Yet behind its friendlier image, Nicaragua is still Nicaragua. The smell of burning brush and garbage fills the distant air on hot summer mornings (a fantastic smell of underdevelopment, by the way—not offensive as some may think), traffic along the highway stops as young boys whiz sticks over their heads to hustle bony cattle across the road into the surrounding fields, and Daniel Ortega—that's right, the same mustachioed strongman whose Sandinista National Liberation Front (FSLN) battled the Ronald Reagan–backed Contras in the 1980s—is again president (see box). It means more anti-imperialist rhetoric and street demonstrations. But no matter who is running things, Nicaragua is a poor country that feels the effects of global price rises first.

Yet despite its sharp edges, "the New Nicaragua," as the country is often billed, has been transformed in recent years by competitive investment incentives, easy foreign-residency requirements, affordable real estate deals, and near-perfect year-round weather (unless you like scraping ice off your windshield in the morning). (See "Residency and Red Tape" and "Real Estate.")

The two most popular parts of the country for retirees—both those who choose to work and those who choose to kick back—are **Granada** and the bustling southern Pacific beach town of **San Juan del Sur**. **Managua**, the sprawling capital city with no center and not many buildings taller than palm trees, is where the working expats live—people such as embassy staff, non-governmental organizations (NGOs), and other professionals. But most foreigners who have a choice about where to live opt for life outside of the capital and travel into **Managua** only to go shopping at PriceSmart or catch a movie.

UPSIDES

1. An inexpensive real estate market, with opportunities for housing and development.
2. The cost of living is less than that of most other Latin American nations.

3. Nicaraguans are very friendly; the country has not yet been "overrun by gringos."
4. Outdoor lifestyle, from hiking volcanos to swimming in lagoons and two oceans.

DOWNSIDES

1. Politically and socially volatile—strikes, protests, and provocative rhetoric from the president are part of life here.
2. If the cost of living is less, poverty is visible and widespread.
3. Occasional blackouts and water rationing are a part of life here.
4. Murphy's Law in effect here: ATM machines go off-line when you are in a rush, internet service crashes when you need to send an urgent email, and so on.

LOCATION

Nicaragua, affectionately known as the "belly button of the Americas," for its central location (and not necessarily its lint problem), is located in Central America, with Honduras to the north and Costa Rica to the south. It is the largest Central American country—about the size of New York State—and has both Pacific and Caribbean coastlines.

CLIMATE

Nicaragua has three distinct climatic regions. The Pacific lowlands, the most populated region of the country (**Managua, Granada, San Juan del Sur, León, Masaya**), has average daytime temperatures in the 90s and nighttime temperatures in the 80s. The north-central highlands (*Matagalpa, Jinotega, Estelí, Nueva Segovia*) is the more mountainous coffee-growing region of the country, with daytime temperatures in the 70s to 80s and nighttime temperatures in the 60s. The Caribbean coast (*Bluefields, Puerto Cabezas, Corn Islands*) is tropical, hot, and sticky, with daytime temperatures usually in the 80s to 90s and hot nights. Nicaragua has a wet season (May through October), and a dry season (November to May), give or take a couple weeks. It is still hot and sunny during the wet season, with tropical showers usually later in the afternoon or evening.

PEOPLE

Nicaragua's population of 5.3 million is predominantly young, though the birthrate has been declining in recent years. The population is mostly mixed-ethnicity mestizo (69 percent), followed by white (17 percent), Black Creole (9 percent), and Indian (5 percent).

There are no official or accurate statistics for the number of North American expats living in Nicaragua; most are here temporarily or on tourist visas. Best guess is between 3,000 and 5,000 North Americans, at least for part of the year. Most "retirees" are younger or "working retirees"; most in good health, not requiring constant medical care.

HISTORY

Nicaragua has a long and tumultuous history with the United States, yet it doesn't affect everyday relations between Nicaraguans and gringos to the extent that one might expect. North Americans first became interested in Nicaragua in the mid-nineteenth century, during the days of the California gold rush, when prospectors were looking for a faster route west. Nicaragua's national hero and Sandinista namesake, General Augusto Sandino, later cut his teeth fighting U.S. Marines. Some fifty years later, a rebel movement carrying his name ousted the U.S.-backed Somoza dictatorship, sparking an eight-year U.S.-funded counterrevolutionary (or contra) war here in the 1980s. The Sandinista government was eventually voted out of office in 1990, only to be returned to power in 2006. Despite the dark history between the United States and Nicaragua, there are many links between the two countries. Many Nicaraguans have family living in the United States and seem interested in life there—sometimes more so than the Americans who left to retire in Nicaragua.

GOVERNMENT

Nicaragua is a young constitutional republic, which has ratified democracy four times since the 1990 elections. President Daniel Ortega, who is often accused of manufacturing mini political crises to negotiate on his terms, provides the country's oligarchy and right-wing press with plenty of opportunity to cry "the sky is falling." But despite the drama and antics, the country's political system is more stable—and entertaining—than many Latin American democracies.

THE SANDINISTA SITUATION:
DEALING WITH DANIEL

In November 2006, facing a divided electorate, former revolutionary leader Daniel Ortega and the Sandinista National Liberation Front were voted back into power after sixteen years out of office. But unlike 1979, when the Sandinistas first took power through the barrels of guns, this time they did it through the ballot box, as a democratically elected party.

As of this writing (2008), Ortega appears to be housebroken. Although he railed against the U.S. for its worldwide "dictatorship" during a visit to the UN, at home he now talks mostly of peace, love, and reconciliation. After winning the elections, which the world agreed were clean, Ortega was quick to reach out to foreign investors, bankers, and other private-sector leaders.

Ortega has also admitted to mistakes of his previous government, namely property confiscations, which created an enormous mess here that is still being sorted out today. Ortega has promised "zero confiscations" by his new government. The Sandinista president has stressed that his government will work to solve the pending land problems that previous administrations left on the table. "We are the ones who understand the land problems, so we are the ones who can fix it," he said.

As president, Ortega is now using his unique historical position to do what he does best: play both sides of the room to his benefit. Ortega has shown that he doesn't have to choose between left and right: in his first months in office, Ortega cemented his friendship with Venezuela's firebrand leftist, oil-rich Hugo Chávez, and at the same time courted the conservative government of the United States.

Venezuela's generous new aid package for Nicaragua has created a curious situation where the conservative countries are now competing for his favor, so as not to lose influence in the region. The United States has responded to Ortega by being more proactive with aid to Nicaragua, and the International Monetary Fund has pledged its continued support. Says René González, president of the Nicaraguan-American Chamber of Commerce, "The Sandinistas are capitalists."

Though there has been concern over Ortega's authoritative nature and apparent plans to reform the constitution to allow him to stay in power after his five-year term ends in 2012, his overtures to investors and the United States helped to restore confidence in the country and its stalling real estate market. Kirk Hankla, president of Coldwell

Banker Nicaragua, said in March 2007 that he thought the market lull was over. "Of the buyers that pulled out of transactions immediately after the elections, most have returned," Hankla said. Although prices softened again in 2008, politics is not a factor, says realtors. "Ortega's victory was like the Y2K scare," said David Brownlee, a real estate broker for Century 21 in San Juan del Sur. "Everyone was scared about it and talked about it beforehand, and then nothing happened."

WHERE TO LIVE

The two most popular retirement areas in Nicaragua are the colonial city of **Granada** and the busy beach town of **San Juan del Sur**.

Located less than an hour's drive southeast of **Managua, Granada** sits

on the northwest shore of the expansive Lake Nicaragua, one of the largest freshwater lakes in the world. It is the oldest continuous colonial city on the mainland Americas, with a legend-filled history and a quaint Old World charm and architecture that led to the city's recent nomination to be named to the UNESCO World Heritage List. The city, located under the dormant Mombacho volcano, is hot and sunny year round.

Two hours south of **Granada** and **Managua** is the hopping beach town of **San Juan del Sur,** which has transformed from a small fishing village to an important tourism and retirement destination in just five years. The town has attracted a lot of hotel and residential development in past years. Large mansions now dot the cliffs overlooking the bay, and several over-sized buildings are being crammed onto the city's main street paralleling the beach. The weather is hot year round, and though the beach at **San Juan** is not the nicest for swimming or sunbathing, the town acts as the coastal hub to all the good swimming and surfing spots to the north and south.

AMBIENCE

From a horse-drawn carriage, tourists snap photos of the colorfully painted adobe homes and colonial-era churches that line the narrow streets of **Granada.** Women pass by on the sidewalk, singing out their inventory of fresh fruit piled in the baskets perched impossibly on their heads. Behind the thick adobe walls of a house down the road, a lion-head fountain cascades water into a courtyard pool, surrounded by a garden flowering with pink ginger and orange hibiscus—the hummingbirds' favorite. Double wooden doors lead out onto a balcony overlooking the red-tile roofs, and a family of green parrots lands in the nearby jocote tree, chattering loudly for several minutes before flapping off toward the Mombacho volcano.

This is a snapshot of Nicaragua, where the pace of life is slow, and the quality of life, for many people on a fixed budget, is good. Here, more than in almost any other Latin American country, the dollar goes further, and the mostly great weather allows for a healthy and active outdoor lifestyle.

As the expatriate communities grow in cities like **Managua, Granada, and San Juan del Sur,** so, too, do the social offerings for foreigners. Some expats have started to form organizations or hold regular parties and events for the local foreign community. There's a women's club in **Managua,** an increasingly active expat community that does fund-raisers and benefits in **Granada,** and a group that started the country's first lending library in **San Juan del Sur.** (See "Volunteering Without Borders.")

Most of the country's cultural attractions—theater, movies, and musical performances—are in **Managua.** But each city has its patron saint festivals. **San Juan del Sur** explodes during New Year's and Holy Week celebrations, when the country floods to the beaches for concerts and partying. And **Granada** is now on the world cultural calendar with its annual International Poetry Festival, held each year in February. The annual event brings hundreds of poets from around the world for a weeklong celebration of the arts. **Granada** is also home to the famous Casa de los Tres Mundos cultural center, which organizes different art, music, and film events throughout the year.

Granada, San Juan del Sur, and **Managua** also have active nightlife scenes, with weekend parties, live music, and dancing (and, of course, plenty of Nicaragua's internationally celebrated Flor de Caña rum).

All three cities also have language schools and intensive Spanish-language immersion programs. Though many Nicaraguans speak at least some English—especially those involved in the tourism sector—it's not imperative that foreigners master Spanish to survive in Nicaragua.

STANDARD OF LIVING

Nicaragua is a grindingly poor country, with a small oligarchy, a pinched middle class, and an enormous lower class. Approximately 80 percent of Nicaraguans live on less than $2 a day. Poverty has many faces in Nicaragua, and as a whole, can be overwhelming to North American sensibilities. Young mothers beg on the streets with dirty infants, barefoot children sell gum late at night at dangerous downtown intersections, hollow-eyed old men push aside bony street-dogs to rummage through garbage put out on the curb, and tough-faced young men gather on street corners with no work and nothing particular to do. The poverty is even greater in the countryside, but the desperation is less.

Nicaragua is a country with rough edges and no visible safety net. For many foreigners, adjusting to the poverty and the sharp contrast between haves and have-nots can be difficult. But for those who want to help, there are lots of organizations, foundations, and other ways to get involved in the community. (See "Volunteering Without Borders.") And many foreigners help the local economy by paying fair wages, rather than the starvation market wages, to domestic employees, staff, and other workers.

In this context, most foreigners, even those on lower fixed incomes, can live well in Nicaragua. By way of comparison, for the amount you would spend to rent a small apartment in downtown Boston, eating macaroni and cheese and sitting on a folding chair while you watch basic cable wearing a sweater because you can't afford to turn up the heat, in **Granada** you could afford to rent a spacious colonial home with flowered courtyards, internet, cable TV, daily maid service, and perhaps a swimming pool. And you could still afford to go out for a steak dinner.

The cost and quality of life are perhaps the biggest factors that lure foreign retirees to Nicaragua. Though the cost of living has increased here in recent years (where has it not?), most find that their money still goes further here and allows them to live a lifestyle that they otherwise couldn't afford.

CULTURE

Nicaragua proudly and quaintly boasts that it has more poets per capita than anywhere else in the world. The country is proud of its cultural contributions and history, and it should be. Nicaragua's most famous son is world-famous poet Rubén Darío, who lived in the late nineteenth and early twentieth centuries. Each year in February, **Granada** hosts the International Poetry Festival.

Nicaragua is also famous for handicrafts such as pottery, rocking chairs, and hammocks. The town of Masaya, a half hour from the capital and **Granada,** is the center of culture and handicrafts. The hammocks made in Masaya are exported all over the world—even to other hammock-making countries such as Costa Rica, Puerto Rico, and the Dominican Republic, where they are resold as locally made. (Ssshhhh, that's a hammock industry secret.)

Nicaragua also has its own culinary flavors, from rundown—a thick stewlike fish dish made on the Caribbean coast—to vigaron, a locally famous dish in **Granada** made from fried pork rinds, shredded cabbage, yucca, onions, and peppers. You eat it with your fingers, which is half the fun.

Drinkers (both booze and coffee, which is usually the same people) will be happy to know that Nicaragua makes some of the best rum and coffee in the world.

LEISURE

Nicaragua has three national sports and pastimes: baseball, politics, and cockfighting—the latter two of which are sometimes difficult to distinguish from each other. It also has two baseball leagues, whose games are a great and easy way to spend an afternoon. Beers cost the equivalent of a dollar, and you can see some pretty good up-and-coming talent and a whole lot of passion. For the strong of stomach, cockfighting is a huge pastime. Said Tanya Ortega, a vegetarian from Minnesota and first-time cockfight-goer,

"I recently decided to go to a cockfight with a friend, and we had an experience we wouldn't have had otherwise, and I plan to go again. And this is coming from someone who hasn't eaten chicken or red meat in twenty years!"

There are many outdoor and ecological activities, such as kayaking on Lake Nicaragua, hiking on Mombacho volcano, and swimming in the crystal clear waters of Laguna de Apoyo. Expats on the coast enjoy surfing on the country's increasingly famous breakers, and visitors to **Granada** can now even practice their golf swing at the country's first floating-ball driving range, which gives new meaning to the concept of water hazard.

While it is common for Nicaraguans to invite friends and family over to their homes for the evening, social life for foreigners usually means going out to restaurants, cafés, bars, and sporting events. The society is accepting of the gay lifestyle.

SOCIAL CUSTOMS

Despite Nicaragua's sordid past with the United States, most Nicaraguans generally do not have an anti-American attitude. In fact, many Nicaraguans have family in the United States, or have lived there themselves, so the social customs usually are not too foreign. U.S media, movies, and music have a strong influence on Nicaragua.

If you are light skinned in Nicaragua, you will be called *chele* (which means "whitey"), just like if you are dark skinned, you will be called *negro,* and if you are overweight, you will be called *gordo.* It's mostly meant to be descriptive, not offensive. "Gringo" is also meant to be descriptive, not offensive. But if someone calls you *yanqui,* that's offensive, and you might be in a situation you shouldn't be, especially if they call you *yanqui, hi'jue puta.*

But Nicaraguans are generally very friendly to foreigners, especially North Americans, to whom many feel more of a cultural or familiar connection. Canadians are not distinguished from U.S. citizens.

Nicaragua is generally a macho culture. It's not uncommon for people passing by on the street to make eye contact and hold it longer than many North Americans are comfortable with. Or for strangers on the street to make comments, like reading your T-shirt out loud or saying, "What's up, Boston?" if you are wearing a Red Sox cap.

Women will often receive *piropos,* or catcalls, which range from creative to lewd. Generally, the catcalls are harmless; the only victim is feminism. Girls, usually young and traveling in herds, also make catcalls, often to men who are much older than they are.

HEALTH CARE/MEDICAL

Although the World Health Organization does not give high marks to Nicaragua's health care overall, its private health care is good, and the state-of-the-art Vivian Pellas Hospital in **Managua** is considered one of the most modern in Central America. Because Nicaragua is a very poor country, the hospital is generally used only by the rich—Nicaraguans and foreigners—which means that very rarely are there lines or long waits to see a doctor. The hospital is inexpensive in comparative terms. An overnight stay costs around $100 for a private room (plus a $300 deposit), a general checkup or medical consultation will cost $15 to $40, and even minor surgery will cost less than $1,000, including medicine.

The prices make medical insurance unnecessary for most, since expats can generally afford to pay out of pocket for most procedures. Some in-country insurance plans are available through the hospitals, but paying out of pocket is usually cheaper and less of a hassle.

As this book goes to press, two new $30 million private hospitals are under construction in **Managua,** including what will reportedly be a world-class children's hospital. Outside of the capital, in places like **Granada** and **Rivas,** the health care is adequate for minor consultations or illnesses. But if you want top care or need to see a specialist, you have to go to **Managua.**

Public health care means long lines, but it is free. (Often the same doctors you would pay to see in a private hospital also work in the nearby public hospital.) The Sandinista government has made improving public health care a priority, and it has its work cut out for it.

RESIDENCY AND RED TAPE

Many North Americans who live in Nicaragua do so on tourist visas, which are good for ninety days but which can be extended at the immigration office. For North Americans who go back and forth to the United States several times a year, the standard tourism card can be the easiest way to come and go. The risk of getting in trouble for living here on a tourist visa is low.

Foreign residency can be applied for under several categories. The two most common ones are known as *pensionado* and *rentista,* both of which apply to people over forty-five. Pensionado is for retirees living off savings or investments, and rentista is for those who have a steady and provable monthly income of $400, plus an additional $100 for each dependent.

For the most part, the paperwork and procedural requirements for all categories of foreign residency are basically the same: certification of income, clean police record, birth certificate, marriage certificate, copies of all used passport pages, a medical exam from a home doctor or registered Nicaraguan doctor, a letter on company letterhead proving employment (for working visa).

Now for the tricky part: all paperwork must be authenticated *first* by the Nicaraguan Consulate nearest to the applicant's hometown, then by the Nicaraguan Foreign Ministry. Those who are approved for residency are eligible for a onetime tax-free import of household goods and a vehicle.

Though Nicaragua has worked to try to make the procedures more transparent in recent years, it hasn't done a good job on either account. Applying for residency can be a very arbitrary, frustrating process.

Working

Nicaragua has two economies: the formal, which is small but growing; and the informal, which is enormous and growing.

Technically, foreigners have to be residents to work legally in Nicaragua's formal economy. With the exception of low-paying "backpacker jobs," like tending bar for a month at a youth hostel, the employment options for foreigners, especially outside of the capital, are very limited. The unemployment rate is 50 percent.

For the most part, with the exception of those who stumble into the real estate racket, where brokers don't need any training or licensing, working in Nicaragua means starting your own business. And despite some red tape and slow bureaucracy, it can be done. Expats have remodeled colonial homes and converted them to B and Bs. New England–style bookstore/coffee shops have been opened on the beach.

Setting up a business in Nicaragua means first forming a *sociedad anónima* (*S.A.*), which would be like creating a corporation in the United States. This process can take about a month and cost about $3,000 in processing and legal fees. All legally registered businesses in Nicaragua are required to pay income and social security taxes. Ignorance of the law in Nicaragua is no defense for those who break it. This is a country where a lot of people cut legal corners, but as a foreigner, you don't want to be the one who gets caught doing it.

COST OF LIVING

The cost of living in Nicaragua is, relative to comparable Latin American destinations, relatively inexpensive. Though the influx of foreign retirees and expatriates has increased the price of living here, creating a parallel economy in recent years, costs are still generally affordable, both in the city and at the beach.

While an apartment or small home can be rented in **Managua** or **San Juan del Sur** for $300 a month, in **Granada** there are mostly centuries-old colonial homes occupied by multiple generations of families, so the rental market generally means remodeled second homes owned by gringos. It is still possible to find a smaller, furnished home in **Granada** with cable TV and twice-weekly cleaning service for around $400 a month, but those deals are becoming rarer. Other colonial homes, complete with a swimming pool, internet, three bedrooms, cleaning service, and all the bells and whistles, rent for $800 to $1,500 a month. As more homes go onto the rental market, the prices in **Granada** could come down, but don't count on it.

Monthly Cost of Living in Granada

Rent for a two-bedroom home, condo, or apartment: $400 to $1,500.

Taxes: 10 percent sales taxes on food, drink. Property taxes are negligible: a decent-sized home would pay about $50 a year; and a mansion in the city, $300 plus.

Groceries for two: $140.

Utilities: Water, $10; electricity, $50 to $70.

Cable TV: $17.

Internet: Basic connection, $40; fast, $80.

Transportation: Inner-city taxi, $0.50; bus to **Managua**, $1; shuttle to airport, $15; taxi to airport, $35.

Maid service: $25 a week.

Restaurants for two: $25 in a midrange restaurant.

Monthly Cost of Living in Managua

Rent for two-bedroom home, condo, or apartment: $150 to $550.

Taxes: 10 percent sales taxes on food, drink. Property taxes are negligible: a decent-sized home would pay about $50 a year; and a mansion in the city, $300 plus.

Groceries for two: $200.

Utilities: Water, $10; electricity, $50.

Cable TV: $17.

Internet: $40 to $70.

Transportation: Inner-city taxi, $1 to $4; inner-city bus, $0.17; bus to other cities, $1 to $5.

Maid service: Minimum $67.
Restaurants for two: $25 to $30 in a midrange restaurant

Monthly Cost of Living in San Juan del Sur
Rent for a two-bedroom home, condo, or apartment: $250 to $500.
Taxes: 10 percent sales taxes on food, drink. Property taxes are
　　negligible: a decent-sized home would pay about $50 a year;
　　and a mansion in the city, $300 plus.
Groceries for two: $200.
Cable TV: $17.
Internet: $40 to $70.
Transportation: Inner-city taxi, $0.50; taxi to Rivas, $6.
Maid service: $50.
Restaurants for two: $20 in a midrange restaurant; $35 in a nicer
　　restaurant.

REAL ESTATE

Anyone can own real estate in Nicaragua. You don't have to be a citizen or
even a resident to own property here.

From 2002 to 2006, the real estate market in Nicaragua had been red
hot, with prices appreciating around 300 percent to 500 percent both in
Granada and along the coast. Gringos were snatching up property in a near
frenzy, buying 10 percent of the homes in **Granada**'s colonial center within
three years.

Then came the 2006 presidential elections. When Daniel Ortega won,
the real estate market's heart skipped a beat. Some expats pulled a panic
sale and cashed out, running for the nearest exit as if their hair were on
fire. The Ortega victory set the market back both on the beach, where
prices leveled off for the first time in years, and in **Granada,** where prices
dropped as much as 50 percent in some cases.

But then, when a new wave of intrepid and educated buyers began
coming back, the market started to recover several months after Ortega
took office. The possibility of his victory, it appeared, was scarier to the
market than his actual presidency. At publication time, the markets were
down, the realtors hopeful.

But buyer beware: Nicaragua's real estate market is full of pitfalls
that were dug by the previous Sandinista government in the 1980s. Due
to land confiscations under the Sandinistas' agrarian reform efforts, many
properties have tricky ownership histories. Some have no clear title, or
multiple titles to the same lot. Buyers should avoid any properties with

provisional titles called *títulos supletorios* (or auxiliary titles) and be extremely leery of any land that was confiscated and then given to a cooperative; even seasoned realtors will often steer clear of these titles. It's imperative for first-time buyers to go through reputable real estate firms rather than try to buy directly from a seller under unknown circumstances.

Retirees generally look for property along the southern Pacific coast or in **Granada** or its surrounding areas. Buying an old colonial home in **Granada** often means buying a street address and then gutting and rebuilding much of the interior. There are, however, more remodeled colonial homes that have been purchased in recent years by gringos, fixed up, and then flipped back onto the market for a markup of 100 percent or higher. Do careful homework before buying anything on the coast. Most of the projects haven't even broken ground. And some probably never will.

There are new condominium projects popping up in **Granada,** with preconstruction costs around $99,000. A colonial fixer-upper may run in the $80,000 to $120,000 range, while a remodeled colonial will go from $150,000 up to $400,000. Gone are the days of the $30,000 to $60,000 deals, though not long gone. Some good deals can still be found. Outside of **Granada,** prime beachfront property along the southern Pacific coast near **San Juan del Sur** is in the $80,000 to $250,000 category, and climbing.

There aren't a whole lot of payment options for foreigners in Nicaragua. Though some banks are now starting to offer mortgages, the terms aren't considered competitive, and you have to be a resident to open a bank account here. Once you purchase a property, it is crucial that you register it in your name with the municipal government, to avoid past owners showing up on your doorstep in the future and claiming they still own the house—which they may if you haven't registered it in your name.

TRANSPORTATION

Daily flights from the U.S. and Spain arrive in **Managua**'s Augusto Sandino International Airport. There are also daily flights on national carriers to more than a half dozen locations in Nicaragua, mostly on the Caribbean coast, which is very difficult to reach by land.

Driving in Nicaragua is not for the faint of heart, however. Streets, even in the capital, don't have names, so directions are by landmark, some of which no longer exist. Drivers are also aggressive and generally insane.

Bringing a car into the country is not impossible, but it is expensive, due to import taxes. It can also be dangerous—highway robbery is not unknown— if you plan to drive it down yourself. Once you're a resident, you are allowed a onetime tax-free import of a vehicle valued up to $10,000.

SECURITY

Though Nicaragua has tried to crack down on corruption and improve transparency in recent years, weak government institutions and starvation wages for lower-level bureaucrats open the door wide to possible corruption. Red tape and general incompetence can also be confused for corruption. Though there is a legal way to do things, it is not uncommon to hear about people paying a "tip" (bribe) to expedite different processes. Offering bribes is a very delicate art; if you try it with the wrong person, you could get in legal trouble.

Contrary to what most people would think, Nicaragua is the safest country in Central America, and **Managua** is statistically the safest Latin American capital city. Though crime has increased in recent years, it hasn't grown as fast here as it has in other countries. The Sandinistas, who created the modern-day police and military, have played an important role in keeping international gangs and organized cartels out of the country. Most crime here is nonviolent theft or cat burglary.

Police generally try to be helpful, but their effectiveness usually depends directly on the competence and leadership of their chief of police. Several cities have implemented a new tourism police unit, which claims to be bilingual and is generally more accessible to questions and concerns from foreigners.

COMMUNICATIONS AND MEDIA

Prepaid cell phones in Nicaragua are now ubiquitous. Email and internet service has improved vastly in recent years. In-home internet hookups cost between $50 and $80 for good service, either through a wireless hookup, satellite, or cable modem.

Nicaragua also has some English-language media. Topping the list is the *Nica Times*, an English-language weekly newspaper. Most movie releases that make it to **Managua** are in English with Spanish subtitles. The movies make it here late, usually several months after being released in the United States, if at all. The one exception is Steven Seagal movies, which, unfortunately, always seem to arrive here a couple weeks after release in the United States.

UP-AND-COMING AREAS

Almost all of Nicaragua, which has gone from zero to discovered in less than five years, can qualify as "up and coming." Even the most popular areas for investment—the colonial city of **Granada** and the southern Pacific coastline—are still far from reaching their ceilings. Despite the recent development boom, Nicaragua is still a country with a nascent economy and infrastructure. The beauty of this country is that it has a lot of space and a lot of unique investment and development opportunities in virtually every type of climate and terrain, from thick tropical jungle on the Caribbean coast to the cool and misty rain forest of *Matagalpa.*

Matagalpa

A two-hour drive northeast of **Managua** will put you in the mountains of *Matagalpa,* the country's main coffee-producing region. The city itself is rustic, and the roads are horrendous. But the mountains are beautiful, and deals can be found on old coffee plantations and other land that was abandoned during the war and is now for sale. It's a cowboy lifestyle here, but those who have dreamed of being a *finquero* (farmer) can make it happen in *Matagalpa.* The weather here depends on the altitude and the surrounding forestry cover; it can be blistering hot and dry in some areas, and misty and cool two kilometers around the bend. In recent years, there have been sprouts of agricultural tourism and coffee plantation development. There are also plans to build the area's first gated community on another nearby coffee plantation.

León

Revolutionary, hip, and hot, the relatively undiscovered colonial university city of León is like **Granada** with a higher education. Two hours north of **Managua**, León is the yin to **Granada**'s yang. The two cities, historical rivals, are similar in some respects and quite different in others. Whereas Granadinos are concerned with what your last name is, how fair your skin is, and who your grandfather was, León is way more liberal and educated. It's also scorching hot (think 100 degrees) and politically left leaning. **León** has some wonderful colonial architecture and the largest cathedral in Central America (a proposed UNESCO World Heritage site). But unlike **Granada,** much of **León** is showing its age, with beautiful old colonial homes crumbling into the cobblestone streets. **León** is getting an increasing number of backpackers and European tourists looking to get away from the gringos of **Granada,** and it is just a matter of time before this fantastic city rises up again to give its conservative cousin a run for its money.

Mombacho Volcano

With cooler temperatures than **Granada,** and only twenty minutes away, the forested heights of *Mombacho* volcano are now being eyed by those who want to be close to **Granada** but not in the city. *Mombacho* is more temperate and elevated, offering great views of the city below. But much of what is being built on *Mombacho* is—as they say here—*a la brava,* or willy-nilly construction without permits. So be careful what you are getting yourself into.

Caribbean Coast

Nicaragua's Caribbean coast is the last frontier, which Paul Theroux made famous in his novel *The Mosquito Coast.* This coast is subject to hurricanes and is ripe for "basement level" investment. Most of the population here is Miskito, Sumo, or Creole, and many people speak Spanish as a second language (the first being an Indian dialect or Creole English). This is the Caribbean—eighty years ago. The coast is reportedly already being eyed by Spanish and other European investors for future tourism development projects. Be extremely careful if buying on the Caribbean, since much of the land is communal or tribal land. The islands, for example, are beautiful, but don't touch!

VOLUNTEERING WITHOUT BORDERS

Nicaragua, a country in need of assistance, has many volunteer opportunities. Dating back to the "solitary brigades" of the 1980s, volunteers generally have a very good image. Locals are welcoming and appreciative of help from expat sources.

- Expat Donna Tabor (through a Pittsburgh-based group called Building New Hope) has started several community projects (www.buildingnewhope.org).
- The largest volunteer organization group in **Granada** is La Esperanza, which works in schools and on health projects on the outskirts of the capital (www.la-esperanza-Granada.org).
- Volunteers at the library in **San Juan del Sur** have created a mobile library with donated books to promote literacy among low-income children (www.sjdsbiblioteca.com).
- Witness for Peace, a long-established activist group, has volunteer opportunities that now focus on economic justice (www.witnessforpeace.org).
- Habitat for Humanity works with partner communities to build homes in various parts of the country.

Tim Rogers, who lives in Granada, is the editor of the Nica Times, Nicaragua's *English-language newspaper, and a contributor to the* Miami Herald *and* Time *online.*

MY NICARAGUA

An Artist and "Political Refugee"

Name, age, origin: Kelly Ann Thomas, forty-one, Texas, Vermont, Massachusetts, and New York. Lived in Europe, too.

Where I live: I rent a house in the town of **San Juan del Sur.**

How long in Nicaragua: Two years.

Previous/present occupation: Interior designer and graphic artist. Now I own a bookstore and sell my artwork online. Small businesses are welcomed and encouraged. My overall business experience has been positive. I live here full-time and go back to the States a couple of times a year.

Reasons for moving here: I have wanted to live overseas again since I left Berlin in December 1989. More recently, I knew after Congress passed the unconstitutional Patriot Act that I had to get out of the U.S. By the beginning of August 2004, we were certain that we would be moving to Nicaragua in the next year. We bought our tickets to visit **San Juan del Sur** the day after Bush stole an election for the second time. We moved here seven months later. Personally, I consider myself a political refugee. Yes, I want to experience different cultures and live abroad, but I feel forced into it because of the illegal wars.

Finances: I moved here with approximately $100K in savings. I receive monthly dividend checks that cover my expenses here without counting my business income. I live a comfortable but not extravagant life.

Costs: San Juan del Sur has the highest cost of living in the country, as well as the highest expat population, save for perhaps **Granada.** The cost of living in **Managua** is slightly lower, but housing in the nicer barrios (*Villa Fontana, Los Robles*) is comparable to what expats pay in **San Juan del Sur.** Most of the expats I know who live in *Jinotega* and *Estelí* and nontouristy places pay about half of what I pay in rent.

My community: I live two blocks from the beach in a town that bills itself as a quaint little fishing village with a gringo problem. Joke. You see oxcarts and BMWs on the streets, more of the former than the latter. It is a small town with a relaxed attitude and a busy pace. Maybe 300 expats. The biggest complaint that the locals have with the expats is that we have priced the locals out of their own town.

Weather: The tourist guides described this area as having a constant breeze from the lake, virtually no mosquitoes, and a year-round temperature range of 70 to 80 degrees. Reality is much different. We have a windy season from December through March, with violent gusts of wind that pound the zinc roofs and leave layers of gritty dust on every surface in the area. March through May are the hot months, with temperatures in the mid-90s in the day, and about 80 at night.

Leisure: I hike the hills, ride my horse, take yoga classes, and walk the beach for exercise.

Culture: Very little. Culture is watching a pirated DVD from the local video store. One restaurant has theme nights once a month, with musicians, food, and sometimes dancing.

Health care/medical: Vivian Pellas Hospital is better than most hospitals I have seen in the USA. I will go there for any problem—routine or emergency. I don't have faith in the other hospitals. I pay $50 for a visit with my gynecologist. The Rivas Hospital, on the other hand, is often referred to as "a place to die." I have no health insurance at present. If something major happens, I have enough money to go to **Managua** or fly to Costa Rica or Panama for care.

Residency and visas: Most people I know have tourist visas. I don't know anyone with a part-time residency visa. Those with retirement visas tended to secure them for moving household goods or cars without customs. I live forty-five minutes from the border. I can cross into Costa Rica for a few minutes and then return to Nicaragua, get my stamp, and be on my way. You can get a ninety-day extension on a tourist visa without a problem.

Crime, corruption: There is a lot of theft, and the bars were on the windows before the gringos moved in. It is accepted as a way of life. I was robbed in my house while I was sleeping. This has happened to five friends as well. I left sandals on my porch one time—gone in less than five minutes. The police are a joke. Usually a call to the police means you'll get a busy signal. On the other hand, serious crimes are treated seriously. After a carjacking in **Managua**—a rarity—the police investigator did his job, and the three men were arrested, tried, and convicted. No problems, no corruption. Traffic cops, of course, take bribes.

No government is free of corruption, but people are more honest about the subject here. But I think the current Ortega administration will be less corrupt than the previous one.

Best: More than anything, I have more time to spend with friends. I also feel as if I have more freedom here, despite Daniel Ortega, the Catholic Church, and the bureaucratic frustrations. I moved from a country that espouses freedom yet monitors my every activity. Here the laws are stricter in some ways, but no one is actively trying to monitor my activities. There are always parties and parades, and people laugh a lot. My rush-hour commute is two minutes, longer if I stop to talk with someone or pet my neighbor's dog. I eat the best pineapple in the world, drink fresh juices every day, and watch gorgeous sunsets every night. It's not all perfect here. I have days when I want to strangle people, especially the ones who keep playing that jukebox across the way.

Worst: Good roads? Only if good is defined as three-foot potholes spaced every four feet. It takes more than two hours to drive to **Managua,** a seventy-mile trip.

How locals drive: Like blind crack addicts trapped in a bumper car ring. Taxi drivers and microbus drivers are the worst.

What I miss most: A working infrastructure—paved roads, reliable water and electricity. I really miss concerts and plays. If I lived in **Managua,** life would be a little more similar to what I left behind. I chose to live in **San Juan del Sur** because of the large expat population; it seemed the best place outside of **León** (too hot), **Granada** (not my vibe), and **Managua** (no way!) to achieve this.

Should other retirees come? The cool people can come, but I prefer that those looking to flip property or build mega resorts or live in said mega resorts just go away. We really need a screening committee! A joke. Honestly, I do my best to discourage many people from moving here. We don't want the kinds of people who are ruining Costa Rica by turning it into a mini-USA. People who move here solely because the cost of living is cheaper than the USA tend to be miserable here. You have to want to be part of Nicaragua to enjoy it. Otherwise it will drive you nuts.

MY NICARAGUA

An "Investor" from Connecticut Who Married a Nicaraguan

Name, age, origin: Scott D., fifty, Connecticut; my wife is twenty-three, from Nicaragua.

Where I live: The city of **Granada,** in a house on a street currently being turned into a walking street with very little car traffic. It is beautiful.

How long in Nicaragua: Six years.

Occupation: Investor.

Reasons for moving here: I wanted to live in a foreign country close to the United States, a third world country that I thought had a lot of potential.

My community: There are all kinds of different people here. Guys who spend all their day drinking; others who are making a contribution to this city and the country. Other people have businesses, which also help the community. I am president of the group called the Amigos de la Policia, which works with and helps the local police. Many foreigners here don't speak Spanish but mostly are not doing anything active. It really helps if you know the language. I understand virtually everything in Spanish. My wife is from **Granada** and can speak Spanish and English.

Weather: Hot all year long.

Culture: Not interested in culture.

Health care/medical: Vivian Pellas Hospital in **Managua** is as good as an American hospital for most problems. I try to stay away from doctors that were trained in Nicaragua. The best doctors are from Cuba or have trained in the United States. An office visit is around $10. As for insurance, for the first time in my life, I do not have any. Costs here are so low that I think you can pretty much self-insure. The only problem is if you have a complicated problem and need to go back to the United States.

Crime, corruption: In **Granada** there is a problem with petty crime; every once in a while, someone gets mugged. Absolutely, there is corruption. I'm not sure if it's any better or worse than the corruption in the United States, it's just a lot more transparent. Also, it is common practice at all levels of government to pay a little money to get things done quicker than they would normally get done. I'm not sure if this is considered corruption.

Drawbacks: Takes awhile to get used to the cultural differences, which include no concept of time, poverty, and lack of education.

Best: People here are much more relaxed and don't have money on their mind every minute of the day. They live like 1950s America—a lot closer to their family. My quality of life is much better here than in the United States. In the States, I am just another middle- to upper-middle-class person trying to keep up with everyone else. Here I live like a king. I just wish more retirees would stay home. We already have enough to go around.

What I miss most: I can't say that I really miss anything. I go back to the United States once a year for a week, and that is enough.

Chapter 12

COSTA RICA

The Peaceful One

BY ERIN VAN RHEENEN

With its jungles, sunny beaches, churning rivers, mountains, volcanos, and enough bird and animal wildlife to make even the staunchest house bunny get up and explore, Costa Rica is best known as a tourist destination for active, tree-swinging vacations. But for a decade or more, this small but varied country of just over 4 million inhabitants has become a major draw for retirees.

Costa Rica lures retirees from up north with an appealing combination of the exotic and the familiar. It's a far-off land less than three hours by plane from Miami, an international destination with a decidedly local feel, a complex country where life is still fueled by basic human warmth. A joke you hear among the tens of thousands of expatriates who live here is that Costa Rica is "Central America Lite," with far fewer of the drawbacks of most other Latin American retirement havens. And after Mexico, it may have the largest population of expats anywhere in Latin America.

There are no reliable numbers on how many North Americans make their home in Costa Rica, but the estimates bandied about range from 50,000 to much higher. Many of them settle in the *Central Valley,* which has at its center the capital city of **San José**. The other big expatriate mecca is the Pacific coast, mostly the area around **Jacó** and *Quepos/Manuel Antonio,* and also up north in *Guanacaste,* along the string of lovely beaches dubbed the Gold Coast.

Most of the new settlers came to Costa Rica for the nature and stayed for the culture. Not culture with a capital *C,* as you'd find in Old World capitals, but a culture of peace, modest prosperity, and a commitment to protecting the land's tropical bounty. Over a quarter of the country is set aside in parks and reserves, where you can see monkeys swarming through old-growth trees or spot a flock of keel-billed toucans on the wing. There's nothing like witnessing a sea turtle the size of a small car laying its eggs on a moonlit stretch of beach, or stumbling upon an idyllic waterfall, or riding a horse to a high, solitary peak. In Costa Rica, there's still time to smell the frangipani.

For the last half century, while neighboring countries dealt with civil unrest and military dictatorships, Costa Ricans, who have no military at all, have been peacefully electing their leaders in multiparty elections. The resulting political and economic stability attracted foreign investment, which further strengthened the agriculture-based economy. Nowadays the economy is fueled by the tourism sector, high-tech manufacturing, farming, and a growing business of telephone call centers for everything from online gambling (legal here) to tech support. Oh, and the retirement crowd.

LOCATION

Bordered on the north by Nicaragua and to the south by Panama, Costa Rica has a 100-mile Caribbean coastline and a 300-mile Pacific coast. At 20,000 square miles, it's the third-smallest country in Central America after Belize and El Salvador.

CLIMATE

For a country about the size of West Virginia, Costa Rica has a remarkably varied terrain. Early April in *Guanacaste* will be hot and dry, while a few hours away, mountain towns like **La Fortuna,** in the shadow of Arenal volcano, are wet and green. The Caribbean coast will be its usual humid and rainy self, while the weather on the slopes above the *Central Valley* will be chilly enough to warrant a sweater. But even in the *Central Valley* (at around four thousand feet), it's usually warm enough during the day to live in flip-flops, if that's your desire.

PEOPLE

Though expatriates no longer enjoy the dirt-cheap cost of living they once did, many appreciate a place with a burgeoning middle class, where foreign newcomers aren't the only ones with wealth. Costa Rica has done a good job of taking care of its own and continues to invest in the medical and educational welfare of its citizenry. There is high-quality universal health care coverage and a well-educated population proud of its country and assured enough to welcome newcomers.

However welcoming, there have been growing pains in a country that perhaps wasn't ready for its own popularity. Costa Rica is still adjusting to increases in the number of visitors and new residents and to the enormous changes in its own population. It has changed from its rural past to a present in which 60 percent of Costa Ricans live in urban areas. Development, not necessarily a bad thing, is now posing problems as infrastructure (roads, water, electricity, waste management) fails to keep pace with all the new houses and condos and businesses.

HISTORY AND GOVERNMENT

Costa Rica's history doesn't presage its current status as the wealthiest and most stable of Central American nations. Sure, Christopher Columbus thought it was a place of riches; when he landed here in 1502, he dubbed the place Costa Rica, or Rich Coast, because the native peoples wore jewelry that Columbus assumed was gold. The gold turned out to be base metal, and Costa Rica's lack of mineral wealth guaranteed it neglect from the Spanish colonists, who tromped off in search of the gold and silver in places like Mexico and Peru.

Many historians believe that Costa Rica's poverty during the colonial era actually helped to lay the foundation for a democratic nation of equals, where everyone struggled equally just to survive and where class differences were not as pronounced as elsewhere. In 1821 Costa Rica threw off the yoke of Spanish colonial rule, and in 1848 the country became its own republic.

By the mid-1800s, coffee emerged as Costa Rica's chief crop, followed by banana cultivation at the end of the century. Coffee and banana growers (most of them American) became the true powers in the country. From the 1920s on, Costa Rica had the good fortune to be governed by three politicians who, alone in Central America, established true democracy: Rafael Ángel Calderón, who established Costa Rica's health and education systems, but who refused to give up his presidency; José "Don Pepe" Figueres, who led a forty-day rebellion in 1948 to oust Calderón and then abolished the army and drafted a new constitution; and President Óscar Arias, whose enlightened governance and role in brokering regional peace earned him the Nobel Peace Prize in 1987.

Many expats have been drawn here because of Costa Rica's unique commitment to peace, preferring to funnel funds into education and health instead of the military. A model for democracy for Latin America, Costa Rica elected president Arias to another four-year term in 2006, and he wants again to be the peace president.

UPSIDES

1. Great weather—fine-tune your climate by moving up or down in elevation.
2. Lower cost of living.
3. Nature, up close and personal.
4. High-quality and inexpensive medical care.
5. Political and economic stability—no army.
6. High literacy.

DOWNSIDES

1. Slower pace can mean inefficiency.
2. Not undiscovered—though real estate prices fell in 2008, they have skyrocketed since 2001.
3. Crime is also on the rise.
4. Lousy roads.
5. Surprisingly, the government has pulled back on some retiree benefits.

WHERE TO LIVE

The Central Valley

Over two-thirds of Costa Rica's population live in the perennially green basin called the *Central Valley*. At four thousand feet and at the center of the valley is **San José**, the nation's capital and its undisputed political, economic, and cultural center. *Ticos* (as Costa Ricans are called) from other areas come here for jobs or educational opportunities, and many expats are posted here to work for international companies. **San José** is where you'll find the museums, theaters, restaurants, shops, and the Latin American headquarters of multinational corporations. If you want to be around other English-speaking expats, the *Central Valley* is the place for you. And for those who prefer to leave the heat and humidity at the beach, the

Central Valley's mild climate is just right. It never gets very cold or very hot here—temperatures average in the mid-70s.

The suburbs and towns surrounding **San José** are popular with expats from up north and from Europe. The western suburb of *Escazú,* with its country clubs and English-language primary and secondary schools, is where the U.S. ambassador lives. Nearby **Santa Ana,** with its lovely old stone church and upscale restaurants, is also popular with expats of comfortable means. To the north, **Alajuela** is a reasonably priced small city near the international airport. **Heredia** is another option; those who like cooler temperatures will appreciate the slopes above the city. Farther afield you'll find **Grecia**, thirty minutes from **San José** but a world apart—it was voted "cleanest town in Latin America." There's also **Sarchí**, the artsy small town where wood furniture and painted oxcarts are produced, and **Atenas,** on the road from **San José** to the Pacific coast, said by *National Geographic* to have the most perfect climate in the world.

Guanacaste and the Nicoya Peninsula

This area's beaches are one if its biggest draws. Surfers, divers, anglers, and loafers flock here. From white sand **Playa Hermosa** up north to rocky *Cabo Blanco* at the southern tip of the *Nicoya Peninsula,* there's something for everyone. *Guanacaste*'s dependable dry season (December to April) makes it the perfect choice for those who want to escape the rain and snow back home.

The increasingly busy international airport in **Liberia** means that visitors can skip a sometimes cranky, crowded **San José** and land less than an hour from the northern Pacific beaches (a four- or five-hour drive from **San José**). The entire Pacific coast area is booming. Condo construction is on the rise, especially in places like **Playas del Coco, Playa Hermosa,** and the former fishing village of **Tamarindo**. It's in these communities, growing at breakneck speed, that you see most clearly the intersection of overdevelopment and underdevelopment. Potholed tracks lead to multimillion-dollar beachside homes. Expensive condo projects route their sewage into nearby rivers (it's illegal, but enforcement is lacking). Infrastructure is overloaded, sometimes to the breaking point. The gap between wealthy newcomers and locals of modest means continues to grow.

Away from the most popular beaches, the building boom quiets a bit. Funky surf towns like **Montezuma** and **Mal País** are growing, too, but not nearly at the rate of their northerly cousins. Beyond northern *Guanacaste*'s Gold Coast, amid a quieter real estate market, you'll meander down back roads to find the old Costa Rica. Prices are more manageable, and everyday life slows to an early-evening amble as the day cools off.

THE CENTRAL PACIFIC COAST

The central Pacific coast is one of the more developed coastal areas in Costa Rica, rivaled only by *Guanacaste*'s Gold Coast. The bigger towns here are **Jacó,** famous for surfing and barhopping; and *Quepos/Manuel Antonio,* a sport-fishing mecca and home to Manuel Antonio National Park, the country's most visited park. Sloths and monkeys hang out in trees that border some of the country's prettiest white sand beaches.

Accessibility is one of the central Pacific coast's strong points. Residents of **Jacó** and **Quepos** are a two- or three-hour drive from **San José** on fairly decent roads. It's very doable to shoot up to the capital for a shopping excursion, or a visit to a well-regarded specialist, or to meet a friend's incoming flight. South of **Quepos** on the central coast, you're getting into more remote territory, though beach towns like **Dominical,** dubbed a "tropical Big Sur," are drawing more and more expats.

AMBIENCE

The best-known phrase in Costa Rica is "*pura vida.*" The literal translation is "pure life," but like so many all-purpose phrases, its meanings are legion. It can be used in greeting, to express agreement, or as a way of saying "Life is good!"

For those willing to adapt to the pace and culture of this country, daily life here can be slower, richer, and more sensuous than the life you were living back home. You can rise with the sun, eat a mango from the tree in your backyard, amble down to the beachside café for a coffee and a chat, visit the monkeys that hang out in the tree near the bridge, then spend all day surfing or reading or noodling away on your computer. (With the slow connections in outlying areas, *noodling* is the word.) When the sun sets, you're ready—you've got a ringside seat for the nightly spectacle, and a cold beer in your hand.

Or, like many retirees, you may find that you're busier than you've ever been: lunching with friends, rehearsing for that play you've just been cast in, driving into **San José** for the symphony, or volunteering your time for one of the hundreds of good causes that need your help. (See "Volunteering Without Borders.")

If the first scenario appeals to you, you're probably thinking of relocating to a beach community. If the second scenario describes you better, the ambience of the *Central Valley* will suit you. In and around **San José,** you'll find dozens of clubs and cultural activities. The *Tico Times,* a weekly English-language newspaper, is the place to look for what's going on, especially in the **San José** area. Choose from among hundreds of options, such as an art film at the Sala Garbo, a talk in English at the University of Costa Rica, an art opening, or the monthly meeting of Democrats Abroad or Republicans Abroad.

Though friendly, Costa Ricans share the Latin preference for family and close friends, so getting to know Tico neighbors requires goodwill and patience. Although English is spoken by Ticos who work in the tourist trade, once you get off the vacation circuit, you'll hear mostly Spanish. True, many movies that come to Costa Rica are in English with Spanish subtitles, phone cards may have instructions in English, and ATM machines have options in English. True, if you live in a community of English-speaking retirees, you could get along knowing little or no Spanish. Trouble is, that world will seem awfully cramped after a while. You'll be safe in your bubble but miss the country around you.

STANDARD OF LIVING

Whether Costa Rica looks rich or poor to you will depend on what you compare it to. If you've been living in a wealthy North American suburb and don't tend to get around to the low-rent districts or the inner cities, Costa Rica will probably strike you as very third world, with tin-roofed shacks on the outskirts of cities and towns and homeless on the streets of **San José**. But if you've traveled in Asia and Africa and the poorer parts of Latin America (or if you're more familiar with the poverty in your own country), Costa Rica will look downright prosperous. Many newcomers, in fact, are surprised that Costa Rica doesn't have the kind of shantytown "banana republic" look that they were expecting to find.

Costa Rica is a moderately prosperous, highly literate, developing nation. The good medical care means that Ticos live long and healthy lives, with infant mortality and life expectancy rates comparable to those in the U.S. and Canada. Though there is poverty here, the majority of houses are in good repair, with healthy children playing in well-tended yards.

Traveling through Costa Rica in the late 1970s, Paul Theroux wrote about the capital city in *The Old Patagonian Express:* "[**San José**] seemed an exceptional city. If **San Salvador** and **Guatemala City** were hosed down, all the shacks cleared, and the people rehoused in tiny bungalows, the buildings painted, the stray dogs collared and fed, the children given shoes, the trash picked up in the parks, the soldiers pensioned off—there is no army in Costa Rica—and all the political prisoners released, those cities would, I think, begin to look a little like **San José**."

Nevertheless, prosperity is relative; the average monthly wage here for someone with a bachelor's degree is still around $400. Ticos tend to assume that all North Americans are rich. So if an expat is living frugally on a pension, people will see him as well-off. Even a gringo trying to make it on a Social Security pension will be seen as having a higher standard of living than the average Tico.

CULTURE

The *Central Valley* (**San José** and its environs) is the place to be for the art scene. It's here that you'll find all manner of theater (in Spanish and English), music (from classical to pop), movies, lectures, poetry readings, and film festivals. You can take part, too: musicians join performing groups; actors can check in with the expat-run Little Theatre Group in *Escazú*. There are several interesting museums as well.

Many retirees have season tickets to the National Symphony Orchestra, which performs in the most elegant building in Costa Rica, the National Theatre. Several decades back, President Pepe Figueres sparked the revitalization of the orchestra, famously asking, "Why should we have tractors if we lack violins?" Ticket prices are very reasonable—even if you couldn't afford theater and the symphony back home, here you'll get your high culture for less than the price of a movie back home.

Costa Rica is not well known for its indigenous crafts, though one that has survived is the kaleidoscopic-bright painting of wooden oxcarts, based in the *Central Valley* town of **Sarchí**. Farmers would decorate their carts in patterns resembling Tibetan mandalas or Pennsylvania Dutch motifs. Miniature painted carts are now popular in tourist shops. Woodworking is also an important craft, with Costa Ricans making full use of the gorgeous tropical hardwoods found here.

While Costa Rican cuisine can be a little, well, monotonous, the influx of international visitors and residents means that you will be able to choose from Lebanese to French to Thai food, especially in the *Central Valley* and in larger beach towns. You'll also sample Costa Rica's astonishing variety of fruits, from the heart-shaped *anona* to the purple-fleshed *zapote*. Coffee, of course, is another Costa Rican specialty. Retirees here like to try all the different brands and then argue about the relative merits of each. And you'll be pleased to know that in most parts of Costa Rica, you *can* drink the water (though it may be undrinkable in some of the overstrapped beach developments dotting the coast).

LEISURE

Residents here are outdoorsy, and so are their leisure pursuits. They hike through the cloud forest, snorkel the calm waters of the Caribbean, fish in the rivers and lakes of both coasts, and scuba dive among the hammerheads off *Cocos Island*. Costa Rica, of course, is world famous for its ecotourism, so for a resident, the world of nature is full time: 850 species of birds, hundreds of varieties of orchids, monkeys, sloths, wildcats, tapirs, crocs, caimans—even the odd manatee.

Tamer pastimes include golf, tennis, swimming, and soaking in natural hot springs. Retirees brush up on their cooking, photography, painting, and writing. As for spectator sports, you need know only three words: *fútbol, fútbol,* and *fútbol.* This is soccer, the world's most popular sport, and Ticos are fanatics. In taxicabs you'll be treated to games broadcast at full volume, the familiar *Gooooooool!* eliciting cheers and the honking of horns. The country went into convulsions of collective ecstasy when the national team made it to the World Cup in 2006.

SOCIAL CUSTOMS

Costa Ricans have long been considered friendly and welcoming. If Ticos get high marks even in the bustling capital city, the friendliness in the *campo* (country) is even more apparent. Despite foreigners' buying up much of the country's prime beachfront, making property ever more expensive for locals, Ticos are still surprisingly gracious hosts. Still, it can be hard to move beyond superficial politeness with Ticos. Long-term expats joke that if you're lucky enough to have a Tico invite you to his house, he won't tell you how to get there. More than one observer has noted the similarities between Asian and Latin American cultures, in that both emphasize social harmony and saving face. Ticos don't much like the American version of blunt honesty, thinking it clumsy and rude.

You'll also encounter other divergences, such as a different sense of personal space and privacy. North Americans tend to like a buffer of space around them, and they enjoy a high degree of privacy. Ticos, usually from large families, don't understand why you'd want to be alone, and they seem to need less personal space. Ticos generally dress a bit more formally than foreign residents, especially in the cities.

As for gender relations, women and men in Costa Rica enjoy absolute equality, at least officially. Women participate in national politics in a higher proportion than do U.S. women, and there are more women than men currently enrolled in the country's universities. But traditions die hard, and in Costa Rica, little girls are taught to serve their brothers at the table. There's still a strong double standard when it comes to fidelity—the men can fool around, the women better not.

Single expat women are treated deferentially, although a woman who hasn't heard a wolf whistle in years may be surprised to hear men murmur sweet nothings as she walks by. There's also a subgroup of North American and European men who come to Costa Rica expressly to meet and sometimes marry a Tica (Costa Rican woman), often half or a third their age.

Costa Rica is known as a gay-friendly place, especially in areas with significant populations of foreign residents. There are many openly gay bars in **San José,** lots of gay-friendly restaurants and guesthouses, and in 2003 the city organized its first Pride Festival, which attracted more than two thousand people.

HEALTH CARE/MEDICAL

Costa Rica gets high marks for the health of its citizens and for the health care available to foreign retirees. Life expectancy here is high, and infant mortality is low, with rates that compare well to those in first-world nations. When Costa Rica abolished its army in 1948, more money was invested in health care and education, and this country is still reaping the benefits of that choice.

A retiree has several options for medical care in Costa Rica. Those who gain residency can become part of the CAJA, the government health care plan that usually costs less than $50 U.S. per month, with no deductibles and including everything—from drugs to dental care. Other benefits of the CAJA are that you won't be denied coverage because of a preexisting condition, and there is no paperwork involved after you're a part of the system. Just present your card at any CAJA facility, and you're good to go.

The downsides of the CAJA? There can be long waits for nonessential services. And although CAJA hospitals are more likely than private ones to have high-tech, expensive medical equipment, basic amenities in these public hospitals can be lacking. Four or six beds might be squeezed into one hospital room, with luxuries like phones or toilet paper hard to come by.

Ticos, along with economy-minded retirees who become Costa Rican residents, may use the CAJA for routine care, then splurge on private care when they get fed up with the CAJA's limitations. Most retirees opt out of the CAJA entirely and take advantage of high-quality private hospitals like CIMA in *Escazú* or Clínica Bíblica in **San José**. They pay out of pocket, or are covered by local or international medical insurance.

Prices at private clinics are often beyond the reach of the average Costa Rican, but retirees from the north will find the fees low, often half or even a third of what one would pay in the U.S. At private hospitals, consultations start at around $45 U.S., and overnight stays start at $175 U.S. (not including procedures, tests, or medications). Doctors at both private and public hospitals are well trained and have often studied in the U.S., Europe, or at the well-regarded University of Costa Rica. Many doctors speak English.

RESIDENCY AND RED TAPE

Visitors from Canada, the United States, and most of Europe don't need to apply for visas in their home countries. You do need a passport, of course, and upon arrival in Costa Rica, you'll get a stamp on your passport authorizing a ninety-day stay. If after three months you're not ready to go back home, you'll need to leave the country for at least seventy-two hours. It's easy to make a quick visit to Nicaragua or Panama; some retirees fly home to see family and friends or to bring down another load of their belongings.

Some people live in Costa Rica like this for years. But if you want a more official status, there are other options. It may be a good idea to avail yourself of them; immigration law is changing. It was easier ten years ago, for instance, to import your household goods duty-free—they've canceled that benefit, and you'll have to pay duties on your furniture and other belongings.

Like many other countries, recently Costa Rica has had to rethink its open-arms policy toward immigration. Immigrants from Nicaragua make up the largest foreign population in Costa Rica; some estimates put the number of Nicaraguans here at close to one million, which would make them about a quarter of the country's entire population. There are also immigrants from all over Latin America, and from Europe and North America as well.

Costa Rica makes frequent attempts to better control this influx, with the result that immigration law—for all—is changing. Even seasoned expat organizations like the Association of Residents of Costa Rica warn that immigration laws are hard to fathom and even harder to keep up with. As an example, in August 2002 the Department of Immigration decreed that residency applications were now to be made in the applicant's country of origin rather than here in Costa Rica. That decree has been inconsistently enforced, and many believe that soon it may be rolled back entirely.

There are four main categories of residency visas in Costa Rica: *pensionado* (retiree/pensioner), *rentista* (small investor), *inversionista* (large investor), and *permanente* (you're here to stay).

The first type, which is most common for retirees, requires proof of at least $600 U.S. income per month from a pension or retirement fund—including Social Security. Also you must stay in-country for a total of at least four months per year. And although you cannot work as an employee, you can own a company and receive income from it.

The other visas escalate in amount of income required, time required in-country, and what must be invested in a bank or a government-approved business, in return for which investors have more rights to employment and corporate income. At the top end, with a visa permanente, a foreigner who has lived in Costa Rica for at least three years may be able to have many of the economic rights of a citizen.

Working

It's relatively easy to start a business in Costa Rica. You can even start and run a business on a tourist visa. Costa Rica officially welcomes foreign investment, especially businesses that create jobs for Ticos. Getting a salaried job is a lot harder, and for most categories of residency, it's illegal. If you have pensionado or rentista status, you can own your own company but can't be a salaried employee in that company or any other. The official penalty for doing so is deportation, and you can't come back for ten years. But enforcement can be lax, especially in jobs that require native English skills, like teaching English, or working in a call center or online betting service that needs English speakers.

If you start that bed-and-breakfast or tour company, you need to hire a lawyer and make it a legal entity. Most businesses here are owned and operated by a corporation; a lawyer can help you set one up, usually for less than $500.

COST OF LIVING

Although Costa Rica is still cheap by American standards, if you feel the need to create an exact replica of your life up north—complete with expensive cars, gourmet food, and high-end liquor—you'll have a hard time living cheaply. Those who are more adaptable will be able to live well on a lot less, perhaps a third less than what they'd spend at home. And if you're *really* frugal, you may be able to live here on half of your previous budget, depending on where you're from.

Many retirees who move to Costa Rica want to simplify: to own less and spend less. That approach will serve you well in a country where simple pleasures rule the day. And if you're over sixty-five, simple pleasures like movies, the symphony, and bus rides will cost even less once you get your gold card—government-mandated discounts for all seniors, foreign and domestic. By the way, seniors in Costa Rica are called, respectfully, *personas de la tercera edad,* or "people of the third age."

Food

If you forego imported items and stick with locally produced goods, two people could eat well for under $300 a month, except in the booming areas of the Pacific coast, where food costs are higher, sometimes by 30 percent.

Utilities

Electricity for a house under 1,500 square feet will run you from $25 to $35 per month.

TV, Phone, and Internet

Cheaper than in Mexico, for instance: cable TV costs about $30 per month; satellite basic programming is $25 per month. Landline telephone service costs about $10 per month, with all calls within the country charged at the same rate. Basic cellular service with one hundred minutes costs $7 per month.

Household Help

Wages for household help are low (about $2 an hour for a maid) but are strictly regulated by the government. As an employer, you provide holiday and vacation pay and pay into your employees' CAJA (social security) account. In December you'll also pay a mandatory Christmas bonus, called *aguinaldo,* equal to one month's salary.

Taxes

Watch it: a 13 percent tax is added to purchases and services. In restaurants, an additional 10 percent service fee is added, making the bill almost a quarter more than the base prices would lead you to believe. The tax on hotel rooms is the usual 13 percent but with an additional tourist tax of 3.9 percent, for a total of 16.9 percent.

Income tax here is paid only on income earned in Costa Rica; the rate ranges from 0 percent to 18 percent. For income earned on investments in this country, you have to pay capital gains tax. For business owners, the tax rate is about 20 percent. Property taxes here are very low and are collected by the local municipal government, which also collects a general tax (also very low) that covers garbage pickup, water, and sewage.

Monthly Cost of Living in a High-end Beach Resort
(Northern Guanacaste and the Central Pacific Coast)

Rent for a two-bedroom home, condo, or apartment: $500 to $2,500.

Taxes: 13 percent VAT; property tax, $275 per year.

Groceries for two: $300 to $500.

Utilities: Water, $5 to $10; electricity, $30 to $40.

Cable TV: $30 to $50.

Internet: Basic connection, $17; fast, $60 to $170.

Telephone: $40.

Transportation: Outside the **San José** area, fewer taxis are metered, so prices are negotiable; local bus, $0.50; bus to other parts of the country, $1 to $15.

Maid service: About $2 to $3 an hour.

Restaurants for two: $25 to $40 in a midrange restaurant.

Monthly Cost of Living in and around San José

 Rent for a two-bedroom home, condo, or apartment: $350 to
    $2,000.

 Taxes: 13 percent VAT.

 Groceries for two: $300 to $400.

 Utilities: Water, $5 to $10; electricity, $30 to $40.

 Cable TV: $30 to $50.

 Internet: Basic connection, $17; fast, $60 to $170.

 Telephone: $40.

 Transportation: Inner-city taxi, $2 to $8 to cross the city; city bus,
    $0.50; bus to other parts of the country, $1 to $15; taxi to
    airport from downtown San José, $12 to $15.

 Maid service: About $2 an hour.

 Restaurants for two: $25 to $30 in a midrange restaurant.

Monthly Cost of Living in a Mountain or Rural Town

 Rent for a two-bedroom home, condo, or apartment: $250 to $800.

 Groceries for two: $250 to $350.

 Utilities: Water, $5 to $10; electricity, $30 to $40.

 Cable TV: $30 to $50.

 Internet: Basic connection, $17; fast, $60 to $170.

 Telephone: $40.

 Transportation: Outside the San José areas, fewer taxis are
    metered, so prices are negotiable; local bus, $0.50; bus to other
    parts of the country, $1 to $15.

 Maid service: $1.50 to $2 an hour.

 Restaurants for two: $20 in a midrange restaurant.

REAL ESTATE

In Costa Rica, foreigners have basically the same property rights as nationals. You can legally buy land here even on a tourist visa (and many people do). One important exception is an area called the maritime zone: beachfront land fifty to two hundred meters from the high-tide mark. Unless you're a resident, you'll need to have a Costa Rican national lease the majority interest, at least on paper.

However—and this is a big however—you need to be aware that realtors here need no license, and there are no government agencies with enough clout to punish unscrupulous agents. It is imperative, therefore, to get a personal recommendation from someone who has had a good experience with an agent. It's also more common here to do without the middle man entirely, striking your own deal directly with the owner of the property. This is especially common in condo developments, which often have their own sales office. As in other developing countries, you need to watch out for the many scamsters riding the high tide of real estate sales in Costa Rica.

Building your dream home in Costa Rica will take a lot of patience and perseverance. The permit process can be complicated and slow, your workers might not show up on time or at all, and cost overruns may dog the project. Mark Drolette, an American expat who built a house in **San Ramon,** says ruefully that he wished he'd known that his "house contract didn't cover the cost of small items like, oh, doors and windows and toilets and sinks." Nail down all the details and put them in writing.

Prices for real estate, once rising quickly, dropped dramatically in some places. As of 2008, new and existing home prices for a two-bedroom, two-bath residence start at $130,000 in the *Central Valley* and the Caribbean coast, $200,000 on the Pacific coast, and as little as $50,000 in the mountains.

As for financing a real estate deal, for all practical purposes, forget mortgages. Costa Rican banks don't make it easy for foreigners to borrow money, and when they do lend to nonnationals, the rates are high. Creative financing is the name of the game here, with many deals done in cash.

Rentals

In Costa Rica, there are many good places at reasonable rents that you can hang your hat in while you take stock of what you want to do.

For your typical American-style two-bedroom house or apartment, you'll pay from $500 up to over $2,000 in the *Central Valley* hot spots like *Escazú,* **Santa Ana,** and the **San José** neighborhood of *Rohrmoser*. In other areas of the *Central Valley*—**Heredia, Alajuela,** and many neighborhoods in **San José** proper, rents are $300 to $1,200. In the popular Pacific coast communities like **Jacó** or along **Guanacaste**'s Gold Coast, rents are high: from around $800 to over $3,000 for beachside luxury. In out-of-the-way mountain towns and along the Caribbean coast, rentals are from $200 to $1,500.

TRANSPORTATION

Costa Rica is less than three hours by air from Miami. Dozens of international flights arrive daily at Juan Santamaría International Airport, the country's main airport, near the capital city of **San José**. If you want to skip

San José, fly into Daniel Oduber International Airport in **Liberia** for quicker access to the Pacific coast beach towns.

But if you want to own a car in Costa Rica, you'll pay for the privilege. Due to high import tariffs, cars here are very expensive, with heavy duties imposed. Costa Rican cities have their share of well-paved streets, but even the highways have potholes, so most roads in Costa Rica could qualify as back roads. As you drive through steamy jungles, up the slopes of dormant volcanos, you might wonder why a relatively prosperous developing nation has such an appalling highway system. The U.S. State Department rates Costa Rican roads and the availability of roadside assistance as "fair to poor," and notes that "Costa Rica has one of the highest vehicle accident rates in the world."

SECURITY

When retirees first arrive in Costa Rica, they are often surprised that many houses have barred windows, and private security guards can be seen everywhere from banks to hotels to that little kiosk at the end of a suburban block.

Statistically speaking, you are safer in Costa Rica than in most cities in the U.S. But crime here *is* on the rise, even violent crime, which used to be almost unheard of in Costa Rica. Law enforcement here is a lot less effective than what most first worlders are used to. There are simply too few police in Costa Rica to do an effective job. And law enforcement is underfunded; some police departments can't afford a police car. There are stories of people calling the police, only to be told that if they want police service, they need to come get the officers or send a taxi.

So people take security into their own hands. They chip in with their neighbors and hire a guard for the block. They put bars on their windows and install burglar alarms. Or they get a dog—probably the single best deterrent to break-ins.

As to corruption, surprise: Costa Rica is far less corrupt than many developing countries, and scores quite high on the rankings of Transparency International, which rates countries' corruption on a worldwide scale. Though greasing palms is not unknown here, offering a *chorizo* (bribe) at the wrong time to the wrong person can have serious legal consequences.

COMMUNICATIONS AND MEDIA

Costa Rica's telephone system is very good. The high concentration of call centers and sports books (online betting agencies), with their reliance on phone lines, tells you that the system is working. High-speed internet access is available in most parts of the *Central Valley* and in the more developed areas of the Pacific coast.

Cable television service usually includes two of the major U.S. broadcast networks as well as basic HBO. There are many Spanish-language daily newspapers in Costa Rica; the most highly regarded is *La Nación,* and the widely read English-language weekly, the *Tico Times,* and the internet-only A.M. Costa Rica (www.amcostarica.com).

UP-AND-COMING AREAS

Beyond the Central Valley

In the low mountains around and beyond the *Central Valley* are many nooks and crannies worth exploring for their relocation potential. These areas will appeal to people who prefer a more temperate climate and who are looking for off-the-beaten-track bargains, which are still out there.

To the north you'll find the highland plain of *San Carlos,* home to Arenal volcano and Lake Arenal. A small community of international expats enjoys the quiet, impossibly green area around the man-made lake known as a premier windsurfing destination. Nearby are the mountain towns of **Santa Elena** and **Monteverde,** the latter founded by draft-resisting Alabama Quakers in the 1950s. Both towns are known for their cloud-forest preserves, where you might spot the iridescent green tail feathers of a resplendent quetzal.

About an hour west of **San José** on the highway to **Puntarenas,** the midsized town of **San Ramon** is beginning to attract a few expats who want the modest amenities it offers: a small mall, a branch of the University of Costa Rica, and a local cultural center that organizes readings and exhibits. Just outside of **San Ramon,** a small group of expats has settled around tiny **Angeles Norte,** taking advantage of the area's mild climate and rural feel.

To the east of **San José** is the former colonial capital of **Cartago,** a bustling and rather traditional town that is *puro Tico* (very Costa Rican). A few select expats have settled here or in the nearby *Orosi Valley,* where glossy coffee bushes carpet rolling hills.

The Caribbean Coast

Costa Rica's wetter and less visited eastern coast attracts a different breed of expat than the more developed Pacific coast. Shopaholics and the pampered need not apply; you won't find upscale malls or luxurious resorts here. What you will find are ramshackle houses painted in tropical pastels, wildlife-rich jungles, and stunning beaches.

This area is more racially diverse than the rest of Costa Rica. Nearly all of the country's small population of blacks, most of its Chinese, and a good part of its indigenous population can be found in the *Zona Caribe,* as the area is known in Spanish. Jamaicans and other Caribbean islanders arrived in the late nineteenth century to work on the railroad and in the banana fields, and their culture now dominates the area. Reggae rules (you'll reach your lifetime Bob Marley limit all too soon), and spicy island-inspired concoctions offer welcome relief from bland Tico fare. A lilting Caribbean English is heard on this coast as often as Spanish.

Puerto Limon (often simply called *Limon,* which is also the name of the entire province) is the biggest city in the area, a bustling and sometimes dangerous port that has more economic than aesthetic appeal. North of **Limon,** swamps and rivers dominate the area. Waterways are the zone's roads, and boats outnumber cars. In the town of **Tortuguero,** for instance, there are no roads. Sand paths connect the wood-frame houses built on stilts, and almost everyone has a dock and a boat or two in his front yard. South of **Limon,** there is one decent coastal road linking the beach towns of **Cahuita, Puerto Viejo,** and **Manzanillo;** most expats settle along this short coastal stretch.

The South Pacific

The southern Pacific coast is much wilder and more remote than the central coast. Most people will enjoy a visit, but only a select few will be drawn to live in this rather torrid zone. The area is dominated by the hook-shaped *Osa Peninsula,* which *National Geographic* magazine calls "the most biologically intense place on earth." This is Costa Rica's Amazon, a tropical rain forest where tall trees drip vines and lianas, macaws screech, and jaguars prowl. Crocodiles lurk in marshy areas, sea turtles lay eggs on deserted beaches, and tapirs amble through the trees.

Better-known towns in the area include **Puerto Jiménez** (where a good number of expats have settled); **Golfito,** a gritty former port and company town for the United Fruit Company; and **Pavones,** home to what surfers say is a hallucinogenically long left-breaking wave.

VOLUNTEERING WITHOUT BORDERS

Costa Rica appreciates and encourages expat involvement in efforts to improve society and preserve the environment. This country has one of the largest and broadest array of organizations, which are grateful for the help of dedicated volunteers.

There are many groups whose mission is to protect the country's fragile ecosystem:

- The Caribbean Conservation Corporation & Sea Turtle Survival League observes and saves sea turtles (www.cccturtle.org).
- **Puerto Viejo**'s Talamanca Ecotourism and Conservation Association (ATEC) studies the ecology of the land and its interdependence with the indigenous peoples (www.greencoast.com).
- Asociación ANAI works in bird conservation (www.anaicr.org).

Community aid projects include:

- VIDA matches volunteers with humanitarian organizations (www.vida.org).
- Habitat for Humanity teaches basic construction to locals, who partner with Habitat to build their homes (www.habitat.org/int/lac/48.aspx).
- The Women's Club of Costa Rica (WCCR) donates supplies to schools and tutors children in low-income areas (www.wcrr.org).
- Voz Que Clama Mission: former Floridian Ginnee Hancock founded this organization, which helps handicapped and indigenous people (www.vqcmission.com).

Erin Van Rheenen is the author of and the creator of the website www.living abroadincostarica.com.

MY COSTA RICA

A Teacher Who Didn't Expect Perfection

Name, age, origin: Alex and Laura James, seventy and fifty, Olympia, Washington, and San Diego.

Previous/present occupation: Laura was a high school English teacher. Now they own a B and B.

Where we live: Lake Arenal, *Tilarán.*

How long in Costa Rica: Three years.

Reasons for moving here: We tried out Australia and found its immigration requirements too formidable. So we researched bed-and-breakfasts in Costa Rica, which Laura had visited the previous year. Of course, the information about Costa Rica on many websites presented the country very attractively.

We didn't expect perfection in Costa Rica—and didn't get it. The apartment in which we stayed in **San José** after arriving clued us into the sexual tourism that is a significant attraction of Costa Rica to many men. We didn't want to stay long in **San José**, with its iron gates, razor wire, and gun-toting guards at banks and stores. Using the internet, we finally tracked down a bed-and-breakfast for sale in the countryside.

Real estate: Many people in Costa Rica buy a condo or home in a gated community built by American developers. There are also many of the smaller Tico homes, which U.S. buyers will usually either remodel and expand or live in while they build a new home on the property. In some ways, it is better to buy an existing home. You will not be adding to the strain on Costa Rica's gasping infrastructure. You can be quite sure that the established residence will not slide down a hillside as new construction might if you are misled as to the dangers of the site.

While nonresidents can easily and quickly buy property, they must beware of incompetence and even scams on the part of sellers, agents, and lawyers. Anyone can portray himself as an agent, as there is no licensing system in Costa Rica. Most of these represent both the seller and the buyer, and then turn the details of the transaction over to a lawyer. While most purchases are completed satisfactorily, there are often tales of a property owner finding that the lawyer—in the common practice of forming a corporation to limit the buyer-owner's liability—has managed to gain control of the property. The buyer should be sure not to let the same lawyer handle both sides of the transaction but instead have a lawyer separate from the seller's lawyer.

Our community: Set in a beautiful mountainous area with moderate weather, *Tilarán* has the reputation of being the cleanest town in Costa Rica, with the widest streets. So we warn people who are looking to settle somewhere about the heat of the coasts and the insecurity and overcrowding of the capital. Anyone planning to move here should realize that in certain areas there is significant crime, and in these and other areas, the heat and humidity can be taxing. Mountain areas such as Arenal, the mountains also near the Caribbean side of **San José,** and *Central Valley* communities outside of **San José** are temperate and beautiful places to live. For those who need heat and/or golf, there is a wide selection of communities on the Pacific coast.

Typical day: Starts at about five-thirty in the morning with checking the internet for business and personal email and reading the news. If we have guests at the bed-and-breakfast, we feed the guests first. Before the housekeeper and gardener arrive, we take a long walk on rural roads up the mountainside with our dogs. Sometimes we play tennis. Often we'll go five miles into the town of *Tilarán* for shopping, banking, and mail. In late afternoon, we often sit out on the deck with a drink, looking at the lake view and watching the birds. If there are guests, we spend time with them, usually discussing their plans for the next day, making recommendations.

Wish we'd known before: In thinking about settling elsewhere in Costa Rica, there were things I wish I'd known before wasting the time. If we'd settled along the Pacific coast, we'd have encountered ecological threats due to overbuilding, insecurity due to drugs and crime, and the potential for future water and electrical failures due to the failure of infrastructures to accommodate the grandiose schemes of developers for resorts, golf courses, and gated communities of condominiums and houses.

Best: Finding a spacious and attractive home in a beautiful and temperate area for much less than we'd have to pay in the U.S. Also, we've found ourselves in a friendly expatriate community, adding extra pleasure to our beautiful surroundings.

Worst: Laura's attempted mugging by a couple on a busy, rainy street in **San José.**

What we miss most: Good roads and Mexican food. Costa Rican cuisine is bland and has little variety.

MY COSTA RICA
An Academic Who Tried Mexico First

Name, age, origin: Josephine Stuart, seventy-seven, Santa Clara, California.

How long in Costa Rica: Thirteen years.

Previous/present occupation: Former director of San José (California) State University International House; now a writer, columnist.

Reasons for moving to Costa Rica: I knew I would not/could not live in the States after retirement, for both financial and personal reasons. I first became interested in Costa Rica when I learned that President Óscar Arias had won the Nobel Peace Prize; I went to a dinner for him in San Francisco. I was further attracted to Costa Rica because it has no military and spends that money on education and medicine.

I visited three times before moving here. I also spent a month with a friend in **Chapala,** Mexico, before making a decision, because she insisted that I would love it there. I did not. I wanted to live where I could speak the language (to some degree), where there were sidewalk cafés, bougainvillea growing, where I could drink the water, and flush paper down the toilet. Costa Rica fit all of these requirements except sidewalk cafés in the city.

Real estate: I don't believe in owning anything here, so I am biased. However, I have talked with some people who have owned homes here and now rent.

Best: I have been able to do my three favorite things and be paid for them: to write, act, and cook. Getting the part of Grandma Prudence in a radio *novela* aimed at teaching children in the campo was probably the best thing.

Worst: Having my apartment broken into and my computer with backup tapes of a memoir and my passport stolen. The next-worst thing was an awful experience in CIMA Hospital.

What I miss most: After almost fourteen years, practically nothing. Well, I do miss not being able to get public television or NPR from the U.S.

Advice: Learn Spanish. Visit first and try different parts of the country to find where you will feel "at home." Don't be too eager to invest in property here. Be very sure of the integrity of the people you are dealing with.

Costa Rica is for some people and not others; one must give it a six-month probation try. I have written my suggestions in my book, *Butterfly in the City: A Good Life in Costa Rica.* Perhaps one cautionary note: just because the Costa Ricans look and dress pretty much like us in the U.S., don't be fooled into thinking they think like we do or hold the same values. That is one of the reasons I moved here.

MY COSTA RICA

A *"Gringo Feliz"* Who Left a Wife and Made a Leap

Name, age, origin: Mark Drolette, fifty, Sacramento, California.

Where I live: In the mountains above San Ramon.

Previous occupation: Former state government analyst.

Reasons for moving here: Then-wife number three said she wanted a divorce. Now-ex-wife number three and I sold our home at the peak of the California real estate market and split the decent-sized proceeds. I was sick of America and wanted to escape.

The thing that first attracted me to Costa Rica was the fact that it hadn't had an army since 1949. The more I read about the place, the more it sounded too good to be true. I decided to move there; friends suggested I might want to visit first. I did, and bought land on my third day in-country. The rest is history: I have a beautiful casa, and I've *not* married again. *Soy un gringo feliz.* I'm a happy gringo.

Real estate: I went completely against the book: I bought land on my third day in Costa Rica; I did not scout out other areas first; I did not rent for six months to see if I could handle living there; I did not check out the bona fides of my developer or contractor or attorney or architect beforehand—and I couldn't be happier. I had a big-time advantage, though: I'd met a woman on the internet who was gracious enough to turn me on to all the trustworthy people she'd met and worked with. In a serendipitous twist, we're now next-door neighbors!

Common misperceptions: One thing I was told was prevalent but I've not encountered, at least in retail establishments: slow service.

Best: Deciding to purchase my half acre.

Worst: Finding out my house contract didn't cover the cost of small items like, oh, doors and windows and toilets and sinks and . . .

Advice: Become as Tico as you can and leave America in America—please. The thing that frosts me the quickest in Costa Rica is when I see or hear of Ugly Americanism here. A personal note to U.S. citizens thinking of moving to Costa Rica: If you wish to come to this exquisite land because you want to enjoy it for what it is and also intend to meld into the culture as much as possible, *bienvenidos.* If, however, you are planning to move to Costa Rica simply because it's cheaper, and you insist on bringing as much of America with you as possible, I've got two words of advice: stay home.

Another piece of advice: Leap, and the next shall appear. (Or it won't.) One thing that drove me forward was knowing that if I didn't grab my golden opportunity to do this, I never would, leaving me to assuredly kick myself the rest of my days, knowing I'd caved in to fear.

Once I decided to carry forward, it was either going to work, or it wasn't. If it did, great. If it didn't, I'd have new information to work with and could then go on from there. And even if this worst-case scenario manifested (which it didn't), at least I'd know I'd not yielded to fear, myriad innate forms of which I'd let stop me most of my life time and time again. This was worth more to me than I could ever hope to explain.

MY COSTA RICA

The Former PR Exec Who Left a Husband and Found a Home

Name, age, origin: Sandra Shaw, sixty, Philadelphia and Washington, D.C.

Where I live: Near **Grecia.**

How long in Costa Rica: Seventeen years.

Previous/present occupation: Former public relations executive. Now teach language; serve on boards of directors of ecological and animal-welfare associations.

Reasons for moving here: My former husband and I were looking to semi-retire in a kinder climate. We happened to meet an honorary consul for Costa Rica and learned that the residency requirements were relatively easy. (At that time, pensionado/rentista status included being able to bring in your household goods and a car duty-free. No more.) We made several trips, singly and together, and we found an attractive former coffee farm near **Grecia**. The whole process, from decision to selling everything in the U.S. and moving, took a year and a half; we finally arrived in mid-1990. We did not consider any other countries.

My first trip was made alone. I figured that if I could travel alone around a country without any negative reactions, I could live there—even without any Spanish. I had never traveled alone in my life before! It was beautiful, of course. The people were kind. The roads were virtually unmarked, and getting around was a real challenge. But I managed and figured that living here would be at least an interesting adventure. I should say that I have always been interested in other cultures, so the idea of living in one full-time was not intimidating. I also have an inherited talent for languages, so the relative lack of English speakers at that time didn't faze me.

Typical day: Up with the sun. Breakfast. Check email. Since I'm active in environmental issues, I usually respond to those online. Once or twice a week, I tutor a student. Go into town, either for errands or a meeting. Lunch with a friend. Organize the logistics for an upcoming spay-and-neuter clinic. If time, try to catch up with all the work needed on my bonsai (I am always behind on this). Play with the dogs. Read *La Nación*. Fix dinner. Read, watch a movie. In bed no later than nine.

Residency and visas: Harder to get than it used to be, and the legislature has been tinkering with immigration reform, which promises to make qualifying for residency more expensive. Know the law before you come. Costa Rica does not smile on "perpetual tourists," people who live here with no residency status and are supposed to leave the country for seventy-two hours every three months. This can be a pain. And coming back into the country, you're always at risk of some sharp immigration official's making things difficult for you. You could even be deported. In addition, Immigration has been tightening up the rules on "marriages of convenience." But the most important advice I can offer here is go to a Costa Rican lawyer who is a specialist in residency issues, and do this before you move here. I can't count the number of people I know who have been ripped off by lawyers who say they can get your residency easily and then do nothing for years.

Common misperceptions: Nowadays, it would have to be the "tropical paradise" thing. Before Costa Rica was discovered and developed, it truly was. There are still places, but they're getting harder to find. The country totally lacks the infrastructure and resources to protect what it has, so much of what is still touted in the tourism ads is very much at risk. Most visitors don't know that so much surface water in the country is contaminated, for example. Nor the fact that many of the beaches suffer from lack of available potable water (in some places, it has to be trucked in). Frequent electrical outages. Heavy Gold Coast development is helping us into a double crisis of energy and water. There's virtually no sewage treatment, either. Next time you look at a high-rise condo, ask yourself where all those flushing toilets lead to.

Wish I'd known before: Nothing—except marrying that husband to begin with. Of course, bureaucratic hassles were horrendous, even more so back in those days before there were computers around. But knowing that in advance wouldn't have changed my decision.

Best: Being forced out of my own cultural mold to the degree that I discovered what my real values are.

What I miss most: After seventeen years here, I don't miss anything. In fact, I feel a stranger *there*, in the U.S. When we first came, there were far fewer interesting food imports and almost no prepared foods, so I had to learn to cook all over again. This was actually fun. Now, however, there's much more available and a wonderful variety of restaurants in **San José.**

Advice: Changing countries and cultures isn't for the faint of heart. It's a major life change and can be stressful, especially if you expect things to be "just like home." Divorces among expatriates are not unusual, because partners deal with these stresses in different ways. Of course, the best advice is to get to know the country first. Travel it, rent a house, spend some significant time both looking for a community you think you can feel comfortable in and then actually living in it for a while.

There are essentially two ways to live here: in a "parallel society," among native English speakers (or German, or whatever), or out there on your own in a Costa Rican community where you are forced to get to know and rely on Spanish speakers. The other-culture experience can be incredibly enriching, but you'll have to commit to learning the language. As a rule, Costa Ricans are very generous with their help if they see you are trying.

Finally, advice which applies to any retiree: find something worthwhile to do. Start a community library. Teach English. Volunteer at the local old-age home. Write for a local paper. Start giving back to life.

Chapter 13

PANAMA

Best Retirement Benefits

By Sandra T. Snyder

Panama, with its spectacular jungle, mountain, and seashore scenery, its excellent urban medical care, its first-world banking and communications, and a robust package of retirement benefits, is arguably the world's most welcoming country for foreign retirees. Central American republics have made efforts to entice North American and European retirees, but it is Panama that is doing the most. (See "Special: Panama's Retiree Benefits.")

It is a fertile, bounteous land of flowering volcanic mountainsides, craggy, picturesque beaches, and green, luxuriant valleys, a favorite of naturalists, environmentalists, and bird watchers. Historically a crossroads for international fortune seekers moving gold and goods by the shortest possible route, Panama is now a haven for gray-haired sun seekers moving *their* goods in from other retirement venues: Florida, Mexico, Costa Rica. (Neighboring Costa Rica has been a more popular retiree destination, but it has pulled back a bit on the benefits it offers foreigners, while Panama is vigorously hoisting a welcome flag.)

Where once the United States sent its armed troops to guard the American-built Panama Canal, or to depose a military dictator like Manuel Noriega (see "History"), the latest invasion is of sandal-clad platoons of aging boomers armed with checkbooks. Panama has a rough-and-tumble history with the United States, a currency not just pegged to—but *is* in fact—the dollar, an economy that is mostly robust, and a solid banking system. (See "Banking and Finance.")

Panama is not only diverse but continues to be affordable despite current record levels of inflation, and that means you may realize your dream in a variety of locations: a cottage on the beach, a cabin in the mountains, or an apartment in a bustling, exciting city overlooking the bay. Within hours you can travel from one region of the country to another and enjoy a change of climate and the variety of activities Panama offers.

Panama is still a small country that has one foot in the first world and the other in the third. In **Panama City,** the influences of its Spanish, French, and American colonial past, its embassies and consulates, and its international businesses have resulted in a worldly sophistication. But corruption is on the rise, safety is on the decline, construction is often out of control, the infrastructure is insufficient, traffic is a nightmare, and tourism is on the rise, while services to support it remain stagnant. There is also a thriving commerce in taking advantage of wide-eyed North Americans who arrive looking for real estate to buy, *fast*. (In fact, the hustlers are not necessarily Panamanian. There is a clutch of slick American operators plying their trade in Panama, often illegally, without benefit of the required license.)

For all of that, serious crime is reportedly low, considerably lower than that of some major cities in the United States. Panamanians are friendly, family oriented to the point of nepotism, and skilled at *juega vivo*—the art of playing the angles. On the Caribbean side of the canal—in the teeming city of **Colon**—and in the lightly populated eastern provinces, life can be primitive and rough. In **Panama City** and the region to the west—*Chiriquí* and *Bocas del Toro*—and along the Pacific coastline near **Panama City,** the living is easier, and that is where the North Americans are heading.

UPSIDES

1. As of 2008, great retirement benefits.
2. Variety of locations—city, mountain villages, beach towns, jungle wilderness.
3. Excellent medical care in **Panama City.**
4. Stable dollar economy.
5. No hurricanes.

DOWNSIDES

1. Sparse medical care outside **Panama City.**
2. Basic infrastructure substandard.

3. Bribery common, but situation improving.
4. Rain, lots of it, can be depressing.
5. Justice system not always just and transparent.

LOCATION

Panama is the crossroads of the world, where the Panama Canal divides a country and two continents. It is located in Central America between Costa Rica and Colombia; it is often thought of as part of Central America to the north of the canal and part of South America to the south. It is roughly the size of the state of South Carolina. Fun fact: because of its geography, the Panama Canal, which should cross the isthmus in an east-west direction, actually runs north to south. In parts of the country, the sun appears to rise in the Pacific and set in the Caribbean.

CLIMATE

The weather is tropical, hot, humid, and cloudy in low-lying regions, but higher elevations bring cooler breezes and temperatures. There are two seasons: dry and rainy. The rainy season is seven months long, from April until December, and the "summer" season, from December to April, tends to be hotter, windier, and less humid. From April on, afternoon showers every few days become daily downpours by November.

A big, big plus: Panama is out of the hurricane belt.

PEOPLE

Panama has a population of roughly 3.3 million, of which about 1 million live in **Panama City**. This population is made up of both locals and foreigners (*extranjeros*) from around the world, many of them descendents of the many nationalities who came to work on the railroad or the canal. Panama also has seven different indigenous populations, including the Ngobe-Bugle and the Kunas.

Most of the population of Panama is of mixed descent, from Spanish men and indigenous women. Panama has a relatively large middle class. Of the total population, half a million live in extreme poverty, primarily in rural areas where they continue to live as they have for generations as subsistence farmers.

Expat Population

No figures are firm. Of the 31,356 foreigners registered with the government (not all do), 17 percent are from the U.S. and Canada. The majority are corporate executives, international business people, and diplomats, with retirees still just a fraction of that number. Not surprisingly, given the rotation of soldiers through the former *Canal Zone,* many retirees coming to Panama were formerly stationed here.

HISTORY

Panama was first explored and settled by the Spanish in the sixteenth century while they used Panama as a staging area for looting Peru's gold. After breaking relations with Spain, Panama joined the Republic of Gran Colombia and remained a frontier of Colombia until 1903. At that time, at the instigation of the United States, Panama seceded from Colombia and shortly thereafter entered into an agreement with the U.S. to build the Panama Canal. With this treaty the U.S. also acquired sovereignty over a fifty-mile-long and ten-mile-wide area that would include the canal and the Panama Canal Zone. The new, "sovereign" Panama became, around its middle, an American colony—indeed, the *Canal Zone* was U.S. *territory,* exempt from local laws.

The U.S. Army Corps of Engineers built the canal between 1904 and 1914. The treaty transferring the canal from the U.S. to Panama was signed in 1977, and over the next twenty years, the transfer was made in stages. In 1989 the U.S. invaded to depose strongman and dictator Manuel Noriega, and a democratically elected government was reinstalled. On December 31, 1999, the remaining U.S. military bases were closed, and total control of the canal was transferred to Panama and the Panama Canal Authority.

GOVERNMENT

The government is a constitutional democracy in which the president and a vice president are elected to serve one term every five years. Corruption is a major concern at all levels of society, from the prisons to the court system to real estate transactions to the man in the street. Transparency International gives Panama a poor ranking: bribes are paid and accepted at all levels of government.

WHERE TO LIVE

Panama City

With its mixture of old-Spain colonial, Miami contemporary, and sleek high-rise skyline, it is a lively, sophisticated city (though its outlying slums, as in so much of Latin America, are a sobering contrast.) It has parks and leafy neighborhoods, good shopping, its historic older buildings are slowly being restored, and you can visit the jungle—where monkeys eat out of your hand—a half hour out of town. The bay is, unfortunately, polluted, and good beaches are only available an hour west of the city. A few of the most popular housing areas in the city for expatriates include:

- *Altos de Golf,* an upscale housing area adjacent to **Panama City**'s largest park.
- *Punta Paitilla,* high-rise buildings, narrow streets, and a convenient shopping area.
- *Punta Pacifica,* newly developed landfill on the bay, upscale.
- *El Cangrejo,* a lovely older neighborhood, being crowded out by new high-rises.
- *Obarrio,* one of the few downtown neighborhoods with single-family houses.
- *El Dorado,* a suburban neighborhood with apartments, duplexes, and houses.
- *Albrook,* in the former *Canal Zone,* with homes converted from military housing.

The Highlands

Life in the pleasant, elevated temperate zone is centered mostly in much-publicized **Boquete,** a tranquil coffee-growing town of 18,000 set in a mountain rise in Panama's breadbasket, *Chiriquí province.* It is nearly an hour's drive from the provincial capital of **David,** itself a fast-growing city an hour's flight from **Panama City.** The town of **Boquete** is a mix of old and new construction, but the housing developments and gated communities that ring the town are spanking new, set among jungle heights, twittering birds, and running brooks. Real estate prices have been on a sharp rise since the early 2000s, but reasonable living costs can still be found in the town's surrounding areas. A few communities:

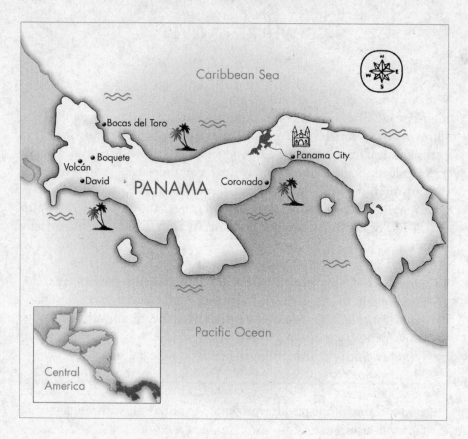

- *Valle Escondido,* a gated community in a pretty, narrow valley close to town.
- *Palo Alto Mountain Club,* a gated community with houses, town houses, condos.
- *Hacienda Los Molinos,* single-family, large-lot houses on the Boquete Road.

The Islands

The big draw is *Bocas del Toro,* the archipelago on the northern Caribbean tip of Panama, where retirees have been flocking for some time to live the seriously hedonistic beach life. It's long been a popular destination for the bohemian set. This island community has a Caribbean flavor and is popular with yachties. Recent completion of a highway to the coastal town of **Almirante** and good airline connections into **Bocas** from the city have improved the quality of life in this beautiful area. On the opposite Pacific coast, the wild and beautiful *Perlas Islands* attract a few hardy retirees but are mainly tourist draws.

SPECIAL: PANAMA'S RETIREE BENEFITS

Panama has an exceptionally full retiree package for their citizens, and foreign retirees who are legal residents can participate fully. New housing is exempt from property taxes for twenty years. Discounts are offered on a wide variety of services, from domestic airfares and medical care to movies, concerts, and restaurants—even fast food. There are some hoops to jump through to get retiree status (see "Residency and Red Tape"), but nothing out of the ordinary (proof of income), and to top it off, you don't have to be of retirement age to be a *jubilado,* or official retiree.

Here is a partial list of Panama's retirement benefits, available to those with jubilado/pensionado visas, aged fifty-five (women) or sixty (men). This might change, so check ahead to update, but start with:

- 25 percent off airfares
- 30 percent off bus, boat, and train fares
- 20 percent off professional services, doctor visits
- 30 percent to 50 percent off hotels on weekdays
- Up to 50 percent off entertainment (movies, theater, sports)
- 15 percent to 25 percent off restaurants, including fast food
- 15 percent off hospital bills (if no insurance)
- 20 percent off medical consultations
- 10 percent off prescription medicines
- 15 percent off dental and eye exams

AMBIENCE

Panama, the city, is the most social place in which you will ever live. Clubs and social organizations of every description thrive: rotary, cultural societies, garden clubs, professional organizations, bridge clubs, community theaters, dance groups, and sports-related clubs. There is a regular concert series as well as numerous visiting performing arts shows in the city.

Depending on your home country affiliation, ethnic interests, and hobbies, you can join a number of clubs and organizations including: American Society, Canadian Society, British Aid Society, Who's New (women's welcome club), Panama Historical Society, Ikebana, Rotary, Elks, Kiwanis,

Balboa Yacht Club, Navy League, Inter-American Women's Club, Harley-Davidson Club, Republicans Abroad, Panama Amateur Radio Association, Ivy League Mixer, Democrats Abroad, Association of the United States Army, Veterans of Foreign Wars, Vino (wine) Club, and many more.

In the interior, the pace is much slower. Locals take time to be polite and courteous in their relations. Thus, they greet one another when entering a store, even entering an elevator. Grocery shopping is a social outing requiring time to stop and chat with friends in the aisles whether in the city or in the country.

Panamanians are friendly and welcoming, and generally have a positive response to North Americans. However, in communities like **Boquete** where foreigners are beginning to outprice the locals, there is a developing feeling of "them and us." The art of juega vivo appears with the two-tier pricing system: one for locals, one for foreigners.

STANDARD OF LIVING

About a quarter of Panama's population is considered to have a middle-class standard of living, which can include owning a home or apartment, a car, and modern appliances. These people usually live in **Panama City,** are mostly of European descent, and work for the government, the canal, in banking, or major foreign corporations. Middle-class families send their children to university in Panama, the U.S., or Europe. While they live and work in the city, they often have beach homes or cabins in the mountains for weekends and vacations.

However, of the total population, a half million live in extreme poverty, primarily in rural and indigenous areas. A recent report on cost of living reported that 70 percent of the population earns $400 or less per month. But in the last four years, unemployment has dropped from 13 percent to 7 percent—a dramatic statistic when compared to most other Latin American nations.

Despite the relative poverty, everyone makes an effort to be neatly dressed and groomed. While it may not be a real Gucci bag or Rolex watch, and the house may not actually be paid for, as long as it can be worn, lived in, and everyone can see it, the person will be thought of as successful.

CULTURE

Panama has more than a dozen art galleries, six museums, and five theaters in the city, and a theater offering English-language productions in **Boquete.** Various embassies and companies sponsor visiting exhibits and shows, including musical recitals, history and cultural exhibits, and dance troupes from all over the world.

Cities in the interior are centers for the famous national dress, the *pollera,* as well as for local fairs, festivals, and carnivals. Additionally, various embassies in Panama celebrate their national festivals during the year.

With so many nationalities represented in Panama, it is not surprising that restaurants of every flavor exist: Italian, French, Panamanian, typical to continental, elegant to a wide variety of fast food. Whether you want a taco or burger and fries, you will find it and often from your favorite purveyor, like McDonald's, Burger King, Kentucky Fried Chicken, T.G.I. Friday's, or Bennigans.

LEISURE

The possibilities for free-time activities are endless. Whether it is a short trip out to the causeway for an afternoon walk with the family, bicycle riding, rollerblading, or jogging, it is only ten minutes from the heart of the city. Numerous national parks are within twenty minutes of downtown. And farther in the interior, there are jungle canopy tours, white-water rafting, mountain climbing, horseback riding, and garden tours.

Panama is a baseball country. Numerous players have made it to the big leagues, and the local teams are wonderful to watch. Nevertheless, soccer is the national sport, and some of their boxers are world class. There is even a cricket team playing in Paraiso on Sundays.

SOCIAL CUSTOMS

Panama has a long history with Americans, dating from the canal days. While the average Panamanian is probably positive about the relationship, political groups primarily connected with the University of Panama blame the Americans for a variety of problems, ranging from a controversial free trade agreement, to interference in internal political actions.

The concept of "political correctness," fortunately, has not intruded on the more relaxed attitudes of Panamanians. Thus you will hear customers address their waitress as *joven* (young lady), call the postmistress *mommy,* address family members as *China* or *chumbo,* female friends as *chica,* and other endearments not meant to be anything but friendly. Panamanian men are macho but perhaps not as blatantly macho as Mexican men. (Speaking of Mexico, the siesta of Mexico and some other Latin countries is not practiced in Panama.)

Panama has had a woman president, and it elicited no comment.

Women hold positions as legislators, port captains, tugboat captains, engineers, doctors, lawyers, business owners, restaurateurs, teachers—even canal pilots—and every other profession imaginable. The two-wage-earner family is the norm at all levels of society.

Panama is very family oriented, and as a result, many social activities revolve around the family. Children are included in activities at private clubs, in restaurants, and at weddings and other social events. In general, acceptance of foreigners is more dependent on proper behavior, correct dress, and speaking the language than on factors such as race, color, or sex.

BANKING AND FINANCE

Panama is a world financial center offering a variety of local and international banking institutions. Checks can be written in English or Spanish. Most expats keep their funds in their home country and transfer money to their Panama account to meet local expenses. But Panama banks offer the convenience of international banking services inside and outside of Panama. You can conduct international transactions and deposit foreign checks, which makes it particularly convenient for foreign retirees. However, all bank accounts on which you are a signatory must be reported to the IRS.

There are also more than 120,000 companies in Panama, most of which trade or hold assets externally or offshore. It is reasonably easy to form corporations, and privacy is assured. This is accomplished by putting the entity in the name of the attorney or someone else, which means that you do not own the assets. Banking and shipping are Panama's two main offshore industries. International concern about money laundering is a regular topic of conversation.

In Panama only locally sourced income is taxed, and there are no tax treaties. Locally sourced profits are taxed at up to 30 percent for individuals. There is no capital gains tax, but gains on real estate count as income. There is a small withholding tax. All foreign-source income is tax-free in Panama.

HEALTH CARE/MEDICAL

Panama has excellent doctors, dentists, laboratories, and especially good hospitals, but *in the city*. Outside the city, plans are afoot to open new hospitals and clinics, but retirees in these isolated locations know they are living with risk.

The Panama socialized-health-care system, the Caja Seguro Social

(CSS), is designed for employees who pay into the system through their jobs. It is a poor system at best, with constant shortages of medications, broken equipment, long lines—but good doctors. The private system is excellent, in the city. Again, keep in mind that anything outside the city is marginal or nonexistent. Out-of-pocket medical expenses are inexpensive: physician office visit, $35; dental checkup and cleaning, $35; cataract surgery, $1,100.

Local health insurance is available—until recently, at a reasonable cost. However, it has limitations concerning medical conditions as well as age restrictions. Medical tourism has existed for specialties such as eye surgery and cosmetic surgery for many years. Prescription drugs are generally available, usually without prescription, except for antibiotics and narcotic analgesics. With the jubilado (retiree) discount of 10 percent to 17 percent, medications are often less expensive than in the U.S.

Note: Panama's wet, tropical climate is not for everyone, especially those with respiratory problems. Rain eight or more months of the year is depressing for some people. Mold is a constant problem everywhere. Pollution, from buses and cars, and concrete dust from building, is a major factor when considering whether retirement in Panama is right for you.

RESIDENCY AND RED TAPE

Panama offers a variety of visas for attaining residential status, the simplest being the jubilado or pensionado visa. Retirees need prove only that they have adequate *guaranteed* income ($500 per month, plus $75 each for a spouse or dependent). Evidence of U.S. Social Security or a government pension and a letter from the U.S. Embassy will meet this requirement. Private corporate pensions require additional proof in the form of copies of monthly checks and bank records. While there is no age requirement, if you are under forty-five, you would probably undergo more scrutiny.

Documents: the usual—obtained *before* you arrive in Panama—a birth certificate, marriage license, clean police report, and, upon touching down, a health certificate from a Panamanian doctor.

Once you apply for the visa, you will receive a *carnet,* a card that indicates temporary status, valid for three months. Use an attorney specializing in immigration, and you should receive your residence status in about three months. During this processing period, you are free to travel to and from Panama, but confirm this with your attorney.

Work permits are possible, assuming that you have a work contract with a local employer, though not for those with a retiree visa. Investor visas require an investment ranging from as little as $40,000 (and other considerations) to $200,000. Investment can be made in an existing Panamanian business for retail enterprises such as a franchise of an existing business or other types of new enterprises in areas needing development, including construction, tourism, and computers.

Panama's government is looking at further visa options to accommodate the potential snowbirds and *residential tourists*—those coming for longer than the thirty-day tourist card allows but not planning on permanent residence. Currently the thirty-day tourist card is issued to U.S. citizens. For citizens of other countries, cards can be renewed for an additional sixty days, but they provide no rights or privileges of residency.

COST OF LIVING

The costs of living in **Panama City** range across the lot. In the better neighborhoods, you can rent a two-bedroom furnished apartment in the city for an average of $1,200 per month. At the low end, acceptable two-bedroom apartments can be found from $400 to $600 per month. Electricity is expensive and explains why most locals do not live in fully air-conditioned housing. And while you might imagine that things would be a little cheaper in the country, this is not really true in Panama because of transportation costs and, recently, a burst of inflation.

Maid service and household help of all kinds are one of the advantages of living in Panama. A full-time live-in maid who works six days a week will cost between $200 and $250 per month. A day maid can be found for between $12 and $15 per day. If they work on a regular basis, they will be eligible for social security benefits, and you will be required to pay a thirteenth-month "bonus." Panama has a very rigid labor code that favors the employee in all cases.

Monthly Cost of Living in Panama City (before 2008 inflation)
   Rent for a two-bedroom home, condo, or apartment: $900 to $1,200 (includes water, trash collection, gas).
   Taxes: 5 percent on everything but food; property taxes, 2 percent of assessed value.
   Groceries for two: $320.
   Utilities: $250.
   TV: $60.
   Internet: $43.
   Telephone: $25.
   Transportation: City taxi, $1; flight to David, $99.

Maid service: Live-in, $200 to $250; $12 to $15 a day.
Restaurants for two: $18 to $35 in a midrange restaurant.

Monthly Cost of Living in Coronado
Rent for a two-bedroom home, condo, or apartment: $2,000 (if it exists, anticipate a waiting list).
Taxes: 5 percent on everything but food; property taxes, 2 percent of assessed value.
Groceries for two: $320.
Utilities: Electricity, $120.
TV: Direct TV, $39.
Internet: $49.
Telephone: Basic, $16.
Transportation: Taxis not readily available; free shuttle bus.
Maid service: $10 a day.
Restaurants for two: $18 to $20.

Monthly Cost of Living in Boquete Highlands
Rent for a two-bedroom home, condo, or apartment: $500 to $800.
Taxes: 5 percent on everything but food; property taxes, 2 percent of assessed value.
Groceries for two: $250.
Utilities: Electricity, $100.
TV: Direct TV, $40.
Internet: Fast connection, $75; basic, $49.
Telephone: $16 (if available); cell phone, $40.
Transportation: Taxi, $1 in town; $5 out of town.
Maid service: Live-in, $200; $10 a day.
Restaurants for two: $10 to $12.

REAL ESTATE

Inflation and the decade-long rise in real estate raises many concerns, and speculation is rife everywhere as to where prices will go. But in fact, in the past Panama real estate has not been easy to resell. Ask any local. Many own the first piece of property they ever purchased, because they cannot sell it. Simplified, there is a preferential mortgage rate for new construction, so anything already built is a less appealing purchase. Further, especially in the city, new buildings are going up daily, all competing to sell to the same customer.

While the overbuilding is evident in the city, it is no less a consideration in the interior. For example, as the need for temporary rental properties increased, speculators arrived to attempt to fill the demand, which will eventually become a glut on the market.

Here in Panama, ask your realtor to produce his real estate license. Only licensed realtors are qualified to legally handle real estate transactions, but there are lots of foreigners who arrived last week and set up shop to make a killing by selling you a mangrove island in *Bocas*. Real estate hustling has built up to fever-pitch in Panama during the past several years.

On the positive side, foreigners are able to buy any property anywhere as long as it is legally titled. Panamanians often live on a property that they do not legally own but they do have the right to attain title. You as a foreigner do not have this right. In an attempt to stop the problem of selling untitled property, in Bocas in particular, the current government is attempting to title more property so that it can be legally sold.

While building, especially in the interior, is popular with foreigners, it is also a long, nerve-racking process. Concrete and steel, in particular, are in short supply with so many construction projects going on all over the country; they will be further limited with the canal expansion demands. Permits and building inspection are cumbersome, sometimes corrupt, or nonexistent.

Housing costs skyrocketed between 2006 and 2008. Half of housing units cost between $1,000 to $2,000 and up per square meter. The top quarter of the housing market, aimed at foreigners, is priced at $300,000 and above. In **Boquete** land costs have also shot up, and now start around $400 per square meter in town (but are still $50 to $60 per meter out of town). Many early speculators bought cheap and now plan to sell newly renovated houses at a profit. Scams and scam artists are rampant, many if not most of them being foreigners.

Property taxes are cheap: a twenty-year-old apartment valued at $145,000 has a yearly tax bill of $380. (New buildings are exempt for twenty years.) Mortgages are possible, but qualifications are more difficult for retirees. All loans are variable rate.

As always, renting first and getting to know the country will pay off in the long run.

TRANSPORTATION

Panama is easily accessible by plane from anywhere in the world. Cruise ships pass through the canal during the season. Driving in Panama is an art, and the skills needed to survive have to be acquired. Generally, traffic is a nightmare. Plan for twice the time you think you need. All your home-town instincts are invalid here: Do not leave too much space between cars, or other cars will cut in front. Do not hesitate at intersections, or you will be honked at.

SECURITY

While Panama has long had a reputation for being one of the safest places in Latin America, a word of caution is now in order. Petty crime, house break-ins, and some crimes previously unheard of—including assassina-tions and kidnappings—have recently become concerns. Attempted car-jackings have been reported in remote areas around **Boquete** as well. Many of these crimes are being attributed to gangs, or *pandillas*.

COMMUNICATIONS AND MEDIA

Both landline and cell service are available countrywide. Of Panama's 3-million-plus inhabitants, 2 million have cell phones. Broadband internet service is also available, and internet cafés and Wi-Fi-friendly locations exist everywhere. Panama has multiple options for TV service, including programming from the U.S., Canada, Europe, and Central America. Movies from the U.S. are available in English with Spanish subtitles within weeks of release.

UP-AND-COMING AREAS

About forty-five minutes from the city, *Ranchos los Sueños* is a small development backing into the hills with subdivided lots that include water and electricity access. A number of Canadian and German retirees are currently building in this neighborhood. While this is an inland development, it is only fifteen minutes from the golf and beaches of **Coronado**.

From **Coronado** westward, developers are planning and building gated beach resorts along the vast stretches of undeveloped coastal areas. Rising out of the sand and jungle, these projects offer building lots, some houses, and some high-rises, planned infrastructure, golf courses, beach access, and the possibility of marinas on this relatively unprotected coastline. These are not towns but developers' projects that will be aimed at an upscale market, probably snowbirds and other short-term users rather than full-time residents.

The *highlands,* including the major communities of **Boquete,** Volcán, **Cerro Punta,** and the surrounding areas, comprise about 350 square miles. A number of gated communities and new developments are in various stages of planning or construction. **Volcán** and **Cerro Punta,** forty-five minutes to an hour from **David,** are more rural and less expensive than **Boquete.** This mountain area is famous for coffee and flowers, and currently attracts retirees interested in buying property to build single-family houses. **Cerro Punta** is literally often in the clouds and is drizzly and chilly.

Other communities in the interior that have some appeal due to their proximity to the city include the greater *Arraiján* area and *Las Cumbres,* a planned community built around a lake and only twenty minutes on the Trans-Isthmian Highway from **Panama City.** *Las Cumbres* offers older homes, building sites, and some new housing. *Arraiján* is an established community of middle-class Panamanians with basic local shopping.

La Chorrera, about twenty minutes from the city across either of two bridges, backs onto Gatun Lake and has recently started to attract retirees interested in building their retirement homes. The *La Chorrera-Arraiján* area is easily accessible by the Corredor Norte and has developing infrastructure and basic services, including water, trash collection, and shopping. However, water is a problem in this area—both too much when it rains, and too little for consumer use. Adequate trash collection is a problem everywhere in Panama and more so in the developing areas.

VOLUNTEERING WITHOUT BORDERS

Basically there are two categories of organizations that recruit volunteers: established international groups and loosely organized expat societies.

The long-established presence of Americans (due to the canal, of course) created many social groups, such as the Panama Expat Society and the Military Expat Society. Many of these societies now have charity arms that support local schools and hospitals. There are also clubs specifically dedicated to fund-raising allied to community-based initiatives in their local area.

- One group spans both categories: the Panama Council of the Navy League of the United States (usually shortened to the Navy League). This group has a wide-ranging number of outreach programs such as repairing schools, orphanages, and community centers. The league funds scholarship programs that finance higher education for high school students (www.navyleague-panama.org).

Worldwide organizations are also active in Panama:

- Fundación Operación Sonrisa (smile), founded in Panama in 1991, has performed corrective facial surgery (mainly on cleft palates) on over two thousand children. Volunteers, working alongside medical personnel, raise funds and provide support services (www.operacionsonrisa.org.pa).
- Habitat for Humanity builds houses in cooperation with families of limited resources and funds seventeen-year mortgages costing just $47 per year. Fifty homes have been built. The Panamanian government estimates that 190,000 are needed (www.habitat.org/intl/lac/155.aspx).
- The neediest children of Panama are the street kids. Abandoned by parents, these children survive by begging and scrounging. In group homes, Casa Esperanza offers food, medical care, and education. Its Family Orientation Program teaches parenting skills. Donations of funds and services are always needed (www.casaesperanza.org.pa).
- Native English speakers are always needed to tutor or teach English.

Sandra T. Snyder is the author of Living in Panama *(visit www.livingin panama.net) and lives in* **Panama City**. *She is the recipient of the U.S. Ambassador's Distinguished American Citizen Award.*

Time out!

CLASS FIELD TRIP!

This book's author-editor, Barry Golson, traveled throughout Panama to see the future—that is, the retirement scene in the country most active in recruiting North Americans. He talked to Americans and Panamanians alike about their experiences. His first-person account, including personal report cards, follows. There will not be a quiz.

Chapter 14

PANAMA'S NEW SETTLERS

BY BARRY GOLSON

On the afternoon I arrive in **Panama City,** citizens are protesting an
unpopular government decree. Traffic is blocked, signs are being waved, a
few stones thrown. Henry Smith, a transplanted Texan and twenty-five-
year resident of Panama who had offered to show me around for the first
couple of days, meets me at the airport and takes it all in stride. Smith, in
his late sixties, lives on the outskirts of **Panama City** with his Panamanian
wife. He takes the long, scenic route, and **Panama City**'s glittering nighttime skyline comes into view: the city of 700,000 has a sleek, modern look,
with tall, slender buildings rising along a palm-lined Pacific Ocean shore
drive. I ask Smith—who has generously offered to squire me about town—
whether we have anything to be concerned about with the demonstrations.

"Nah," he says. "They never protest after dark, and they take the weekends off. This is Panama."

This past decade, there has been a torrent of media ink about Americans
flocking to **Panama City** and to its "islands and highlands," lured not only
by its climate and natural beauty but by generous retiree discounts, tax
abatements, and liberal immigration policies. I previously explored the
retirement scene in Mexico (*AARP,* February 2004) before moving there,
and began hearing more about Panama as the next hot spot—not only
Panama City but such places as **Boquete, Volcán,** and **Bocas del Toro,** in
the country's hinterlands.

In often breathless prose, press reports, promotional newsletters, and
websites have touted Panama as the cheapest, warmest, friendliest, most
Americanized retiree destination anywhere. The question is, how does it all

work out in practice? Though I will hear my share of testimonials to the good life in Panama, I am interested as well in a newer phenomenon: the real estate hustle. You're not in Panama long before you begin to hear stories about real estate sharks going after retiree minnows. I ask my expat guide, Smith, what he's been seeing among new arrivals. He says, "People are falling in love too easily. Panama's an old pirate station—it goes way back—and there are still a lot of pirates around. But instead of cutlasses, they're using the law and for-sale signs."

Over the next few weeks of traveling and talking with both Americans and Panamanians, it is a refrain I am to hear from one end of the country to the other: don't do anything in haste. Tales abound of Americans "who leave their brains at the border" and overpay for a house or buy unsuitable or untitled land. One newcomer, who lived for several years in Costa Rica and now works for an American firm in **Panama City,** says, "It's the same in both countries: you get off the plane, your eyes glaze over, you are so in awe of the natural beauty, the setting is so exotic. The real estate broker tells you the places are going fast—so you jump."

My first impression of **Panama City** is that it resembles Miami. Panama's relationship with the United States, as long and sinewy as the canal that bisects the country, is in evidence everywhere. Many commercial signs are in English. At the airport, I see only a few official references to the national currency, the balboa—a gentle fiction expressed in their coinage, though the folding stuff is strictly U.S. dollars. With **Panama City**'s mixture of old-Spain colonial, South Beach contemporary, and the usual Latin American perpetual-near-collision traffic (stop signs are ignored throughout the country), it strikes me as a lively, sophisticated city.

Kevin Bradley, also generous in clueing me in to Panama's scene, is red haired, cheerful, and Irish tongued. He was born in the *Canal Zone* and seems to be the insurance agent for every second gringo I meet in Panama. We are at a dinner on the scenic causeway joining **Panama City** to two islands. He is laughing about some of the scams he has witnessed.

"Sure, Panamanians love juega vivo, and it's easy to get hustled, but I'm in touch with a huge range of Americans down here, and the vast majority have retired without problems. There are a few scoundrels here—both American and Panamanian—but that's not the rule." Bradley suggests a golf outing, which I take him up on. We play at the Summit course, a relic of the zone days, where the fairways lie parallel to the canal. Just over the ridge, supertankers laden with containers glide silently by on their way to the Miraflores Locks.

Nancy Hanna lives in a red-tiled three-bedroom house converted from officers' quarters in the "reverted" *Canal Zone*. She bought it for $130,000 in 2004. She is an unabashed Panama booster and edits the tourist-targeted *Panama Planner*. Hanna praises the country's "first-world infrastructure" and stable democracy. Hanna picks up on the Panama-Miami comparison: "less crime, no hurricanes, and Americans are more popular in Panama!" She also praises medical care in **Panama City** as being close to U.S. standard, an opinion shared by every resident I talk to during my visit. Here doctors give patients their cell phone numbers and make inexpensive house calls.

Other residents are less chipper and warn against gringo provincialism. An old-timer says, "Americans ought to be cautious about coming down here, wrapping themselves in a little air-conditioned bubble, and ghettoizing themselves." He is critical of some gated communities. "The *Canal Zone* was a big gated community," he says, recalling a 1964 incident in which anti-American riots caused twenty-seven deaths. "If these places just market to Americans and isolate them arrogantly, you become an inviting target for a demagogue."

On my way to Panama's domestic airport, I solicit the best expert advice you get in any country—from my cab driver. Maximo Trejos, forty-six, drove soldiers and civilians who ran the canal twenty-five years ago, and he drives tourists and retirees today. Thinking about the old-timer's remarks, I ask Trejos if there is any chance that anti-American feeling could again fester.

"In the past, there *was* some real resentment, but much less now," he says. "Many of the soldiers stationed here had everything paid for—housing, food—and so they had a lot of money to throw around and to be arrogant with. They would tear up bars, order Panamanians out. Civilians who lived in the zone were better behaved, especially after the canal treaties were signed, and that is what most of the Americans I meet today are like."

Panama City Report Card
  Looks: A– (skyline, old city)
  Weather: B (warm but humid; lots of rain)
  Shopping: A– (A+ in Colon free zone)
  Culture: B–
  Medical facilities: B+
  Other Americans: B (cosmopolitan atmosphere)
  Wow factor: Amazing canal and nearby rain forest
  Quick review: Miami—with more English!

• • •

Boquete is a tranquil coffee-growing town of 18,000 set in a mountain rise in Panama's breadbasket, *Chiriquí province*. It is nearly an hour's drive from the provincial capital of **David**, itself an hour's flight from **Panama City**. The country's airlines have kept air travel cheap, and residents of the mountain communities look at the trip as a commute. The town of **Boquete** is a bit frayed, but home construction and the new cafés and restaurants that now dot the town's main street suggest that things are on the upswing. As are the real estate prices, which doubled and then redoubled between 2002 and 2008.

Erin and David Ross, silver haired and short sleeved, are having a late breakfast at Café Punto de Encuentro, a popular expat spot. They left Sacramento on a get-acquainted tour of Latin America, stopped for a few days in **Boquete**—and canceled the rest of their itinerary. David, a former air force officer, says, "We looked in Costa Rica, we looked in Mexico, but we were so taken by the beauty of the area, and the people, their willingness to help—plus the cost is about half of what it is in Sacramento." Erin adds, "It also had to be affordable enough that I can be an eight-times-a year grandmother, flying back to see my grandkids. And you get twenty-five percent off your flights!" A hummingbird hovers in the air at a nearby flower bush. David, a first cousin of the Grateful Dead's late Jerry Garcia (but who prefers jazz), says, "A lot of people feel there is a spirituality about this land, a place they were meant to be."

I stay to talk with the owner of the café, Olga Rios. A native of **Boquete**, she has run the café for eight years. She talks about her mostly American customers. "The majority of retired people who come to my café are good people, not arrogant," she says. "Most just want a tranquil life here. Unfortunately, there are also speculators, and that is not good." Rios says that many of her friends had to move out of town when rents and real estate began shooting up, and that she had hoped to buy some land for a small home, but "we can't afford it." Just a few years ago, she says, homes cost $25,000; now they're $250,000 and up. "I don't want to see **Boquete** change too much. There used to be a general store where people would tie up their horses and sit and talk to each other. Now it's being made into a hotel for foreigners."

One foreigner in **Boquete** everybody knows is Sam Taliaferro, the American developer of *Valle Escondido* (Hidden Valley), a gated community on the fringe of town. A guard waves me through into a little world unto itself. Tucked into a little gorge flanked by steep, lush ravines, a brook meanders through its middle, a nine-hole golf course straddles the property, and the flowering foliage is boisterous with twittering birds. It is positively Disney-esque. Homes look expensive, and the biggest is a ten-

thousand-square-foot mansion at the head of the valley, where Sam Taliaferro reigns over his domain.

"I'm as libertarian as you can get," Taliaferro tells me as he gives me a
driving tour of the valley. (This is a sentiment I hear often in Panama.) "I
made my money in the States in tech and cars, and I burned out on all the
taxes I had to pay." He moved his business offshore and married a Panamanian woman who was born near here. "I fell in love with the place and
decided I would build my ideal community." Taliaferro says he wanted to
create a "Galt's Gulch," the fictional utopia for entrepreneurs, isolated from
an overregulated world, described by Ayn Rand in *Atlas Shrugged*.

Taliaferro, an energetic man with a persuasive salesman's patter, is
described by many as a visionary. Besides **Hidden Valley**, he has interests
in other developments and hotels as well as grand marketing plans to make
Panama the premier destination for affluent boomer retirees. "Retirement
is going to be bigger for Panama *than the canal*!" he declares, waving his
forefinger. (The canal and associated businesses are thought to provide
about 40 percent of Panama's income.)

I ask about Americans being isolated in a gated community.

"What owners really want," he says, "is first-world amenities. They want
less maintenance, fewer headaches." He drives us through the gate, down
into **Boquete**. "When we go out this gate," he says, "you see homes that have
no sewage, the water system is horrible, the roads are falling apart. Why?
Government doesn't have the funds. We take care of everything—our own
water and roads. Also, if you live outside this community, your chances of
being robbed are high." He points to a local home. "Look at the bars on
those windows. What's the difference between living in a gated community
or a gated house? I'd prefer not to see those bars on my windows, and just
have to go past *one* bar."

Lower on the living scale is Allen MacDonald, sixty-eight, whom I
meet at another small café in town. He lives on his Social Security check
with a Panamanian wife twenty years younger and her two kids. They rent
a sixty-foot-square ranch a few miles out of town for $250 a month, and
his stepchildren attend the local schools.

I inquire if this is his second marriage. "At *least*," he says with an imp-
ish grin lacking in one or two front teeth.

MacDonald bemoans the rise in prices and says that he could not now
afford to live closer to town. "Breakfasts that used to cost three dollars in
Boquete now cost six dollars," he says. But he likes his life. "I sleep and eat
when I want to, and I can blast my music from the porch, and nobody
minds." He does not own a car but takes 35-cent taxis into town. He has
Panamanian insurance, which runs him $54 a month for his family of four,

but admits the service is basic. "You have to take a bus down to David and stand in line at six in the morning just to make an appointment." When he visits David, he often has a McDonald's hamburger; it costs him 85 cents with his 25 percent retiree discount.

The village of **Volcán** is around the other side of the (potentially active) volcano, and is **Boquete** before the land rush. It is talked about as the "next" highlands retreat, with perhaps a hundred hardy foreigners living a life far from supermarkets and department stores. The pastoral country-side is rich with red cedar, silver-dollar eucalyptus, and amaryllis. There are a dozen kinds of hummingbirds, and, in the right season, a lucky hiker can spot the rare green-and-red-crested quetzal.

I meet John and June Bennett at a breakfast place along the main street. John and June are originally from Florida and are another refugee couple from Costa Rica, where they retired first. John says, "Besides cutting back on benefits, Costa Rica raised import duties on your car from five percent to fifty percent—who needs that?" The couple is no kinder to Florida. June says, "It's sunny, it's warm, it's dull. And the property values—I don't know how the average person can live in Florida anymore."

John, a former marine and air-conditioning salesman, says they moved to **Volcán** "to be free." They rented, then paid $48,000 in 2005 for an A-frame in a modest neighborhood, where they immerse themselves in the lives of their Panamanian neighbors. June says tartly, "I don't miss the Wal-Mart life; I love the little stores. It's not for everyone. If you're a woman with the nails and the hair and the waxing, you might want to stay in **Panama City**." John adds, "This is a small town like I remember it in the fifties. Not Little Amer-ica, but the same feeling I remember. Everybody waves at you—the people, the police, the Indians." The neighborhood they live in happens to be called *Nuevo California*.

Not far away, Melodie Barkara lives in a plain, comfortable home by a pasture. Barkara is well known online as the founder of another Yahoo group, Viviendo en Panama, but which she now disowns "because there are too many people posting with too many ulterior motives." For my ben-efit, she gathers a group of four other American residents to discuss their impressions of life here in the mountains.

Like the people I talked to in **Panama City,** they love their new lives but are exercised at the real estate hustling that is going on, even here in the boondocks. The group also agreed that hype had reached this pastoral venue as well. "If you read the websites, it's eternal spring here," said one woman. "But they don't talk about the six months of rain, and the winds that can blow your roof off." The group also talked about poor potable water and a strained water supply. It occurs to me that these lovers of the isolated life may be discouraging more newcomers.

Mountainside Report Card
   Looks: A (volcanic beauty)
   Weather: B (warm, often rainy, windy)
   Culture: F
   Medical facilities: D
   Shopping: D
   Other Americans: B (libertarian slant)
   Wow factor: The flowers! The hummingbirds!
   Quick review: Idyllic, spare living for the hardy

My final stop will be *Bocas del Toro,* the archipelago on the northern Caribbean tip of Panama, where retirees have been flocking for some time to live the seriously sybaritic beach life. It is a series of islands that the *Lonely Planet Panama* (the only decent guide to the country) calls a "biologist's fantasy," because of its rare wildlife and unique jungle biosphere. Painted houses and seafood joints under palapa roofs perch over the water. Expats loll in hammocks, and dogs run free.

For some retirees, it has been less a fantasy than a nightmare. In a well-publicized series of real estate transactions a few years back, retirees who overlooked Panama's restrictions on owning island property were rudely awakened when a government agency declared their land purchases invalid. A crooked American developer was arrested and jailed.

Bocas has a countrywide reputation for high tolerance: it attracts the more idiosyncratic breed of expatriate. Somewhere between 300 and 400 foreigners are thought to live there, but it's not the kind of place that encourages a census. English is widely spoken as a first language. Boats are the main mode of transport, as residents ply the waters to visit one another on outlying islands.

One such resident is Claude Talley, seventy-two, the African-American owner of Angela Hotel, a seaside inn and restaurant. Originally from Memphis, Talley worked at IBM and came to Costa Rica in 1997 "to go fishing on my boat for a year." He grew to dislike Costa Rica and sailed his boat down to Bocas. "I docked and just took a walk through the town park. People would walk down the middle of the streets, and taxis drove *around* the people. I thought, What a serene place. It's still that way. There are some Ugly Americans here, but they haven't managed to rile the people—yet."

If anyone can be said to have lived both the dream and the nightmare in *Bocas del Toro,* it is Susan Guberman-Garcia and her husband, Izzy Garcia. The couple is from San Jose, California, where Izzy was a consultant and Susan a successful civil rights lawyer. They pick me up by motor launch at a town dock, and we cross the bay to a near-deserted island. There they live in one house at the edge of the island jungle while they build a bigger one. It is indeed the wayfarer's dream: "When I first saw the land," says Susan, "there were monkeys in the trees and the sounds of the jungle all around me. I couldn't believe we could actually own a place here!"

Their joy turned sour. What they paid for in **Bocas** was not a land title; they understood they could not own property outright on a Panamanian island, but Susan hired Panamanian attorneys who told her that "rights of possession" were a safe first step to eventually getting title. They paid the sale price and obtained what they thought were the proper certificates, but last year the new government in **Panama City** invalidated the agency issuing the documents. After much wrangling, the case—and many others like it—is in limbo, though Susan is confident it will work out and expects to continue living on "their" island. She acknowledges that as a lawyer she should have been especially careful, but she relied on what she thought were well-recommended professionals.

I ask them what they do about health care from such a remote location, especially in case of a medical emergency. "Well, if your number's up, your number's up," says Susan, laughing. "Health care in **Bocas** is rudimentary, so you have to fly to **Panama City,** where the care is excellent and affordable."

Bocas Report Card
    Looks: A– (raffish seaside charm; fabulous natural scenery)
    Weather: B+
    Culture: F
    Medical Facilities: F
    Shopping: F
    Other Americans: B (hang-loose ethnic mix)
    Wow factor: Archipelago natural paradise
    Quick review: Panama's Key West, still relatively cheap

I spend a couple of days back in **Panama City** before flying home. One afternoon I go to the Miraflores Locks at the canal and watch the fascinating water duet of a large oil tanker waltzing slowly into the lock—with only a foot to spare on each side—then being lowered by hydraulics and gravity into the Pacific. It is pretty much the method used in 1903, back when

Teddy Roosevelt first cooked up the independence of Panama from its mother country, Colombia. On another day, I realize how close **Panama City** is to its surrounding jungle when I take a taxi thirty minutes to the Gamboa Rainforest Resort and find myself feeding howler monkeys on overhanging branches from a rented skiff. I also spot what my guide tells me is a three-toed sloth, basking immobile in the sun. He reminds me of a couple of laid-back retirees I'd seen in the **Bocas** sunlight.

Panama also has a glamorous minister of tourism: Rubén Blades, international star of stage, screen, and salsa music, with a degree from Harvard Law School. He is out of the country during my trip, but when I return to the States, we email each other. In answer to my question about the difficulty of finding reliable information on retiree topics, Blades says he is pushing to establish a special government office, unique in Latin America, that would serve as a clearinghouse for advice and complaints from retirees and second-home owners. He says he is also sponsoring the first new property census since 1973 "to clarify to one and all what land and coastal areas can be bought, sold, or given in concession in Panama." He adds, "This will make it tougher for hustlers to bamboozle unsuspecting buyers." Blades claims that Panama's retirement benefits are unmatched and believes retirees come to Panama for spiritual, as well as financial, reasons. "Retirees come to Panama to *live,* not to die," he says.

Panama Retirement Report Card

Overall: B+, with a deduction for hustles

Quick review: The benefits are enticing. If we hadn't already chosen Mexico, whose depth of soul and culture we prefer, we might have considered Panama.

MY PANAMA

A U.S. Army Vet Who Can't Take Cold Weather

Name, age, origin: Edward Lesesne, sixty-seven, Florida.

Where I live: *Diablo* and *Albrook,* Panama City.

Previous occupation: Officer and civilian manager, U.S. Army.

Reasons for moving here: I came down here in 1964 between tours in Vietnam. I retired here in 1980 and have been here ever since. I love the weather, fishing, the people, and my standard of living, which I couldn't have the same in the U.S.

Finances: I am retired three times (army 24 years; civil service, 18 years; and SS; plus I'm 100 percent disabled by the VA). I guess you could say I'm well off.

Costs: I couldn't afford what I have here in Panama in the U.S. I have an apartment on the Panama Canal that would cost millions in the States, and I also have a house in *Albrook.* I own all my property outright. I usually cook, but when I go out, the cost rarely goes over $40. I was in Las Vegas and had a dinner for two at the Top of the World restaurant, which cost $297!

Weather: Great. One of the main reasons I'm here. I got shot up in 'Nam and can't take the cold weather.

Health care/medical: Excellent. In some ways better than the U.S. All of my doctors have been U.S. trained.

Crime, corruption: Very low. I've learned not to put myself in harm's way and have thus far avoided being robbed.

Common misperceptions: People who haven't visited here think it's still a banana republic. Nothing could be further from the truth. You could compare **Panama City** with Atlanta, Georgia.

Best: I live on the Panama Canal, and the view is great. I like the two seasons, as they give us some variety. I love the rainy season best because everything is so green. Also, the dry season gives us beautiful flowering trees and bushes. A long time ago at the Panama Canal Yacht Club, we had a wet jockstrap contest, and I won.

Worst: Traffic. A terrible messy divorce.

Happiest when: I'm fishing and in my church.

What I miss most: Home Depot.

MY PANAMA

A Former Engineer Who's Happy but Hates the Hustlers

Name, age, origin: Paul (pseudonym), sixty-five, San Mateo, California.

Where I live: Panama City.

Previous occupation: Engineer.

Reasons for moving here: Spent years visiting in Central and South America, and while I loved Mexico, I kept coming back to Panama. I love sailing, the climate, the mountains to hike, and proximity to volcanos to climb.

Finances: Comfortable investment income and U.S. Social Security.

Costs: You need $30,000 minimum, $50,000 to live well. Many people are coming here on just Social Security, but they can't afford the social life, constantly complain, dress poorly, and are shunned by locals.

My community: I live in the hills in the city with a great view in a forty-year-old building. Local neighborhood is small; few outsiders except the occasional corporate exec, ambassadors. Mixed friends, from Panama, Nicaragua, Europe, U.S., Canada. Locals friendly, social.

Weather: Panama City is rainy from April through December, but it's the best time of year, as it is clean, fresh, green, and cool. I hate the dry season when it is dusty, hot, boring.

Leisure: Sailing, running, hiking (close enough to get to the highest peak in Costa Rica). My wife loves the social life, and we belong to everything. Black-tie events regularly from August to January.

Culture: Symphony season, visiting performers like Kenny G, dance troupes.

Health care/medical: I have a history of kidney stones and have ended up in the ER in California, Virginia, Florida, and Mexico. In Panama, too, but what cost $2,000 in the States was $200 here—and I got the same treatment and results. Excellent doctors; they speak English and have time for and an interest in their patients.

Crime, corruption: I don't worry about crime, although it is there. Generally I go anywhere and do everything any time of day or night. However, every week recently I have a friend whose house has been broken into—iron gratings are crowbarred, and dogs are sprayed to keep them quiet. Another had his new car stolen by the son of the maid while they were on vacation.

The seller of a house or car or TV will raise the price while you are writing the check because he decides you would have paid more. The government changes the rules after you have built the house because it changed the set-back laws. Anyone at any time can go to the police and file a *denuncia* accusing you of anything. If the judge thinks it reasonable or is a friend of the person filing the complaint, or doesn't like you, he can enforce the denuncia. Theoretically, they can decide to attach your possessions, although only those relevant to the complaint. It is up to you to prove your innocence and try to get your stuff back. So: avoid having a high profile, avoid getting involved in legal situations.

Locals' attitudes toward gringos: Positive in general, but their culture assumes that *everyone* is a mark—juega vivo. Not even their grandmother is safe if money is involved. I learned the hard way about how people do business here and will take advantage of you until you scream. You will make friends, fit in, and enjoy the people and their family-oriented culture, but superficially so. Below the surface, everything is corrupt all the time.

Wish I'd known before: How tax preferences affect resale of property values in the city—there's no appreciation on old houses. The apartment across from us sold three times in ten years, each time for $145,000.

Best: Social life, close to everything a city has to offer, shopping, restaurants, friends.

Worst: Traffic, day and night; noise from traffic, car alarms; buses spewing black unburned fuel. Everything has black greasy soot on it all the time, even outside the city, for some reason. In **Bocas,** my friends complain about the same thing, and they live on an island in the middle of nowhere!

Happiest when: Out sailing.

What I miss most: A really top-rate restaurant. A really good bookstore.

Expected to miss but didn't: Work, but found lots of volunteer opportunities.

MY PANAMA
A Former Canal Worker Who Moved to the Mountains

Name, age, origin: Sally (pseudonym), sixty-six , Massachusetts and New York.

Where I live: *Palmira,* **Boquete,** in the mountains above **David.**

Previous occupation: Retired from Panama Canal Company.

Reasons for moving here: I worked here for twenty-three years and expected to spend the first post-retirement decade sailing around. But when my husband experienced several serious health problems, we decided we needed a home base and chose the country we know best.

Finances: A decent U.S. civil service pension and investments.

Costs: You can spend a lot but you can also live inexpensively. Close in to **Boquete,** rents are up, with a close neighbor paying $1,200 a month for a very nice U.S.-style house. Others are renting for $600 to $700. Dinner for two in a high-end restaurant is $20 to $30 without alcohol. There are expats living reasonably here on $2,000 a month. If you want to eat out, travel back to the U.S. once a year, play golf, drive to **Panama City** every couple of months, and entertain, a couple needs about $50,000 a year or more.

My community: Friendly local people, great expats with an incredible mix socially, culturally. Recently been a real influx of newly arrived expats.

Weather: Mostly perfect, except for the rains. For the most part, you can spend most days outdoors, and there's little need for heating or cooling.

Leisure: Hiking, gardening, woodworking, getting together with friends. The Pacific Ocean is about an hour away. There's good river rafting and several equestrian centers. Many volunteer opportunities.

Culture: A few concerts and plays during the holiday season. Still, it's not like being in **Panama City** with many more cultural events.

Health care/medical: Reasonably good for such a small population. For complex cases or those requiring sophisticated equipment, you need to fly to **Panama City**. That said, the local people in **David** (forty-five minutes away) do a good job of stabilizing cases before they head to PC.

Crime, corruption: Not a problem for us, but a growing problem in the larger community. The government has few resources, and thieves know there is little chance of being caught and going to jail. A lot depends on where you live, how your home is protected, and what your relationships with your neighbors are like.

Locals' attitudes toward gringos: Generally very friendly. They tend to judge each person individually, which is good, since we do get some Ugly Americans.

Common misperceptions: That life is all wonderful here in **Boquete**. **Panama City**, which is one hour's flight or a six- to seven-hour drive, is where you have to go to find really good medical care, shopping, cultural events, and international flights. If you want fast access to all this and can't afford to fly and stay in hotels, **Boquete** isn't for you. Also, not many new people focus on the fact that it takes two days' travel for friends and family to get here. Those with one week's vacation can't come to visit easily.

Volunteering: Almost anything you can think of. With the poverty among the indigenous population, there are orphanages, places for battered women and children, a group that helps housebound older people, a group that collects food for the poor. All of them need help and money.

Best: Meeting my current husband, who is a local institution. Or, should I say, belongs in an institution.

Worst: Losing my first husband overboard from our sailboat anchored in **San Blas**.

Happiest when: The sun is shining, and my husband is busy.

What I miss most: Nearby sailing. Easy access to good ice cream.

Advice: Some people say they came here for the low cost of living, but are spending everything they saved traveling back to visit kids or to aging parents. Bottom line: don't move anywhere based solely on cost of living. You need to be prepared to miss your family and make friends in a completely new place.

EUROPE

Note: Costs in Europe are in euros (€) because of dollar-to-euro volatility.

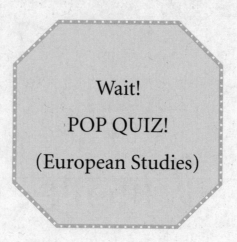

Wait!

POP QUIZ!

(European Studies)

Now, class, your final quiz: Are you a candidate for retiring to France? The results will reflect on your aptitude for other European locales as well. *Bonne chance!*

SHOULD YOU RETIRE IN FRANCE?

Test yourself, mon ami

1. **How familiar are you with France?**
   a) I've visited France many times. I toured the country from *Bourgogne* to *Languedoc.* I minored in French in college. I've read the *philosophes* and Molière and Malraux. I rent DVDs starring Daniel Auteuil and watch them in French.
   b) I've been to France twice, for one week each time. Last visit we toured the château country. I took two years of French in high school; we read *Le Petit Prince* in class. I've rented a few French DVDs, all starring Gérard Depardieu.
   c) I spent a week in France a couple of years ago and liked it, but I've only seen **Paris.** I know some words in French. I like Beaujolais and know the tune to "La Marseillaise," and I've seen all the Pink Panther–Inspector Clouseau movies.
   d) We stopped in **Paris** for a few days on a two-week tour of Europe. I liked **Paris,** but not the traffic. They eat late there. I don't know any French,

but most people speak English anyway. I'm glad to see they have a McDonald's near the big arch.

2. **Why are you moving to France?**
   a) I've dreamed of moving there; I want to be a part of French life: the food, the culture, the history, the beauty. I'm willing to live more modestly than in the U.S. because of the high cost of living in Europe. I also admire the French health system.
   b) I want to experience a different culture, and I think French life may be the way to do it. I'll have to cut back a bit, but I'm willing only up to a point. I can probably get affordable health coverage there.
   c) I like the idea of living in France, as long as there are other U.S. people around me. I'll have to see about this high cost of living—if it's too high, I'm outta there. I hear there's free health coverage.
   d) Well, I read this book about retiring in France some years back, and it says you can live really well on $800 a month because of the lower cost of living. I also need a hernia operation, and I'm not covered in the States.

3. **How do you feel about meeting French people?**
   a) I certainly hope to make friends among the French people. If I show them respect, friendliness, and a bit of humility, I think they'll be open and friendly.
   b) I don't expect to make too many friends among the French people. For one thing, my French isn't very good. I'm apprehensive.
   c) How will the French people treat *me*? I hear they're kind of aloof, and I don't know how I'm going to react to that.
   d) I hear the French are arrogant as hell, and I'm not going to take any crap.

4. **After two earlier visits to the prefecture to get your residency permit, you wait in two different lines, then are told to come back next week with additional documents.**
   a) I shrug and do it.
   b) I complain good-naturedly and do it.
   c) I complain bitterly and decide I won't do it at all. I'll coast on my tourist visa.
   d) I elbow my way to the front of the line and offer the chief official a bribe.

5. **You and your spouse are driving through the Dordogne and see a small museum that's off the beaten track.**
   a) We're both delighted. We visit the museum, talk to the guide inside, have a lunch in its courtyard.

b) I don't know if I have the time, really, but we stop and give it twenty minutes.

c) I can't find it in *Frommer's,* so we drive on.

d) I don't like museums.

6. **You're on the beach in Nice. The women are topless, the men in skimpy briefs. Your reaction:**
   a) I enjoy the view. Different strokes.
   b) I stare wide-eyed.
   c) I'm kind of shocked. I had no idea.
   d) I put two fingers in my mouth and give a loud wolf whistle.

7. **You have a chance to rent a charming old farmhouse in Provence, though it will need some renovation.**
   a) Perfect!
   b) OK, but I'm not a handy person, so this is going to be strictly hands-off for me.
   c) Nice, but I'm the apartment type.
   d) Looks like a teardown to me.

8. **How will you walk down the Champs Elysees?**
   a) As slowly as possible, window shopping, people watching, maybe stopping at a café.
   b) I stroll briskly; nice stores, interesting people, but been there, done that.
   c) I walk fast, head down; I'm in a hurry to get to the metro.
   d) Taxi!

KEY: *Give yourself 5 points for every "a" answer, 4 points for every "b," 3 points for every "c," and 0 points for every "d."*

35–40 points: *You're a thoughtful, open-minded, and promising candidate for moving to France.*

25–35 points: *With a bit more study, visits, and on-the-ground experience, you may become a candidate for moving to France.*

15–25 points: *You need to learn a lot more before you consider doing anything more permanent than visiting France as a tourist.*

0–15 points: *Go to Epcot.*

Chapter 15

FRANCE

La Grande Dame

By Beth Arnold

Every man has two countries, his own and France.
—ATTRIBUTED TO THOMAS JEFFERSON

Self-contained, poised, cultured, and sensual to the bone, France has historically been a seductress of expats beckoned by her splendid culture and the promise of one of life's richest experiences. A nation seemingly without regrets, gloriously self-reliant, France trusts her palette, her eye for color, her sense of what is or is not required of her. Expatriates of a certain kind are attracted by her hard-to-get airs. They like to drop her name, as in, "We have a cottage in **Arles**," or "We winter in **Cannes**." For them, France is the ultimate challenge, the pièce de résistance!

From *pommes frites* to champagne, from couture to culture, this is a country that knows instinctively how to sate an expat's tastes. Steeped in style and savoir faire, her charms are legendary, beginning with her reverence for food and wine—for long lunches washed down with a fine vintage; colorful open-air markets with their tumbling heaps of fruits, vegetables, artisan cheeses, roasting chickens, breads, and confections.

Food, of course, is just the appetizer for France's panoply of high culture and civilized life. The French care about taste and beauty—they encourage it, subsidize it, and preserve it—and this is one of the threads by which expats are inexorably pulled, sometimes planning for decades before they finally move here. Would-be expats dream of France for her arts and her respect for them; they fall for her storybook villages and historic cities; they daydream about the natural splendor of the French countryside. They lose their hearts to the French art of life.

One sixty-year-old Californian artist found the village of her dreams during a trip through the *Languedoc-Roussillon,* when she was looking for a life change. She fell in love instantly, but went steady first; she rented on and off for three years. Finally she took the plunge and bought her village house just a minute's walk to the Mediterranean, nestled amid the hillside vineyards. "I've wanted to live here in France since I was twenty-one years old!" she said, still not quite believing it.

Another expat, sociologist Cathy Greenblatt, who now lives in Nice, recalls, "When I was twenty-two years old, a year after graduating from Vassar, I made a European summer tour with a college friend. I remember being in Nice, driving along the corniche (cliff road) toward Monaco, and I said, 'This is gorgeous. I have to live here some day!' Thirty-nine years, and many visits to France and to the *Riviera* later, my husband and I chose to move to Nice. I found our apartment on the fourth day of looking, knowing exactly what we wanted. When people asked, 'How could you buy a place in four days?' I said, 'It wasn't four days. It was thirty-nine years.'" She and her husband now live in a high-end high-rise with a *Côte d'Azur* view to die for.

Sweetening the pot further for expats is France's excellent health care system—the best in the world—a sophisticated telecommunications network, a fine-tuned, moderately priced public transportation system for which retirees receive a discount, and an extensive, superbly maintained national highway system. And if for some strange reason the expat feels the need to take a vacation from France, the country's location as an inter-European hub is celebrated with an assortment of discount flights.

Unfortunately, nothing is perfect, not even France, where the devaluated dollar is no equal to a healthy, growing euro economy. For Americans arriving with dollars—even lots and lots of them—the day of cheap cafés and penny baguettes is over.

So, yes, life in France is more expensive than it was, and the grueling exchange rate is a fact of expat life. But a generation of North American affluence has made it possible for at least the more prosperous baby boomers— the ones who tended their 401(k)s and protected their nest eggs—to renew the traditional quest to seek a richer life in France. For despite its reputation for $10 cafés-au-lait, France, according to many expatriates, is still less expensive than many higher-end parts of the U.S. Affordability continues to be a factor in their decision to settle in France. Though Nice has become a very expensive city, even for vacationing Parisians, resident Cathy Greenblatt says, "Our taxes, insurance, and maintenance are a lot less than in New York."

Paris and **Nice** aside, North Americans of more modest means, squeezed by rising costs in their home cities, find that they can still afford to rent or buy in the less-traveled parts of France. "The quality of life is so much better here even if you're not terribly well-off," says longtime resident Karen Fawcett, owner of Bonjour Paris (www.bonjourparis.com), an engaging website about life in France. "There are ways of living nicely. You have to be flexible and resourceful. State of being and frame of mind really count. There's more freedom in France not to have to live with certain expectations, to explore."

UPSIDES

1. An immense and rich culture
2. Great quality and art of life
3. Beautiful cities, villages, and landscape
4. Living history, especially **Paris**
5. Attention to and respect for good food and wine
6. First-rate health care

DOWNSIDES

1. Bad dollar-to-euro exchange rate
2. French bureaucracy
3. Lack of understanding of the pleasures of ice and air-conditioning
4. Occasional haughty attitude—in France the customer is *not* always right

LOCATION

France has the largest landmass in the European Union, though it's smaller than Texas, extending from the English Channel to the north, south to the Mediterranean, east to the Rhine River, and west to the Atlantic Ocean. It is bordered by Belgium, Luxembourg, Germany, Switzerland, Italy, Monaco, Spain, and Andorra.

CLIMATE

France's climate is predominantly temperate—with the exception of the north, where it rains a lot, and the Atlantic Ocean can play havoc with weather patterns. The climate of central France is continental. **Paris** winters are cold but not frigid, while skies are notoriously gray. Summers are mild, though the last few years have included several weeks of blazing heat. Savvy Parisians carry umbrellas in case of sudden showers and dress in layers half the year, as temperatures can change on a dime.

The south is renowned for its brilliant blue-sky sunny days. Summers are hot and dry, though in some parts of *Provence,* evenings require sweaters. The mild winters are known for few rainy days, especially along the Mediterranean coast. The famed mistral winds careen down the *Rhône Valley* and whip through the south throughout the year.

PEOPLE

With around 61 million people, modern metropolitan France has a diverse European population; about 10 percent of French citizens are foreign born. The largest groups of immigrants are Arabs, Africans, and Indo-Chinese from the former French colonies, as well as Portuguese, Spanish, Italian, Turkish, German, British, Belgian, and Polish.

About 100,000 Americans and 60,000 Canadians live in France. Approximately 50 percent reside in **Paris,** and of the other 50 percent, most have taken up residence in *Provence* and along the *Côte d'Azur.* Remaining expats are scattered in various parts of the country, including *Normandy, Brittany, the Dordogne, Burgundy,* and in the *Languedoc-Roussillon.*

HISTORY AND GOVERNMENT

The Celts arrived from central Europe and inhabited ancient Gaul, modern France, in 600 BC. Julius Caesar came, saw, and finished the job of conquering the Celtic tribes. Eastern Germanic tribes—the Franks among them—eventually toppled the Roman Empire. As Christianity later became dominant, France grew from a feudal society into a proper nation—rich, artistically innovative, and ruled by divine-right kings.

The French monarchy reached its peak under Louis XIV, the Sun King, who built Versailles. In 1789 the French people rebelled against royal excess, and the French Revolution climaxed with the beheading of Louis XVI, Marie Antoinette, and legions of aristocrats. Soon afterward Napoleón Bonaparte rose to power, conquered most of continental Europe and crowned himself emperor. Bonaparte was defeated at Waterloo in 1815. France remained the second-largest global colonial empire after Britain throughout the nineteenth and early twentieth centuries.

World Wars I and II were both fought on French soil, and though the allies were victorious during the first, France was devastated. During the second, France was partially occupied by the Nazis. The Free French under Charles de Gaulle joined the Allies and liberated **Paris,** but World War II left deep scars on the country. By the 1960s, with its colonies released, France's élan returned (though not without a burst of revolutionary fervor during 1968). Today France is a founding member of the European Union, has traded in the franc for the euro, and, despite debates over its generous if costly welfare system, is among the world's most prosperous countries. A new president, Nicolas Sarkozy, elected in 2007, promised a warming in the always fractious Franco-American political relationship. (See "Social Customs.")

WHERE TO LIVE

Americans are scattered throughout France; *where* depends, of course, on the landscape and experience they want, the region or village that catches their fancy. One couple recently bought a house in *Champagne,* romantically, in the village where they'd met thirty years before. Some choose *Normandy* or *Brittany* for the cooler weather and proximity to **Paris**. Others prefer *Burgundy* for its emphasis on living the good life, gastronomy, and impressive wines.

It is difficult to pinpoint places that are specific retirement destinations, because in France, Americans do not necessarily seek out other Americans. Especially in *Provence,* where probably half the American expats live. Said one former Arkansas resident, "We're not like the British. We don't travel in packs." She adds that in some of the less-known regions, Americans do not socialize with other Americans or encourage their countrymen to move there. That is why they moved in the first place.

Americans are to be found mostly in:

Paris: With a little more than 2 million inhabitants and another 10 million in its metropolitan area, **Paris** is the most visited city on earth—vibrant, diverse, sophisticated. Grand monuments and wide boulevards characterize some parts, while others are laced with narrow cobbled streets and small parks. The city's superb architecture, its shaded sidewalks, splendid churches, and fanciful shops and markets make it one of the world's finest walking cities. A leader in business, fashion, arts, and politics, **Paris** is a luxurious international hub with all the accoutrements.

Provence and the *Côte d'Azur:* In this ritziest corner of southeastern France, the regions of *Provence,* the Alps, and the *Côte d'Azur* lie along the Mediterranean Sea, bronzed and relaxed. Fashionable **Nice** and **Cannes,** glamorous **Saint-Tropez** and **Antibes,** and scores of smaller though equally chic villages dot the splendid coastline. Inland, *Provence*'s rocky mountains, olive groves, and bright fields of sunflowers and lavender crowd the canvasses of the world's greatest artists, who came to capture the area's astonishing light. If **Paris** is the heart of France, then *Provence,* with its inimitable landscape, Roman ruins, medieval fortresses, and array of cultural activities, is its soul.

AMBIENCE

Paris: The City of Light has separate worlds, each with a distinctive atmosphere, in its many neighborhoods (*quartiers*). A multitude of arts offerings—exhibitions, concerts, opera, dance, theater—stretch across the city in museums and other institutions, performance venues, parks, churches, and little clubs. The American Library in Paris is the English-language book lender, and several good English-language bookstores are scattered about the city. All offer literary events.

Though expats in France most often emphasize that they are there to live among the French, not to stick to their own, the desire for comradeship in one's own language or culture is universal. But with such a diversified Parisian population, friendships are struck with a wide array of nationalities. Language fluency isn't necessary, but it makes life easier and opens the door to French friends.

Provence and the *Côte d'Azur:* In *Provence,* life is slower, and people take the time to smell the lavender, or while away an afternoon with a long lunch or a game of *pétanque.* Summer offers a myriad of arts festivals scattered throughout the region, and there is a permanent roster of museums, galleries, concerts, presentations, and productions. Sports clubs are available everywhere, and hiking is terrific. There aren't any expat retirement communities per se but, again, English speakers will find a lot of company. There are nearly 500,000 Britons who own second homes in France, and resources for them abound. Several English-language weekly and monthly publications cover the south. Riviera Radio broadcasts in English. Because of the heavy tourism here, English is widely spoken.

Provence has been gentrified, but life there can still be celebrated in simple pleasures—food, wine, nature. Note: half of the businesses in tourist villages shut down in winter after the season is over. They reopen again in spring.

STANDARD OF LIVING

France has the sixth-largest economy in the world. There is a solid, rising middle class; money and its accompaniments are as French as apple *tarte.* Nevertheless, cracks in the prosperous fissures are apparent in the ethnically concentrated suburbs just outside **Paris.** There, poverty and a high unemployment rate frustrate and disaffect French-born children of immigrants who've lived in this country their entire lives. Immigration, integration, and French identity are hot political topics in France.

Comparing the American and French standards of living, cultural differences come into play. Despite criticisms by politicians about the French work ethic—their working week is thirty-five hours; everybody has a vacation of at least one month—France's social insurance system is notably humane. The public at large is protected against catastrophic effects of poor health or out-of-control medical bills. (See "Health Care/Medical.")

"The standard of living is high for everyone because of free health care and education," wrote Adrian Leeds, owner of Parler Paris (www .parlerparis.com), another information gateway for expats who are thinking of moving to France (see "Resources"), "all thanks to high taxes and a social democracy. There is not as much difference between the rich and poor here."

Paris: Americans live in tiny apartments or take over whole floors, depending on their financial resources. The European concept of space is different from that of Americans. Parisians are used to living in small places and live more of their lives on the street. It's **Paris,** after all, and the café society is also a big part of what expats come to get. If Americans downscale, some find it difficult to adjust to more cramped quarters, while others find the minimalist zen liberating. (See "Real Estate.")

Provence and the *Côte d'Azur:* Some expats find dreamy old country houses (*mas*) already renovated or do the work themselves; a huge number of them write books about it. Those who want to be part of village life and walk down the street to cafés and weekly markets buy houses or apartments in any number of charming communities. *Riviera* city apartments are the choice for those who desire urban amenities, sunny days, and the sea on their doorsteps.

CULTURE

Bonanza! **Paris** has it all, in abundance, whether fine arts, music, opera, dance, museums, or theater. No city compares with it.

Of course, Paris largely shuts down in the summer, and that is when *Provence* shines. While tourism is booming and second-home owners are in residence, every city and village in *Provence* has festivals and spectacles scheduled. Just about anything you can think of is a cause for celebration in summertime France. Music floats through vineyards and châteaus; food and wine are ballyhooed. Other seasons aren't devoid of events, but lusty summer is the queen of arts here. *Provence*'s multitude of art galleries and good museums are open year round, many worth *un détour* on their own, since so many artists lived in the region.

What the French call *artisanal* products are a part of their cultural heritage. The *Auvergne,* including **Laguiole,** is the home territory of artisan cutlery makers. **Dieulefit** and **Moustiers** produce handsome pottery. **Vallauris**'s art scene was indelibly stamped by its most famous resident, Pablo Picasso. **Brittany**'s Quimper is another famous variety, and, of course, the porcelain at **Limoges** and **Gien** is internationally coveted. Lavender and its products are also well-known Provencal handicrafts as well as herbal soaps and other bath products. Elegant and wildly colorful table linens are found in nicer shops wherever tourists go, and exquisite French papers line the shelves of **Paris** (and many other towns) stationery and art supplies shops. A chichi group of perfumers also have fabulous Parisian boutiques.

Artisan producers of truffles (**Provence** and **Périgord**), foie gras (especially **Périgord**), pâtés, and thousands of varieties of cheeses, sausages, olive oils, candies, and chocolates abound. Wine, cider, champagne and other sparkling wines, along with cognacs, Armagnacs, Calvados, eau-de-vie, and pastis (**Marseille**) are sold everywhere.

Good food and wine are gifts of the gods in France. Today you see people munching sandwiches or pastries walking down the street when time is short, though some French consider this ill-mannered. Fast-food chains exist—including Quick, McDonald's, Pizza Hut, and Kentucky Fried Chicken—but even they offer menus with courses. A bottle of water is OK to carry along, but the French think go-cups are bizarre. Why would anyone drink coffee on the run?

Dinner begins earlier in the country, but in **Paris,** crowds start between eight-thirty and nine. Meals can last for hours anywhere in France, and unless you're in a formal venue, they're apt to be lively occasions.

LEISURE

Travel, sightseeing, and museum-going are not just tourist pastimes but everyday resident pleasures. North American expats take up photography, book clubs, bridge games, poker, gardening, hiking, tennis, boating, dance classes, cycling, and soccer, and, in the Midi (the south), a fine French substitute for shuffleboard, pétanque. France is also known for the Tour de France, whose doping scandals are as famous as its uphill climbs, and for the 24 Hours of Le Mans sports-car endurance race.

In **Provence** and the **Côte d'Azur,** expats describe their friends as multinational, including the local French—if you speak French. People get together for events and often have friends over or go out for aperitifs. There are places that have exclusive expat cocktail circuits, although many want no part of it. Dinners at home on the terrace or at intimate restaurants (including those with well-known chefs) are part of the lifestyle. More modestly priced plates can be found, but dining out adds up in France.

Both regions are highly gay friendly. "The cuter the town," one expat reports, "the more gay men live there."

SOCIAL CUSTOMS

During the last few years, the French have gotten a bad rap in the U.S. Americans were *not* treated shoddily in France when, during the run-up to the Iraq war, American airwaves and editorials were full of xenophobic rants against France and French fries. France and the U.S., of course, have had friendly relations for centuries, and the French seem to know this more than Americans do. Older French persons readily say they're grateful for the American liberation of their country in World War II.

The French may have loathed George W. Bush and his policies, but generally speaking, they avoid lumping in American residents and tourists with unpopular administrations. Says expat Mary Whitfield de Vachon, "Ah, the French may gripe about us, but deep down they like us."

As far as issues and leaders go, the French will tell you that their country has its own problems. The young and disaffected French are outspoken about their disapproval of the role America has played in the world in recent years, but their harshest criticism is often for their own country. What is true: the French respect and love their culture, and want to protect their country from being completely overtaken and homogenized by American popular culture. Also true: a lot of the criticism for the French boils down to their "service" attitude, which is not the "the customer is always right" and delivered-with-a-smile American variety. Even the French would like their countrymen to provide better service without the haughty disinterest that sometimes is offered.

Jerks can be found anywhere, including France, but many longtime expats will say they're the exception rather than the rule. Despite campaigns to improve French attitudes toward tourists, longtime expats will say that the French are generally hospitable and generous, and can be enormously friendly, if more formal than Americans. Friendliness, respect for the culture, and trying to say a few French words go a long way as social lubricants. Knowing the French code of manners (For example, it's correct to say "Bonjour, madame" or "Bonjour, monsieur" rather than just "Bonjour") is a valuable tool, especially as a resident.

Dress in **Paris** has become much more informal, though style is in **Paris**'s DNA, and the perfectly dressed and coiffed Parisian woman can still be seen on city boulevards and in village squares. Comfort is a consideration these days everywhere, although it's common to see a French woman pushing a stroller while clacking down the street in high heels and a fabulously sexy dress.

France can be a haven for single women, expat women report. "There's

a civility about France," Karen Fawcett offered. "Old people are not thro
out the window. A woman alone is respected. France is liberated as far as
a woman alone goes."

HEALTH CARE/MEDICAL

French health care has been ranked number one in the world by the World
Health Organization for the last decade. The French medical insurance system, or Sécurité Sociale, is available to every citizen, for which they contribute a little more than 20 percent of their salaries.

To be eligible for the national medical coverage in France, an expat
needs to prove legal residency, which would be with a *carte de séjour* (temporary permit) or *carte de resident* (residency permit). When an American
comes to live in France, he must show proof of his own U.S. or international
insurance (but only short-term) before obtaining a residency permit. A
number of American companies offer this type of health insurance for
expatriates. After three months, you become eligible for coverage under the
French system—but must obtain a residence permit. After qualifying as a
resident (see "Residency and Red Tape"), you must pay for this national
insurance, as do French citizens, according to a sliding scale. Your contribution is determined by your income in the previous year (not current
earnings). If you retired in the U.S. with an income of $100,000 (in the year
before your move to France), but live in France on U.S. Social Security in
the current year, you would still pay $7,500 for basic health coverage in this
first year. After this initial period, all official residents (French or American) pay a 7.5 percent tax on their income from whatever source. (There
may be an additional premium for non–European Union foreigners.)

As a resident, you will be eligible for basic health coverage, which covers 70 percent of doctors' visits and 80 percent of hospital costs. However,
most residents (French and American) also opt to buy "complementary"
coverage, which pays the balance of medical costs, visits to specialists, and
better dental and eye care. Complementary health insurance is similar to
Medigap policies in the U.S. If you are not settling permanently in France
or will be traveling back and forth several times a year, international travel
insurance may be the best option.

RESIDENCY AND RED TAPE

For North Americans who plan to reside in France no more than three
months (ninety days) during a six-month period, it's easy: no visa is

this is considered a short stay. Three months on, three
problem.

European Union countries, France requires a carte de séjour
rmit) for visitors staying longer then three months. But U.S.
apply for these permits in the U.S. at the French consulate
diction over the state of their residence, and it must be done
before they move to France. No one, the law says, can change his or her status from a tourist to a resident while in France.

That said, many expats advise not bothering with a carte de séjour. They say French bureaucracy is a huge pain, and getting into the system has drawbacks. But does the system go to great lengths to check on how long someone stays in France? Not usually, say insiders. As long as expats are paying their way, contributing to the economy rather than relying on France's generous government benefits, there should be little problem. (Immigrants of lesser means are another matter.)

The carte de séjour is nevertheless a constant topic among expats, even among those who forego getting one. For those who prefer sticking to the letter of the law, there are several categories of carte de séjour. Fortunately, the long-stay kind that most retirees seek is manageable, if time consuming, to get.

Visa de long séjour: must be requested in the U.S. at a French consulate. This enables Americans to immigrate to France and, therefore, be issued the related immigration status—the carte de séjour—once they arrive in France.

Carte de séjour temporaire: most nonretired Americans are issued this immigration permit, which must be renewed every year. Proof of private medical insurance and financial means are among the requirements. The local *prefecture* demands yearly proof that you still comply with this.

Carte de séjour mention visiteur: the one most retirees get—if they get one. You are allowed to live, though not work, in France, if you have the financial means, have private comprehensive medical insurance coverage, have a place to live in France, and a clean police record. You will not belong to the French national health system with this.

Carte de resident (long-term residence permit): similar to an American Green Card, it grants permanent and complete right to live and work in France as well as the right to apply for the medical coverage of the Sécurité Sociale. Those who have lived here for at least five years can apply for the carte de resident. After many conditions are met—including French language skills and knowledge of French culture, proof of financial means, and more—and the applicant is approved, it is valid for ten years and is renewable.

Working

Do *not* think you can move to France and find a job, then change your visa status. Employment must be arranged ahead of time, approved by the French Ministry of Labor, and a long-stay work visa acquired before coming here. The French government *definitely* cares about this topic. Some people do work under the radar, but they're taking a big risk. Getting caught working without a permit can mean criminal sentencing, which is mostly impressive fines.

COST OF LIVING

Trying to give an idea of costs in a country as large, varied, and prosperous as France is an inexact science. The following financial estimates give an idea of what an expat's monthly expenses might be in three locations: **Paris,** the *Côte d'Azur,* and **Provence.** The figures are in euros, the exchange rate of which in 2008 was approximately $1.5 to €1, and will, of course, vary. So, a few snapshots:

Monthly Cost of Living in Paris
   Rent for a two-bedroom home, condo, or apartment: €2,000 to
      €3,000.
   Taxes: €50 to €300.
   Groceries for two: €200 to €600.
   Utilities: €75 to €300.
   TV, telephone, internet: €33.
   Annual TV tax: €115.
   Transportation: €20 to €80 for metro tickets and occasional
      taxis.
   Maid service: €160, or €10 an hour.
   Restaurants for two: €70.

Monthly Cost of Living in the Côte d'Azur
   Rent for a two-bedroom home, condo, or apartment: €800 to
      €1,400.
   Taxes: €250.
   Insurance: €60 (for around €100,000 coverage).
   Groceries for two: €300 to €600.
   Utilities: €80 to €300.
   TV, telephone, internet: €33.
   Annual TV tax: €115.

Transportation: €130 per bus trip; taxis more expensive; total cost for
  a car, €250.
Maid service: €76 to €288, or €11 to €18 an hour.
Restaurants for two: €70.

Monthly Cost of Living in Provence
Rent for a two-bedroom home, condo, or apartment: €800 to
  €1,200.
Taxes: €250.
Insurance: €60 (for around €100,000 coverage).
Groceries for two: €300 to €600.
Utilities: €80 to €300.
TV, telephone, internet: €33.
Annual TV tax: €115.
Transportation: Total cost for a car, €250.
Maid service: €192, or €12 an hour.
Restaurants for two: €70.

Car expenses are similar to those in the States, with lower gas mileage
offset by higher gas prices. Telephone expenses reflect a basic rate for telephone, television, and internet packages that include unlimited calls to
Europe and North America, which various companies offer. Cell phones,
about the same cost as in the U.S., are ubiquitous, and free Skype is becoming more common. TV, by the way, is taxed once a year.

REAL ESTATE

Foreigners can buy property anywhere in France. Mortgages are available
to residents and nonresidents alike and are generally low. One big difference for prospective American buyers is that there are no multiple listings,
so brokers have the incentive to sell the properties they represent. Real
estate agencies (*agence immobiliers*) abound, which means there are a multitude of contacts to make for a property search, though the internet saves
prospective buyers time and trouble, and property consultants will search
for apartments, help with loans, and manage purchases for a fee.

No one, it seems, comes to France to build a new house. "They want old,
old, old," wrote Adrian Leeds of Parler Paris. "They almost always renovate."

Paris: The price of property is at an all-time high and growing. Depending on the *arrondissement* (neighborhood), apartment averages per square
meter range from €4,500 in the nineteenth arrondissement to €8,500 in
the sixth (mid-2007). The annual appreciation has been 9.9 percent. The

sixth is one of the most popular American neighborhoods, probably owing to the Lost Generation mystique of onetime **Paris** residents Ernest Hemingway and Gertrude Stein. The percentage of nonresident foreigners buying property in **Paris** is growing, and there are unofficial reports of up to €10,000 to €12,000 a square meter in the trendy *Marais* (the third) and up to €20,000 on the *Île Saint-Louis* (the fourth). Other central historic areas are also highly prized.

Provence and the *Côte d'Azur:* British writer Peter Mayle ruined the real estate market for everyone when he wrote *A Year in Provence* and popularized the area. The British started buying up houses and properties en masse, sometimes acquiring virtually whole villages in some regions of France that they populated—and prices skyrocketed. Price estimates:

Villas and Houses
Coast, €3,900 to €8,900 per sq m   Average, €5,600
Inland, €2,200 to €5,800 per sq m   Average, €3,300

Apartments
Coast, €3,600 to €7,700 per sq m   Average, €4,800
Inland, €2,200 to €4,500 per sq m   Average, €3,000

TAXES

Before buying property in France, it's *imperative* to have good legal counsel in deciding how to set up ownership, which like everything else in French bureaucracy has complex implications—in this case, for inheritance issues and tax rates associated with them, which are designed as incentives for family property to remain within the family. But they can be worked through and solved. Briefly, spouses or partners aren't automatically considered legal heirs. French inheritance laws determine how property will be divided upon an owner's death—regardless of how he or she has spelled it out in wills or trusts.

Capital gains tax: Like all business in France, capital gains can be a tricky subject. Briefly, the tax rate on gains is 26 percent for French residents and 33.3 percent for owners of property who reside outside the EU. As in the United States, the principal private residence may be exempt, depending on the length of residence.

Property taxes: There are two principal taxes on residential property in France, the *taxe d'habitation* (residence tax) and the *taxe foncière* (real estate tax). A property owner must pay the taxe foncière, and the renter pays the taxe d'habitation. These taxes are assessed and determined in their locales, and rates can vary markedly, often higher in cities than small villages. "Taxes in **Nice** run over twenty percent," says resident Mary Whitfield de Vachon. "One of the most expensive spots in France."

Income tax: As for income tax issues related to Americans living in France, U.S. tax is based on an American's citizenship. France's tax is based on residency. But the U.S. has a treaty with France to avoid double taxation. This treaty permits offsetting one country's taxes against the other.

"Research health insurance, tax, and estate issues thoroughly," says Anne Woodyard, a food writer now living in the *Languedoc*. "You may *not* want France to be your principal residence."

TRANSPORTATION

Besides the international direct flights that serve **Paris, Marseille,** and **Nice,** a host of European airlines fly within France and the region. Plane fares in Europe used to be expensive. Now very cheap flights are available on easy-Jet, Ryanair, Blue Air, Wizz Air, Vueling Airlines, and others to destinations within Europe.

Trains run by the French rail system, SNCF, are comfortable (especially the high-speed TGV), and all seniors (over sixty) get 25 percent to 50 percent ticket discounts within France and 25 percent off inter-European travel. The national highway system is excellent; major autoroutes charge tolls. The French drive fast, though not as insanely as Italians. Motorcycles are the biggest annoyance. The **Paris** metro is justifiably famous for its punctuality and cleanliness. In smaller villages and the *Provencal* countryside, a car is a necessity. Sure, it's possible to bring your car into France, but why? It's much easier to buy a car than to go through the process of making it legal, and perhaps paying taxes.

SECURITY

France is a safe place to live, and expats feel secure here. Pickpocketing and purse snatching are the most common variety of petty crimes, and they usually occur in cities or at major tourist attractions, though no more so than in other European countries. It's wise to leave tempting objects out of sight and lock the car if one is traveling anywhere in Europe, especially in cities. The crime rate is predictably far lower in rural areas than in the cities. The gendarmes (police) are generally helpful, honest, and nonthreatening.

COMMUNICATIONS AND MEDIA

France Telecom Orange is the national supplier of telephone lines. The company also sells cell phones and contracts, and packages of telephone, internet, and TV services. Broadband is available in many areas, especially where retirees usually head. Snail mail can be efficient, though packages sent overseas can be either fast or seemingly take forever. Be careful: the postal system asks you, absurdly, to declare what a package contains, so if you enclose something valuable, it may never arrive. Buy insurance, but prepare for a long wait for payouts.

In **Paris,** you can subscribe to various channels (TPS and Canal +) that show a lot of English-speaking movies; from time to time, there are French-purist crusades to limit the amount of English spoken on broadcasts. In rural areas, especially where there isn't a huge population of Anglophones, there may be fewer—or no—English TV channels broadcasting in English; you have to hook up to a satellite. In the right spots, satellites pick up British programming.

UP-AND-COMING AREAS

The *Dordogne* and *Le Lot,* with their wide, lazy rivers, fairy-tale villages, and Cinderella châteaus have drawn large numbers of English and Americans. But the real contender in the southwestern region is the *Languedoc-Roussillon,* the curl of Mediterranean coast that begins west of **Marseille** in the salty plains of the *Petite Camargue* and stretches to the Pyrenees and the border with Spain. The region includes *Provence, Alpes-Maritimes, Côte d'Azur, Rhône-Alpes, Auvergne, Midi-Pyrenees, Gard, Herault, Lozère, Aude,* and *Pyrenees-Orientales.*

Provence was once part of the old province of *Languedoc,* the land where the Occitan language (the *langue d'oc*) was spoken, and Occitan is one of the major *Languedoc-Roussillon* influences. It is a land of rocky, craggy hills, silvery olive trees, and vineyards—seven hundred thousand acres of them. These delicious wines are not as legendary as *Bordeaux* and *Burgundy,* but they are becoming better known and appreciated. The *Languedoc*'s landscape is not as beautiful as *Provence,* its markets not as luscious. But it has other advantages; for instance, its coastline isn't stamped with villa and apartment sprawl (except for *La Grande Motte*). When tourists do descend during August, there are

247

nd off-the-beaten-track villages that provide a means

)ccitan *Languedoc-Roussillon* starts near Vincent
loops up and around to include **Nîmes,** with its
monuments, and the graceful village of Uzes. Far-
is **Montpellier,** thriving, diverse, and architecturally elegant.
ere, and in the surrounding fields and vineyards, are to be found a
growing number of English speakers.

The Canal du Midi, the most famous inland waterway of France,
snakes through the countryside from the vibrant city of **Toulouse** to
the *Languedoc* seaside villages of **Agde** and **Sète.** It goes by the extraordinary citadel of **Carcassonne** and becomes an aqueduct through
the town of **Beziers. Toulouse** may not technically be in the *Languedoc,* but it's the commercial and cultural center in the west of the *Aude*
department. Like **Montpellier,** expats are enthusiastic about **Toulouse**
and its surroundings. Sleepy **Albi,** a town of about 65,000 people
northeast of **Toulouse,** is one such destination. This is another good
area to look for a home, though the scenery isn't as striking as the more
storied retirement locales.

The *Languedoc* has historically been remote. It's a long way from
Paris, though the high-speed TGV now stops in **Montpellier.** The
Pyrenees have always proven a natural barrier and ensured isolation,
which is a plus for the region's residents who don't want their lovely
hideaway spoiled. It's not gentrified—yet. The farther inland you go,
the more prices drop, especially in the isolated mountains that take
your breath away.

The region isn't completely undiscovered. The British have moved
in, and the Dutch, Scandinavians, and other nationalities also have a
presence. Americans are here in less evidence. Says one American,
"The English speakers do band together—in good spirits. The local
population is welcoming, as long as you are respectful of their culture
and can speak some French. Nobody likes the loud, boring expats!"

Like *Provence* and anywhere else in France, more than half the
shops, restaurants, and hotels in the country and coastal tourist towns
close for winter. Some people like this quiet time of year better, but little happens then. It's about a two-hour drive to **Montpellier** and a little longer to **Toulouse** to get a city fix.

Montpellier: Another hot up-and-comer, **Montpellier** is a dynamic city with a famous university, thousands of students, an exciting range of arts offerings, festivals, and good museums. The city's energy feels young and alive, while the classical architecture affords visual grace. The old town has a sophisticated mix of trendy shops and fine ethnic restaurants, reflecting the diverse population. Many refugees from the Algerian war—French as well as North African—moved here after the conflict ended in 1962. Long, sandy beaches are very close, and the region abounds with vineyards and beautiful old manor houses. The small airport is convenient, as is public transportation. Property prices have risen 25 percent in the last five years in and outside of **Montpellier**, and they continue to go up as the *Herault* becomes increasingly popular. But they're still a lot cheaper than *Provence* or **Paris**.

Montpellier Area Apartment Rent: €600 to €1,200.

Property Prices:
An apartment in a classical building in the center of **Montpellier**, €3,000 per sq m.
A terraced village house in the area, €2,000 per sq m.
A farmhouse inland in the mountains, €2,000 per sq m.

Perpignan: Perpignan isn't as big or as fashionable as **Montpellier**, but it has a smaller, stylish old town with cool shops, bars, and restaurants, lovely monuments, and busy town squares. Catalan culture is widely felt here. The sphere of small bijou villages around **Perpignan** is a nonstop source of entertaining festivals and sightseeing opportunities. It has a small airport serving inexpensive airlines. You definitely need a car.

Perpignan Area Rent: €400 to €1,100.

Property Prices: €1,500 to €1,905 per sq m.

Côte Vermeille: The *Côte Vermeille* below **Perpignan** has a wonderful corniche and a string of picturesque villages. **Collioure** is the most famous, with its gaily colored fisherman's houses, gentle harbor, and a profusion of shops. It's also the most sought after and highly priced. Matisse and Derain began the Fauvist movement here, and it retains its roots with a thriving community of artists and galleries. (There is one scenic vantage point in **Collioure** that they *all* paint.) Winter population is 3,000 to 4,000, while the summer population is 30,000 to 40,000 plus day-trippers. It can be crowded and tight.

Argelès-Plage has a wonderful, long, wide, sandy beach, a rarity along much of the Mediterranean. It lacks **Argelès's** loveliness but has a quiet and charm of its own. **Port Vendres** and **Banyuls** are on the coast between **Collioure** and the Spanish border, real working towns without the tourism, their shops and restaurants serving the locals year round. **Port Vendres** is a port town, and **Banyuls**, known for its namesake wine, has a charming main street by the sea. The road from there leads to the *Costa Brava,* as it's known beyond the Spanish border, and then to **Barcelona**. It's a beautiful, sometimes frightening drive. For those who live along this coast, shopping for staples is done in **Perpignan**, or across the border in Spain, where prices are cheaper. Air travelers arrive via **Perpignan's** small airport, or at **Girona**, in Spain. Again, a car is a must.

Côte Vermeille Rent: €750 to €1,200 a month.

Property Prices:
   Argelès: €2,500 per sq m.
   Collioure: €4,100 per sq m.
   Port Vendres: €2,500 per sq m.
   Banyuls: €3,000 per sq m.

Toulouse: Toulouse is one of the largest cities in France, known as *La Ville Rose* because the bricks of the Italianate mansions and other buildings go through a chameleon-like transformation to pink, orange, and red as the light changes throughout the day. The *Place du Capitole* simply shimmers with elegance, and, like **Montpellier**, Toulouse is brimming with university students who give a vibrant feel to the city. It is also the center of the French aeronautics business. As in **Montpellier**, there are trendy shops and restaurants to visit, museums to see, and fine antiques to buy. The arts are an important part of the city's life.

Public transportation is good. The **Toulouse** airport is close, and the city is a major rail center.

Toulouse Area Rent: €600 to €1,150; up to €2,100 for a large
   country house.

Property Prices:
In the best neighborhoods, such as *La Côte-Pavée, Le Busca,* or *Minimes,* homes can be €400,000 or more, and over €250,000 in areas like *Le Mirail.* Apartments range from around €150,000 in the modest **Albi** suburb to €270,000 in **Toulouse** proper.

VOLUNTEERING WITHOUT BORDERS

France has such a strong social welfare system that the kinds of volunteer organizations common in the U.S. are not here. And problems arise if the volunteer activities could be interpreted as depriving someone else of paid employment. But if you are willing to volunteer and speak French, many more opportunities exist.

Some foreign residents have created opportunities by volunteering within their own expat communities. For example:

- WICE is a nonprofit, volunteer-based association that provides cultural and educational programs and services for the international community in **Paris** (www.wice-Paris.org).
- The American Cathedral in **Paris** welcomes anyone (even tourists) to help at the Friday lunch for the homeless. It also has a Love in a Box program, which provides holiday gifts for needy children (www.americancathedral.org).
- The American Church in **Paris** has a wide-ranging number of social action and service opportunities by providing volunteers to partner organizations (www.acparis.org).
- International Habitat for Humanity and France's Habitat et Humanisme have joined forces to combat poverty-level housing in France and around the world (www.habitat-humanisme.org).
- The Association of Americans Resident Overseas (AARO) welcomes expats who wish to reinvent their lives abroad by sharing their interests and activities (www.aaro.org).

Beth Arnold is an award-winning writer who has lived happily in France for the last five years. A member of the Association of American Residents Overseas, she wondrously calls **Paris** *home.*

MY FRANCE

A Boston Couple Who Eat
Five-hour Dinners in Provence

Name, age, origin: Karen Fawcett and Victor Kramer, fifty-nine and seventy-nine, Boston.

Where we live: Apartment in **Paris**, a house in *Provence*.

How long in France: Twenty-one years.

Present occupations: Own and run BonjourParis.com, about life in France.

Reasons for moving here: Victor had a job here; I fell in love with the diversity of France's culture. The U.S. is too vanilla, small minded. I was also nervous about the U.S. government and the Christian right.

Finances: Well, they were fabulous when we first got here! Today, I'm not sure I'd retire here on dollar income. We live on a small trust and investment income, plus real estate income that I've managed. If you have kids, you should have enough to bring them here or fly over there.

Having said that, there are ways of living here nicely. You can still find a house for 20 percent of the price of houses in the expensive parts of the U.S.—New York and Connecticut. Did you know the price of baguettes and coffee are fixed?

Leisure: The time frame. We tend to spend time eating five-hour dinners. It can take twenty minutes to buy a newspaper, stopping and chatting with everyone. Pastis at eleven at night. Stay up till two in the morning talking. Concerts, movies, clubs.

Wish we'd known before: Besides better language skills—not much. You can overresearch this. You can know too much.

Best: The quality of life here is *so* much better. Americans who want to retire here don't come just because of the cheap wine and the sun. They love the culture. They don't sit around. Did you know you can get a card that gets you into every museum in the world? And France really does respect age. Old people are not thrown out the window. France is liberated, too: a woman alone is respected.

Happiest when: Dealing with all the perspectives and cultures that France embodies. In D.C., where I stayed with the same people, I had to look for it.

What we miss most: Family. Cheap fares.

Expected to miss but didn't: Size 10½ shoes.

MY FRANCE

A Gentleman Farmer with Family Who Can't Retire

Name, age, origin: David Fries, sixty, from a farm in Pennsylvania.

Where we live: In the northern rural part of France. Beautiful rolling hills, extravagantly lush greenery, good cheap wine, extremely civilized citizenry, over-rated restaurants, dazzling architecture, endlessly fascinating cities and towns, lots and lots of cows.

Reasons for moving here: I first started spending time in Europe in the 1960s, and I don't recall ever allowing more than a year or two to pass between visits, many of which were extended. Starting in 2001, most of our extended visits were to France. My wife, June, our three daughters, and I finally decided just to stay, if only to avoid the disruption travel caused.

Finances: I freelance in the publishing industry. One of the unforeseen difficulties of starting a family late is a lack of predictability. With three children all still in school, retirement much before seventy or so isn't an option, and unexpected draws on our resources are common.

Costs: Figure suburban Los Angeles or Connecticut, then add 50 percent.

Weather: Summer in France in the north is quite English. In the south, it's quite hellish. Winter in the south is quite temperate. Winter in the north is still quite English.

Leisure: We like museum hopping and city exploring. The children often play in pickup soccer games and the like. Walking French country lanes is a daily ritual.

Health care/medical: Extraordinarily good.

Residency and visas: Can be quite a nightmare, if you try to do it by the book. Trying to work with French consular officials in the States before you come, as the law states, is a pain. Many French consulates simply cease answering their telephones in the summer and restrict their hours in the winter. As a result, the limits put on tourist visas are often widely ignored. It is highly unlikely that an American violating the terms of a tourist visa will get in much trouble. The French are a practical people, and their government does not see American tourists as a national threat. In fact, they spend a lot of money convincing Yanks to come visit—money that might be better spent augmenting their visa offices abroad.

Locals' attitudes toward Americans: Especially in small, rural villages, Americans are still a kind of novelty. There is no overt anti-Americanism; that's reserved for Parisian politicians anxious to make a headline or two. In even the smallest hamlet, there are vestiges of American culture: brands, celebrities, ad slogans, jackets, jeans. Americans will notice that even the poorest Frenchman will dress as well as he can and observe proper etiquette in greeting others, especially on entering a room or shop. Americans can do themselves a service by skipping T-shirts and low-riding blue jeans and dressing as though they are employed.

Common misperceptions: The biggest misperception about France is the notion that the government and its policies reflect the sentiment of the general population. There is an almost complete disconnect in France between the ruling class and those who are governed. In fact, the best way to get a perfect Gallic shrug is to ask about taxation or foreign policy. Most French people do their best to disregard both.

Best: There really is a distinctly French style of living—rather like a serious version of Italy, with all the plusses and minuses that suggests. It's also almost overwhelmingly middle class, with a very strong conformist tradition.

There are a lot of "best things" that happen to anyone visiting France, and almost all of them involve interaction with everyday French citizens, many of whom will go to great lengths to help a visitor, especially one who at least attempts to speak French. Even in **Paris,** as famous for incivility as Manhattan, the prevailing sentiment is one of understated politesse. Everywhere you go, manners matter—except on the roads, where suddenly a dark side of the French psyche is revealed.

Happiest when: Sitting in a café, sipping a coffee, reading a paper, and commenting on passersby with my lovely wife.

What we miss most: Everyday doses of Fox News and Bart Simpson.

MY FRANCE

A Single Woman in Sunny Nice

Name, age, origin: Mary Whitfield de Vachon, sixty, Harlan, Kentucky.

Where I live: An apartment in **Nice**, which I own.

How long in France: Twenty-nine years.

Reasons for moving here: I married a Frenchman.

Finances: Not much. I live on the income of my personal investments. I have no pension either in France or the U.S. I do not feel "retired." I still struggle.

Costs: Expensive! The young French can no longer afford to live in town. Rich foreigners buy the villas and apartments at any price. Groceries cost a lot more since the dollar fell against the euro. But I can still find nice restaurants for €15 for an enormous plate of antipasto.

My community: I live on a major street in what used to be the "working section" of town but is becoming increasingly chic. It has its own neighborhood markets. Everything I need is within a few blocks. When I walk by with my dog, storekeepers speak to me. My dog and I walk to the port of **Nice** in less than ten minutes and can be at the beach in about twenty minutes. I live by myself. I am still quite agile. Hope this lasts. My close friends in **Nice** are French. But I am an active member of the Anglican Church in Monaco, so I am constantly with English speakers; mostly British there, although there are a handful of Americans. I am totally integrated with both communities.

Weather: Sun and warmth most of the year. When it rains, the Nicois stay home until it stops and usually are in a bad humor.

Leisure: Swimming in the Mediterranean, cultural outings with a group, weekly bridge with French friends, the ballet in **Monte Carlo,** symphony, museums.

Health care/medical: A problem if you are not in the French system.

Wish I'd known before: Well, I am divorced from my French husband.

Drawbacks: The can't-do mentality rather than find a solution. The lack of initiative. The bureaucracy. I cringe whenever I have to deal with anything administrative. Papers, papers, papers.

...unteering is not especially in the French mentality, ...ding. You can find this through American associations.

...llar so low against the euro, I think I could live bet- ...now but obviously health care there would be a worry. ...way for so long, I can no longer compare.

...My French family (even though I am divorced), my French friends, ...ny American and English friends, the beauty of the country, the climate.

Worst: Unmet expectations—namely a happily-ever-after ending to the fairy tale.

MY FRANCE

A Couple Who Found the "Other" South of France

Name, age, origin: Anne and Kirk, fifty-six and fifty-four, Woodyard, Reston, Virginia.

Previous/present occupation: Kirk, business capture consultant, founder of Music and Markets Tours (www.musicetc.us); Anne, formerly with a worldwide ministry organization, now pianist, music teacher, travel and food writer.

Reasons for moving here: France was an easy decision for us—not a stretch, mentally. We have lots of friends who have homes in France. The ease of flying here from the U.S. East Coast also entered into it. We had spent a lot of time in Europe and felt comfortable in France. We were originally looking for a rental investment, and chose the *Languedoc* because it was an up-and-coming area—not an already discovered one such as *Provence,* but still had the beaches and climate that would make it attractive both to us and to weekly renters. As we explored villages within the circle we had drawn in the south of France, we ended up finding a lovely village house that we fell in love with.

Our community: The *Languedoc* is the "other" south of France. Similar in climate to more-known *Provence,* miles of sandy beaches, just a few hours' drive to Spain. *Provence* makes for easy day trips. Beautiful cathedral towns and historic villages nearby. The most wine production of any region of France, with quality getting better. We enjoy visiting vineyards.

Typical day: Listening for the morning bells and the *"Ça va?" "Ça va!"* of villagers walking down our lane. Shopping for daily meals is always a pleasure. Market day in our town is twice a week, and that's always a special treat. If it's warm enough, we'll eat all of our meals in the flowery courtyard—just love that place! Go to the beach for a while, walk along the Canal du Midi, explore a new spot in the area, or visit an old favorite.

Common misperceptions: We did a lot of research before buying our place and visited the village at all times of the day and week. So there have not been unpleasant surprises: we *expect* things to be different. A common misperception is about French rudeness: well, folks in our area are very friendly and welcoming and helpful.

Best: The groove of weekly rhythms; the oft-mentioned, and very true, *qualité de la vie* (quality of life)!

Worst: Cold in the winter; no central heating, and since it's more a summer fun area, no fireplace. The old stone house takes a *long* time to warm up when we arrive!

Advice: Avoid getting so involved in an expat community that you miss out on the "Frenchness" of life and company. Also, research health insurance, tax, and estate issues thoroughly—you may *not* want France to be your principal residence.

MY FRANCE

A Couple Who Moved to a Chic Mediterranean Fishing Port

Name, age, origin: Cynthia and Ian Gillespie-Smith, sixty-one and sixty-nine, Maryland.

Where we live: Bandol, a town near **Toulon.**

How long in France: Sixteen years.

Previous/present occupations: Photographer/photo editor/photo workshop director. I continue to photograph but no longer run workshops.

Reasons for moving here: Since my first trip to Europe when I was nineteen, I have been a passionate Francophile. The language, the history, the art and architecture, the style of the people, and the sheer beauty of the country all inspire me.

Finances: Comfortable. Generally speaking, in this part of the country, you'd need perhaps €50,000 to €70,000 a year per couple. Could get by on less, but . . .

Costs: Dinner for two with wine would normally cost between €70 and €90 at a medium-priced restaurant, although at some of the best places, you could pay that much for the fish alone! Gasoline is about $8 a gallon, tolls on the autoroute are expensive, food in the markets is expensive. In part this is because the dollar is so weak, but Europeans spend a lot of their income in order to live well. Thankfully, excellent wine and cheese are generally less expensive here than in the U.S.

Our community: Bandol is a pretty town of 8,000 on the Mediterranean coast. (Until recently we lived in the *Luberon* part of *Provence,* but made our move to the coast this year. An excellent move for us.) It's still a fishing port, but the main industry is probably tourism or the fine **Bandol** wines. Within a five-minute walk of our apartment, we have every service imaginable: gourmet shops, caterers, wine shops, cafés and restaurants, hair salons, the post office, veterinarians, dry cleaners, and the daily outdoor food and flower markets.

Weather: Sunny 320 days of the year, we are told. Warm into December, and spring comes in early April. It can be quite windy, however.

Leisure: Ian joined the tennis club and plays frequently. We also have a sailing club that rents different types of boats. We belong to the BLC (Bandol Loisirs et Culture), which offers many cultural activities, including bridge, hiking, cooking, computer help, and so much more. **Bandol** also has a cultural center with activities, including free French lessons.

Typical day: Breakfast in the sunshine, a hike, a lovely lunch, a chance to play the piano, time to read or make some nice pictures, a chat with friends, a lovely bottle of wine and dinner.

Health care/medical: Considering quality and cost, the health care system in France is probably the best in the world. (This statement is based on surveys I've seen, not only my opinion.) Contrary to what many Americans have been told, there is not a long waiting period for health care in France as there can be in many other countries with socialized medicine. I can normally get an appointment within a few days or a week. For a specialist, I might expect to wait a few weeks, although if you explain that there is a special problem or that you are going away, often you can be slipped in more quickly. We've never been hospitalized in France, but we have many friends who were completely satisfied with their treatment in French hospitals.

Residency and visas: I got my first residency card in 1993, and it was difficult enough. Today it may be even worse. As usual, just when you think you've produced every scrap of paper necessary, some bright bureaucrat will think of something else. It takes a long time to acquire whatever you are after, from a driver's license to a name change at the bank. One just gets used to it.

Other expats: There are not many expats in **Bandol,** and most are European. The local people are polite, helpful, and friendly. In a few months, we've met a lot of people and have been welcomed into several homes. Most of the people we've met are sophisticated, curious, well traveled, and happy.

Crime, corruption: There is a lot of theft in the Mediterranean area. Purses and cameras are snatched from under tables and off chairs. Cars and houses are broken into. Personal safety is much less of an issue than in the States, but people need to be aware.

Common misperceptions: That the French are rude. I am not sure how this got started, but in sixteen years in France, I have seen very, very few rude French people. My experience is that with certain exceptions in large cities (probably from tolerating too many rude tourists), the French are among the most consistently polite people I've met.

Best: The physical beauty of the country, the style and elegance of the large cities, and most of the French people. In **Bandol** we appreciate the multitude of activities and the ease with which we can pursue them.

Worst: The bureaucracy and dog poop on the sidewalks.

Happiest when: With Ian in the sunshine in **Bandol.**

What we miss most: Hard-shell crabs.

Chapter 16

ITALY

La Dolce Vita

BY KATHY MCCABE

Fair Italy!
Thou art the garden of the world, the home
Of all Art yields, and Nature can decree.
—LORD BYRON

Long before Frances Mayes wrote her bestseller *Under the Tuscan Sun,* foreigners, particularly artists and writers, have been drawn to Italy by the
promise of *la dolce vita*—the fine, sweet life of lore. Some would even say that
the country, shaped like a gallant cavalier's boot and surrounded by a rocky,
tumultuous sea on three sides, is as well known for its famous expatriates—
Lord Byron, Elizabeth Barrett Browning, Robert Browning, Henry James,
Edith Wharton, George Eliot, Mark Twain, Charles Dickens, Gertrude Stein,
Mary McCarthy, Gore Vidal, and Jan Morris—as it is for its pasta.

Fortunately, Italy's hands-on approach to its rich, spirited past lends
the same texture and vibrancy to the daily lives of today's expats as it did
to those who came before. Like Byron, they walk through foggy Venetian
mornings, navigating la Serenissima's narrow, winding walkways, following the scent of espresso to their favorite local bar. They own villas nestled
in Tuscan vineyards where they raise and harvest their own grapes, sometimes stomping them into smooth liquid under a warm autumn sun, pour-
ing the sweet red wine from them for visitors throughout the year. They
rent cottages on the banks of *Lake Como,* houses in the countryside out-

side of **Naples,** small condos along the *Amalfi coast.* They swim and sail and smell the lemon trees. Whether in the shadow of the Alps or the now placid Mount Vesuvius, twenty-first-century expats are discovering once again the Italy they read about in the sonnets, the one they dreamed about from the first time they ate spaghetti in an Italian restaurant back home in Texas or Minnesota or New Jersey.

Italy retains its traditional roots within a highly modern state. So don't expect to get your morning cappuccino in a paper cup. Not in Italy, where daily rituals and a strong sense of community are reflected in the local bars; there workers gather to sip espresso out of thin white cups and chat about politics before heading off to the office. Slow down, expat, smell the coffee, think about lunch, about your *passagieta*—your predinner stroll. In Italy, as in France, food is lifestyle, and in all but the largest cities, most stores close for lunch and never stay open past dinner.

Italian writer and social commentator Luigi Barzini theorizes that many foreigners fall in love with Italy because they want to be free of the shackles of their own society. "In the heart of every man," he wrote, "there is one small corner which is Italian, that part that finds regimentation irksome, the dangers of war frightening, strict morality stifling, that part which loves frivolous and entertaining art, admires larger-than-life-size solidarity heroes, and dreams of an impossible liberation from the strictures of a tidy existence."

Such was the case for Lois Smith, who moved to **Verona** with her husband in 2005, and says, "My own country had come to seem inimical to my ideals, seemed to be on the wrong track. I wanted to experience something completely different, something I thought would be more simpatico with how I felt inside."

Still, if some American expatriates and Italians are not aligned with U.S. foreign policy, the ties between the Italian and the American people remain strong. With 1 in every 10 Americans boasting some Italian blood, and the memory of the allied soldiers who came to Italy's aid during World War II still vivid, the country continues to extend hospitality to bases of the U.S. Army (**Vicenza** and **Livorno**), Air Force (**Aviano**), and Navy (**Naples**) with their total population of 16,000 military personnel.

UPSIDES

1. The savoring of life; la dolce vita is vitally alive and well in Italy.
2. The sense of community and the noisy warmth of family life.

3. With three thousand museums and 60 percent of the world's art, Italy is culture heaven.
4. Good, affordable health care.
5. The mild Mediterranean weather.

DOWNSIDES

1. The dollar's fall against the euro makes Italy expensive.
2. The wheels of bureaucracy turn excruciatingly slowly.
3. You need to be in pretty good shape; Italy is not disabled-friendly.
4. Great Italian food, but little variety in ethnic dining.
5. Corruption: Italy does not get high marks from Transparency International.

LOCATION

Italy, its famous shape in the form of a boot, is flanked by the Tyrrhenian Sea on the west and the Adriatic Sea on the east, and is bounded by France, Switzerland, and Austria to its north. Sicily and Sardinia are the largest of its islands.

CLIMATE

Italy has mild Mediterranean weather south of Florence, while the northern regions (**Milan, Turin**) are more like continental Europe—cold and snowy in the winter, temperate the rest of the year.

PEOPLE

The Italian population, some 58 million, are fairly homogeneous. Eighty-five percent of Italian citizens are Catholic, but freedom of religion is guaranteed under the law. In the past decade, an influx of immigrants from Eastern Europe and Africa have made the population slightly more diverse. Italy has the fifth-highest population density in Europe. The country's birthrate is alarmingly low, and its population is aging rapidly: nearly 20 percent of Italy's citizens are over sixty-five, compared to 12 percent of the U.S. population.

Expats

Some 67,000 Americans live in Italy and can be found in every corner of the country, although **Rome, Florence,** *Tuscany,* **Umbria,** and *Campania* are among the most popular areas for expats to settle. There are no specific statistics on the number of American retirees living in Italy, but they definitely have a growing presence in the expat community.

HISTORY

Rome was founded on the seven hills. Caesar came, saw, and conquered, and the procession of emperors through the fifth century AD give Italy the most fabled history this side of Greece. The history of modern times, including the creation of the world's first fascist state under Benito Mussolini, is less glorious. Despite the centuries of empire and conquest, today's Italy is a relatively new country, unifying only in 1861. Therefore Italians, especially those who are older, feel more allegiance to their home city or region—twenty in all—than to the national state. There is a large disparity in economic prosperity between the predominantly industrial north and the rural south; long-standing prejudices against southerners still fester.

GOVERNMENT

Italians might have pride in their nation, but that does not necessarily extend to their government. Since the end of World War II, Italy's parliamentary majorities have changed with dizzying speed, its parade of presidents ushered in and out of revolving doors. Though Italy has had a large bloc of working-class Communist voters, it is the Christian Democratic Party that has dominated the landscape. History, corruption, and the constant turnovers in leadership have led Italians to generally mistrust the government.

WHERE TO LIVE

Tuscany is the area that immediately comes to mind when Americans dream of moving to Italy. As the birthplace of the Renaissance (**Florence** in particular) and home to enchanting medieval cities such as **Siena, San Gimignano,** and **Pisa,** *Toscana* is one of the most celebrated regions of Italy, and its popularity has now made it one of the most prosperous—and

expensive. Tourists and expats alike are drawn to its olive groves and world-famous vineyards. Stringent building rules (in *Chianti,* for instance, new building is not allowed; only an existing structure can be refurbished) have left *Tuscany*'s undulating green hills unspoiled, but real estate at a large premium.

Yes, real estate prices have gone through the tile roof; a renovated home in *Chianti* is unthinkable for less than a half million euros, and that's for a small house, if you can find one. You're more likely to be spending €1 million and up. John Rennie of the property website KeyItaly.com, says, "*Tuscany* has never been a struggling rural economy, but, rather, a very successful and affluent one, as you realize when you gaze at vineyards and olive groves that date back hundreds of years. It means you *don't* have to rough it. There will always be a good restaurant, a newsagent, a hospital, a pharmacist, within reachable distance."

Diane and Peter Voigt, former educators from Florida, chose *Lunigiana,* which is less expensive than other parts of *Tuscany,* because although it is a rural area in the mountains, it takes only thirty minutes to reach the coast and is within a few hours of **Pisa, Genoa, Florence,** and **Parma.** Says Diane, "We have ancient towns and one hundred castles, but we also have amenities like *supermercati* (supermarkets), ATMs, and a wide selection of pet supply stores—which is very important, since we brought our ten rescued cats with us."

During the late 1990s, *Tuscany*'s neighbor *Umbria* gained the title of "the next *Tuscany,*" and American and British expats started buying property there. With similar, though slightly more mountainous, terrain, *Umbria* remains *Tuscany*'s low-key sister. Those who have their hearts set on *Tuscany* but can't afford the time, money, or energy to refurbish a hilltop villa often find *Umbria* an excellent alternative; apartments with views of Lake Trasimeno sell for €165, 000 to €185,000.

The Etruscan city of **Orvieto,** which hosts the Umbria Jazz Festival every winter, is not only beautiful but conveniently located on both the A1 autostrada and the **Rome**-to-**Florence** train line. Also worth considering is *Umbria*'s capital city, **Perugia,** home to the Università per Stranieri di Perugia (University for Foreigners), and offering the affordability and cultural opportunities of a college town.

Rome, Italy's capital city, is ideal for city-loving expats seeking diversity and a vibrant expat community. Few cities in the world can offer a more tantalizing mix of ancient and modern culture than the Eternal City, but the budget-conscious retiree needs to know that living here comes at a very high price.

Thousands of American expats of all ages, from students, to young families on work assignments, to retirees, call **Rome** home. For many, the city's American Catholic church, Santa Susanna, is the place that brings them together. There's no need for a car in **Rome,** as you are only an hour by train from the beach or the countryside.

The average monthly rent for a two-bedroom apartment in **Rome** is €1,600 in the center of town, with flats in the areas surrounding the Spanish Steps and Piazza Navona going for much more. The *Parioli* neighborhood, not far from the Villa Borghese, is a quiet expat haven, but pricey as well. The farther out from the center, obviously the more reasonable the rents and real estate prices. Buyers should expect to spend at least a few hundred thousand euros for even a small Roman hideaway.

AMBIENCE

The allure of la dolce vita is not a false promise for those who come to Italy. The sweet life isn't just the grand sweep of living well, but also small everyday rituals that evoke tradition and respect, and while Italy is modernizing, these traditions aren't about to disappear. Take the old men sitting in any city or village piazza. Don't be surprised if most are wearing suits, even though the biggest outing they will have all day is just to sit right here. The pride they take in their appearance is a throwback to earlier times.

Take the ritual of a big Sunday lunch with the family. While you might find a few stores in some of the major cities open on Sunday, nearly everywhere else, they're closed. Extended families gather for an elaborate afternoon meal, whether they're in **Rome** or on the beach in **Rimini**. At about one o'clock on a warm Sunday in a small Italian village, you'll hear cheerful conversation and dishes and glasses clanking through the open windows.

The wine those families drink probably doesn't come from a store or even a labeled wine bottle. It might come from grapes grown in their own backyards or a neighbor. In fact, it is quite possible that none of the basic ingredients came from a store, but, rather, from the local farms and markets.

Speaking very broadly, Italians are creatures of habit. Come August, for example, a typical Italian family will head off for several weeks at the same beach they went to last year and the year before; in fact, the father may have been sitting on the same patch of sand every summer for his entire life. Italians seem to hold on to this continuity in spite of or perhaps because of growing pressures in the modern world. For most Italians, August vacation is a birthright. Those American retirees who had to postpone vacations during their working life or never took the full amount might be surprised but secretly pleased at the Italian attitude about time off.

Though not apparent at first, settle in Italy, and you'll discover that Italians are a study in contrasts. The same easygoing shopkeeper who lets you pay for your food whenever you get around to it can turn into an impatient, pushy curmudgeon behind the wheel of the car or standing in a long line. Discovering how much more there is than meets the eye with the Italian people can be fascinating.

Expats universally wish they had learned more of their host country's language before making the move. While many Italians who live in the major cities and more visited areas speak some English, most Italians in smaller towns don't speak any. Italians are generally warm and patient with those attempting to speak Italian and seem to genuinely appreciate any effort to do so.

Yet while Italian locals may be friendly, the lack of efficiency can make new American arrivals crazy. Old hands urge patience. One expat says that she has come to an abiding acceptance of the Italian bureaucratic ways and has developed a "two-trip rule." "It takes at least two visits to do anything," she explains. "If you go to the *comune* (municipal) office in **Massa**, it will take at least two visits to accomplish your goal. This can be very trying until you realize that this is just the way it is, and you start to plan on getting something done in two trips not one."

STANDARD OF LIVING

Italy's average per capita income in 2005 was $30,010, compared to $43,740 for the United States. There's a large gap in the Italian figures between the north of Italy and the south, especially *Sicily*. The average per capita income in southern Italy is just 56 percent of that in the north.

The unemployment rate tells a similar story. Italy's current unemployment rate hovers around 9 percent, but it warrants a closer look. As a U.S. State Department report states, "Unemployment is a regional issue in Italy—low in the north, high in the south." The report goes on to explain, "The overall national rate is at its lowest level since 1992. Chronic problems of inadequate infrastructure, corruption, and organized crime act as disincentives to investment and job creation in the south. A significant underground economy absorbs substantial numbers of people, but they work for low wages and without standard social benefits and protections." Only about a quarter of Italy's unemployed qualify for any kind of unemployment assistance. Unemployment benefits are extremely limited, as the common understanding is that the family is responsible for taking care of any out-of-work family members.

CULTURE

Abbondanza! In a contest between France and Italy as Europe's center of culture, UNESCO gives the nod to Italy, citing its three thousand museums and *60 percent of the world's art*. (Retirees please note: those over sixty-five are eligible for free museum entrance.) Italians are also music lovers, and some of the world's best opera venues are found in Italy, including **Milan**'s Teatro la Scala, **Venice**'s La Fenice, and Teatro di San Carlo in **Naples**. During the summer, numerous festivals pay homage to music and the arts.

Arts fans need not travel to the big cities or special events to enjoy culture. Even the smallest towns in remote regions host free concerts in their piazzas. Among the most noteworthy events for many expats are the celebrations surrounding feast days, a holiday centered around a town's or city's patron saint. This is when locals join together for one of the biggest parties of the year, and it can be a moving experience for new residents, one that really sums up what they love about Italy.

Some holidays are celebrated in multiple cities. While **Venice** may be most famous for its large *Carnevale* festivities, many smaller Italian cities celebrate the pre-Lent period with parades and parties. Many locales have their own special yearly events, such as **Siena**'s Palio horse race, pitting citizens of various city districts against one another.

Those interested in period architecture and archaeology are in for a surprise around every corner. Italy's towns and cities produce crafts unique to their areas: there's papermaking in the town of **Amalfi,** mosaics in *Sicily,* masks made in **Venice.** Many of the specially trained artisans creating these items are happy to demonstrate and teach their skills, whether in a formal class or an impromptu visit.

LEISURE

Expats say their retirement activities are much like they would be in the States, but much more interesting. Says an expat in **Rome,** "We do errands, and our walks usually take us past the Forum, Pantheon, Colosseum, or through many of the famous piazzas." Retired expats can re-create most of their hobbies in Italy, though some might take more effort than others. For example, golf is not as popular here as in the States, but there are definitely some good courses, mostly in the north.

They report housework, cooking, reading, and pursuing hobbies as part of their everyday activities, but also studying Italian, taking long drives, visiting museums, working on community projects, and emailing friends and family back home.

Outdoor enthusiasts will be happy to know that Italy is home to many national parks and miles of beaches. Hiking trails are usually available just a short drive outside any major city.

SOCIAL CUSTOMS

Life in Italy revolves around the family in strong part because of tradition and, in other ways, due to necessity. For economic reasons, many Italians live at home until they marry, and family connections are still essential. In Italy, "it's not what you know, it is who you know" is definitely a truism.

While women have made great strides in equality—in the workplace, especially—the country lags behind the United States in true equality for women. Take a look at any small village piazza in the afternoon, and you might see plenty of men (especially older ones) but few women. They are at home, taking care of the house and family. Women rule the home, but men still run the workplace. Because of the inflation of past years, many Italian women are forced to work full time (with the children, the *bambini,* in the care of Grandma; day care is still rare here) to help support the family. This is one reason Italy has one of the lowest birthrates in Western Europe.

Nevertheless, Italian men can still be macho, true to their reputation, and some American women say their flirting, compliments, and advances make them feel more "womanly" than back home. Despite a few exceptions, many Italian men know where to draw the line, especially when a woman signals that she is not interested.

HEALTH CARE/MEDICAL

All Italian residents have the option of joining the national health service, *Servizio Sanitario Nationale* (SSN). As in France, Americans who wish to join are required to show the previous year's tax return and will be asked to pay 7.5 percent of their net incomes to join the national plan. The minimum yearly payment is €400 per person. Local branches of the national system administer the services. Visits to primary care physicians are free, while tests and visits to specialists require a small copayment. (An MRI, for instance, might come with an out-of-pocket cost of €35.)

Some expats choose to keep up their American or international health insurance if they can; many U.S. policies will not cover expenses abroad. Those policies that do provide international coverage usually require that the patient pay out of pocket in full and be reimbursed later. Former Kentucky postal worker Barbara Skinner and her husband both chose to join the Italian SSN *and* to maintain their American insurance. "It's a Blue Cross Blue Shield policy that also covers us here in Italy, so anything not covered by the Italian system is paid for—or at least eighty percent of it!—by our BCBS policy," says Barbara Skinner. "It's too good a price for us to drop it, and if we ever do return to the States, we'll be covered."

Americans should keep their U.S. health coverage or take out a temporary policy until after they have completed all of their paperwork in Italy. Why? You need to show proof of health insurance in order to receive a stay permit. And you don't get Italian health insurance without a stay permit.

RESIDENCY AND RED TAPE

If you're a U.S. resident and planning to stay in Italy for less than ninety days, technically you're supposed to register with the local police department and receive a "stay" visa within eight days of arriving. Few people actually do this, however. This stay visa can be renewed for an additional three months.

If you're planning to stay six months or longer, you will need a *permesso di soggiorno per dimora* (residency permit). The process is similar throughout EU countries. To do this, you have to plan well ahead. The process begins with obtaining a residency visa *before* you leave the States. You will be required to show proof of independent income and a clean criminal record. The exact income requirement can be hard to pin down, as it seems to vary with the location. You will also need to show an Italian rental agreement— ahead of time—or proof of ownership of Italian property.

Once in Italy, you must pay a visit to the local police department to fill out an application for the residency permit. You will need to bring three passport photos, a *marca di bollo* (an administrative tax stamp you can get at the local post office), and proof of health insurance.

Working

It is extremely hard for foreigners to be granted a work permit in Italy. Retirees moving here shouldn't expect to be able to work; they may find small jobs that pay "under the table" (*in nero*) or decide to start their own small businesses (especially catering to American tourists visiting Italy) once established in the country. One American retiree says that many local officials look the other way when it comes to working under the table; one even asked this expat, who doesn't have a work permit, if he could hire her to teach him English.

Unsurprisingly, starting a small business in Italy can be a complicated endeavor, filled with procuring permits and registering with various offices. But where there's a will there's a way, and American expats have successfully started cooking schools, publications, bed-and-breakfasts, and other businesses here.

If you want to work in Italy, it helps to be of Italian ancestry. An American of Italian descent might qualify for citizenship under any of the following circumstances: he or she (1) has an Italian grandfather and was born after 1947; (2) was born in Italy and is over the age of twenty-one; (3) has Italian parents; (4) is married to an Italian citizen; or (5) has lived in Italy for more than a decade.

COST OF LIVING

Retiring in Italy used to be especially attractive to Americans because the cost of living was traditionally somewhat lower than in other leading European countries. Due to the euro conversion, inflation, and the weakened dollar, those days are over. A true comparison, of course, depends on where in the U.S. or Canada you come from, but it now costs about the same to live in Italy as in the United States—more in cities like **Rome, Florence,** and **Milan,** and far less in rural villages and hill towns.

Cristina Fassio, the founder of the ExpatsinItaly.com website (see "Resources"), sums up what costs more and what costs less: "Wine is less expensive, and gasoline is much more expensive. Electricity, phones, and heating are all at least double what you would pay in America. Food can be less expensive, but international foods are considerably pricier."

One category where costs are obviously much higher today is housing, whether you decide to rent or buy. (See "Real Estate.") This is especially true in the big cities. A recent study concluded that rental rates in Italy have doubled since 1999. **Rome** and **Florence** had the largest increases, an average of 128 percent. In general, the farther south you travel in Italy, with the exception of perhaps the *Amalfi coast,* the cheaper the cost of living, sometimes up to 20 percent less.

The lira-to-euro conversion followed by the weakening dollar was a one-two punch for expats and those considering the move. Various surveys have estimated the cost of living increase brought about by the lira-to-euro conversion at 10 percent to 20 percent. Those who moved here postconversion have seen the weakening dollar take a bigger and bigger bite out of their bank accounts and have had to adjust accordingly.

Monthly Cost of Living in Umbria

Rent for a two-bedroom home, condo, or apartment: €500 to €700.

Taxes: There is a 20 percent Value Added Tax (VAT) on just about every purchase in Italy. Property taxes can be as little as €50 a year.

Groceries for two: €320.

Utilities: Water (usually included in rent or condo fees), €18 to €20; electricity, €50.

Cable TV: €35.

Internet: €20.

Telephone: €35.

Maid service: €7 to €10 an hour.

Restaurants for two: €25 for a night out in a midrange restaurant.

Monthly Cost of Living in Rome

Rent for a two-bedroom home, condo, or apartment: Starts at €1,600.

Taxes: There is a 20 percent Value Added Tax (VAT) on just about every purchase in Italy. Property taxes can be as little as €50 a year.

Groceries for two: €400.

Utilities: Water (usually included in rent or condo fees), €18 to €20; electricity, €30.

Cable TV, telephone, internet: €100.

Transportation: City taxis about €10 for a fifteen-minute ride.

Maid service: €10 an hour.

Restaurants for two: €40 for a night out in a midrange restaurant.

Monthly Cost of Living in Verona

Rent for a two-bedroom home, condo, or apartment: €800 to €1,000.

Taxes: There is a 20 percent Value Added Tax (VAT) on just about every purchase in Italy. Property taxes can be as little as €50 a year.

Groceries for two: €360.

Utilities: Water (usually included in rent or condo fees), €10 to €15; electricity, €50 to €100.

Cable TV: €84.

High-speed internet, telephone: €100

Transportation: Taxi to airport, €28.

Maid service: €7 to €10 per hour.

Restaurants for two: €40 for a night out in a midrange restaurant.

Monthly Cost of Living in the Marche (see "Up-and-Coming Areas")

Rent for a two-bedroom home, condo, or apartment: €400 to €600.

Taxes: There is a 20 percent Value Added Tax (VAT) on just about every purchase in Italy. Property taxes can be as little as €50 a year.

Groceries for two: €350.
Utilities: Water, €18 to €20; electricity, €50.
Cable TV: €60.
Internet, telephone: €50.
Maid service: €7 to €10 an hour.
Restaurant for two: €25 for a night out in a midrange restaurant.

REAL ESTATE

There are no restrictions on who can buy property in Italy, although foreigners find it can be a frustrating process, filled with plenty of paperwork and endless negotiations. Expat retirees should be realistic about what they want and put time into finding the proper people to help them.

Sheila Leavitt, who calls herself the Italy House Scout (www.italyhouse scout.com), is an American who owns her own home in **Sarteano, *Tuscany*.** She helps Americans find properties for sale as well as navigate the ins and outs of the buying process. Sheila urges her clients to think hard about whether they really want to own a home in the countryside and consider all of the upkeep that property may require. "Some people think they want a villa in the country, but it's a lot of work and can be isolating," she says, suggesting that clients look at buying in the center of smaller towns, especially in more affordable southern *Tuscany*.

While prices vary, an apartment in need of restoration may sell for €80,000 and cost the same amount to fix up. Many more of these apartments are going on the market as the Italian population ages and the birthrate drops.

Due in part to extremely restrictive building laws, there is very little new construction in Italy. The choice usually comes down to purchasing a modernized property for a higher price or spending a small amount on a home in need of restoration and planning on putting the money in on your own modifications.

Renovating a home in Italy is no easy task, as readers of innumerable construction narratives know well. It requires both patience and cash. Renovation is more expensive than in the U.S. because the required building materials are heavy brick and stone. A typical renovation in central *Umbria,* for example, costs about €1,200 to €1,500 per square meter. Permits are also a challenge: they can take months, even years, to obtain, especially if your property has a historic design or might be in the vicinity of ancient ruins. One family has tried for a decade to get a permit to build a swimming pool to no avail, as there are Etruscan ruins lying beneath its land.

The Voigts in *Lunigiana* say they hesitated because of the plunging dollar but went ahead anyway, paying €320,000 for a three-bedroom, two-bath renovated house that was in move-in condition. They appreciated that the house had all of the modern amenities, a huge terrace overlooking a river, and no land to maintain. Elaine Markell and her husband, from Laguna Beach, California, still rent their furnished two-bedroom apartment in **Rome**'s *Trastevere* neighborhood (at €2,800 per month) but insist that local help will be crucial to finding an apartment they would like to buy. "But we've put that off indefinitely until the dollar recovers some." The Skinners, who live in *Umbria* on their $2,500-a-month pensions, have put their house up for sale. They purchased it when one euro was the equivalent of 94 cents, and plan to move to a smaller apartment to reduce their monthly mortgage payment. They've had to give up on their travel plans, but they're not giving up on Italy.

Mortgages as we know them in the U.S. are relatively new in Italy but are not difficult to secure. In order to get a mortgage, you have to secure a *codice fiscale* (Italian tax number), and women must present copies of their birth and wedding certificates showing their maiden name, as under Italian law, all house and car purchases are always in a woman's maiden name. You will need the codice to open a bank account.

Once you find the property you like, you sign a *compromesso,* a private contract between you and the seller signaling intention to buy, and make a deposit of about 20 percent of the purchase price. The *notaio,* a public notary who does not represent either party, witnesses the closing and presents the new owner with a *rogito,* a deed of sale. Annual property taxes in Italy are very low.

Rentals

Since apartment and villa rentals are popular choices for tourists, numerous agencies can help you secure a place for a few weeks. For rentals, also check the classifieds of Italian and expat publications and/or go through an Italian broker. Because of the way the law is written, Italians actually prefer to rent to foreigners. (Keep this in mind in case you decide to move to Italy and continue to rent rather than buy.) If an Italian citizen can prove that there is no other place to live in the vicinity of a rental he currently occupies, he cannot be evicted. These housing laws don't apply to foreigners. Many rentals come semi- or fully furnished.

TRANSPORTATION

Living in the birthplace of Ferrari, Maserati, and Lamborghini, it is no surprise that Italians love their automobiles. Italy actually ranks third in the world for the number of cars per capita. Yet non-Italians can sometimes find it a laborious process to buy a car and get an Italian license.

"All you need to buy a house is money," says Cristina Fassio of Expats in Italy. "But to buy a car, you have to first get the visa to enter Italy, then the *permesso di soggiorno,* then residency, which will give you a *carta d'identità.* It might take three months to a year, depending on where you apply."

Another daunting aspect of driving in Italy is the price of gas. Filling the tank of a small hatchback car costs as much as €55. Tolls on the country's main autostrada, A1, are comparably higher than back home. Car insurance is also a cost to take into consideration; expats say it starts at about €1,000 per year. You get the drift. Consequently, expats living in urban areas may want to forgo owning a car altogether and use car rentals to travel.

Trains are often the best, most affordable way to get from city to city. Eurostar trains connect the major cities and can get you from **Naples** to **Milan** in six and a half hours. Smaller trains connect outlying towns to regional cities; buses are the only form of transportation in many rural areas. Budget airlines that fly within Italy have begun to appear on the scene.

SECURITY

Despite some stereotypes in American media, Italy has a low crime rate, and violent crimes are rare; the majority of crimes are thefts or muggings. Americans living abroad should take the precautions they would take at home. Bear in mind that Italians are somewhat suspicious of police—as they are of the government. This attitude is more prevalent in *Sicily,* for example, because of Mafia corruption. Transparency International gives Italy a poor ranking in its corruption survey. (See appendix 1.)

COMMUNICATIONS AND MEDIA

Italians are just crazy about their *telefonini* (cell phones). They call one another for no reason at all and always end their conversation with a string of good-byes (ciao, ciao, ciao, ciao). The popularity and affordability of cell phones here have alleviated some of the pain of waiting to have a landline installed. Expats who came here years ago had to wait months and months for a phone, although recently things seem to have improved.

The best deal for phoning home to the States is a €5 international calling card at the local *tabacchi* (tobacco and convenience store). It can be activated using a toll-free number and provides several hundred minutes of calling time. One of the best bargains in *Italia*!

Although use of the internet is not as widespread here as it is in the U.S., internet connections are available in most areas. The Italian postal service has long had a reputation for inefficiency and slow delivery times.

Standard Italian television includes several RAI channels showing news, American TV programs dubbed into Italian, and wacky game and talk shows.

UP-AND-COMING AREAS

Le Marche

Le Marche has become much talked about as Italy's next hot region, especially for expats seeking an affordable alternative to *Tuscany* and *Umbria*. It is bordered by the Adriatic Sea to the east, *Umbria* to the west, *Emilia-Romagna* and *San Marino* to the north, and *Abruzzi* to the south. For those looking for an escape from it all, they should know that *Le Marche* is rustic and sparsely populated compared to other Italian regions. The trade-off is isolation, distance from major urban areas, and, perhaps most important, from major airports.

Yet the region has its cultural offerings. After all, the small city of **Urbino** was the birthplace of great Renaissance artists Bramante and Raffaele, and the city's Palazzo Ducale is a UNESCO World Heritage site. The port city of **Ancona** (with ferry connections to other Mediterranean ports) has a growing collection of archaeological treasures in its Museo Archeologico Nazionale delle Marche.

A restored four-bedroom farmhouse in move-in condition with a pool, nice views, and a little bit of land might be priced at about €450,000 in an attractive area of *Le Marche*'s countryside. This is about half what an equivalent property in *Tuscany* might sell for. Rents are correspondingly priced.

Puglia

This long strip of land comprising the heel of Italy has a unique landscape devoid of mountains and covered by plains and hills. Farms devoted to vineyards, olive trees, and vegetables are separated by neatly constructed stone walls. The giant olive trees, several feet in diameter, twisted and towering, are startling. The travel media has labeled *Puglia* "the new *Tuscany*," and indeed Tuscans have come here to buy land. The Tuscan wine family the Antinoris, have purchased a number of vineyards in this region.

The area surrounding the town **Alberobello** is dotted with *trulli*. These small conical buildings, first built in the thirteenth century, are created out of limestone and are unique to *Puglia*. Foreign buyers, especially the British (who can take budget flights from the United Kingdom to the region's major cities of **Bari** and **Brindisi**), have snapped up trulli. To get an idea of pricing, a four-bedroom trullo, in fairly good shape, on eight thousand meters of land, is currently selling for €250,000.

Puglia's sandy beaches are a big draw to this area; three-quarters of the region borders the sea. **Savelletri di Fasano** and **Polignano a Mare** are charming seaside towns where buyers can find a villa or a former *masseria* (a sighting tower built in the Middle Ages just inland from the coast in order to warn of attacking Turkish pirates). **Lecce**, a city of 100,000 near the very bottom of the region, reigns as one of the most beautiful cities in southern Italy, and has been called "the Florence of the south" and "the Athens of *Puglia*."

Sicily

The size of Vermont, legendary *Sicily* claims to be Italian, but that's a recent development. For thousands of years, *Sicily* was under the domination of outside forces, including the Greeks, Arabs, Romans, and Normans. Their influences are layered throughout the Sicilian lifestyle—from the architecture to the cuisine—and have produced a complex, clannish, beguiling region. *Sicily* offers a little bit of everything at an affordable price. There are well-preserved Greek ruins, beautiful beaches, an evocative volcano, and much more. *Sicily* probably isn't the place for neophytes, but expats who have some grasp of the language (not the same as northern Italian) and its social customs may want to move here. Among those customs is a traditional wariness of strangers; this is, after all, the birthplace of the Mafia. Though recent efforts to root out the mob have eased local attitudes, expats should not generally expect to be invited into Sicilian homes for wine and confidences.

While many tourists are enthralled by the seaside village (and shopping mecca) of **Taormina**, this is actually one of the more expensive places to buy on *Sicily*—or Italy. There are many other more affordable beach locations, and going inland presents even better bargains. Italian airline Eurofly offers seasonal nonstop service between New York and **Palermo**, and many European budget airlines offer good fares on connections to mainland Italy and other countries.

VOLUNTEERING WITHOUT BORDERS

Because of the primacy of family life, Italians have traditionally been wary of outside institutions such as the state or large organizations. This is why volunteerism hasn't been an essential part of their culture.

But this is changing. About 12 percent of the population currently work as volunteers, which is on a par with other West European countries. (By comparison, Americans volunteer at twice this rate.)

- Expats will find most opportunities at the local level: teaching English to schoolchildren, heading up a project for the local church, or helping with the town festival. Americans shouldn't be discouraged by the lack of formal opportunities but should follow in the footsteps of previous expats and approach their own communities, church, or school leaders to volunteer their services.

Kathy McCabe is editor and publisher of the subscription newsletter Dream of Italy *(www.dreamofitaly.com), recommended by* USA Today *and* National Geographic Traveler.

MY ITALY

A Couple in Rome Who
Don't Mix with Other Expats

Name, origin: Elaine Markell, Laguna Beach, California.

Where I live: Rome. We rent a condo in the popular *Trastevere* neighborhood.

Previous occupations: I was an executive in mortgage banking, and my husband was a biologist.

Reasons for moving here: We chose Italy because of the beauty of **Rome** and the relaxed lifestyle. Our entire lifestyle changed; we don't drive a car or use a clothes dryer (yes, my laundry goes on the rack outside like everyone else's)—the list goes on. Everything is different, and that is what we love about it, the daily adventure. Plus, Italy is a great home base for travel throughout Europe.

Finances: We sold our house in Laguna Beach and retained a property in San Diego that is a vacation rental. We paid off the San Diego house with some of the Laguna Beach house proceeds, which leaves us with no debts in the States and a comfortable amount in investments.

My community: We do not know or see any other expats. We live among the Italians, who are a very accepting people and have made us feel very welcome.

Typical day: After we get up, we check the internet for news, get dressed, and walk the dogs. Every day we walk to a beautiful piazza and enjoy a leisurely cappuccino at an outside table. We are regulars at the café and chit-chat with the waitresses. We have many places to choose from to go to for lunch, and afterward we either go home or sometimes to a movie or run errands. We walk a lot, and our errands take us past the Forum, Pantheon, Colosseum, or through many of the famous piazzas of **Rome**. My husband is the cook in the family, so in the afternoon we go to the butcher shop, the vegetable stand, and the bread store and pick up the ingredients for that night's dinner. After we eat, we stroll through our neighborhood and get a gelato. In the evenings, we watch a DVD or read.

Common misperceptions: I am embarrassed to say that I did not realize the cultural differences would be so great. Aside from the language barrier, the Italians look at things with a very different perspective than Americans. I appreciate the differences, and after two years, I am still discovering new ones every day. An open mind is essential.

Wish I'd known before: Learn Italian! Everybody does not speak English. Second, the customer is not king here. Many times customer service is nonexistent. Losing one's temper only makes it worse so patience, patience, patience!

What I miss most: Malls.

MY ITALY

A Couple in Verona with Second Thoughts

Name, age, origin: Lois and Samuel Smith (pseudonym), sixty and sixty-two, New Jersey.

Where we live: Verona, in a rented apartment in a restructured palazzo in the *centro storico*.

How long in Italy: Two years.

Previous occupations: Executive secretary; Samuel was an exec with an insurance company.

Reasons for moving here: I am half-Italian by descent from my paternal grandfather. My husband and I had traveled to Italy before moving here, and we decided this was the place to be. My husband is an avid amateur cyclist, and the *Veneto* is cycling heaven. **Verona** seemed to be the best choice in the north, for three reasons: it is a small city with all the cultural diversity of services you might desire; there is *not* a huge expat community (we wanted to live an Italian life); and it is a good transportation hub, since we made the decision to live here without cars.

Also, I had a desire to leave the United States. My own country had come to seem inimical to my ideals, seemed to be on the wrong track in most things cultural and political. I wanted to experience something completely different, something I thought would be more simpatico with how I felt inside. I actually said, before we came, that "I feel more at home in my skin when I am in Italy."

How wrong I was.

Finances: My husband's pension is $100,000. I will be taking Social Security soon.

Our community: There's not much of an American expat community here; more Brits.

The English speakers who settle in Verona seem to want the same thing we wanted, to live an Italian life interacting with Italian-speaking people, not to live in the derisively termed "Chiantishire" of *Tuscany*, for instance. The Italians, without exception, are pleased that we chose their city but absolutely do not understand why we did it. They still ask, "But why did you move here?" Many Italians still dream of America as the land of opportunity, a place they want to visit or move to; yet most Italians never leave their hometown or home province. So it is a puzzlement to them that we picked up everything and moved here to retire. Not only that, we left our only child (age thirty-three) behind in America—that really blows their minds. We joke that our daughter's parents ran away from home, and we get blank stares. Lost in translation, I guess.

Common misperceptions: This is an alien country, a totally different cultural milieu, from anything that an American has experienced at home in America. Being of Italian descent does not—repeat, does not—prepare you for living in Italy. That is something that I think very few prospective emigrants can understand. I have never felt so "American" as since I moved to Italy.

Best:
- To be able to travel at will to all the places in Europe that I have always wanted to see, and share this with our adult daughter on her twice-yearly visits.
- To enjoy the festivals of the holiday months.
- To learn to eat the Italian slow-food way. To appreciate seasonal variations in the food markets, to buy the freshest food without additives. (Of course, the air pollution cancels that out, but, hey, you can't have everything.)
- To walk across the bridges of the *Adige*. To enjoy the beauty of the old city on a clear day or a crisp, frosty night at Christmas.

Worst: Italians seem to have no personal-space boundaries. People make jokes about the Italians' inability to form a queue, their lack of courtesy passing you on the sidewalk (it's called shoulder bumpering), but not funny when you encounter them in daily life. We had the horrible bad luck to lease an apartment with next-door neighbors who embody all those traits. When our neighbors cough, talk, yell, abusively scream at their sons at one in the morning, we hear it all, and they do not care who else hears them.

Second, bureaucracy. Most of the procedural problems we encounter in our daily life here are due to an apparent lack of flow-charting skills. The Italians want to talk everything to death. This strange society cannot seem to find its way out of a paper bag. Our right-wing mayor thought he would discourage immigrants by forbidding people to walk about and eat, aimed at the Middle East and Greek food vendors. It turns out that by that rule, eating a gelato in the town square is forbidden. On the national level, there's the residence permit problem: they changed a rule, didn't think it through, and now there are a half million permits backlogged. Sometimes when *stranieri* (foreigners) get together and talk, we wonder whether or not the Italians have just rested on the laurels and achievements of the past so much that they can't be in the present.

What I miss most: *Who* do I miss the most: our daughter, though we "talk" every day with lengthy emails. *What* do I miss the most: American personal responsibility, American customer service—instead of throwing up your hands and shrugging, "Not my fault"—American honesty and directness, American efficiency. I miss most of all about America the openness of our people. I miss the ability to laugh at ourselves and not take everything so seriously.

Advice:
- Really examine your heart and be honest with yourself about why you are doing this or thinking about it. Don't be *leaving* somewhere, be *going* to somewhere.
- Don't jump too fast. I wish we had not brought *everything* we owned—it cost us $17,000 in a supersized ship container—thinking we could make a smooth transition into Italian life. There is a catch-22 to this, however, since the Italian government gives you only six months from your arrival date to bring in your household goods without paying exorbitant duties.
- If your significant other has serious questions about the wisdom of making a life-changing move, listen—he or she might be onto something.
- Lower your expectations and then lower them again. Tell yourself one hundred times that you, as a lady, promise not to be offended if you walk into a restaurant unisex toilet and find a stall door ajar and a well-dressed man urinating in plain sight. Tell yourself that.
- Make friends. You may find that your friends will not be other Italians (unless you are absolutely fluent in Italian) but other

stranieri who can share your laughs and cry with you when you need to cry.

- Practice respect for elders when you are elbowed in the ribs in the queue at the fruit stand by the cute little old lady with the white hair and gloves.

Plans: We are planning to return to the States in approximately five years. We will have had seven years in **Verona** and we will be sixty-seven and sixty-five. I hope that we will have done everything that was in our hearts to do. I hope that we will have outsmarted our neighbors from hell.

Most of all, I hope that my memories of Italy, like memories of childbirth, will be mellowed by time.

MY ITALY

Cat Lovers Who Found a 900-year-old House in Tuscany

Name, age, origin: Diane and Peter Voigt, sixty-three and seventy-one, Ormond Beach, Florida.

Where we live: We live in **Pieve di Crespiano,** in an area known as *Lunigiana*. We're in the northwest corner of *Tuscany*. We bought a 900-year-old house, which is built *into* the wall of the *borgo* and overlooks the Taverone River.

How long in Italy: One year.

Previous occupations: Both of us are retired federal employees, and we worked for the Department of Education in the Office of Student Financial Aid. Luckily, we don't have to work in Italy.

Reasons for moving here: We have dreamed about moving to Europe since we retired in December 1996. But for family reasons, we couldn't, and we traveled throughout Europe instead. After a trip to Italy in 2003, we decided that this was where we wanted to live. I discovered *Lunigiana* on the internet through a local real estate site. The description sounded so perfect to us that we came to see for ourselves. While here, we fell for the area and the people. It is rural Italy, but close enough to major cities—**Pisa, Genoa, Florence, Parma**—that we always have access to big-city attractions. It is in the mountains, but only thirty minutes to the sea. There are craggy mountains, deep valleys, and rolling meadows. We have ancient towns and hundreds of castles, but have amenities like supermercati, ATMs, and a wide selection of pet supply stores—very important to us, since we brought our ten rescued cats with us.

Our community: While very few of the locals speak any English, they are patient with our attempts to speak Italian and have welcomed us with open arms. There are a reasonable number of English-speaking people here from the UK, U.S., Netherlands, and Denmark, and with the Italians, we have quite an international social set. The expats here are part of the local community. All of us socialize with the Italians, participate in community activities, and feel as if we belong here. The locals are so warm and so friendly, and they really appreciate just how much we love their country.

It also helps that the majority of people here are liberals, like us, and as opposed to Bush and the Iraq war as we are. (To be honest, it was the Bush win in 2004 that provided the final push for us to make the move. We didn't want to live in a country that would choose such a government.)

Best: When you wake up in the morning to the sound of the river, singing birds, and the church bell pealing out the hour, you realize that you are living a fairy tale. When the villagers invite you to join them in an impromptu *festa,* and you spend an evening drinking local wine, eating local food, and singing all the songs they have been singing for generations, you know you are not in Kansas any longer!

Worst: My husband's stroke. We are so lucky that he suffered no long-term physical effects, but when it happened, it was very scary. I felt completely helpless, unable to understand what the doctors were telling me and not knowing how to ask the questions I wanted to ask. We came through it OK, but it was not a good time.

What we miss most: Family and friends first. Then ethnic food.

Advice: Rent first. Since we had ten cats to accommodate, we didn't have that luxury, so we bought immediately.

Also, don't be afraid of following your dreams. We asked ourselves what would happen if we didn't like living in Italy and reached the conclusion that we'd just come back to the U.S. After a year, we are so glad that we took this chance and made this move. It is a dream come true for us, and we love it.

MY ITALY

From Kentucky to a Hill Town in Umbria

Name, age, origin: Art and Barbara Skinner, sixty-one and fifty-five, Louisville, Kentucky.

Where we live: San Venanzo, a small village in *Umbria*.

How long in Italy: Four years.

Previous occupations: We both worked for the U.S. Postal Service. Art also worked for Churchill Downs racetrack, and continues to work there when we visit the States.

Reasons for moving here: We first visited Italy in 2000 because my son was stationed here with the marines. Though we didn't realize it, we had fallen in love with Italy. We began to use any chance to get back here: a special frequent-flier offer, an extra week of vacation, whatever. We soon realized that our time in the States was just marking time until we earned enough money and vacation time to get back to Italy. After five visits in two years, we finally figured it out: we just needed to live in Italy. It wasn't a lifelong dream, it wasn't inspired by Italian heritage (neither of us has a drop of Italian blood), it wasn't to escape American politics or to find a simpler life, it was just that we *needed* to live in Italy. We tell people that we didn't choose Italy, Italy chose us. We didn't even consider it a decision, just an acceptance of what was supposed to be.

Finances: Approximately $2,500 per month from two pensions and retirement savings.

Costs: Rent for a two-bedroom home or apartment, about €500 to €700. Groceries maybe €400 a month. Restaurant for two: €25 to €40. Had the dollar remained strong, our life here would be equal, possibly better than our life in the States. When we moved to Italy, we hoped to be able to travel throughout Italy and Europe, but the decline in the dollar has meant the loss of our travel budget. Art retired at age fifty-seven, and I simply quit work, so we knew sacrifices would have to be made. We have one car. We eat at home much more often. We don't go out to movies. I don't wander the aisles of Target or Costco, buying stuff I don't really need. We make do with what we have, enjoying a glass of wine on our patio, sharing a gelato, and strolling down the street.

Our community: We live in a small, agricultural Umbrian hill town. Our area is covered with fields of olive trees, vineyards, sunflowers, and hay. *Umbria* is the green heart of Italy, and we see it all around us. The town has all the necessary stores and services to make living here very easy. We don't have to get in the car and drive to the grocery or the post office or the hardware store. Our biggest disappointment (maybe the only one) is that we don't have a central piazza where everyone gathers for coffee and shopping and people watching.

Our town has a population of about 1,500, and although people are very set in their ways, they're also very friendly and welcoming. A few Moroccans living here, but otherwise we are the only non-Italians in town. Many of the people here are farmers, and everyone has a small plot with a few tomato plants, herbs, olive trees, and grapevines. When I share my pesto with our neighbor, she reciprocates with fresh eggs from her hens.

Culture: There's always something going on; it's just a matter of staying informed. We visit the museums and churches in **Perugia, Spoleto, Montefalco**. Nearby **Montecastello di Vibio** has the world's smallest theater, offering concerts. **Deruta,** not far from us, is famous for ceramics. **Orvieto,** one of our favorite cities in Italy, is one big open-air museum with many things to see and do.

Health care/medical: As residents, we belong to the Italian health care system, which charges us 7.5 percent of our income, so general office visits cost nothing. A visit to a specialist may cost €25 to €40. We've been pleased with our doctor here, but he smokes. When Art was hospitalized for three days, the total cost was less than €2,400. Because one never knows what's coming next, we've also kept our health insurance in the States. It's a Blue Cross Blue Shield policy that also covers us here in Italy, so most of what's not covered by the Italian system is paid for.

Residency and visas: We have an elective residency visa. The financial requirements seem to be a big secret. You need to show some assets and income, but how much is a big secret. The requirements seem to vary from consulate to consulate. When we applied for our visa, we showed our bank statements with our monthly pension deposits, and also showed our retirement savings accounts.

Crime, corruption: In our time here in **San Venanzo,** there has only been one incidence of crime. Of course, it was generally agreed that it was "the Albanians." Overall, the Italian government is notorious for payoffs. Knowing someone who knows someone is the way to accomplish *anything* in Italy, from fixing a parking ticket to getting permission to work on a building.

Locals' attitudes toward Americans: Wonderful. Everyone has been so friendly and welcoming. The plumber has come to the house on a Sunday morning, then refused to accept payment. Our neighbor makes sure we know about the local festivities. The woman in our local bar pushes back Art's money when he stops in for coffee. The postmaster helped us get a car loan and pushed through the paperwork for our carta d'identità. The ultimate compliment came the other day when our neighbor, a farmer about seventy years old, asked *me* what I thought about his ailing rosemary bush.

We've encountered no bad attitudes because we're American, though we always tell our Italian friends right away that we don't like George Bush. On the contrary, older Italians still seem to love all Americans; I guess because they still remember our help during the war.

As to American influence here, it's happening. Change is coming. When stores start staying open all day, people won't be able to go home for lunch with the family and a nap, so the importance of the family will gradually be eroded, just as it has in the U.S. When larger chains open more stores, the smaller mom-and-pop stores won't be able to compete. Change can be good, but eventually Italy might lose those things that make it uniquely Italy, and not the United States.

Best: We hadn't spent years dreaming of life in our dream villa, so life in this village could not have turned out better. We were simply drawn to Italy and knew that as long as we were together, everything would be OK. We also came with the attitude that if it truly didn't work out, we'd simply return to the States.

What we miss most: Grandchildren. English-language newspapers, books, and magazines. Just being able to go into a bookstore and browse through the books!

Plans: Will we stay forever in **San Venanzo**? Or explore another part of Italy? We love this village, but being retired doesn't mean you just sit still. So we're asking ourselves, Are we missing a great opportunity if we don't explore our options?

Chapter 17

CROATIA

The New Frontier

By Hank Brill

Let's save you some time by being blunt from the outset: Croatia is not for everyone. If you prefer to follow the well-trod path from which all the pitfalls have been removed, you should move on to another chapter, or wait five years for Croatia to reach the point where retirement havens such as Spain are now. If your idea of retirement is hanging out with people like yourself doing things you've done all your life, you'll hate Croatia.

This little country of fewer than five million, located in the heart of Europe, is better suited for those who held on to their Davy Crockett coonskin caps for fifty years, waiting for an opportunity to explore a new frontier or two. It's not that Croatia is an uncivilized wilderness. Its rich and varied culture is measured in millennia, not centuries. (See "Culture.") Nor is it a backward place where the water is questionable and electrical power is intermittent. Even the minimal disparity between the quality of Croatia's infrastructure and that of nearby European countries such as Austria and Italy is being remedied rapidly.

What makes Croatia a challenge is its newness as an expat destination. Croatians themselves cannot quite get used to the new reality that their country is attracting Germans, Austrians, Brits, Russians, and increasing numbers of North Americans who want to live here year round. After all, only a decade ago, it was the Croatians who were looking to move elsewhere to escape the war in the Balkans.

288

LOCATION

Croatia, at the crossroads of the Mediterranean and the Balkans, is a crescent-shaped country with borders on Slovenia, Hungary, Serbia, Bosnia and Herzegovina, and Montenegro. Its rocky seashore and picturesque Dalmatian Coast are on the Adriatic, across from Italy.

CLIMATE

If you're along the *Adriatic coast,* the Mediterranean climate provides a long, mild spring and fall on either side of a cool, dreary winter. The effects of the sunny summer's heat are moderated by the low humidity and nearly constant sea breezes. Those who prefer a mountain climate with plenty of snow and cool summers will enjoy Croatia's Dinaric Alps, and may even be able to find a spot that includes the bonus of a spectacular sea view where the mountains meet the water. Croatia's capital of **Zagreb** has its share of expats, but most are there for business rather than the Continental climate with its cold winters and hot summers very similar to those in nearby Budapest or Vienna.

PEOPLE

Today, after war and displacement, the Croatian population is 90 percent Croat, with a remaining minority of Serbs. They are overwhelmingly Catholic and their language, Croatian, is Slavic and uses the Latin alphabet.

HISTORY AND GOVERNMENT

When Croatia declared its independence as Yugoslavia began to come apart, the Yugoslav government headquartered in Serbia objected, and sent soldiers and artillery shells in an unsuccessful attempt to subdue the Croatians. Croatia's independence and its opportunity to rebuild were finally assured by the Dayton Peace Accord, which the United States helped broker in 1995.

The road to recovery has not been easy. Croatia had been, along with neighboring Slovenia, the most advanced, industrialized, and wealthiest part of former Yugoslavia, but the war decimated the economy. The nationalist government that held power from 1991 until 2000 didn't help matters either, since its policies discouraged foreign investment and hampered the recovery of what had been a booming tourist industry before the war.

The far-rightists suffered a resounding defeat at the polls in 2000, and the turmoil in Croatia has been replaced by political stability under a parliamentary democracy dominated by center-left and center-right parties. The current government has worked hard to improve relations with neighboring countries. European tourists have returned by the millions, and the European and American press are rediscovering this little gem of a country and dubbing parts of it the "New *Tuscany*" and the "New Monaco."

But still, a little of that Davy Crockett or Daniel Boone spirit can come in handy. Some parts of Croatia are a new frontier in the most basic sense of the term. Frank and Betty Freestone are a British couple in their fifties who originally came to Croatia hoping to buy a holiday home for a reasonable price. They ended up purchasing a centuries-old ruin on thirteen acres atop the highest mountain on the *Istrian Peninsula,* miles away from power lines and paved roads, and have now turned the building—which housed a family and their 150 sheep—into a beautiful lodge with electricity and hot water provided courtesy of the sun.

For others, the nemesis is a Croatian bureaucracy unused to dealing with "strangers," as expats are called in Croatia. Frank and Alice Poynter, an American couple in their sixties, fell in love with the little island of *Vis,* Croatia's outermost inhabitable island in the Adriatic, and joined with local residents and some South African investors to bring much-needed jobs to the area. In three years, they've managed to navigate successfully through the Croatian commercial and bankruptcy courts and are ready for the next step: building permits for the two abandoned factories their development company purchased.

Prospective expats with an eye to the future are also attracted by Croatia's prospects. Croatia's old and close friendship with Austria and Germany (it was on the side of the Nazis in World War II) has moved Croatia to first in line for EU membership by 2010. As EU accession approaches, real estate prices will rise, as they have in all other European nations that have joined the Union. It is the "pioneers" who will enjoy the greatest benefits of that appreciation.

UPSIDES

1. Mediterranean climate along the coast; mild winters.
2. Location, location, location: **Florence, Milan, Vienna, Munich,** and Budapest, less than eight hours away by car.
3. Very hospitable people.

4. Diversity: Croatia has lived under **Rome, Venice,** the Austro-Hungarian Empire, and Italy. Each left its mark on the culture.
5. Gorgeous coastline.
6. Timing: business, property opportunities prior to EU membership.

DOWNSIDES

1. Bureaucracy: top beef listed by all expats. It's not hostile, just creaky.
2. Cost: it's still Europe, not Florida or Central America; prices higher than either. But still much cheaper than Italy or southern France.
3. Fewer expats: can be either a plus or minus, depending on your preferences. Expat community diverse, with Austrians, Germans, and British.

WHERE TO LIVE

Istria

While over 150,000 Americans visited Croatia in 2006—up nearly 40 percent from the year before—fewer than 10,000 live here as legal residents. Outside of the government and corporate types who reside in the country's capital, **Zagreb,** most expats live in *Istria,* the little heart-shaped peninsula located in the northwest corner of Croatia next to Slovenia and only a few miles from Italy. Though smaller than Rhode Island, *Istria* offers much variety. The west coast is fairly flat and sprinkled with miniature versions of **Venice,** such as the island towns of **Rovinj** and **Umag,** which were in fact built by the Venetians in the fourteenth and fifteenth centuries. The southern tip of *Istria* is dominated by **Pula,** the 3,000-year-old city, where the Venetian Gothic city hall stands next to a nearly intact Temple of Augustus, built in 2 BC, and a Roman arena now features musical artists like Sting instead of gladiator fights.

The less-developed east coast of *Istria* is a beautiful, rugged place reminiscent of northern California in both terrain and climate. *Istria*'s interior, the one called the "New *Tuscany*" because of its vineyards and olive groves, contains the fairy-tale medieval villages of **Motovun** and **Groznjan,** which

stand perched atop hills and are still surrounded by walls. *Istria* has Croatia's most developed real estate market, with many brightly colored new seaside condos and even two new golf course developments close to completion. Its people are also used to foreigners, having hosted European vacationers for decades, and their desire to be good hosts (and businesspersons) has given many of them the ability to shift easily from Croatian to Italian to German to English. *Istria*'s location is another plus. With a reasonably early start, you can enjoy lunch in **Venice** (by car or boat) or hit the slopes of the Italian Alps shortly after noon. Spending the weekend in **Florence** or **Milan** or Munich or Vienna or Budapest is also easy since they are all within an eight-hour drive.

Dalmatian Coast

The next largest expat population resides in Croatia's long, beautiful *Dalmatian coast* or on one of its more than one thousand islands. The city of **Dubrovnik** has become a major jet-set destination in the past few years, and actor John Malkovich, of Croatian ancestry himself, was one of the first to buy a run-down villa—at a price of more than $5 million. Perhaps the view allows him to see the yachts of Bill Gates and Steven Spielberg as they explore the Adriatic waters around the city in the summer.

Zagreb

Finally, Zagreb is an option for the urban-oriented adventurer. It's a city of about one million residents within its metropolitan area, and offers most of the culture and shopping that one would find in other European capitals. Property is still much cheaper than in new Eastern European hot spots like Prague in the Czech Republic, but the city is much more affluent and developed than the new EU cities of Sofia, Bulgaria, and Bucharest, Romania.

AMBIENCE

After "*Dobrodošli*"—that is, "Welcome"—the next Croatian message to all Western European and North American arrivals is "Chill." The pace is definitely Mediterranean. Lines at government offices will just have to wait during midday breaks, which the Italians here in *Istria* call *pausa*. Many retail businesses close for the early afternoon, as they do across the Adriatic in *Italia*. And on holidays, forget about it. Everything is closed, and people are home with their families.

Most Croatians have the attitude that there must always be time for a good cup of coffee or glass of wine accompanied by a chat with friends. Throughout the year along the coast and in **Zagreb,** the outdoor cafés fill on sunny days as people take their pausa and catch up on the latest.

It would be an overstatement to say that there is something so substantial as an expat community in Croatia. There are too few as of yet, and they're too scattered. But they are finding ways to learn of one another's presence. Nationality matters less.

Which brings up the subject of language. Language experts declare Croatian among the most difficult languages to learn. It does use our Latin alphabet with a few additional consonants (č and ć = *ch*; š = *sh*; ž = *s*, as in "pleasure"; đ = *j*; the omnipresent j = *y*), but it is highly inflected, meaning that nouns and adjectives change spelling and pronunciation depending on their function in a sentence. Most challenging to English speakers is the proliferation of consonants and lack of vowels. You may have to travel through four or five letters in a word before reaching the first *a, e, i, o,* or *u.*

Expats are thankful that Croatians are so good with languages. Especially in **Zagreb** and the tourist areas of *Istria* and *Dalmatia,* many people speak three or four other languages well, usually English, Italian, and German. For the past decade, all schoolchildren begin English in elementary school, and the academic emphasis is reinforced by television programming that is more than 50 percent American and British productions with Croatian subtitles. The largest telephone company, the German-owned T-Com, has help lines staffed by fluent English speakers, and their cell phones have a full English option (unlike Italy).

STANDARD OF LIVING

Croatia had a state-owned economy from the Second World War until independence in 1991. Even now, most Americans would consider it a socialist country, with its national health care system and fairly generous social welfare. The result is a country without great extremes between rich and poor. In fact, the vast majority of Croatians are in the middle, even if that middle is less affluent than the median in the U.S. or most of Western Europe.

The economy is currently growing at a faster rate than the economies of the U.S. or Western Europe, and an upper middle class is beginning to appear in numbers large enough to support the burgeoning number of BMW and Audi dealerships in the country. While former President Josip Tito was a Communist as he ruled Croatia and the rest of Yugoslavia from 1945 until his death in 1980, he did plant the seeds of a market economy by subdividing government-owned land into building lots, which were then given to individuals. The typical Croatian pattern was to build a house on that land, which was later enlarged to include additional apartments and often a first floor used for some small business like a bakery or café. Now these Croatians own their buildings free of a mortgage, and can afford expensive new cars and other luxury goods.

Expats living in Croatia fall into two categories. There are some very wealthy Europeans and a few American celebrities who live quite luxuriously here. Andreas von Bismarck, a descendant of the German chancellor, has a place in *Istria.* More common are working expats who have businesses and live much as the Croatians around them do. The number of middle-class expats who live well but not extravagantly will increase when the large golf course developments begin to fill with Europeans and North Americans.

The housing options in *Istria* and *Dalmatia* are basically the same. There are many small condo-style developments called *apartmani* that offer European-style accommodations, meaning limited square footage and amenities. Prices range from €1,200 to €2,000 per square meter. Larger luxury condo developments are just beginning to appear. A step-up from that are the villas that still have European dimensions, but often include a pool and some garden space. These are often built in small communities of ten to twenty villas, but few are gated in Croatia, where crime is not an issue. Villas with views of the Adriatic, mountains, or vineyard-covered hillsides command higher prices.

All over *Istria* and *Dalmatia,* expats are buying stone ruins for €60,000 to €70,000 and restoring and updating them. A British couple, Frank and Alice Freestone, bought an old farm in the midst of the Učka Nature Park. Its condition was what is described here as an "old Istrian house," meaning that plumbing, wiring, and roof are all add-ons. Since then, it's been like living in their own personal remake of *Under the Tuscan Sun.* A British reality television show called *Build a New Life in the Country* chronicled the Freestones' adventure for English TV.

CULTURE

Croatia's history has molded a culture that is a combination of Slavic, Italian, and German elements. Cities like **Pula** and **Split** retain many Roman buildings and ruins, some of which, like **Pula**'s arena and Diocletian's Palace in **Split,** remain in use today. The powerful city-state of **Venice** ruled much of Croatia's coast in late medieval and Renaissance times, and the Lion of St. Mark can be found on many Croatian seaside buildings. The heart of cities like **Zagreb, Rijeka,** and the coastal resort of **Opatija** are reminiscent of Vienna, with their Wien Art Nouveau architecture and manicured gardens.

Croatian food shows these influences as well. On the coast, there is plenty of risotto and pasta with seafood, while the interior favors potatoes and meats like breaded veal. *Istria* and *Dalmatia* compete to cure the best *prsut,* a salty, dry ham that is sliced thinly and often enjoyed uncooked. Croatians laugh about the way their truffles, an underground fungus renowned for its strong flavor and Viagra-like effects, are smuggled across the border and packaged as the better-known Italian truffle.

North Americans will be somewhat disappointed at the limited choice in types of restaurants. There are few establishments featuring non-Croatian food, and you may have to look hard for a Chinese, Mexican, or Indian restaurant. But never fear, McDonald's and Subway are here to showcase their "American" food.

Croatia is proud of its wines, and each region claims its own as the best. The wine industry is growing, and Croatian vintners are traveling around the world, including to California and France, to learn how to improve the quality of their product even further. The fruit of the vine is an important part of a Croatian meal, from the opening course of *supa* (in which friends dip pieces of grilled bread in a mixture of Teran wine and olive oil) to the closing toast of "*Zivio!*"—that is, "To Life!"—made with small glasses of grappa, a Croatian brandy.

LEISURE

Croatia's history as one of Europe's favorite playgrounds for decades has created a leisure industry that satisfies nearly every active adult. Along the coast, there is an abundance of sailboats, dive shops, fishing charters, beaches—naturist and otherwise—and currently the hottest water sport: sail boarding. Inland, there are biking and hiking trails, rock climbing, paragliding, and ballooning. Tennis facilities include the tennis center in **Umag** that hosts an ATP clay-court tournament every summer. If you're a golfer, you may have to be patient a little longer. There's the Jack Nicklaus course on its way just north of **Pula,** and other courses are planned as well.

If you're looking for something uniquely Croatian, Betty and Bob Poytner, Arizonans who opened an inn in *Istria,* have a summertime recommendation. On nights with a full moon, *Vis* residents and their guests gather in the village of **Rukavac** and climb into small boats for the short trip to the Green Cave, a sea-level cavern whose name comes from the way that its walls are lit by sunlight bouncing off the sea floor. At night, however, there is no green cast, only candles that have been placed on the cave's walls. Once there, the musically competent among the hundred or so that have gathered sing Dalmatian *Klapa* tunes about life and love and the joys of being on the island.

SOCIAL CUSTOMS

There is not a lot about Croatian social customs that will shock North Americans, except, perhaps, how very polite Croatians are. Everyone says "*Dobar dan*" ("Good day!") when they meet. The children address adults with the Croatian version of "sir" and "ma'am." Everyone uses "please" and "thank you" and "you're welcome" abundantly.

The one exception to this politeness is apparent when waiting in line.

Some Croatians say it's a holdover from Communist days, when shortages meant that one's place in line might determine whether you got fresh bread that day or not. Whatever the reason, many Croatian Dr. Jekylls transform into Mr. or Mrs. Hydes when it's time to queue up for something, pushing and shoving and cutting in. If challenged, though, they're likely to revert back to their normally polite selves.

In the areas where expats live, Croatians are used to foreigners after hosting international tourists in large numbers for decades. (It's having those foreigners stay year round that is taking some getting used to.) The tourist economy has also made them quite open minded about different lifestyles and cultures. Nude beaches started in Croatia before anywhere else in Europe, and the locals are fine with it. The beautiful Istrian coastal town of **Rovinj** has a thriving gay community, as does **Zagreb**. It's commonplace to see Bosnian women wearing the *hijab* (Islamic head scarf). Dark-skinned people are a curiosity here still, but there are few reports of racial prejudice.

HEALTH CARE/MEDICAL

Croatia has a national health care system supplemented by a relatively new private, market-based segment. The national health system is available to foreigners who pay its monthly cost of about $60 through either their employer or as individuals. Coverage includes major medical, doctor visits, dental care, prescription drugs, and a portion of eyeglasses costs.

Croatians tend to complain about their health system because of waits for elective and nonemergency care, the quality of facilities, and alleged corruption. Americans may find the facilities outdated, but the quality of the professional staff is high and the cost of care is astonishingly low.

RESIDENCY AND RED TAPE

North Americans who would like to spend no more than a few months here during the year will find it quite easy. Your U.S. or Canadian passport will gain you entry for up to ninety days out of any six-month period, and starting local nonresident bank accounts for both local and foreign currency, complete with debit cards, takes only a passport.

Croatia does not yet have a nice, neat retiree category for immigrants. If you want to reside here for six or twelve months a year, it will be necessary to demonstrate a vaguely defined ability to support yourself in addition to the other internationally standard requirements of no criminal liability and provision for housing.

For "permanent" renewable one-year residency, you form a company.

But it's imperative that you check the official websites; these regulations are subject to change.

Route 1: Temporary Residency
- Begin this process in the U.S. by contacting the Croatian Embassy in Washington, D.C.
- Requires birth certificate and clear criminal report, and means of support established through Social Security benefits, private pension, or cash assets.
- Grants one year of residency, which is renewable annually with the option to obtain permanent residency, and even citizenship, after five years.

Route 2: Business Visa
- Form a Croatian company with 20,000 kunas (about $3,750) in start-up capital that is fully available for use once the company is registered (about two to three weeks).
- Obtain a business visa with proof of company registration.
- Grants one year of residency, permission to earn money in Croatia through the company, full national health insurance benefits for $60 per month, and tax rebates.
- Renewable annually with the option to obtain permanent residency, and even citizenship, after five years.

Working

If part of your retirement dream is to pick up a part-time job at the local Wal-Mart, forget about Croatia. We don't have Wal-Marts, and they couldn't hire a foreigner for a part-time job anyway. Work laws are still restrictive, since Croatia is not at full employment. A work permit is required, and that can only be obtained on your behalf by a Croatian company or a foreign company licensed to do business here. They will have to show that workers like you cannot be found among the Croatian citizenry, and the red tape discourages companies from fooling with foreign workers.

If you're interested in a second or third or fourth career, though, and one with plenty of challenges, Croatia could be just the thing for you. It is relatively easy to form your own company with the proper guidance, and you and other foreign directors can all earn money through it. With Croatia's growing economy and upcoming EU accession, you may find that being a native English speaker gives you some advantages in dealing with the portion of the market coming from abroad. (See "Real Estate.")

COST OF LIVING

The cost of living in Croatia is roughly comparable to such American cities as Houston and Atlanta, making it among the less expensive cities in Europe. Our expats estimated the monthly expenses for a couple from a low of $1,200 to a high of $2,000 for a middle-class lifestyle. You can expect energy and food prices to be higher, housing costs to be about the same, and medical care to be much cheaper than in the U.S. There are no personal or real property taxes. Expats not earning money here will be burdened only with the Value Added Tax (VAT) of 22 percent on all goods and services except books, bread, and milk. If you purchase through your Croatian company, you can avoid that tax bite on everything from cars to computers.

The main variation in the cost of living within Croatia comes from differences in housing costs. In housing-short **Zagreb** and the sought-after *Adriatic coast,* real estate and rentals are higher, with the most expensive being around **Dubrovnik.** Basically, the farther away from the sea, the cheaper the property. (In non-euro Croatia, prices will be given in U.S. dollars.)

Monthly Cost of Living in Zagreb
Rent for a two-bedroom home, condo, or apartment: $500.
Groceries for two: $400.
Utilities: $100.
Cable TV: $60.
Internet, telephone: $70.
Maid service: $5 per hour.
Restaurants for two: Around $35.

Monthly Cost of Living in Istria
Rent for a two-bedroom home, condo, or apartment: $550 to $600.
Groceries for two: $450 to $500.
Utilities: $100 to $125.
Internet, telephone: $75 to $100.
Maid service: $4 per hour.
Restaurants for two: Around $35 to $45.

Monthly Cost of Living in Dalmatia and Islands
Rent for a two-bedroom home, condo, or apartment: $400 to $500.
Groceries for two: $350 to $400.
Utilities: $100.
Internet, telephone: $75.

Maid service: $4 per hour.
Restaurants for two: Around $25 to $35.

Cost cutters will do what the Croatians themselves do: take on some of the renovation/construction work themselves; grow some food during the year-long growing season; rent out a room occasionally to the tourists. Americans dependent on pensions paid in dollars have to hope for the best.

REAL ESTATE

Croatia is becoming one of the hot international real estate markets. Impending membership in the EU has always brought rapid real estate appreciation to other European countries, and Croatia, with its beautiful coastline and mountains, could follow that pattern.

Would-be investors do need to be aware of some caveats. As of 2008, foreigners must obtain permission from the Ministry of Foreign Affairs before they can have title transferred into their own names. The real estate industry is completely unregulated; no broker's license is required. There is a 5 percent tax assessed against the sales price of all real estate and paid by the buyer. Croatian land is surveyed, and land records are computerized and available online. There remain, however, title issues with many properties, particularly in rural areas, because of a frequent lack of care in transferring title when the owner dies. There is no such thing as title insurance yet.

Only the most adventurous of the adventurous should consider building a new home. There is a great deal of sensitivity about inflicting damage on the environment. Obtaining a building permit for vacant land is very difficult. The mortgage market is in its infancy as well.

Prices are low by European standards but higher than many resort areas in the U.S. You can expect to pay €1,800 to €3,000 per square meter for housing, whether it's an apartment or villa. But property purchases are arcane and can be very complicated. Most expats try to buy property and establish residency by starting their own company. Croatia makes it fairly easy to establish a limited liability company here. Start-up capital in the amount of 20,000 kunas (about $3,750) is required, and the process takes less than a month to complete. Once the company is registered, the start-up capital is fully available for the owner to use or even withdraw. The new company can purchase real estate without limitation. The majority owner of the new company can obtain a business visa with minimal documentation that allows the holder to live here year round and even earn money through the company.

Croatia wants foreign investment and entrepreneurs. Its constitution guarantees foreign investors both equality before the law and the inalienable right to withdraw funds and profits from the company after taxes and debts are paid. Tax laws are becoming more business friendly and feature a flat 20 percent tax on profits, with no additional tax on distributed profits. The number of governmental English-language websites with useful information for expat businesses is increasing, and there is a drive to reduce the red tape necessary to get a business up and running. (See "Working.")

TRANSPORTATION

The number of flights to Croatia increases almost weekly as the reputation of the place spreads around the world. It has a number of international airports to most European cities. Low-cost fliers like Ryanair, EasyJet, and Wizz Air are adding flights, and direct flights to and from the U.S. can't be far behind.

By car, Croatia is near the center of the European superhighway system, and the European cities of **Florence, Milan,** Innsbruck, Munich, Vienna, Budapest, and Austria are all less than eight hours away. **Zagreb** is easily accessible by rail from Munich or Vienna, and that line will soon be extended to the coastal port of **Rijeka.** The *Adriatic coast* is served by ferries from Italy's **Ancona** and **Venice,** and fast catamarans provide daily service between Istrian towns and **Venice** in the summer. The country is spending a lot of money to improve the quality of highways within its boundaries.

As to public transportation. **Zagreb** has an extensive trolley and bus system. Older Croatians love public transportation because their ride is free once they reach sixty-five. Every morning the buses fill with chatting retired folks headed to do their morning shopping at the city market and have a cup of coffee or glass of wine with a few friends. At midday they climb back aboard the bus with a sack filled with a cabbage or a few potatoes, a loaf of bread, and piece of meat. With this kind of independence, there are few senior citizens in nursing homes here.

SECURITY

Croatia's crime rate is low by American standards. Its rates of violent crimes and property crimes are closer to Japan's than to those of the U.S. One thing expats find most striking is the Croatians' own lack of concern about crime. Women in particular show no reluctance to travel by themselves at night using public transportation. Parents have no problem letting young children walk down the street by themselves to play with friends.

But corruption *is* a big issue in Croatia. Croatians usually rank their country high in corruption on international surveys, and there must be some truth behind that self-perception. But few expats have reported witnessing corruption personally in the form of someone demanding a bribe. The European Union is taking a very close look at the Croatian judiciary and bureaucracy over the next two years, so at the least, everyone will probably be on his or her best behavior for a while.

The lasting effects of the sins of the fathers can be seen in Croatians' attitudes toward the police. Marshal Tito was ruthless, and his political enemies did not fare well. The police were the tool he employed to keep control, and older Croatians still evince some fear of the cops.

COMMUNICATIONS AND MEDIA

Everything is up-to-date in Croatia when it comes to communications and media. The old state-owned telephone company was bought by Deutsche Telekom, and its service is reliable and very foreigner friendly if you're an English speaker. Cell phones work as well here as in any populated area of the U.S. DSL is as fast as is available in the U.S.—and at a comparable price—and more and more villages are being brought online.

Watching television will make you feel right at home, if perhaps in a time warp back to 1990. Every afternoon you can watch *Married With Children* and *Family Matters* with Croatian subtitles. At night, there's all the *CSI*s and some BBC mysteries.

UP-AND-COMING AREAS

If your profile and bank account balance aren't lofty, the Dalmatian city of Split or an island like *Hvar, Vis, Korcula,* or *Brac* may still be within reach. *Hvar* claims to have the most sunny days of any place in Europe and has been named among the ten best islands by several travel magazines.

Vis

Outermost among the inhabited islands is *Vis*. It is a land for the bold expat, ready to live at the very edge of a new frontier, an option for those who want to be the first to cut a new trail. Europe's Alps stretch to their southern limit in Croatia, at some points running right

---

into the Adriatic Sea. Rising to more than a mile high from a base close to sea level, these mountains' peaks are covered with snow for half the year. European tourists are just beginning to discover the area, and land is still quite cheap. Infrastructure is not as developed as in *Istria* or *Dalmatia*, but autobahn-style superhighways provide excellent access to the region from elsewhere in Croatia and beyond.

VOLUNTEERING WITHOUT BORDERS

A variety of organizations sponsor volunteer work in Croatia.

- Locally, museums and art and craft galleries welcome English speakers to help with tours. And every town has the usual assortment of community and church organizations that extend a welcome to "strangers."
- The International Women's Club of **Zagreb** gathers women from many countries who raise money and lend their services to local charities (www.iwcz.hr).
- The Society for Dolphin Conservation, together with veterinary faculty from the University of Zagreb, is working to save the last 220 Adriatic dolphins from extinction.

  The society aims to establish sanctuaries and a conservation center (www.delphinschultz.org/grd-english).

Hank Brill dons his coonskin cap every morning to help foreigners and foreign companies get started in Croatia. (See "My Croatia" #3.)

MY CROATIA

Arizonans Living on an Island in the Adriatic

Name, age, origin: Betty and Bob Poynter, sixty-one and sixty-two, Payson, Arizona. Lived in twenty countries before settling here.

Where we live: In an apartment in **Vis Town** on the Croatian island of *Vis*. The island is ninety square kilometers in the middle of the Adriatic Sea; the town's population is about 1,500.

How long in Croatia: Four years.

Present occupations: Consultants specializing in international development.

Reasons for moving here: We wanted a change of culture. We liked the climate. We were already doing quite a bit of business in the Balkans. And the politics in the U.S. was a factor; we marched against the Iraq invasion. We have worked and lived in over twenty countries—including, on and off since 1999, on the Balkan Peninsula. We appreciate the opportunity to explore the rest of Europe from a convenient home base. We enjoy daily life with our Croatian/Dalmatian friends on *Vis*. We have become involved on a daily basis with the thousands-of-years-old traditional life on this island. In essence, our four years have been an experience of discovery, and we've "learned how to live."

Here's what I mean by learn how to live: We spent most of our lives in the U.S. living in urban environments. Here on *Vis,* we head off at ten in the morning to buy some bread at the local bakery. Along the way, we run into someone we know who's headed to go fishing or crush grapes or pick olives. They say, "Come with us," and we do. We end up participating in activities that go back thousands of years. People really touch the earth here. They're more in balance with nature. Look, life on this island can be difficult. It's isolated. And I have to admit that there are times when we are back in the U.S. on a visit or living elsewhere because of work that we question why we are here. But when we return to *Vis,* it's very obvious why we stay. We fall back in love with the place.

Finances: We have income from Social Security, investments, and the work we are still doing.

Costs: You can rent a two-bedroom house or apartment for €350. Groceries cost about €700, and a night out at a restaurant for two is €40.

Our community: The population in the winter is 99.9 percent Croatian. During the summer months, there's an influx of tourists from the rest of Croatia and other parts of Europe primarily, though there are some Americans, Australians, and Canadians. The bulk of the Croatian population is elderly people who have lived on the island all their lives. However, there are more and more younger Croatians who enjoy living here year round and have found ways to make a living.

The relationships among expats is friendly, but there aren't many expats who are here for long periods of time. When they are, they eat out in local restaurants, hire locals to work for them, and enjoy life on the island and surrounding sea. Most of the expats are British people who already knew each other before they came to *Vis,* so they tend to spend time with one another. A small percentage of local people speak English. With the local population, it helps to speak Croatian; relatively few speak English. We're good at languages, but Croatian is the most difficult. But Croatians are not like the French. Croatians will explain things. The people here have time for that.

Living on an island any place in the world creates special challenges, as the residents tend to be more inward. In the case of *Vis,* which was isolated for many years because it was a military base, this is accentuated. *Vis* residents are struggling—trying to create a vision for the future. Like many places in Croatia, there's pressure to sell real estate at an accelerated pace, at very high prices.

Leisure: We enjoy boating, hiking, tennis, fishing, diving, swimming, yoga, and exploring caves. We also do lots of local traditional activities with our friends, like crushing grapes, picking olives, and hunting for mushrooms.

Culture: Not on the island, but in **Split,** accessible by ferry: symphony, movies in English, ballet, art museums and galleries, opera, jazz, and indigenous culture.

Drawbacks: (1) learning a new language, (2) understanding the culture of living on a small island, (3) decline of the dollar against the euro, (4) inflating real estate costs.

Best: The natural beauty; traditional way of life on *Vis;* spontaneous joy in doing seemingly insignificant things; getting to know people who are in tune with their environment.

What we miss most: A well-equipped fitness center.

Expected to miss but didn't: Access to a wide array of social and entertainment offerings.

MY CROATIA

British Innkeepers Who Bought an Old Lodge

Name, age, origin: Frank and Alice Freestone, fifty-one and fifty, Cambridge, England.

Where we live: Brest, *Istria,* in a house we renovated and turned into an inn. It was a 200-year-old lodge that originally housed a family and its 150 sheep. The coast is only forty-five minutes away, as are the larger towns, so we have the best of both worlds: remote yet with everything accessible.

How long in Croatia: One year.

Previous/present occupations: Frank was a contractor; now we're innkeepers.

Finances: Savings and sale of our home in England.

Reasons for moving here: Mainly, we were unhappy with the rat race in the UK. We came over three years ago looking for a holiday home. At the time, Croatia was a real bargain, and not many British people knew about the "Pearl of the Adriatic." So cost was one of the deciding factors. We landed in **Trieste** after making appointments with estate agents in various parts of Croatia, and armed with our printout from the web, we set off—not knowing if or where we would find a place.

We traveled through Croatia down as far as **Split,** viewing properties all the way. On our last booked viewing in **Split,** knowing all the properties viewed so far were not suitable for us, we were feeling totally disappointed and disheartened.

We started our homeward journey and stopped overnight in **Opatija** and saw a tourist magazine in the hotel. We found an article on Croatian national parks and nature parks, including Učka. We sifted through our mountain of web printouts of properties, and found it listed as a stone ruin with thirteen and a half acres of land in the Učka Nature Park.

With one day left before our flight back to the UK, we had nothing to lose in taking a look. We rang the owner and agreed to meet the next day to view it. The drive up to the property was stunning, through woodlands and open meadows. We arrived, and there the stone house stood. It was certainly a ruin, but we fell in love with it immediately and decided then and there that it was for us. We basically started the purchase in a day. A year ago, our plans evolved into making a permanent move here and turning the property into an ecotourist destination.

Leisure: Boating, hiking, biking, fishing, horseback riding, rock climbing, paragliding. Walking the parks in Croatia is wonderful, and they are being looked after so that they can be enjoyed and preserved.

Crime, corruption: Low.

Locals' attitudes toward expats: We are the only expats in our small village; we seem to have been accepted, although they did call us the "mad British" for wanting to live as isolated as we are. We try to fit in with the community, as it is up to us to change if need be, as we have moved to their country. English is widely spoken, but as far as speaking Croatian is concerned, we're limited to asking if they speak English.

Other expats: As far as other expats we've met, it's surprising how many British people have made the move to *Istria*. We are constantly making new contacts, the latest being a couple in **Novigrad** attempting to kick-start golfing in *Istria*. Believe it or not, they come from the same small village in England as we do (small world after all).

Drawbacks: Bureaucracy.

What we miss most: Cheaper English tea bags.

Expected to miss but didn't: TV.

MY CROATIA

Brought His Wife and Kids to a 3,000-year-old Town

Name, age, origin: Hank and Kaye Brill, fifty-two and fifty-one, Chicago.

Where we live: An apartment in **Pula,** in a quasi-suburban neighborhood within one kilometer of the sea. **Pula** calls itself a 3,000-year-old town, and it has the Roman ruins to prove it. For a town of 70,000, it's a fairly cosmopolitan place, with internationally known entertainment in the summer, a university, and an increasing number of expats.

How long in Croatia: Eighteen months.

Reasons for moving here: We wanted to pursue lifelong dreams of living abroad. We also felt that our children would benefit from exposure to a different culture. Finally, we thought it was a good time to leave after the 2004 elections and all that had gone before.

Finances: Sale of home and savings. Retirees receive no benefits in Croatia. But there is a constitutional guarantee for foreign investors that they will receive equal treatment and can always take their money out of the country.

Costs: About €750 to rent a two-bedroom apartment. Groceries €600 a month. Depends on where. **Dubrovnik** is for the jet set—very expensive. The rest of the *Dalmatian coast* is comparable to *Istria*. In *Istria,* the east coast is less expensive than the west coast and interior. As for taxes, there is a 5 percent tax on real estate transfers and a sales tax on new apartments, but there is no real or personal property tax like in the U.S.

Our community: It's 90 percent Croatian in the winter, and packed with tourists from all over Europe—and more recently, the world—during the summer. The expats here generally feel lucky to be here "ahead of the crowd," because property prices are rising. Here in *Istria* where we live, there is a lot of Italian, German, and English spoken. Young people all take English in elementary school. And at least half the programming on the Croatian broadcast networks is American and British. Our daughter is in school here. They have made a strong effort to accommodate her as she learns Croatian.

Leisure: Walks by the sea; fishing.

Culture: In the summer, we have everything from Russian ballet to Sting performing in the arena. There are musical events throughout the year, including jazz at a couple of local clubs, and classical music at the university.

Health care/medical: My wife has glaucoma, and needed to find a doctor shortly after we arrived. To date he has done more to explain her illness and its treatment to her than any doctor had in the U.S. Tests are done on a new German machine more advanced than what she had used in the U.S. The cost was $15 as opposed to $300 out of pocket. Prescription drugs can cost about 15 percent of what they cost in the U.S.

Drawbacks: Some social isolation; friendships with local Croatians difficult. The slower pace is both a plus and a minus.

What we miss most: Ethnic restaurants. Ice and lots of hot water for baths.

Expected to miss but didn't: TV (because everything is available by download anyway).

Chapter 18

SPAIN

The Possible Dream

By Benjamin Jones

Sunshine filtering through the drapes outside your bedroom window wakes you up well into the morning. The rattle of castanets from last night's free flamenco show in the town square still resounds in your head, where it keeps company with the slight ache that reminds you of that last, perhaps ill-advised, tumbler of sangria as a 1:00 a.m. nightcap. No matter. A portion of hot, crispy churros washed down with a *café con leche* down at the sidewalk café around the corner will get you going again. Then it's a stroll along the Mediterranean beachfront, a quick visit to the internet café to check your email, and a trip to the *mercado* to load up on groceries. Lunch with friends follows at a seafood restaurant at the little fishing port in town (the three-course *menú del día* costs $12) and then the ramble home for a siesta.

It's another day in Spain, a country whose rich heritage, pleasant weather, sophisticated cities, fine beaches, leisure activities, great food, and warm people draw tens of millions of travelers each year. And a growing number of foreign visitors, including an estimated 12,500 North American retirees.

"What I like about Spain can't be defined in tangible terms," says retired teacher, labor relations consultant, and journalist Henry Marquez, seventy-three, from Denver, who now owns a small vineyard near the southern town of **Puerto de Santa Maria**. "It's the ambience and the atmosphere. It's the only country in the world where people enter a restaurant and wish total strangers '*Buen provecho*,' which means 'Bon appétit.' Spaniards are friendly, outgoing, and they sure know how to live!"

Physically, Spain is a land of mountains, high steppes, magnificent river valleys, and beautiful coastlines. The weather is just as varied. Spaniards can be wading through waist-high snowfalls in the north during the deep winter at the same time that people in the far south are splashing about in the Mediterranean under balmy skies.

Once isolated both politically and economically from the rest of the continent, Spain today is an integral part of Europe and a thoroughly modern country. But while eagerly embracing change, Spaniards still hold on to their age-old traditions of strong family ties, allegiance to their geographical origins, a tolerance of others, and the refreshing attitude that pleasure and relaxation are just as important in life as work.

LOCATION

Southwestern Europe, in the *Iberian Peninsula*. Spain is about the size of Texas with forty-five million people.

CLIMATE

Continental, with harsh winters in the northern and central regions, and hot and dry summers in the center and the south. The northeastern Mediterranean coast can be very humid in July and August. Winters are very mild along the Mediterranean and in the *Balearic Islands* and *Canary Islands*.

PEOPLE

In ancient times, every conquering power in the region traipsed through Spain at one point or another, leaving a racial legacy of olive skin, dark hair, and brown eyes. Indigenous ethnic groups—which consider themselves separate from (and sometimes superior to) the rest of the folks, and who even speak their own languages—are the Catalans (18 percent), the Galicians (8 percent), and the Basques (3 percent). There are 9 million foreigners, many of whom are recent immigrants from Africa, the Arab world, South Asia, and Eastern Europe.

An estimated 12,000 U.S. retirees live in Spain, as do 500 Canadians, mostly along the Mediterranean coast and in **Madrid**, the *Balearic Islands,* and the *Canary Islands*. There are scores of thousands more Britons, Dutch, Scandinavians, Germans, and other Europeans.

HISTORY AND GOVERNMENT

Spain's glory days were in the sixteenth and seventeenth centuries, when it was a major European power and vast wealth flowed in from its colonies in the New World. However, political and economic stagnation followed the loss of its European territories in the eighteenth century, a crippling war against the occupying French in the early 1800s, and independence throughout their colonies in Latin America.

Spain was largely on the sidelines of history until the Spanish-American War in the late nineteenth century, when it lost its remaining colonies in Asia and the Americas. A crippling civil war, which ended in 1939, deeply divided the country, and the psychological scars are just now beginning to heal.

Right-wing dictator Francisco Franco was the victor in the war, and despite his pro-Axis sympathies during World War II, he was embraced by the West as a staunch anticommunist during the Cold War. But Spain did not really return to the international fold until the restoration of democracy following Franco's death in 1975.

A constitutional monarchy was established after Franco died, and since then Spain has enjoyed a stable government with regular elections to choose a parliament and prime minister. There are at least a dozen parties in the national parliament, which makes Spain more politically diverse and therefore more democratic—in theory at least—than the United States.

WHERE TO LIVE

The Coast

It's the beach, with its azure sea, brilliant weather, and year-round activities, that attracts the majority of expats to the Mediterranean coast, the most popular spot to retire.

Running from the French border in the north all the way to Portugal in the south, the *costa* offers a variety of landscapes, distinct features, and attractions for the retiree. In **Catalonia** in the more humid north, pine-studded hills speckled with huge stone farmhouses march down to coves and picture-perfect fishing villages. The greenery, the wonderful restaurants tucked away on rural back roads, and the local Catalans' devotion to good food and wine remind one of nearby France.

As you travel south toward the city of **Valencia,** the land becomes drier, homes are whitewashed with red tile roofs, and it begins to feel like Spain. Almost every seaside town and hamlet from here on down the coast

contains foreign retirees, and some places (like **Benidorm, Javea, Calpe, Denia, Torrevieja, Fuengirola, Marbella, Estepona,** and **Sotogrande**) are filled with people from abroad of all ages and nationalities who have found their place in the sun.

The Cities

There are pockets of retirees in the big cities such as **Madrid** and **Barcelona,** exciting metropolises filled with vibrant cultural life and all the conveniences of any city in the world. Elegant **Madrid,** located in the exact geographic center of Spain, boasts some of the best art museums in the world, fantastic performing arts, a nightlife that goes on forever, and great restaurants. **Barcelona,** with its modern and fin-de-siècle architecture, bohemian traditions, and the Catalan love for the good life, is a hedonistic delight.

Rural Spain

More intrepid foreigners are choosing the challenge of restoring tumble-down farms and village houses far from the madding crowd. Many foreigners have found homes in the hills above the coasts (with an easy drive to the well-stocked supermarkets, movie theaters, and other attractions there), while others are truly breaking new ground in tiny, isolated pueblos deep in the Spanish interior.

The Islands

For those seeking a relaxed lifestyle but with plenty of opportunities for active leisure pursuits, the *Balearic Islands* group—*Majorca, Minorca,* and *Ibiza*—located in the Mediterranean, and the *Canary Islands,* off the North African coast, are ideal.

Foreigners have been attracted to the *Balearics* for a long time, from composer Frédéric Chopin and author George Sand, who set up house together in *Majorca* in the nineteenth century (scandalizing the locals), to the hippies and disco denizens of *Ibiza* today. Despite their charms, which include lovely old towns and fine beaches, both are largely overrun with resident foreigners and tourists, making the third main island, *Minorca,* the preferred choice for many retirees. It also is a favored destination for visitors, but it's a bit less hectic, and a tad more sane than its sister isles.

UPSIDES

1. The weather. Sometimes called "the Florida of Europe," but without the hurricanes!
2. A laid-back lifestyle.
3. Fascinating history and culture around every corner.
4. Large numbers of welcoming fellow retirees.
5. Slumping real estate is an opportunity for buyers.

DOWNSIDES

1. The Latin "mañana" attitude can be frustrating.
2. Cultural differences: siestas, Vespas, and dinner at ten-thirty, anyone?

3. Prices for many goods and services are higher than in the U.S.
4. Large numbers of welcoming fellow retirees.
5. Slumping real estate is bad for resale opportunities.

AMBIENCE

Spain has long been almost a byword for unhurried, relaxed, take it easy. The Spaniards, after all, invented the siesta, and it is still practiced. The country is also known for its "mañana" attitude, which can be maddening to those from more punctual cultures. However, these days Spaniards, well aware that they are now an integral part of a more hurried world (for better or worse), are shaking off the torpor and making some progress toward arriving on time at appointments, for example.

Still, the time-honored tradition of a long two-hour lunch survives, and sometimes it appears that no serious business gets done in the afternoon. And weekends are worse. Take a walk down the street or through the square at four o'clock on a Saturday or Sunday, and it looks like the place has been abandoned en masse. But not to worry: everyone is still at home enjoying a massive lunch *con la familia,* snoozing, or tuning into a soccer match.

Spaniards like foreigners and in general are warm, open, and helpful, but they can be shy in forming solid relationships with expats. Making friends with other retirees is easy. Where foreigners gather along the coasts and on the islands, there is a plethora of clubs for almost every interest, from gardening, literature, and amateur dramatics to jazz appreciation, animal rights, and sports. The intensity of your social life is up to you.

English is widely spoken on the coasts and in the islands, where most retirees choose to live, as these areas are longtime destinations for tourists, especially the British. But the locals appreciate it when someone makes an effort in their language, even if barely comprehensible, and Spanish is indispensable in villages and rural areas.

STANDARD OF LIVING

Since joining the European Union just over two decades ago, Spain has been transformed economically from what was once an almost third world nation to enjoying equality with its once more prosperous neighbors.

And this progress is evident everywhere and not just in the statistics (Spain's per capita annual income: $25,000). Freshly built condominiums crowd the outskirts of cities large and small; high-class restaurants that could stand on their own in New York or Miami are sprouting like mushrooms. More and more Spaniards are driving the latest Mercedes.

There is relative poverty in some urban areas and even in the villages. But well-financed social programs, free and universal health care (see "Health Care/Medical"), support from extended families, and an extensive network of charities ensure that almost no citizen goes to bed hungry or is homeless.

Expats tend to cluster in solidly middle-class and upper-class areas, and some of the latter are very tony, with their marinas, pricey boutiques, multimillion-dollar homes, and championship golf courses. Most foreign retirees can afford domestic help and gardeners, even if only for one or two days a week.

Things changed dramatically for expats in 2008, when a combination of overbuilding and international housing problems hit the Spanish vacation real estate market hard. (See "Real Estate.") The drop in vacation house prices left a lot of expats, especially those who had bought at the peak of the market, unhappy and frustrated. But one expat's unhappiness is another's break, and the situation in Spain presents ample buying—or renting—opportunities for newcomers in the forseeable future.

CULTURE

Culturally Spain is a microcosm of the Mediterranean world. The Romans' main legacy besides their ruins is the Spanish language, with its Latin roots. Later came the Jews, and the Moors, who also influenced the language as well as Spanish architecture and cuisine.

Cervantes, Velázquez, Goya, Picasso, Celo, Dalí, Miró, Casals, Segovia. Spain has no shortage of universally great cultural figures, and the arts are accorded great respect at all levels of society. For culture vultures, the big cities such as **Madrid, Barcelona, Valencia, Bilbao,** and **Málaga** offer up a smorgasbord of museums, art galleries, opera houses, orchestra halls, dance troupes, and jazz clubs, attracting both local and international talent.

And thanks to generous subsidies from the government and private businesses, art exhibits, concerts, recitals, folklore performances, and cultural festivals are regular events even in some of the remotest pueblos. Typically the local government sponsors a summer festival that might include a Mexican dance group, a Ukrainian women's chorus, a chamber orchestra from **Madrid,** or a troupe of clowns, all performing under the starlit skies in the plaza beside the thirteenth-century church.

Spain's wonderful cuisine is also regionally diverse, with *Catalonia* and the *Basque Country* acknowledged as the best places to tuck in. A prestigious culinary magazine recently chose El Bulli, located on *Catalonia's Costa Brava,* as the best restaurant *in the world* for the almost surrealistic kitchen creations of its chef/owner, Ferrán Adrià, who likes serving up sardine foams, tomato ice cream, and other innovative delights. And the Basque city of **San Sebastián** boasts more Michelin-starred restaurants than any comparable area in the world, even in France.

But earthier, and still delicious fare, is the norm. Paella, the rice-based casserole of shellfish, saffron, and vegetables (and sometimes rabbit and snails!) rules in **Valencia,** while Andalusians love to douse fresh fish in flour and fry it up quick in bubbling olive oil. In the center of the country, roast meats are the main course, and spring lamb grilled over a fire of grapevines is the star attraction.

Wherever you are, tapas, the bite-sized bar snacks, are the perfect accompaniment to a glass of *vino tinto* (red wine), *vino blanco* (white wine), or sparkling *cava* wine from any of Spain's award-winning wine-growing regions.

LEISURE

There is a surfeit of leisure activities for retirees in Spain, whether outdoor or indoor, with sports at the top of the list. Fishing, sailing, swimming, and jogging or taking long walks along the excellent beachside promenades that front most coastal towns are favorite pastimes for those who have opted to live by the sea.

And for those who like their physical activity dry, there is tennis or golf. Spain is the leading vacation destination for European golfers, and there are many world-class courses within easy reach of just about anywhere retirees settle. Green fees, however, are more expensive than in the United States and start at around €50.

A little known fact: Spain is Europe's second-most mountainous country after Switzerland. Trekking, horseback riding, and canoeing in the high country are on offer throughout the year, and for those who want to emulate Ernest Hemingway, the trout streams beckon. For skiers, the slopes of the *Sierra Nevada* in the south are a wonderful winter getaway.

A less strenuous leisure pursuit is sightseeing, and it is always a delight to pack a lunch, hop in the car, and see what wonders await you down the road. Spain boasts a long and glorious history, and there are reminders everywhere. The old Roman city of **Mérida,** with its intact open-air theater and aqueduct, along with a museum filled with treasures from two millennia ago, is a great place to explore.

Granada's amazing Moorish glories, **Seville**'s orange-tree-shaded plazas, the old Jewish quarter of **Córdoba**, and that odd, part–Olde England, part-Mediterranean territory of *Gibraltar* are all just a few hours away. Farther afield, there are the conquistador cities of **Extremadura**, bohemian **Barcelona**, the cosmopolitan glitter of **Madrid**, and the green wilds (and great cuisine) of the northern Atlantic coast.

And there are always fiestas to attend. Every city, town, and village has its own big blowout at least once a year, with religious processions, folklore performances, fireworks, gastronomic fairs, sports competitions, and, at night, dancing and drinking in the main square until way, way late.

SOCIAL CUSTOMS

In general, Spaniards are unfailingly polite and will bend over backward not to offend. Old World courtesy is the rule: Spanish men open doors for women and men alike, it's considered rude not to greet an acquaintance with a hearty *"Buenos días,"* and a friend will almost become violent if you deny him the pleasure of picking up the tab for a round of drinks or even a meal.

Spain gave us the word *macho,* and the concept is certainly evident in some aspects of life, although in its more benign forms. Example: construction workers hollering out harmless and occasionally quite witty flirtatious remarks at passing females. "I want you to be the mother of my children!" "Columbus conquered a continent with a sword, you've conquered my heart with just a glance!" That kind of thing. In general, Spain is a very safe place for single women. Manifestations of extreme machismo, such as fisticuffs over a contested parking space or a perceived slight in a bar, are rare.

Most Spaniards are Roman Catholics (although church attendance is dropping steadily) and are very family oriented. Children rule and are warmly indulged even when they are making nuisances of themselves in restaurants. But the focus on the family does not extend to intolerance of alternative lifestyles, and Spain was one of the first countries in Europe to allow gay marriage.

Spaniards have a long love-hate relationship with America. More than one hundred years after the fact, the loss of Spain's colonies to the U.S. in the Spanish-American War still grates, as does Washington's support for right-wing dictator Francisco Franco as a bulwark against Communism during the Cold War. Recently, after a railway terrorist attack, Spaniards virtually forced the government to pull its support from the U.S. war in Iraq.

But America is still deeply admired for the vibrancy and appeal of its popular culture and for its business acumen, while Canada is seen as the sanest and most civilized of the Anglo-Saxon nations.

HEALTH CARE/MEDICAL

Health care in Spain has improved dramatically over the past decade and is now as good as, or even better than, the rest of Europe. Indeed, many citizens of other European Union countries travel to Spain for operations and other procedures because the care is good and the waiting list is shorter. Hospitals and health care services around Europe eagerly recruit Spanish doctors and nurses because of their professional qualifications.

Spain has both public and private health care systems. Almost every Spaniard and foreigners who have registered with the authorities are covered by the public system. This not only provides free doctor visits, surgical procedures, and hospital stays, but also heavily subsidized prescription medicines.

Expats living in Spain with any type of visa can join the public health care system. You go to your city hall and *empadronarse,* or register yourself, as an official city resident. This will give you the right to apply for a local health card, which you use for visiting the clinic in your town or neighborhood and scheduling doctor visits.

Spanish hospitals in general provide good care although there is sometimes a problem of overcrowding at big city hospitals and long waits to see a specialist. Even small villages have clinics that state doctors visit several times a week for walk-in visits. Emergency services cover the entire country.

However, many expatriates opt for private health insurance, which is widely available from both Spanish companies such as Sanitas, and British or Dutch companies that have special packages for overseas residents, including Americans and Canadians.

RESIDENCY AND RED TAPE

The Spanish government issues what is called "a residence visa for retirement," good for five years and renewable. The most important requirement is proof of permanent retirement annual income of at least $10,000, plus $1,700 from an "official institution" for each dependent family member. This means Social Security, a private source or corporation, and proof of any other income source and/or properties in Spain.

You'll also need: proof of medical insurance coverage in Spain and a statement typed on a physician's letterhead verifying you are in good physical and mental health, free of contagious diseases, and not a drug addict; and a clean police criminal record from the state authorities, which must be verified by fingerprints. All documents must be photocopied at least three times and translated into Spanish by an officially recognized translator. Visa approvals require authorization from **Madrid**, and that process takes an average of five months.

After one full year in Spain, North Americans can ask for residency with the right to work. There is also what is called a temporary residence visa for those planning on staying more than ninety days in Spain but less than five years, but this does not allow you to work. Some retirees from North America opt for entering Spain as tourists and hop over the nearest border or fly out of the country to get their six-month tourist visas renewed. This is technically illegal and not advised, as someday a zealous border official may turn you back, and who needs that kind of adventure?

Working

Although the situation is improving, Spain is one of the most difficult countries in the European Union for starting up one's own enterprise, because of the red tape and paper chases involved. "Work possibilities certainly exist, but they are very limited," says Donna Domingo a former executive secretary from Seminole, Florida, who retired to the Atlantic seaside town of **Rota** twenty-four years ago. "I *could* start my own business. But I haven't. It is very hard with all the paperwork and the bureaucracy."

To work at all, a North American retiree would have to obtain a residency permit with permission to work, proving that no Spaniards could fill the position. An alternative is to obtain a self-employment visa, or *visado de trabajo por cuenta propia*, with which you can set up your own company or open a business such as a restaurant or bed-and-breakfast.

Spanish residents are taxed on their worldwide income, but one can deduct taxes paid in his or her home country, and there is a tax treaty between the United States and Spain that covers the issue of double taxation.

COST OF LIVING

Spain's not as cheap as it used to be, but where in the world is? And the worsening dollar-euro exchange rate makes prices for most goods and services in Spain appear high indeed when compared with those in North America. But by applying a little common sense, avoiding the exact duplication of one's lifestyle back home, and bargain hunting, Spain is certainly affordable.

Monthly Cost of Living in the High-end Mediterranean Resort of Sotogrande

Rent for a two-bedroom home, condo, or apartment: €700.

Taxes: Property taxes vary according to location but are all high; no sales tax on food and drink.

Groceries for two: €400.

Utilities: €75.

Satellite TV: €40.

Internet: €30.

Telephone: €30.

Transportation: Taxi to airport, €30.

Maid service: €8 an hour and up.

Restaurants for two: €50 for a night out in a midrange restaurant.

Monthly Cost of Living in Madrid

Rent for a two-bedroom home, condo, or apartment: €1,000.

Taxes: Property taxes vary according to location but are all high; no sales tax on food or drink.

Groceries for two: €400.

Utilities: €80.

Cable or satellite TV: €40.

Internet: €30.

Telephone: €30.

Transportation: Taxi to airport, €18.

Maid service: €9 per hour and up.

Restaurants for two: €40 for a night out in a midrange restaurant.

Monthly Cost of Living in a Rural Village

Rent for a two-bedroom home, condo, or apartment: €350.

Taxes: Property taxes vary according to location but are all high; no sales tax on food or drink.

Groceries for two: €400.

Utilities: €40.

Satellite TV: €30.

Internet: Basic connection, €15 (most villages do not have broadband).

Telephone: €30.

Transportation: Bus to nearest city, €8 and up.

Maid service: €7 per hour and up.

Restaurants for two: €25 to €30 for a night out in a midrange restaurant.

To put it all in perspective, according to a report on costs of living around the world in 2006 by Mercer Human Resources Consulting, **Madrid** and **Barcelona** were ranked forty-third and forty-sixth respectively, and sandwiched between the two Spanish cities were Los Angeles at forty-fourth and White Plains, New York, at forty-fifth.

REAL ESTATE

It is perfectly legal for North Americans to buy property in Spain, and there are no restrictions whatsoever, whether it's a beachfront mansion, resort town villa, big-city apartment, or rural fixer-upper.

Searching for that perfect property is relatively easy. All real estate agents in the most popular retirement spots advertise in the local English-language publications, and if you Google terms like "real estate *Costa del Sol*" or "real estate *Canary Islands,*" dozens of websites, mostly in English, will pop up. Some of these sites provide detailed and regularly updated information on what steps will be involved in buying a house, obtaining a mortgage, and changes in tax law. (See "Resources" chapter.)

Another method is to saunter around the place you think you would like to live and look out for *Se Vende,* or For Sale, signs on attractive properties. There are also at least a half dozen Spanish real estate magazines in English covering the most popular areas.

Once you find your dream home and are ready to deal, it is absolutely essential to hire a bilingual lawyer, or *abogado,* to represent you and steer you through and explain the bureaucratic channels, plus a certified financial expert to handle the tax issues. One of the most important tasks your lawyer will perform is searching through the municipal registry to make sure the seller actually owns the property and that it is free of liens. In years past, unwitting foreigners have bought residences that the sellers didn't own or purchased a plot of land for a future home only to find out it was not zoned for residential use.

Local experts will also know that the stunning view of the beach from the house you have your heart set on is about to be blocked by a new four-lane highway.

Along with the cost of the house or apartment itself, there are various taxes (transfer, value added, and stamp duty) that depend on the property's value plus fees for the notary and property registration. These official costs usually amount to around 10 percent of the property's value.

Spain has a very competitive lending market, and some banks have set up special departments to service expatriate home buyers. Through a variety of lenders, one can obtain interest-only mortgages, fixed-rate mortgages, variable-rate mortgages, or a combination.

But as in the United States, the days of easy mortgages and rising house prices came to an end in 2008. Prices of houses fell by 30 percent or more in many expat locations, leaving many of Spain's large number of European retirees and snowbirds holding negative mortgage equity. The problem will continue to be severe for some; for others, it is an opportunity.

But Spain will almost certainly remain an attractive destination for vacation home and retirement buyers for years to come, so it's highly likely that an affordable purchase still makes sense. And that's the crux: What can you afford? Much of it depends on where you want to live.

Although falling values will affect these prices in 2009, a one-bedroom apartment in a complex with pool in the booming *Costa Brava* resort town of **Benalmádena,** for example, will set you back €150,000, but a similar property in the less-developed Mediterranean region of *Murcia* costs €100,000.

In the *Canary Islands,* which boast temperatures of about 75 degrees year round, prices for a simple, refurbished two-bedroom bungalow with patio and garden in a four-star development start at €175,000.

City prices, naturally, are steeper. In a recent look through the newspaper property section, a two-bedroom apartment in one of the newer neighborhoods of **Madrid** was listed for €350,000.

In the luxury resort towns like **Marbella** or **Sotogrande,** average prices can range from €400,000 for a condo to €1 million for a four-bedroom house with garden and swimming pool. There are, of course, homes that can cost much, much more.

If roughing it is your thing, a *finca,* or rural property, with a three-bedroom, 60-square-meter house on 10,000 square meters of land in the hills of *Málaga* province was recently listed for €125,000.

Rentals

Rental properties in those areas most popular with retirees are widely available, both for short-term and long. The prices are all over the place, and can range from a few hundred dollars a month to several thousand, depending on location and type of dwelling.

TRANSPORTATION

There is international air service between **Madrid** or **Barcelona** and many U.S. cities; it's seven hours from New York. A growing number of low-cost carriers like Ryanair and EasyJet now serve not only **Madrid** and **Barcelona** but smaller destinations closer to the popular retirement centers, with flights from all over Europe.

Getting around the country by train is the preferred choice of many Spaniards. Trains are fast (bullet train service is expanding rapidly), clean, and relatively cheap, and many boast meal and drink service similar to that of airlines. Buses are sometimes necessary to reach more out-of-the-way destinations.

But if you want to see this country at your own pace, stopping at that crumbling castle on the hill or trying out a restaurant in an isolated village that you've heard about, driving is best. Despite some black spots, Spanish highways and roads are quickly improving, thanks to the billions of euros pumped into transport infrastructure over the past two decades. One drawback: gasoline is very expensive, which is a good argument against shipping over your gas guzzler from home, and for buying a car locally.

SECURITY

Many foreigners taking their cue, perhaps, from the reputations of Latin American countries, believe that corruption is widespread in Spain. But try to slip a Guardia Civil €50 to avoid a traffic beef, and you'll be tossed in the pokey. Corruption does exist at high levels of the "Here's one hundred thousand euros, let me build a housing development on that protected land" variety, but that rarely involves expatriates.

Crime is another matter. While the rate of traditional violent crime (murder, bank robberies) is low compared to the United States, there is a worrisome increase in muggings of foreigners and a recent wave in home invasions of expatriates by Eastern European gangs, which are quite common on the coasts.

If you're a victim, the Spanish police will be sympathetic and helpful, but if it's a mugging, regular burglary, or auto theft, they're likely just to go through the motions, and there will be little follow-up.

COMMUNICATIONS AND MEDIA

Telephone service in Spain is good, and cell phones are ubiquitous. Spaniards have the maddening habit of chattering away loudly into their handsets about their most personal business while on the bus or sitting in a café. Broadband internet is widely available, except in some rural areas where residents can opt for their own rather pricey satellite reception. The postal system is neither better nor worse than at home, with mail to and from North America usually taking around a week to arrive.

There are TV cable and satellite systems that provide an ever-expanding choice of channels from around the world. Spanish television, both free-to-air and subscription, shows some films and American and British series in English.

UP-AND-COMING AREAS

Longtime expats bemoan the overbuilding along the Mediterranean and on some of the islands, which shows no sign of letting up as European baby boomers hit retirement age and head south. They speak wistfully of moving on to some yet pristine paradise before the developers arrive.

With the coast pretty much played out, some have opted for the quieter islands in the *Balearics* and *Canary* archipelagos.

Minorca in the Balearics has managed to avoid the total takeover of neighboring *Majorca* by foreigners (where German is more commonly heard than Spanish) and the youth/drug/raver culture Mecca that is *Ibiza*. If you're the outdoors type, this is the place for you. *Minorca* is a UNESCO-designated Biosphere Reserve, and there are beaches ranging from long, sandy strands to tiny, isolated coves with just enough space for a blanket, an umbrella, and a picnic basket, plus breathtaking scenery perfect for long hikes in the interior.

Fuerteventura, in the Canary Islands (known to the Romans as "the Fortunate Islands"), is the new hot spot. It's the closest of the islands to the African coast and on the same latitude as Mexico and Florida. It is the second-largest of the *Canaries* but has the least population density. The most popular areas to live are *Corralejo, Betancuria, Caleta de Fuste,* and *Lajares.* Water sports include surfing, wind surfing, deep-sea fishing, and sailing. The balmy weather ensures perfect conditions for golf, tennis, and horseback riding. As on islands everywhere, prices are higher as goods have to be shipped over from the mainland. Expect to pay between 15 percent and 20 percent more for goods and services.

Andalusia, in the mountains of the southern region, is seeing more and more foreigners arriving, attracted by the isolation, the cheaper prices, and the convenience of popping down to the nearby coast when civilization beckons. There are few, if any, real residential developments here, so that means rural abodes or village homes for rent or purchase.

Finally, some expats literally head for the hills. They follow in the footsteps of those who have abandoned civilization as we know it, to make a home in the hinterlands of the Spanish mainland. Several have written books about their often comical and frequently exasperating experiences of finding a place to settle while dealing with recalcitrant builders, bothersome neighbors, and wayward wildlife.

VOLUNTEERING WITHOUT BORDERS

Many charity organizations in Spain, especially those in areas where retirees tend to gather, are run by English-speaking foreigners and welcome new volunteers. Some more ambitious projects, such as the dolphin headcount, require a fee—but most just seek a helping hand.

- Pueblo Inglés is an organization where American volunteer tutors run intensive immersion programs in picturesque villages in Spain. These programs are attended mainly by business middle managers who need English to run international businesses (www.puebloingles.com).
- Sunseed Desert Technology is a British nonprofit that develops, demonstrates, and communicates low-tech methods to live sustainably in the desert province of *Almería*. Each year more than three hundred volunteers, living communally, serve up to several months (www.sunseed.org.uk).
- The Asociación de Málaga de los Sanctuarios del Burro rescues abandoned and injured donkeys, dogs, cats, "and almost anything that walks or flies." It has undertaken over six thousand rescues since 1995 (www.refugiodelburro.com).

Benjamin Jones has worked as a journalist in Spain for a number of U.S. and foreign publications and broadcast outlets since 1980.

MY SPAIN

A Volunteer from California

Name, age, origin: Samantha Carlin, fifty-four, San Diego.

Where I live: Estepona, *Costa Brava.*

Previous/present occupation: Formerly personnel manager, currently freelance lecturer.

Reasons for moving here: Just one visit! But I did want a place in Europe, and so I researched for about a year until I found the region I wanted.

Real estate: Never, never buy without a good local lawyer; preferably one who has been recommended. Complete the transaction before a notary: buying country property takes a great deal of additional research to ensure legality. I wouldn't build. It requires, to my mind, a great deal of fortitude, and at least a rudimentary knowledge of Spanish.

Culture: In Estepona, the town hall provides a full calendar of concerts, exhibitions, ballet, opera, films (in English, Spanish, and other languages), an annual jazz festival, car rallies, and other activities, many of which are free. On New Year's Eve, they put on a super fireworks display in the town, with grapes and festive hats, tooters, and all the rest.

Typical day: I have been involved in volunteer work of one sort or another since I arrived. If retired, I find that it gives structure to a life that might otherwise flounder. For three years, I volunteered at a charity in *Málaga* province that provides hospice care for terminal cancer patients of all nationalities. Volunteering in an environment that was Spanish, but where a number of volunteers were other nationalities, was rewarding as well as social. I found that most Spanish helpers and customers, while they may have been noncommittal at first, warmed very quickly as they saw that we were sincere in our efforts. I am now a committee member for one of three more charitable societies on the *Costa Brava.*

Wish I'd known before: The weather! Far cooler and wetter in winter than I had previously believed. (It's not always summer on the *Costa Brava*!)

Advice: Try to learn Spanish as soon as you are able, even if it's only a few words. Attend local *ferias,* fiestas. It's not only fun, but you learn a lot about the local traditions in your area. I've found that participation is a key word. Consider volunteer work. It not only improves your Spanish, but it puts you in contact with local residents.

MY SPAIN

A Single Woman Who Moved Alone, Knowing No One

Name, age, origin: Nora P. McNulty, sixty-seven, Chicago.

Where I live: Altea, Valencia, *Costa Blanca.*

Previous occupation: Retired accountant.

Reasons for moving here: At home I was in a rut at work, long hours at the office, shoveling snow in the winter. Years earlier I had checked out Mexico, but health care was an issue. I chose Spain after a visit to my daughter-in-law's Spanish family. Since I have dual citizenship in the U.S. and the UK, I knew that I would be able to participate in the national health care system; Spain is of course an EU country. While visiting her family for Christmas holidays, I checked out the area. I checked out apartment prices, all seemed feasible, and I was ready for a challenge in my life.

Finances: When I moved here, it was pesetas, not euros, then, and the dollar was strong. Life is not so easy financially now. I bought my place and live mostly on Social Security.

Real estate: There are many scams and unfair land-grab laws, especially in *Valencia* province. Use a reputable lawyer and be sure that you understand any agreement, most of which will be in Spanish. Have a very good interpreter who is taking care of your interests. Check with AFPO—Association of Foreign Property Owners—in most towns. (See "Resources" chapter.)

Typical day: Catch the news on CNN.com—English-language papers are very expensive in Spain. Walk along the beach, have a coffee in an outdoor café. Meet friends for lunch or go to a club gathering. *Menú del día* is a very inexpensive lunch. Play *boules* on the beach. Dinner in or out with friends, occasionally a concert or opera. We have a very good venue in **Altea,** and seniors get discounts on tickets.

My community: Altea is a very old, beautiful village. But on the *Costa Blanca,* there are very few Americans or Canadians. Lots of British, Dutch, Norwegian, and Germans. I belong to several expat clubs, and I take Spanish and painting classes.

Wish I'd known before: About renting. I bought my house and have since found that rents are very low and that there are many places to rent. Also wish I'd learned Spanish before I came.

Best: I learned that I could move to a foreign country, alone, knowing no one, not knowing the language. That I could develop friendships, and find a comfortable life for myself. I was free to be whomever I wanted to be—no one had any pre-conceived opinions about me.

Worst: I had a serious accident and was in the hospital for ten days, not able to communicate with the medical staff. Medical care, however, was the very best and cost me zero.

What I miss most: Summer in Chicago. Knowing the ropes: who to call for help; how to get a plumber, a window cleaner, a car mechanic, a daily newspaper delivered to the door.

MY SPAIN

An Artist with Political Convictions

Name, age, origin: Laura Mason (pseudonym), seventy, Pebble Beach, California.

Present occupation: Artist.

Reasons for moving here: I considered other countries, especially Italy, as it is full of artists, but I did not like it as much as Spain.

Finances: Social Security and earnings from sculpting.

Real estate: Rent first, check out the neighbors. Then, if you decide you can put up with them and Spain, buy the best renovation you can find.

Typical day: Getting warm in the winter, riding my horse in the summer early before it gets too hot. Mostly taking care of necessities in the morning and creating in the afternoon.

Wish I'd known before: Spanish before I came to Spain. The Spanish used to respect Americans and liked us, now no one likes us. Also, I should have brought more money. The dollar went down against the euro to pay for the costs of the Iraq war.

Best: To become acknowledged for my art in Spain.

Worst: Bush being elected for a second term.

Advice: Make sure you like the sort of people living around you. I expected more culture, more sophistication, but found mostly expats living for the sun only. I found a certain element of fairly common English who look down on Americans, yet Spain is full of low-life English. The few Americans I know here all came with some resources, but I see English, Dutch, and Germans coming to Spain without anything to offer but schemes for what they can make or take from Spain.

MY SPAIN

*A Former Engineer with a
View of the Rock of Gibraltar*

Name, age, origin: J. Douglas White, eighty-four, New York, Washington, D.C., and California.

Where I live: Torreguadiaro, *Cádiz.*

How long in Spain: Thirty-three years.

Previous/present occupation: Former electronics engineer, presently an author.

Reasons for moving here: Change of culture. I was living in England, and age and climate convinced me that a change was due. So I moved to Spain. I found **Gaucín**, a village in *Andalusia* (population, 2,000, including 50 expatriates), and an even more enjoyable lifestyle there (read my book, *El Camelot*). Developers discovered **Gaucín** and ruined it with new buildings of phony *rústico* design. Prices soared along with the cheap glamour, and most old friends left. I sold out and moved to the *costa*. The whole *costa* is being overbuilt with cheap apartment buildings. It is fine now, but the future of this particular area looks bleak (in contentment, that is).

Senior benefits give you a 25 percent discount on public transportation, free flu shots, and an invitation to the mayor's Christmas dinner (which includes a gift: usually a small poinsettia plant or a calendar).

My community: Torreguadiaro is a small town in the shadow of **Soto-grande,** the Beverly Hills of *Cádiz*. My condo is on a beach of the Mediterranean; my terrace has a ninth-floor view of Gibraltar and Morocco. There is harmony among the expats (very few Americans) and the Spanish; we depend on one another.

Weather: Inland, mountain winters are colder; summers cooler. The typical Spanish traditional house is built to stay cool in summer and warm in winter. Heat is from fireplaces or gas heaters, and can be very uncomfortable. The new houses on the coast have air-conditioning, but there is no natural gas for central heating.

Leisure: There are always new restaurants to sample, exhibits or charity shows to attend, or picnics and sightseeing. A favorite Sunday trip is on our little train into the mountains for a four-hour lunch (good wine at $2 a bottle), waterfalls, and dramatic cliffs on the way. There are plenty of charities to join, and lectures by London experts on different types of art.

Culture: Art and crafts classes in every town, mostly by and for expats. There are several American clubs on the *costa,* which do luncheons and charities. All Spanish cities have excellent orchestral concerts, operas, and ballets by famous companies. In summer the hills are alive with music festivals. For those who like their steak rare, there is a *plaza de toros* in almost every town.

Health care/medical: Americans don't get the benefits of those from EU countries. In England health care is free for Americans, but not in Spain. Insurance is fairly reasonable: I pay €2,200 a year. Office visits €25 to €50. Doctors, excellent. In a Houston hospital, I had an ear tested for a minor problem; it cost $3,700, and I was given pills that made me very ill. Back in Spain, I took the pills to my local doctor, who found they were for scarlet fever. His pills: €6, and they cured my ear problem.

Residency and visas: A *residencia* permit gives you all the privileges of a national, except for medicine and other socialized benefits. You also have to pay income tax on your worldwide income—or as you report it. The benefits are that your death duties are 5 percent rather than 45 percent for a nonresident, and you have such advantages as: if you're in a car accident, the "resident" receives preferred treatment over the nonresident. The rule for non-residencia holders is that you must leave the country every six months, but many foreigners choose to ignore it, with no problems. But rules keep changing. I renew my residencia every five years, which allows me to work here, or own and operate a business.

Locals' attitudes toward Americans: Most Spaniards on the coast speak English, or at least I never have trouble being understood. I now speak Spanish conversationally. But it isn't absolutely necessary. Unless you're extremely gregarious (or romantic), most of your friends will be English or American anyway.

Best: The flower-covered hillsides in springtime were unexpected; a real bonus. Living here I've learned the joy of life, coming to appreciate things for their value, not their cost.

What I miss most: Cranberry sauce, buttermilk, and oyster crackers.

Chapter 19

PORTUGAL

Touch of Old Europe

By Holly Raible Blades

Everyone comes to Portugal for the sun. And the beach, of course. The endless golf season. The easy life: leisurely meals at seaside restaurants, cheap, good wine, lingering over coffee or beer at an outdoor café. It's a bargain for Northern Europeans. It's not dirt cheap like it used to be, but costs are still easily at least 30 percent lower than in most other Western European countries. Portugal offers a highly civilized European lifestyle mixed with a sweet, slow, resort-style beach life, frost free, all year round.

You'd have to be a little bit in love with the idea of Europe, though. You'd have to be drawn in by the castles and the wine and the romantic stories, the beautiful old buildings, history so rich and real and present that sometimes you feel as if you've fallen through a crack in time. You'd have to like the idea of an early morning on a cobblestone street, stopping by the *padaria* to pick up warm bread, maybe stopping at the café to down an espresso and practice your Portuguese with the barman. Later you might walk down to the sea wall or the beach to see what the fishermen are catching, then meet up with some expat friends for lunch outside or a game of bridge. Take a bike ride, swim, play a little tennis or a round of golf, go sailing, attend language class, paint. The light is very good here.

UPSIDES

1. Cultural heritage and stability of Old Europe with a lower cost of living.
2. Mild climate and hundreds of miles of spectacular coast.
3. Large international community, and English is widely spoken.
4. Good wine is cheap, even with a lousy exchange rate.
5. One of the five safest countries in Europe.
6. Good health care.

DOWNSIDES

1. The expats are welcoming, but integrating with the Portuguese community is difficult.
2. Laws to protect workers mean it is expensive to fire anyone, regardless of performance.
3. The longtime Salazar dictatorship created a sense of sorrow and passivity.

LOCATION

This tiny country in the southwestern corner of the *Iberian Peninsula* has the added advantage of a somewhat shorter flight to North America than other European destinations, while at the same time providing a convenient jumping off point for traveling farther in Europe. The Spanish city of **Seville**, for example, is a one-and-a-half-hour drive from the *Algarve,* Portugal's sunny southern coast. London is a two-and-a-half-hour flight from **Lisbon. Paris** is overnight on the train.

CLIMATE

Portugal's long, open Atlantic coast means it's kept warm by the Gulf Stream in the winter and cooled by the trade winds in the summer. Temperatures in the interior are more extreme, but on the coast—and Portugal is mostly coast—winters average in the 50s and 60s, summers in the 70s and low 80s. Even in the *Algarve,* the region which famously enjoys three hundred days of sunshine a year, the temperature rarely gets above the mid-80s. Summers are long and dry and can be windy. Winters are humid and rainy, but gray days are frequently interspersed with balmy. In the areas most likely to attract expats, a light jacket or sweater is usually sufficient, even in the coldest part of the year.

PEOPLE

For all the globe-trotting, the Portuguese don't seem to have brought home much foreign DNA. It's a homogenous country. It's a conservative, traditional place where the customs and formality of Old Europe persist. The people have a reputation for being kind and tolerant. They've been receiving foreign visitors for a long time, and a backlash of living under a dictatorship for much of the twentieth century is a reluctance to try to tell anyone how they should live. "Life is free here," affirms Patricia Westheimer, a former teacher from San Diego who has lived in the resort town of **Cascais** for sixteen years. "People leave expats alone."

Even during the dictatorship, the foreigners kept coming. The **Estoril** coast, in particular, just north of **Lisbon,** became known as a home base for royals in exile in the 1950s—Spain's King Juan Carlos waited out the Franco dictatorship here. Portugal is rife with the sense of lost kingdoms and elegantly faded grandeur, the wistful nostalgia that is so much a part of the Portuguese soul. It's a bittersweet melancholy that they call *saudade,* and explains the plaintive national song, the fado.

In the areas where expats tend to cluster, the community is highly visible. In 2005 Portuguese Immigration listed ten thousand official North American residents (approximately eight thousand Americans, two thousand Canadians). It is likely that the number actually in the country is significantly higher, but the appeal of expat life in Portugal is the international nature of the community—significant numbers of British, Dutch, Irish, German, and Scandinavians.

HISTORY

Portugal feels exotic. It's Europe, yes, but with a Moorish influence, and bits and pieces of a once far-flung colonial empire: Brazil, Macau, Goa, East Timor, Angola, Mozambique, Cape Verde. It is a history lover's paradise. The Portuguese themselves are sometimes accused of living in the past, but in their defense, it was a glorious past.

The twentieth century was hard on Portugal, though. The centuries-old monarchy was overthrown in 1910. A military regime took power in 1926, and Portugal spent almost the next fifty years under a dictatorship, mostly led by extreme conservative Antonio Salazar. Portugal escaped the

ravages of World War II, but Salazar conducted long, unpopular wars in an attempt to hang on to the African colonies. In 1974 a group of army officers staged a bloodless coup to end the dictatorship, which had outlived Salazar, who died in 1970. The colonies were liberated, and almost a million refugees poured into Portugal (a country with a population of only 9 million at the time), seemingly overnight. A volatile period followed, but when the dust cleared, Portugal was a stable parliamentary democracy and a European Community member, barreling into the twentieth century as the twenty-first was nearly beginning.

WHERE TO LIVE

The areas in which expats tend to congregate (and where one can pretty much get by without speaking any Portuguese at all) include:

- The *Algarve* is the southernmost strip of the country and is the region many people think of when they think of Portugal. Resort heavy, it is to Northern Europe what the Caribbean is to North America, and it is practically an expatriate colony within Portugal. Directly across from North Africa, the climate is the most reliably perfect in the country. The coastline is still the Atlantic but, calmer and warmer, it feels more Mediterranean. Prices tend to be higher here than anywhere else in the country except perhaps the **Estoril** coast outside of **Lisbon,** but it is extremely popular. Some areas have been overdeveloped and cater to cheap package tours from abroad; others are ostentatiously aimed at a luxury tourist market. Finding the perfect balance for living here rather than vacationing may require a bit of a hunt.

- In the **Lisbon** area, the vast majority of foreigners live on the **Estoril** *linha* (the towns along a commuter train line running westward along the coast), notably including the beach towns of **Estoril** itself and neighboring **Cascais.** Roughly twenty minutes from the metropolitan delights of **Lisbon** by car when there is no traffic (frequently over an hour in rush hour) or thirty minutes by train, this area offers beaches, access to rural landscapes, historical sites, public transportation, many restaurants, bars, a casino, cinemas, major shopping, golf, a marina, and other sports facilities.

- The charming villages in the nearby **Sintra** hills, about the same distance from **Lisbon** on a different commuter line, have their own set of beaches and are also historically popular with foreigners. Leafy, romantic **Sintra** was a Moorish stronghold and later was where the Portuguese royal court summered to escape the heat. It is chockablock with old palaces and wonderful houses, but is notoriously damp.

- **Lisbon** itself is an intriguing city, and parts of it are highly atmospheric, but like most cities, it is crowded, noisy, and dirty. Parts are horrid byproducts of urban regeneration in the 1960s and 1970s, unfortunately, but for those attracted to cities, there is a lot going on, and there are pleasant areas. Nice sections to live include *Lapa* and *Príncipe Real,* and maybe *Campo de Ourique.*

- The northern city of **Oporto,** with its long ties to Britain and the rolling vineyards nearby on the banks of the Douro, has a smaller outpost of expats. It is a cosmopolitan city, a rich city, with green areas spreading out around it. Harry Potter author, J. K. Rowling, lived here during her brief stint in Portugal. It's hard to believe her student wizards were not inspired by the sight of the college students here dashing up steps in their traditional black robes, and there is certainly something magical in the medieval villages that dot the region.

The areas most attractive to foreigners are also the areas where real estate prices are most likely to have risen the most. In the tourist zones, even a coffee and a pastry will cost double what they do in a more Portuguese neighborhood.

Trying to integrate into a more Portuguese community carries an emotional price. There is a comfort factor in being close to other foreigners, especially for someone not fluent in Portuguese. But for a person who drives and prefers to amuse himself, living twenty minutes away from an expat hub may not be an issue. Even such a small distance could make a significant difference in prices or in what you can get for the same money.

AMBIENCE

Life in Portugal is generally peaceful. Rush-hour traffic around the major cities—and trying to cross the bridge out of **Lisbon** on a long weekend—is the main exception.

Most foreigners find that making friends with Portuguese nationals can be a long process. And although the Portuguese are polite to foreigners, this is not a particularly open culture. In Portugal the extended family fulfills the role of the community. People tend to spend time primarily with their families and a few close friends that they've had since childhood. In the international community hubs, on the other hand, there are numerous clubs and activities that make it easy to become involved and meet people. Less encumbered by family and "real world" responsibilities, most expats are up for meeting newcomers and available for socializing.

English is widely spoken, especially in the tourist areas and cities and by younger people, who study it in school. You can certainly get by with just English in the *Algarve* and the *Estoril* area, but you will feel more in control of things and connected if you make an attempt to learn at least basic Portuguese. Any efforts to speak Portuguese will be met with extravagant compliments on your language prowess from your Portuguese hosts—usually delivered in flawless English.

STANDARD OF LIVING

Most expats enjoy a very high standard of living. The Portuguese who can afford to live in the areas where most expats live are generally well off. It is routine for expats to rub shoulders with some of the richest people in Portugal, but Portugal is traditionally a poor country, and a lot of people live on wages that would make North Americans cringe. Still, they get by. Parents help their children for a long time; most people live at home until they get married, or even after. To avoid that situation, some engaged couples will put off the wedding for years while slowly outfitting an apartment; that is changing as social barriers to living together before marriage fall. Poverty often takes the form of ugly high-rise buildings where people live in tiny apartments, relics of 1960s social programs. Some shantytowns remain in urban areas. Poverty in rural areas may be less obvious, but some live in barely habitable conditions.

CULTURE

There is, of course, a virtually endless supply of palaces, castles, gardens, wineries, ancient ruins, convents, and churches to tour. All cities of any size offer cultural riches: museums, galleries, exhibitions, film festivals, dance performances, classical and pop music concerts, sporting events. In **Lisbon** and the *Algarve,* there are English-speaking community theater groups. Throughout the country, even in rural areas and small towns, one can find music, folklore, medieval handicraft, agricultural, and religious and gastronomic festivals. Summer months, especially, give rise to colorful celebrations of local feast days.

In the more agricultural regions, summer is also the season for bullfights, which throws in a certain Hemingway-esque aspect for those who like that sort of thing. Unlike the Spanish version, the bull is never killed in the ring, and the major part of the contest is conducted on horseback. (The bull is normally taken to a slaughterhouse afterward.)

LEISURE

There are numerous cultural diversions, as mentioned above, but many expats say that their leisure activities revolve around sports: walking (and exploring new neighborhoods), biking, all water sports, going to the health club, tennis, golf, horseback riding. Many say they discover a passion for soccer (the other Portuguese national religion)—watching it, at least, if not playing. The climate is a joy for gardeners, for whom there is always something blooming. Many expat social clubs organize regular lunches, coffee mornings, talks, and sometimes short courses, as well as outings and other activities. Courses and lectures in English are more available in the *Algarve* than in other areas.

SOCIAL CUSTOMS

Latin men may have a reputation for machismo, but in Portugal women have the same level of equal status that they would have in North America. Women can feel perfectly safe traveling alone. North Americans are generally well regarded. Older Portuguese remember with gratitude the role they believe the U.S. played in helping to avert a Communist takeover in the 1970s. This is also a country that traditionally emigrated, so many Portuguese have family or friends in the U.S. or Canada. Portugal is a U.S. ally and founding NATO member with a large American military base in the *Azores,* but most Portuguese were not happy about American foreign policies after 2001. They are almost universally too polite to mention it unless you bring it up first, though. They have no such compunction about telling you that you are fat, however, and expressing shock at the general fatness of Americans.

People at all levels of society like to be well dressed even if they are just dashing to the supermarket. When you meet and depart from friends in Portugal, for the first time or the millionth, men shake hands, and women exchange kisses on the cheek with both men and women. Saying good-bye in a group can take considerable time because it is obligatory to go around and kiss everyone. North American expats are universally uncomfortable with this kissing custom at first, then fall into it so that expats go into frenzies of air kisses with one another.

HEALTH CARE/MEDICAL

Portugal has an overextended public health system that provides universal health care to Portuguese citizens and to other resident EU nationals in Portugal who register for it. It is available to non-EU residents only if they are working and paying into the Portuguese social security, although in an emergency—a car wreck, for example—one might be taken to a public hospital and then reimburse the system. (See "Working.")

The general Portuguese attitude is that if something is really wrong with you, you are better off in the public system (except, perhaps, in the more remote areas). They believe that the public hospitals have the money for the most up-to-date equipment. Many doctors who work in the public system also have private practices, so you could see the very same doctor privately if you wished.

The public hospital may look threadbare and certainly won't be coddling anyone, but when push comes to shove, it gets the job done. But there can be long waits, both hanging around in a health center waiting to see a doctor or for needed surgeries. People who can afford it often go private for the sake of convenience, comfort, and a greater sense of calling the shots, often paying out-of-pocket because private health insurance is not a cultural standard for the Portuguese.

The vast majority of the foreigners who do get accepted to the public health system probably do much as the wealthier Portuguese do: use it when it seems cost effective or to stretch out limited private insurance. (As an example, an office visit for an enrolled user costs €2.50.) Being enrolled in the system means getting a *cartão do utente* (user card) at the local health center and signing up for a "family doctor" whom you see when you go in for checkups and who will make referrals for specialists or testing.

A private system exists in parallel with the public system. Foreigners, particularly Americans, tend to have more faith in the private system, probably for cultural reasons. The private system is quite good—especially in urban centers where private hospitals and clinics are proliferating—and costs less than in North America. In areas with a lot of expats, there also tend to be groups of foreign-born doctors who cater to the international community.

An office visit with a private doctor averages around €60. A two-day stay in a private hospital for a hernia operation, for example, runs €1,750. Most people describe feeling safe and well cared for, although at first glance, some facilities may look old-fashioned. Medicines are significantly cheaper than they are in the U.S., and many are available without a prescription. Pharmacies are generally excellent, and by law there is always at least one pharmacy in any given area open all year, twenty-four hours a day.

RESIDENCY AND RED TAPE

To enter Portugal for stays of less than ninety days, U.S. and Canadian citizens need only a passport valid for at least three months after the end of their stay. While deciding whether Portugal is really where they want, visitors often arrange to cross a border and get a stamp in their passport every few months in order to just . . . keep staying. That does not violate the letter of the law, but if it goes on too long, it does violate the spirit and essentially amounts to living as an illegal immigrant. Though stories abound of people who have been doing it for thirty years, Portugal, like everywhere else, is tightening up the borders.

The process of applying for a residence permit begins in the country of origin at the closest Portuguese consulate. One applies for a residence visa there, then applies for authorization for residence at the closest *Serviço de Estrangeiros e Fronteiras* (*SEF*, Foreign Nationals and Border Service) office to where one is staying in Portugal. This has to be done before the validity date on the residence visa runs out.

The basic documents needed to apply are the same as in most European countries. Portuguese legislation is not specific on the income requirement, but they want to see that you have enough that you are not going to be a burden on the state. To give an idea of what it costs to live in Portugal, a salary of €17,500 a year (about $24,000 in 2008) is considered not bad at all, even for someone with a college degree and experience. Two people can live very comfortably on that much, even in expensive areas.

Working

It is possible to find some work, such as tutoring or teaching English privately, that one could do under the table. Most companies, however—including language schools—require freelancers to obtain an official receipt called a *recibo verde* ("green receipt"). When you sign up for green receipts, you must also sign up at social security. The minimum social security payment on green receipts, regardless of how much you make, is €150 per month. This is another way of gaining access to the national health system, so it may be worth it.

Starting a business is bureaucratically daunting, but people do it. Foreigners must follow the same rules as nationals and must be in the country legally. It will require the help of a good accountant and a lawyer who knows the system.

Residents in Portugal must pay taxes in Portugal on their worldwide income. Not everyone does it, but that's the law.

COST OF LIVING

There is a very wide range of choice available in the level at which an expat might choose to live in Portugal. In general, expats go higher end rather than lower, but it is possible to live simply and still have a good quality of life. Senior citizens, including foreigners, are eligible for discounts, including half price on train tickets and deep discounts on rooms in the national *pousadas* (hotels in historic buildings or typically regional places), entrances to historical and cultural sites, and movies. Rates for "citizens of the third age" are usually posted, and it is enough to show a photo ID with a birth date.

Monthly Cost of Living in the Algarve

Rent for a two-bedroom home, condo, or apartment: €500 to €1,800.

Taxes: Value Added Tax (VAT, or *IVA* in Portuguese), a sales tax on all goods and services; 5 percent for necessary goods (example: basic food in a supermarket); 12 percent or 21 percent most typical.

Groceries for two: €200 to €320.

Utilities: €100 to €140.

TV, internet, telephone: €50 to €100.

Transportation: Car to airport (**Cascais** to **Lisbon**) €30.

Maid service: €7 an hour.

Restaurants for two: €30 in a midrange restaurant, including wine and tip.

Monthly Cost of Living in Lisbon

Rent for a two-bedroom home, condo, or apartment: €400 to €800.

Taxes: Value Added Tax (VAT, or *IVA* in Portuguese), a sales tax on all goods and services; 5 percent for necessary goods (example: basic food in a supermarket); 12 percent or 21 percent most typical.

Groceries for two: €200 to €300.

Utilities: €100.

TV, internet, telephone: €40 to €100.

Transportation: Taxis start at €1.75.

Maid service: €6 an hour.

Restaurants for two: €30 in a midrange restaurant, including wine and tip.

Monthly Cost of Living in a Rural or Mountain Village

Rent for a two-bedroom home, condo, or apartment: €300 to €400.

Taxes: Value Added Tax (VAT, or *IVA* in Portuguese), a sales tax on all goods and services; 5 percent for necessary goods (example: basic food in a supermarket); 12 percent or 21 percent most typical.

Groceries for two: €200 to €300.

Utilities: €100 to €130.

TV, internet, telephone: €40 to €100.

Transportation: Buses and trains; cost depends on destination.

Maid service: €4 an hour.

Restaurants for two: €35 in a midrange restaurant, including wine and tip.

REAL ESTATE

Foreigners can buy anywhere in Portugal but must have a Portuguese bank account. Opening one requires a fiscal number, which is also needed to arrange for utilities. In Portugal debts are accumulated against the property, not the owner, so someone knowledgeable needs to search whether there are any liens against the property before the sale.

All properties over €85,000 are subject to property purchase tax based on a sliding scale up to properties worth €521,700 and 6 percent for properties over that value. Mortgages are available but usually won't extend past the borrower's sixty-fifth birthday. There is capital gains tax on the sale of property, and this is higher for nonresidents than for residents.

Real estate is available at an enormous range of prices, but as an example, Susan Michael's two-bedroom, two-bath apartment in **Lagos** with a common swimming pool and view of the sea has a market value of €225,000. A typical three-bedroom villa in **Lagos** in the *Algarve* would cost approximately €350,000 and up. Prices are lowest in the countryside away from the ocean. In central Portugal, you can find a broken-down ten-bedroom palace (a *real* palace) listed for €125,000 negotiable, ideal for converting into a bed-and-breakfast. The process of restoring a place like that, romanticized in so many expat memoirs, might drive you to an early grave, but the possibility exists.

Rentals

It is popular nowadays for the Portuguese to buy, but there are still many short- and long-term rental properties available, and foreigners are extremely desirable as tenants because of a history of strong renter protection laws that traditionally made eviction difficult and expensive. Landlords assume that foreigners will eventually leave of their own accord; they won't end up having to pay to get them out.

As everywhere in the world, desirable location is really what jacks the price up, and beach areas, especially, have become extremely desirable for foreigners. It's still possible to find reasonably priced housing, but you might have to look around a bit.

Building

Most people, even Portuguese, would advise building from scratch only for those with a high level of patience and good humor, because frustration and delays will certainly be part of the project. It's advisable to buy a property that already has an approved plan, because gaining permission to build or renovate can quite literally take years. You could always write a book about the experience later, though.

TRANSPORTATION

Most North Americans regard driving in Portugal as insane, though anyone who has ever driven in Boston should be able to take it in stride. Portugal is routinely cited as having the highest road fatality rate in Europe, though the situation has improved markedly in recent years. Highways are usually excellent, but local roads may be badly maintained. Signage is often deplorable.

If you live in the country for more than six months, you will have to trade in your foreign driver's license for a Portuguese license. This is usually something that foreign residents resist, but the fine if you get caught is exorbitant.

The good news is that in most places public transportation is readily available, very good, and inexpensive.

SECURITY

Portugal has one of the lowest crime rates in Europe and is very safe. There is a fair amount of opportunistic petty crime—purse snatching, pickpocketing, car break-ins—especially in areas popular with tourists, but not a lot of violent crime. The joke is always that if a thief happens to break into your house while you're actually there in Portugal, he will apologize and offer to come back when you're out.

There are always reports of police corruption, but the vast majority of expats who end up dealing with them seem to be well treated. "I've only dealt with them once," a recent transplant says. "They were helpful. Not necessarily fast acting, but effective."

COMMUNICATIONS AND MEDIA

Internet service is widely available and very good except in more remote areas. Cable television and satellite give access to foreign channels (including CNN, Sky News, BBC World and BBC Prime, Fox, and movie channels), but Portuguese television buys many American and British series and movies.

UP-AND-COMING AREAS

The *Alentejo* is the large agricultural region of Portugal that stretches across the country, north of the *Algarve* and south of Lisbon. This is the region that many Portuguese dream about as a getaway, a place to buy and restore an old farm worker's cottage or, if they are a little more flush, a stately manor farm. The coastline of this region is less developed than the *Algarve,* dotted with small towns that the Germans and the Dutch seem to be particularly fond of. It has a more back-to-nature feel, with sandy coves of beaches at the base of dramatic cliffs. The area along the border with Spain, that traditional enemy of old, is lined with castles. It can be blazingly hot in summer and bitterly cold in winter, and storks nest at the top of every church tower. Simple and rough, in a country where life moves slowly, this is where it moves so slowly, it almost goes backward.

Central Portugal is being talked about as the new *Provence,* with Northern European buyers scooping up ruins to renovate. The region's capital is **Tomar,** on UNESCO's World Heritage List. This is a largely undeveloped rural area, the kind of place where one could pull off the road near the river, wander down through the tall weeds, and jump in for a dip a few feet from the ruins of a Roman aqueduct. Towns in this region are ninety minutes from the Lisbon airport on good highways. However, property prices here have been appreciating at an astounding rate—a ruin with a small plot of land near the Castelo do Bode Lagoon and the Zêzere River sold for less than €40,000 five years ago; now the few ruins still available sell for three times that.

For those who enjoy island life and a bit of an adventure, the natural, unspoiled beauty of the archipelago of the *Azores* is reputed to be a buyer's market. The bulk of Portuguese who emigrated to the U.S. and Canada in the early 1970s (a peak period) came from the *Azores.* In the last five years, many of them and sometimes their children have begun coming back to retire in Portugal. That and a U.S. military base in the *Azores* means a strong English-language culture. This really is in the middle of the Atlantic Ocean, however, so you may feel isolated. There are far fewer civilized amenities and entertainment than might be desirable in a permanent living situation.

Madeira is a tropical volcanic island off the coast of north Africa, renowned for its stunning cliff walks and for its vegetation, especially orchids. They call it "the floating garden," and it's justly famous for its wine. There are no beaches on *Madeira* itself; beach life revolves around the sandy neighboring island of *Porto Santo*. *Madeira* is a more traditional, quiet spot than the *Azores*.

VOLUNTEERING WITHOUT BORDERS

Portugal does not have a strong culture of volunteering, but there are a number of opportunities for expats to contribute in meaningful ways in cooperation with their new neighbors.

- Habitat for Humanity has a well-organized chapter based in **Braga,** which unites locals and expats in home building in this low-income area of the country (www.habitat.org/intl/eca/163.aspx).
- The International Women in Portugal group organizes numerous charitable initiatives (www.iwponline.org).
- The expat-founded Laço Association in **Lisbon** operates a breast cancer treatment and awareness project that has launched several national advertising campaigns and donated mobile mammogram units (www.laco.pt).

Holly Raible Blades is senior editor at People & Business, *a Portuguese magazine. A Pennsylvania native, she went to Portugal on vacation in 1989 and . . . stayed.*

MY PORTUGAL

A Couple Who Started a
Winery in the North of Portugal

Name, age, origin: Carol and James Barber, sixty-seven and sixty-five, St. Helena, California.

Where we live: In the north of Portugal, on a small farm in the country. We also rent an apartment in the city.

How long in Portugal: Thirteen years.

Previous/present occupations: Carol, formerly a catering company owner; James, an enologist. Both are now in the winery business.

Reasons for moving here: Different pace of life, change of culture, boredom with living situation in the USA, and wanting new and exciting challenges.

Costs: Food and restaurants still a bargain compared with the rest of Europe. The country is very cheap but very low in quality. We rent our apartment in the city for €700 a month. We own our home in the country, where electricity is extremely high, about €400 per month. As seniors, we get cheaper film tickets, transportation rates, and special offers at national pousadas.

Our community: We live part-time in a big city on the ocean in an apartment and in a house in a very rural and remote area of great natural beauty but extremely isolated. The city offers cultural events, shopping, and restaurants. The farm is lacking in "civilized" amenities and lonely. People are peasants and uneducated, and there are very few foreigners to socialize with in the area. We socialize with retired foreigners, who number around fifty. We find ourselves being friends with people we would not ordinarily have been friends with in the USA. We all share our "horror stories" of less than pleasurable encounters and red tape in our adopted country.

Leisure: See films, walking, bike riding.

Culture: Concerts, films, folk fairs.

Health care/medical: Our private Portuguese health insurance (*Médis*) is both cheap and excellent. We pay €350 a month for two people over sixty-five, and have major medical coverage. We find the private doctors and hospitals are very good. Despite what you hear, we find the public hospitals are horrible, and we try to keep out of them.

Crime, corruption: We have the lowest crime rate in Europe. We never feel afraid here as we did in California. The police seem pretty lazy, and their reputation says they are corrupt at times. But we behave and stay clear of them. The local government is corrupt, like all over Europe. People make small salaries and can be bribed to make things happen faster. The national government is a joke and has squandered away the EU money on the wrong things while hospitals and schools are bad.

Wish we'd known before: People are more conservative and only friendly on the surface. They only want to be close to their families. Most of our close friends are other foreigners.

Drawbacks: We have had to live with a totally different work ethic. People here are very different than Americans in the way they work. They are often lazy, don't show up, and many have no pride in their work. The red tape of doing business is overwhelming.

Best: The slower pace, sweet nature of most of the people, kindnesses extended on a daily basis, and the feeling that older people are valued as a wise and important part of the society. We get more respect than older people do in the U.S. and feel we are not just people to be thrown away!

What we miss most: American efficiency and the spirit of pulling together when things get tough.

Expected to miss but didn't: A more comfortable life in terms of cars, houses.

MY PORTUGAL

*A Former Airline Executive
Who's Having Too Much Fun*

Name, age, origin: Milchen Mey de Casconsuelos, sixty-one, Houston and Atlanta.

How long in Portugal: Two years, but traveled here often. My husband is Portuguese.

Previous/present occupation: Airline executive. Still work.

Reasons for moving here: My husband, born in Portugal, had businesses in the U.S. We never intended to stay for thirty-five years in the U.S. We had always planned to retire in Europe, and strongly considered France. But the climate, beauty, and cost of living in Portugal did it for us. I had researched health care and would not have moved here if it were not affordable and good. When George Bush was reelected, we did *not* want to remain in the U.S.

Finances: We have funds, liquidated our U.S. home at a profit, and I'll be starting SS soon.

Costs: Rent is €1,250, a maid is €5 an hour, our favorite restaurant costs €30 for two.

My community: Cascais, near **Lisbon,** directly on the ocean, with a fabulous view. We wanted to be near a metropolitan area and an airport, a must for us. We're close to the beach, hiking trails, major shopping, and an active English-speaking community. The spirit here is wonderful. We have every nationality, and the clubs and groups—Americans in Portugal, Democrats Abroad—give me great new friends.

Leisure: Though I work, I can be relaxed 24/7 because Portugal has so much to like. I hike, swim, show people around (we have *so* many houseguests now), pursue new hobbies, and follow soccer—a religion in Portugal.

Drawbacks: None, absolutely none. Although Portugal is very welcoming to most foreigners, I have seen some prejudice toward Brazilians, which shocked me. But that's the exception. And oh . . . how long it takes Portuguese to say good-bye.

Best: All of my expectations were fulfilled, and thank *God* I escaped the Republicans on TV so much!

What I miss most: My daughter, nothing else.

Expected to miss but didn't: Junk food, music, friends.

MY PORTUGAL

A Teacher and Writer
Who Feels Portugal Has Changed

Name, age, origin: Patricia Westheimer, fifty-six, Baltimore and San Diego.

Where I live: In **Cascais**, near **Lisbon**. I rented for six years, then bought an apartment (good decisions, both).

How long in Portugal: Sixteen years. I visit the States occasionally, but the longer I'm here, the less frequently I go back.

Present occupation: Teacher, writer, seminar leader, director of Westroots Business Writing Seminars.

Reasons for moving here: As a teacher, I'd always traveled during the summers throughout Europe, mostly France. I'd never been to Portugal but kept hearing it was affordable, had good weather, natural food, and kind people. All true!

Finances: When I moved here sixteen years ago, I had saved enough for $2,000 a month in income, and I lived on that easily. Today the dollar is *much* lower and the expenses much higher.

My community: Our seaside town, once a fisherman's village, has everything I need and want—shopping, restaurants, lovely walks, movies. For better or worse, it's become increasingly chic. Lots of expats close by. My husband heads the Americans in Portugal group, and there are luncheons, lots of expat activities. I miss intellectual stimulation, though. I lived in **Paris,** where they had great expat classes. We hardly have any here. It's a low-key, friendly community.

Weather: As some say, "Portugal is a cold country with a hot sun." It's lovely and sunny but can get cold in the winter, as the older homes are not insulated. Still, sunscreen advised all year round.

Health care/medical: Good private medical care, but you have to pay for it. Not easy to get on national health if you're not Portuguese or don't have a work contract. Anyway, long waits, and you have to speak Portuguese. If I couldn't afford private health insurance, I wouldn't move here. I know some expats who've gone back to the States to get Medicare there.

Drawbacks: I loved Portugal when I first moved here sixteen years ago, and still do. But life has changed a lot: it's more expensive, and the Portuguese do not seem as proud of their country, nor do they work as hard as I sense they once did. Salaries are very low here, and the economy is not good for the average Portuguese. I think that contributes to a low level of joy on the part of the locals. *I* feel joyful because I can enjoy the best this country has to offer, but my financial situation is quite different from the average Portuguese's. Also, Portuguese families are kind to us on the streets but are not very open to us— I've been in three Portuguese homes in sixteen years. It's changing, but slowly.

Other drawbacks: Phones have been expensive, but change is finally coming. Cell phones are costly; I use text messaging to keep down the fees. I use Voipstunt for free computer calls to the States. Also, I had a Portuguese maid, and then it got complicated. Now I use a domestic service.

Best: I feel less stress, work less, enjoy life more, have learned to see the human side of life, and live more soulfully. This country has a less materialistic emphasis, and I welcome that.

MY PORTUGAL

Fell in Love with a Portuguese Man—and the Algarve

Name, age, origin: Susan Michael, sixty, Maine.

Where I live: Lagos, a coastal town in the *Algarve* region. We own an apartment and will move into a house soon.

How long in Portugal: Lived abroad for three years, moved to Portugal in 2002.

Previous/present occupations: International development consultant; now editor/writer. My husband and I still work.

Reasons for moving here: After living in Europe, I wanted to continue my sojourn abroad. I met and fell in love with a Portuguese man and chose to make my home here. I appreciate the change from a faster-paced, more overtly competitive U.S. Frankly, over the years, conventional middle-class U.S. society did not show me much. I like being in a culture that still reveres family (and not just as a political slogan) and civilized discourse, a country that by and large has remained true to its national ethos of living life simply. While I did not stay in Europe as a conscious attempt to avoid U.S. society, this move has been very beneficial for me.

Finances: Combined income of €50,000 a year.

Costs: Rent for our apartment is €500 to €600 a month, unless you want to go high end. In that case, the sky's the limit. The market value of the apartment is probably €225,000. Prices are lower inland. Groceries run us €250 a month (we eat well) and utilities average about €100. We can eat out for two for €25. Don't forget Europe's famous VAT sales tax: 21 percent. On the other hand, we currently don't pay any property tax, due to a Portuguese tax exemption on a primary residence for seven years.

    The cost of living here is one of personal choice. Our expat friends tend to live quite simply; they choose typical Portuguese restaurants and eat simply. Other expat communities farther east in the *Algarve* tend to attract expats that want a more expensive lifestyle—the area around **Faro** has high-end, more exclusive, golf-oriented, gated villa communities and amenities, such as more expensive restaurants. One of the pleasures of the *Algarve* is that it provides expats a clear choice of the financial level at which they wish to live and entertain themselves.

My community: We're in a coastal town, and our apartment is within view of the beach. We're moving farther inland, to a house we're building in the countryside. There is a large expat community of English, German, Dutch, and others in the *Algarve* region. The British are the most numerous, and given their critical mass and their penchant for creating colonies abroad, the British are by far the most organized, visible, and tightly knit group of expats. All other groups operate on a much lower key, and unlike the British, they generally learn some level of Portuguese and mix with others. The Portuguese shopkeepers and restaurateurs are extremely solicitous hosts, but by and large do not mix with expats in large numbers. All told, there are relatively few North American expats.

Leisure: Sailing, swimming, exercise at a health center, visiting local town and village festivals, films, gallery browsing, travel in the region, dining in and out with friends, working for a local charity.

Culture: I actively seek cultural activities here and in **Lisbon**. **Lisbon** is a treasure trove of history and culture. There are galleries and museums galore in **Lisbon** and a respectable number in the *Algarve*.

Health care/medical: Portugal has a public health system but has developed over time a two-tier arrangement, public and private. If a person needs elective surgery and goes the public hospital route, it often requires a long wait— up to six, nine months. Many Portuguese (like my spouse), who can afford the more expensive private clinics and hospitals, opt to do so to avoid the wait.

Because I hold a full-time Portuguese residence card, I have a health card that allows me access to the Portuguese medical clinic. For general medical care, I use both systems: a private-practice English-speaking doctor for annual exams, and the Portuguese medical clinic for simple problems like colds. When I go to the Portuguese medical clinic, I ask for a doctor who speaks English and generally find one. Many expats who can go to Portuguese medical clinics avoid it because they operate on a wait-your-turn basis and can have long lines. I don't mind the wait; the price is right:

Cost of an "expat" doctor visit, €60.
Cost of a Portuguese medical clinic visit, €2.50.

Many expats are openly disdainful of the Portuguese medical system. I've found medical care to be excellent, though I am in a privileged position in that my spouse knows the local doctors. But I've found my approach to medical care has evolved over my expat years. When I first moved to Europe, I held the opinion that the U.S. system is first-rate and could not be duplicated. I do not think this now. With my current non-U.S./Canada plan, I have the entire continent of Europe to rely on for medical care. I think the general North American public is fed a bill of goods about the preeminence of U.S. medical care.

Locals' attitude toward Americans: I think we Americans are admired for our ingenuity, our resourcefulness, and our sheer inventiveness. We are admired for producing quality goods. But as a country, we are also feared—or at least our political leaders are feared. The Portuguese, like most Europeans, are unsettled and uneasy about the global intentions of the U.S.

Drawbacks:
1. The bureaucracy in Portugal is entrenched and daunting. This is a "paper culture." The paperwork involved in the simplest of registrations is endless. Anecdote: A Canadian friend decided to apply for a real estate license to go out on her own. Not only did the bureaucracy require old school records, it insisted that she produce her grammar school records from New Brunswick, Canada. And as frustrating as the bureaucratic mentality can be, the delay in processing is equally so. It took me over two years to get my formal residence card.
2. This is silly, but I am an impatient person. I miss the instant gratification of buying books and products ASAP. I have had to learn to be patient and wait for U.S. goods that I order online.

Best: The lessons learned as an American abroad—I think I am a richer, wiser person for living here. It has increased my sense of what it means to be an American, both the good and the bad. Living abroad has taught me—and continues to teach me—new things about myself, who I am, where I come from, and where I am going. This opportunity to have new experiences is a blessing, particularly at my age.

What I miss most: U.S. bookstores, Hanes underwear, Orville Redenbacher microwave popcorn with butter, Pepperidge Farm herb stuffing, and all seafood from my home state of Maine.

Expected to miss but didn't: U.S. TV and films; we get CNN, the BBC, Sky News for English-language news, and movie channels. U.S. films in theaters are late reaching here, but they arrive. I thought I would miss the Boston Red Sox, but I can get live baseball games on MLB.com for a small fee. (Of course, I am up in the middle of the night watching these games, but you can't have everything!)

Chapter 20

ALSO CONSIDER . . .

A Sampler of Other Retirement Destinations

ARGENTINA

Argentina, still staggering a bit from its 2002 financial meltdown, is at once the most sophisticated of Latin American countries and among the very cheapest for retirees. To the casual visitor, it seems to have it all: a capital city that rivals many European capitals in culture and architecture; a diverse, four-season geography that offers every possible sport and activity; a real estate market that is, for the moment, appealingly underpriced; and a culture rich not only in the arts but in music, dance, and nightclubbing—with the tango as its high point.

Though Argentina has become a mecca for younger artists, writers, and entrepreneurs, the older set has yet to discover it in the numbers its appeal would suggest. Lingering anxiety about the country's economic prospects, the rise in crime, and uneasiness about Argentina's politics in the past (a harbor for former Nazis, the upheavals of Peron-ism, the harsh military rule of the 1970s) have kept retiring North Americans at bay. It may not make Americans feel as comfortable as other Latin American countries do, looking, as it does, toward Europe for inspiration rather than to *El Norte*. European retirees have known about Argentina for years, and now even East Asians have discovered its retirement allure—and its cost benefits.

The economy has been recovering steadily since its nadir in 2002, but even in 2008 a four-course meal complete with a bottle of fine Argentinean wine and a world-class steak is $20. A 1,600-square-foot, two-bedroom, two-bathroom apartment in the chic southern city of **Bariloche,** with a lake and mountain view, sauna, gym, and pool sold in 2007 for $150,000. In the higher-end neighborhoods of downtown **Buenos Aires,** apartments range from $165,000 to $300,000. (Rentals are somewhat less attractive, with one-bedroom, one-bathroom apartments costing anywhere from $800 to $2,500 a month.) Public transportation in and around metropolitan **BA,** where one-third of the country's population and most expats live, is extensive, efficient, and cheap.

The weather in Argentina is mild and springlike throughout much of the country, with warmer and cooler spots depending on the altitude. (And latitude: Argentina stretches more than five thousand miles north and south.) The most populous parts of the country see three hundred days a year of sunshine. Argentina in winter (July) is a skier's paradise, with sprawling Andes Mountain resorts offering fresh powder for all levels, and a golfer's nirvana the rest of the year; there are over sixty private courses around **Buenos Aires** alone, many of which charge less than $20 a round.

Argentineans are immensely proud of their European connections, maintained in part by large communities of German, Spanish, and French residents going back a half century or more. Its cities are home to splendid cathedrals, opera houses, and museums, as well as broad, Haussmannesque boulevards and parks where residents of all ages can be seen strolling about until the early morning hours. Dinner in **Buenos Aires** frequently starts around ten or eleven at night, and most restaurants will continue to serve until daybreak.

Long-term residency in Argentina is relatively simple, requiring the usual, such as a birth certificate, notarized confirmations of residency and employment/income, and a clean criminal record. After living in Argentina for more than six months, the average expat will pay around 35 percent in income taxes, assuming he forgoes the usual Argentinean practice of not paying them.

Natural beauty, a lively and diverse population, and high standards of living on a tight budget. It seems inevitable that more Americans will discover the retirement potential of Argentina—and it virtually defines the meaning of a summer-winter snowbird destination. Until then, Argentineans can justifiably consider theirs the most truly *European* of South American countries.

AUSTRALIA

It's no wonder Americans have an affinity for Australia (and, usually, vice versa). As large as the continental U.S., with a rich topography, a temperate climate, terrific beaches, and an affable, casual, hey-mate! society, it reminds Americans of America as it once was (or was thought to be). So you hear a lot of talk from North Americans dreaming about retirement in **Sydney, Melbourne,** or becoming sundowners in the outback.

There's one problem, and it's the reason we don't name it among our primary destinations: unless you are financially very well off, or fall into very restricted and specific categories, you cannot retire there.

You can adopt the stay-awhile plan, getting a visa for three to six months, and then move on to another venue, returning six months later. (You can sometimes get the visa extended to twelve months, but that's hard to get.) But as for retiring in any permanent way, consider:

- You must have assets of around $600,000 if you're going to live in a city.
- You must invest that much in Australia.
- As a couple, you must have income of about $50,000, such as a pension (less in rural areas).
- You must bring your own health plan with you.

If you have those kinds of assets, then Australia may be for you. The land Down Under offers extremely high, North American–level quality of life at Northern European–level prices. Housing, food and drink, medical care, and locally produced goods are generally less expensive than what you would find in Western Europe or any major American city, though many manufactured goods (especially cars) can be 25 percent to 100 percent more expensive if they are imported. Australia is, after all, an island nation, a twenty-four-hour, $1,500-plus flight from New York, and not the easiest weekend visit for friends or grandkids.

Australia has much to offer the well-off retiree, especially if you're the outdoors type. Australians love barbecues, open-air concerts, water sports, and public parks, and the country's sparsely populated inland retains a frontier feel very much akin to the nineteenth-century American West. Australia's big cities, which account for the vast majority of the country's population, contain a vibrant mix of urban center and suburban sprawl, characterized by Victorian-era residential areas, low-slung beach neighborhoods, leafy hilltop mansions, teaming ports and harbors, and modern steel-and-glass skyscrapers, all connected by an efficient and (thanks to the 2000 Olympics) recently revamped public transportation system. **Melbourne** has been voted "The World's Most Livable City," and **Sydney**'s downtown attracts some of the world's best restaurateurs, entertainers, museum exhibits, and beautiful people of every walk of life.

Housing prices range predictably according to location, with **Sydney, Melbourne, Brisbane,** and their suburbs being the most expensive (a brand-new three-bedroom, three-bath home several miles from downtown **Sydney** starts at under $170,000 USD; a one-bedroom, one-bath apartment with a great river view in **Brisbane** goes for around $200,000 USD), and more reasonable apartments and homes farther inland.

If it weren't for the rigid visa and income restrictions, Australia would certainly be at or near the top of our list of places to say G'day! to your mate for the rest of your days.

THE CARIBBEAN

The Caribbean islands, arguably, deserve their own chapter. Extending more than 2,500 miles from the *Bahamas* to *Trinidad and Tobago,* there are thousands of small islands—most uninhabited—and hundreds that have residents. They enjoy tropical weather (*Bermuda* and the *Bahamas* are subtropical), with sunny skies over three hundred days a year. Their exotic vegetation, picturesque towns and villages, mountains and waterfalls, and clear blue waters have long made the Caribbean one of the world's favorite playgrounds.

As to their aptitude for retirement, here's what can be said generally:

Well-inhabited islands can be potential destinations for North American retirees. Indeed, many thousands have already taken up residence there—for hundreds of years, if you want to get historical about it. There are probably few global regions where, taken together, more expats and part-time expats of all nationalities are gathered in one "region." Most larger islands have something hedonistic to offer the North American retiree. Some smaller islands have an appeal to a certain type of retiree: sublime isolation.

Here's the kicker, and it may be the reason the Caribbean doesn't always figure on retirement lists: for those looking to make a permanent residence on most islands, the cost of living ranges from pretty expensive to prohibitively expensive. That is, expensive for island living, without offering the cultural attractions of our also-expensive European choices. Imported food, housing, cars, appliances, and clothing are all expensive. Retired life in the Caribbean is usually not much more "foreign" than life on Key West, Florida, or even Hawaii. *St. Barts* can seem like Beverly Hills. For the most part, you retire in venues given over entirely to tourism, for all the pleasures and drawbacks (mega hotels, cruise ships) that suggests.

Are there less-visited, less expensive, more "foreign" islands that are exceptions to these generalities? Of course. Life in the *Dominican Republic* or *Dominica* is more reasonably priced. *Martinique* and *Guadeloupe* offer a "foreign" life, as full-fledged departments of France. And like Latin America, not Europe, most currency is tied to the dollar, which is reassuring to North Americans.

More points to ponder, again, speaking generally:

- Housing costs—purchases and rare long-term rentals—have quadrupled in the past three or four years on many islands. Beachfront property is prohibitive. Prices on the tonier islands (*British Virgins*) may start at $1 million, with transaction costs up to 20 percent.
- Though residency is possible on most islands (if you're an American of average means, best forget *Bermuda;* ditto the *Bahamas*), hurdles can be as bad as or worse than Latin America or Europe: waiting periods, investment requirements, taxes, permits. Sometimes you even need character references, like joining a country club.
- Airfare on and off the islands can be reasonable, due to high tourist traffic, which makes it easy to be a part-timer and skip all the legal complications above.
- Health care is good on some islands; again, thanks to tourism. It can be poor on the smaller islands and require island hopping.
- Roads are generally good, except on the poorer islands.
- Crime is rising throughout the Caribbean.
- Taxes. Ah, yes. Now, *there's* a reason to live there. Consult an offshore expert.
- These islands have experience with retirees and therefore offer a balance of amenities: *Antigua* and *Barbuda, Bahamas, Barbados, Caymans, Grenada, Guadeloupe, Jamaica, Martinique, Montserrat, Saint Kitts-Nevis, Saint Lucia, Saint Martin, Saint Vincent, Trinidad and Tobago, Turks* and *Caicos, British Virgin Islands.* (*Puerto Rico* and *U.S. Virgins,* not listed, are U.S. territories.)
- Speaking of *Puerto Rico,* even though it's part of the U.S., the island also has many of the natural attractions and cultural differences of the Latin American countries covered in this book—with the considerable added appeal of U.S. infrastructure, judicial system, and Medicare. Not exactly "abroad," but not to be overlooked.

ECUADOR

Ecuador has been making the retirement lists for some years now, and with good reason: it has natural beauty, great affordability, a surprising number of first-world amenities, and, like Panama, a currency that isn't just linked to the U.S. dollar—it *is* the U.S. dollar. Though a small country straddling the equator, no bigger than Washington State, Ecuador contains 10 percent of the world's plant and animal species and is home to the *Galápagos Islands,* where Charles Darwin spent some memorable time. The smallest of the Andean nations, it has a picturesque Pacific Ocean coastline with knockout beaches; thick, mountainside forests; and high, steeply peaked volcanos. A wanderer can hit all three regions within a couple hundred miles.

There has also been a fair amount of political turmoil, including a financial crisis in 1999, which may be one reason Ecuador is not on more retirement rosters. As recently as 2006, the latest of a long line of presidents was ousted. But its reputation for instability may be a bum rap. The Central American republics we've covered have had more than their share of political upheaval (with the exception of Costa Rica), and the answer always seems to be: foreign residents aren't affected. And now that the dollar is the official currency, politics won't affect your savings, either.

It also comes as a pleasant surprise how modern and up to date things are in **Quito** and **Guayaquil,** Ecuador's main cities. Everything from Big Shopping to first-rate communications are available, there are amusements aplenty, and hotels and restaurants offer first-class room and board. Residency requirements are about the same as they are in other Latin countries, real estate is still very reasonably priced, and the rental market is good (in other words, affordable). You can rent a modern two-bedroom home or apartment in the city for $500 to $700 a month; amazingly, you can get it down to $300 to $400 in the sticks.

It's far away and has a relatively small conclave of North American retirees, so there's that to consider. But if there had been room for an eleventh "major" chapter in this book, it might have gone to Ecuador. Oh, and one last fact: the Panama hat originated in Ecuador.

GREECE

It's a rare traveler who has taken a cruise of the Greek Islands without sighing about how glorious it would be to retire somewhere in Greece. We, your authors, are one such couple. On a cruise that included **Athens,** the Peloponnesus, *Rhodes, Crete,* and the tourist islands of *Mykonos* and *Santorini,* we decided to jump ship on the tiny, tidy island of *Syros.* (The captain of our cruise ship was so amazed, he accompanied us down the gangplank to make certain this is what we wanted to do.) We stayed on in *Syros* and sank into the life: swimming in the bright, clear Aegean, eating grilled octopus washed down with ouzo, living modestly amid the whitewashed homes in a village near the city of **Hermoúpolis.** We stayed two months and wished it were longer.

We weren't about to stay longer, and neither will most Americans without working hard at it. While in theory there is a way to apply for residency and even work permits, it is far easier for fellow EU nationals to succeed than it is for North Americans. There is the usual proof-of-income, clean-medical, and police-record documentation, but the process can be discouraging. Here's an official government quote: "It should be expected that residence permits for stays beyond the six months may not be easily granted, and the Greek authorities will not give advance assurance that the individual will be permitted to prolong his/her stay. All applications to the local aliens authorities will be forwarded to the Ministry of Public Order for consideration."

There's more: not only is **Athens** among the thirty most expensive cities in the world, life on the islands is now *very* costly. Websites in late 2007 were reporting huge (20 percent) hikes in the costs of groceries in the previous six months, and room and board was also skyrocketing. Staples could cost two and three times what they would cost in North America. As elsewhere on well-known islands, everything that must be imported is becoming more and more pricey, to the point where the dream of retiring to a warm, welcoming island is becoming just that: a dream; at least for those of average means.

But if you have the patience and deep pockets, retiring to that Greek island is still the dream to beat.

HONDURAS

Honduras's white sand and Caribbean-blue paradise has much to offer the independent-spirited retiree. This Central American diamond, sandwiched in a rather rough neighborhood with El Salvador to the west, Guatemala to the north, and Nicaragua to the east and south, boasts miles of pristine beaches, a warm climate and warmer population, and a remarkably high standard of living on the cheap, even compared to the rest of the region. Add to that decent (if inconsistent) medical services, a basically stable democratic government and economy, and increased transportation options to and from the country via newly opened airline routes, and the work-in-progress Honduras will be an option for those looking for something off the beaten Caribbean path.

The natural attractions of Honduras are typical of a tropical coastal nation: fantastic water sports; seafood; hiking and biking through topography that includes lush rain forests, misty mountaintops, and cloud forests; ancient ruins; and, of course, miles and miles of beaches. Honduras's prime seafront locations are the *Bay Islands* of the northeastern coast, where bottlenose dolphins, manta rays, parrot fish, and whale sharks populate the maze of corals that make up the Mesoamerican Barrier Reef system.

The three islands (*Roatan, Guanaja,* and *Utila*) are accessible from the mainland via air or ferry, and are the most heavily frequented by North Americans. Property prices have risen steadily on the islands since Hurricane Mitch devastated the local economy in 1999; however, prices are still far below what you would pay in other parts of the Caribbean.

The Bay Islands are not only a haven for frugal expats but also for swarms of mosquitoes and the dreaded sand gnats, making insect repellent as vital an accessory as sunscreen in the summer months. On the mainland, most visitors and locals can be found in and around the capital of **Tegucigalpa** (**Tegus,** to the natives—try saying "Tegucigalpa" five times fast!) or the busy city of **San Pedro Sula**. Each offers nearly all of the creature comforts of North American life, including major shopping centers, multiplexes, four-star hotels, and international restaurants.

As is the case with Nicaragua, which is back on retirees' radar—and other Central American republics, such as the militarily ravaged, deeply impoverished countries of Guatemala and El Salvador—Honduras is among those countries within a reasonable distance of the U.S. that will undoubtedly show up in retirement itineraries of the future. For now, though, they are likely to remain primitive, challenging, and, of course, affordable.

NEW ZEALAND

Like Australia, New Zealand often makes North Americans' retirement dream lists for two reasons: its extraordinary and varied natural beauty, and its charming and welcoming Kiwi citizens. Oh, yes, and it probably doesn't hurt that the U.S.-New Zealand dollar ratio still favors the U.S. dollar. The cost of living is reasonable compared to North America, and the crime is as slow as you could wish for. Plus, you may see a hobbit or two (it's where the *Lord of the Rings* trilogy was filmed).

Despite its appeal, New Zealand's immigration rules are so restrictive that the vast majority of U.S. retirees are ineligible for long-term residence. Like Australia, unless you live in a Commonwealth country, New Zealand's immigration laws have a point system that heavily favors the young, the highly skilled, and the wealthy investor. You not only have to show income, you have to put substantial funds to work in New Zealand—several hundred thousand dollars.

But for those rich, highly skilled seniors who can clear the hurdles . . .

New Zealand consists of two main islands: the North Island and the South Island. On one or the other of the islands, there is a microclimate and natural setting for just about everyone. A retiree can live among or easily visit cities as large as the New Zealand capital of **Auckland** or as small and remote as **Golden Bay,** as well as fjords, glaciers, native bush, snow-capped mountains, trout streams, rugged rocky or smooth sandy beaches, the high plains, wineries, orchards, horse farms, ski resorts, fishing villages, and seal/penguin/albatross colonies. Bungee jumping may not appeal to the typical retiree, but New Zealand has hundreds of golf courses, as well as nature walks for all degrees of fitness. Kayaking, fishing, trekking, and bicycling are also popular pastimes in New Zealand.

Those coming from crowded big cities will appreciate the sane pace and absence of congestion found throughout New Zealand. Outside of the largest cities, the highways crisscrossing New Zealand are mostly scenic two-lane roads with few other cars. Modest signs identify bed-and-breakfast options as well as local crafts (pottery, wood carving, blown glass, and so on). Food service consists of family-run taverns and restaurants as well as roadside "takeaways" (food to go). Roadside picnic tables are easy to spot. McDonald's has arrived, but its locations are few and far between.

THE PHILIPPINES

The Philippines, a sprawling island nation, *should* have a lot going for it as a retirement haven: tropical weather, lush scenery, great affordability (**Manila** has an extremely low cost of living), and a certain familiarity for U.S. citizens. Not only was it an American colony, but it had the largest U.S. military base overseas in Subic Bay until its closure over two decades ago. As a result of these military connections, a good number of former servicemen have made the Philippines their home in retirement.

Websites advertise a two-bedroom condo in one of the upscale "villages" in **Makati City** for $400 per month, claiming that you can dine out on average at a three-star restaurant "for less than $10, including tax and tip." Maid service is about $100 a month, and a chauffeur (which you might need; see below) will cost about $200 a month. English is widely spoken. Health care is a puzzle: though it's not highly ranked by the World Health Organization, some of its hospitals are very highly regarded, and visitors from elsewhere in Asia come to Manila for complex medical procedures.

Despite all its good points, there are reasons the Philippines does not figure in most retirement lists. For one thing, crime is a big problem, and unlike much of Latin America, here tourists and foreign residents are not necessarily spared. Bodyguards and personal chauffeurs are widely used, and every day brings press reports of muggings, kidnappings, and worse. For another thing, political stability can be a sometime thing: a history of coups and insurgencies, added to regular terrorist outbreaks, makes for a jittery existence. Transparency International also ranks the Philippines as the most corrupt of the nations we cover in this book. Finally, buying property is officially restricted to those who apply for, and are granted, a special retirement visa, which includes among its requirements an investment of $50,000. These visas are otherwise not hard to obtain, and include the now-familiar proof of income and clean police record.

And yet the Philippines has its firm supporters: the substantial crime, as in Latin America, is concentrated to certain regions and certain neighborhoods; the people are friendly toward Americans; the weather is terrific; and the cost of living, again, is practically unmatched in its affordability. General Douglas MacArthur said, "I shall return," during World War II. So, too, are Americans, particularly former military types, who return to make a home in the Southeast Asian tropics.

THAILAND

Thailand, with its rice paddies, Buddhist temples, lumbering elephants, and murmuring monks in saffron robes—as well as its big-city restaurants, mad traffic, bespoke tailoring, and bargain-priced sapphires—has long been Southeast Asia's most popular tourist stopover. Now some tourists are staying longer, as Thailand has built a modest reputation as an appealing place for Europeans, Asians, and North Americans who seek to retire in Southeast Asia, including Americans who discovered the country during the Vietnam War.

Aside from the Vietnam-era GIs who went on R & R to the fleshpots of **Bangkok** and **Pattaya,** Americans in general know little about Thailand. Restaurants ("Let's go eat Thai tonight") and movies (*The King and I, The Beach*) appear to be the main influences in learning about the ancient kingdom of Siam, whose King Mongkut modernized the country in the nineteenth century—and probably did not dance, à la Yul Brynner, with the real Anna.

So it can be a pleasurable surprise for a North American visitor to be exposed to Thailand's exotic diversity. Foreigners gather in vital, crowded, chaotic **Bangkok,** with its slums and soaring five-star hotels. Or in the northern university town of **Chiang Mai,** with its artisan galleries, elephants, and gardens. Or in the southern tropical islands of *Koh Samui* or *Phuket,* with their hordes of backpackers and beach-chic visitors. Or even in **Pattaya,** which GIs turned into a seedy brothel, but where a Times Square–like cleanup may yet prove successful. In these areas, and others, Thailand's rich artistic and religious traditions, tolerant culture (to a point—don't speak ill of the king), and often suitably modern medical, electronic, and business resources make it a target of choice for the more adventuresome of senior settlers. Health care in the major cities is considered good and inexpensive, with English-speaking doctors generally available.

Holidays and holy days are a swirl of color and incense in curved-roof temples and monasteries, as monks celebrate and tourists gawk. Food is available at street stands and at four-star restaurants alike. Sports are of the kickboxing variety, although Western recreations—sailing, tennis, biking, scuba—are there to be tapped as well. English is widely spoken, and house and apartment rentals are widely available and, for the most part, still reasonable. Property sales are another matter. Villas in the resort areas can go for multiples of a million dollars, while apartments in rich enclaves in *Phuket* can be in the single-million range. But in villages a few miles inland, prices drop dramatically, and houses are available for $75,000 and up. (Houses can be had only with thirty-year leases; apartments and condos can be owned outright.) Mortgages are tough to get.

On the negative side, Thailand's government has been far from stable in the past decade, and its currency is not rock solid, either. There have been isolated instances of bombings. Most water is not safe to drink and must be bought bottled. Sexual tourism can make for an unappetizing breed of visitor seen descending into some of Bangkok's anything-goes neighborhoods.

But in 2001 the government decided to get serious about the retiree business by making it far easier for the over-fifty-five crowd to settle in Thailand. Retirement visas, renewable annually, are issued without a lot of fuss to foreigners who can show clean records and suitable income (it varies, but about $18,000 a year usually suffices). Even that isn't written in granite; if your funds are more modest, you may be able to apply for a residence permit with a bit of legal help. Once you've managed to stay in the country legally for three years, you can get permanent residence.

Chapter 21

VOLUNTEERING
WITHOUT BORDERS

WHY VOLUNTEER

Many of us arriving at our retirement destination in Latin America have made that taxi drive from the airport to our hotel and felt unsettled by the poverty we see along the way. We become aware of the contrast between the standard of living of the local population and that of the expats.

Volunteering is a way to broaden and deepen an understanding of your new country, to become part of the community, to enlarge your circle of like-minded expat friends, to help change the perception of expats from "obnoxious Americans" to "concerned neighbors." In short, to give something back.

HOW TO VOLUNTEER

In general, there are two types of volunteer opportunities.

Before you leave home, use the internet to research which of the well-known, worldwide organizations are active in your new country (see below). On their websites you will find the countries in which these charities work, descriptions of the kind of programs they run, and the type of volunteers they recruit. These "umbrella" charities can be easier to join because they welcome expat volunteers.

Once you're on the ground in your new town, seek out the local groups. However, many expats are surprised to find relatively few community self-help projects. In many countries, there is no tradition of organized charitable associations. Over centuries, residents have become leery of civic or government-sponsored efforts. The cultural tradition is that neighbors help neighbors to improve schools or build a youth center.

Because North Americans *are* "joiners," you may learn that a number of charity organizations have been spearheaded or founded by expats. Whatever their origins, at the end of each country chapter, the section "Volunteering Without Borders" gives you a sampling of local groups involved in efforts, from feeding children raised in the slums of **Puerto Vallarta** to saving the dolphins in danger of extinction in Croatia.

It is also worth mentioning "volunteerism," the fastest-growing section of the travel industry for the over-fifties. A "vacation with a purpose," these are relatively short trips (from two weeks to several months) in groups organized to work alongside volunteers in already existing programs, from ecology conservation in China to teaching English as a second language in Italy.

The short excursion works with our suggestions to stay awhile to scope out a country before a long-term commitment and to rent before you buy (or *never* buy) while you're there. If you plan to spend only several months in the country, it may not be realistic to join a long-term charity enterprise. However, spending two or three weeks working in less-developed parts of the country can give you an insight into a part of the society you're not otherwise likely to see.

And the last and most important advice on how to volunteer: seek out your community's civic, religious, and business leaders. Follow in the footsteps of your fellow expats who know where there is a need and have worked to fill it. Joining an organized charity may not be the best way to give back. Working personally, neighbor to neighbor, may be the most rewarding way to help—and become a part of—your adopted community.

WHERE TO VOLUNTEER

Besides the local groups listed in the individual country chapters, the following are the worldwide organizations that are "senior friendly": up to half of their volunteers are over fifty years old. (You need to read carefully between the lines of books featuring hundreds of overseas volunteer opportunities; the vast majority of such opportunities are for young people.)

Cross-Cultural Solutions

www.crossculturalsolutions.org

Cross-Cultural Solutions is an international NGO (nongovernmental organization) that places volunteers working with local grassroots organizations in twelve countries. Its focus is on health care, education, and community projects. CCS is highly respected and has been awarded special consultative status by the United Nations. Retirees make up 35 percent of its volunteers.

Programs are active in: Brazil, China, Costa Rica, Ghana, Guatemala, India, Morocco, Peru, Russia, South Africa, Tanzania, and Thailand.

Elderhostel

www.elderhostel.org

Although the Elderhostel service program was initiated in 1993, these volunteering programs are not as well known as the long-established travel and study programs. Elderhostel partners with Global Volunteers and other well-respected groups to enlarge and support projects ranging from reforesting the watershed in Nicaragua to teaching English in southern Italy. Multigenerational families and groups are encouraged, but at least one member must be fifty-five or older.

Volunteers, who work in teams, are placed in over eighty countries located in Africa, Asia, Australia, Europe, Latin America, the Middle East, and the South Pacific.

Global Volunteers

www.globalvolunteers.org

Volunteers work in teams assisting local organizations in child care, health care, community building projects, and educational programs. This group, which has been called a private Peace Corps, works with one hundred host communities in twenty countries worldwide. Over half of the volunteers are in the over-fifty population, and boomer families (intergenerational family groups) are encouraged to apply. It has been granted special consultative status by the UN.

Programs are active in: Australia, Brazil, China, Cook Islands, Costa Rica, Ecuador, Ghana, Greece, Hungary, India, Ireland, Italy, Jamaica, Mexico, Peru, Poland, Portugal, Romania, and Tanzania.

Habitat for Humanity International

www.habitat.org/gv

Habitat for Humanity, one of the best-known volunteer organizations, recruits groups and individuals for Global Village work teams in over one hundred countries. Team members work alongside low-income families to construct and renovate homes. Trips are two to three weeks long, and cost ranges from $1,200 to $2,000 (airfare excluded), depending on location.

Work sites are typically in underdeveloped countries. No prior experience is necessary, and senior volunteers are welcomed.

Programs are active in: Argentina, Bolivia, Botswana, Costa Rica, El Salvador, Ghana, Guatemala, Honduras, Hungary, New Zealand, Paraguay, Portugal, Romania, Thailand, Uganda, and Zambia.

International Executive Service Corps (IESC)

www.iesc.org

The IESC is the largest nonprofit economic-development organization that provides technical and managerial assistance to countries worldwide. Its thirteen-thousand-member roster includes retired senior executives and paid consultants who ally their management expertise with local businesses to advance globalization, prosperity, and financial stability. Unlike most volunteer groups, IESC pays all expenses (airfare, hotels, health insurance). If a project is longer than a month, spouses' expenses are also covered. Volunteers (typical age is sixty) are assembled into teams for individual projects according to the needs of the local business.

Programs are ongoing in about sixty developing countries worldwide.

VOLUNTEER HEAVEN

By RUTH ROSS MERRIMER

Is there a Volunteer Heaven? A special place reserved for those who spend a good part of their lives—especially their retirement years—volunteering for good causes? Is it genuine altruism or a means of filling the empty hole that retirement has left in their lives? I don't think the reason people volunteer really matters. What matters is that the lives of the receivers and the givers are changed forever for the better. At least, that was my experience as a reporter covering the *Lake Chapala* social scene—meaning, in large part, volunteer and charity events—for ten years.

Volunteering has a special importance wherever you find a substantial number of Americans living in a country like Mexico. Between the scarcity of paid employment for foreigners and the lack of extensive social services by the Mexican government lies the opportunity for expats with time on their hands.

In our two towns of Ajijic and Chapala the foreign population is burgeoning, as it is all over Mexico. They are building houses using Mexican labor, purchasing building supplies at Mexican-owned businesses, buying their clothing, food, and all they need to make a home at Mexican places of business, and here, at least, most adult Mexican heads of households now have steady work. Despite some tensions, life for the Mexicans has improved; if a Mexican wants to work, work is available. At the same time, energetic expats who may have come down here without a clear idea of what to *do* in their new home have found a new reason to get out of bed in the morning. It can be a virtuous cycle for both Mexicans and expats. In a word, volunteering takes on a special meaning down here because it takes place where it's most needed.

Though Mexico is considered the richest of all the Latin American countries, it's an open question how much is dispensed to sick and disabled children. Mexico has thirteen billionaires, but in my twenty-eight years in Mexico, I never heard of their billions building and subsidizing new hospitals or opening new schools. (I'm not saying they haven't; just that I've never seen any local evidence of it.) It took Canadian and American volunteers to do that.

There was no trade school in Ajijic. A group of Canadians proposed to build one; American expats joined in and agreed to contribute funds, and the project took off. Volunteer participation went beyond fund-raising: many put in ten-hour days working alongside Mexicans. It was finished, swiftly accredited, staffed, and opened in 2004.

Another point of pride in **Chapala** is the Old Folks Home. It was originally begun years ago by an American couple. After their deaths, the home went into Mexican hands and became just another empty, dilapidated building. Eight years ago, an American widow took on the job of bringing it back to worthiness. With volunteer funds, she re-opened it to a capacity of forty Mexican elderly folks. She receives an annual payment of $50—total—from the Mexican government to go toward feeding, housing, clothing, and providing medical care for elderly in the home. She got one or two local markets to donate their unsold produce, secured the services of a couple of Mexican doctors to attend to their medical needs, and rebuilt the structure with the help of expat volunteers.

Each charitable group is run like a business; this appeals to former fast-track North Americans used to the organized work they once did in the States. They are busy and productive again. They elect officers and decide where and how to dispense funds and volunteer effort. The biggest subcommittee, perhaps unsurprisingly, is tasked with organizing fund-raisers that will bring in the crowds.

And so the parties go on—and on. All the important American, Canadian, and Mexican holidays are an occasion to have a fund-raiser. One week they may throw a "Black and White Ball," where the women put on their party best, the men dress in tuxes—and a few Scots arrive wearing formal kilts. Another week it may be a "Ginger and Fred" dance, the floor prize going to the best dancers. "Back to the Fifties" dinner dances are popular, and there is competition for open weekends by sixties and seventies aficionados.

For many, the fund-raisers are a social scene they are only too happy to join. For others, the interminable rounds are a drag. A common phenomenon I observed was "social burnout," which caused expats to retreat from the scene, or, in some cases, to return to the U.S. Nevertheless, many who left wrote that they found themselves volunteering in the States because of habits they picked up in Mexico.

Much of the volunteer work is done by expats working solo. There is the retired carpenter who teaches boys the art of cabinetmaking; a retired computer programmer who teaches computer use; the artist who holds classes for children and sells their work to locals and tourists, the proceeds going to the young artists themselves.

Those who retire find that, after a period of doing what they thought they wanted—kicking back and doing nothing in the sun—they become eager to do something productive again. This combination—a system that discourages paid work by foreigners; an undefended social services sector; a population truly in need; and foreign residents who want meaningful work—comes together to make volunteering a central part of "retiring" abroad.

Ruth Merrimer lived in Ajijic, *Lake Chapala, for twenty-eight years, covering the expat beat for local publications.*

Acknowledgments

We wish to thank the hundreds of expats and international travelers who gave us so much time, practical advice, and great stories over the past four years. Although bylines accompany each country chapter, we want to express our gratitude to our contributing writers, as well as to the many expats who freely answered our questionnaires so generously—and vividly. In Mexico, *gracias* to Barbara Kirkwood and Eileen Pierce. In the States, thanks to Michael Pixley for the maps; Paul and Cindy Prewitt for advice; my nurturing agent, Ellen Geiger; and of course our editor, Beth Wareham, and associate editor, Whitney Frick, at Scribner, and our copyeditors Kathleen Rizzo and Phil Bashe.

The Charts

Americans Living Abroad: Selected Countries
From the Bureau of Consular Affairs

Compiled in July 1999. Does not count U.S. military or government personnel.

Note: *Since so many Americans live overseas part-time, or in multiple locations, or without registering with consulates, these numbers are decade-old approximations at best. They especially do not reflect the numbers of Americans believed to be moving to Latin America since 1999.*

This list is meant only to give a *relative* idea of the pattern of expatriation. How many are retirees is unknown; the vast majority are assumed to be Americans working for local or international firms.

Argentina	27,000	Honduras	10,000
Bahamas	7,000	Italy (four cities)	170,000
Barbados	12,000	Mexico (nine cities)	1,000,000
Belize (one city)	3,000	Nicaragua	5,000
Costa Rica	20,000	Panama	20,000
Croatia	2,000	Philippines	100,000
Dominican Republic	82,000	Portugal	2,000
Ecuador (two cities)	13,000	Spain	100,000
France (three cities)	105,000	Thailand	20,000
Greece (two cities)	72,000	Uruguay	3,500

Quality of Life: Countries

Selected from the Economist Intelligence Unit
(Numbers in parentheses = rank on overall lists)

Best to Worst
Based on costs versus average wages, crime, health, available goods, and services
- Measured in 2005
- Out of 111 countries

- Ireland, Switzerland #1 and #2
- Worst: Iraq and Zimbabwe

Italy (8)	Greece (22)	Argentina (40)	Croatia (49)
Spain (10)	France (25)	Thailand (42)	Ecuador (52)
USA (13)	Mexico (32)	Philippines (44)	Nicaragua (76)
Canada (14)	Barbados (33)	Uruguay (46)	
Portugal (19)	Costa Rica (35)	Panama (47)	

Quality of Life: World Cities

Selected from Mercer Surveys

Best to Worst
(Economic and political strength, freedoms, climate, distribution of health care, food, housing)
- Measured in 2007
- Zurich, Switzerland, and Geneva, Switzerland, ranked #1 and #2; Baghdad, Iraq, last #215
- Out of total of 215 countries

Paris, France (33)	Buenos Aires, Argentine (79)
Lyon, France (34)	Panama City, Panama (92)
Barcelona, Spain (41)	San José, Costa Rica (106)
Madrid, Spain (42)	Pula, Croatia (107)
Lisbon, Portugal (47)	Quito, Ecuador (118)
New York, U.S. (48)	Manila, Philippines (123)
Milan, Italy (49)	Mexico City, Mexico (188)
Rome, Italy (61)	Managua, Nicaragua (170)
Montevideo, Uruguay (76)	San Pedro Sula, Honduras (180)
Athens, Greece (78)	

Ranking of Health Systems

Selected from the World Health Organization (WHO)

Best to Worst
- (a) general health level, (b) health inequalities, (c) system responsiveness, (d) distribution of responsiveness (how system serves all people), (e) proportionate costs
- Out of a total of 191 countries
- Last surveyed in 2000. Latin American countries, especially Mexico and Panama, considered to have improved.

France (1)	Canada (30)	Philippines (60)	Panama (95)
Italy (2)	Costa Rica (36)	Mexico (61)	Ecuador (111)
Spain (7)	USA (37)	Belize (69)	Honduras (131)
Portugal (12)	Croatia (43)	Nicaragua (71)	
Greece (14)	Thailand (47)	Argentina (75)	

Total Crimes per Capita

Selected from UN Survey, 2000

Highest <u>Reported</u> Crimes to Lowest

(Special Note: *This list is a better indication of <u>crime reporting</u> than of actual crimes.*)

- Out of 60 countries surveyed
- Largest *total* of crimes reported: USA

U.S. (8)	Italy (19)	Uruguay (30)	Greece (45)
Canada (12)	Portugal (21)	Mexico (39)	Thailand (45)
France (14)	Spain (28)	Costa Rica (41)	

Cost of Living: World Capitals

Selected from Mercer Surveys

Lowest to Highest
- Measured in 2006
- Most expensive city in world: Moscow

Buenos Aires, Argentina	Mexico City, Mexico
Manila, Philippines	Pula, Croatia
Montevideo, Uruguay	Melbourne, Australia
Quito, Ecuador	Athens, Greece
San José, Costa Rica	San Juan, Puerto Rico
Santo Domingo, Dominican	Madrid, Spain
Republic	Miami, U.S.
Panama City, Panama	Paris, France
St. Louis, U.S.	Milan, Italy
Lisbon, Portugal	New York, U.S.

Perception of Corruption

Selected from Transparency International (www.transparency.org)

Least Corrupt to Most Corrupt
- Measured in 2006
- Out of 163 countries surveyed
- Finland, Iceland, New Zealand #1
- Worst: Iraq, Myanmar, Haiti, #163

Canada (14)	Italy (45)	Panama (84)
France (18)	Greece (54)	Argentina (93)
USA (20)	Costa Rica (55)	Dominican Republic (99)
Spain (23)	Thailand (63)	Nicaragua (111)
Portugal (26)	Croatia (70)	Honduras (121)
Uruguay (28)	Mexico (70)	Philippines (121)

Global Peace Index

Selected from Vision of Humanity

Most Peaceful to Least Peaceful
(Measures twenty-four indicators, including ease of access to guns, military expenditure, local corruption, war and conflict, homicide, and the level of respect for human rights.)
- Out of 121 countries measured
- Norway #1
- Russia, Israel, Sudan, Iraq, #118 to #121

Canada (8)	France (34)	Nicaragua (66)	USA (97)
Portugal (9)	Greece (44)	Croatia (67)	Honduras (98)
Spain (21)	Panama (45)	Mexico (79)	Thailand (105)
Costa Rica (31)	Argentina (52)	Ecuador (87)	

Appendix 2

Trend Spotting

A Chat with the Professor of Expatology

At fifty-seven, sporting a ponytail and the look of a rock musician (which he was), David Truly, PhD, is undoubtedly a leading expert on the behavior habits and patterns of North American retirees in Mexico—in **Lake Chapala,** to be exact. A short ride from **Guadalajara,** "Lakeside" is a chain of small villages around a picturesque body of (sadly, polluted) water, inhabited by an estimated 25,000 gringo retirees, more part-time. It's thought to be the largest single group of retirees outside of American and Canadian borders. Truly, whose doctorate is in geography and is affiliated with Central Connecticut State University, has lived in the Lakeside village of **Ajijic** with his wife and two young children.

In academic terms, Truly has been conducting a one-of-its-kind "longitudinal analysis of international retirement migration." In plain English: Who *are* those expats? It's a specialty that only a mother—or perhaps a prospective expat—could love. Truly has researched the region's expatriate habits over a ten-year period, interviewing hundreds of expats and Mexicans in the area. His studies, still underway in early 2008, are the first in-depth look at the movements of retirees across borders, at the types of people who become expatriates, and at what they do after they've moved. His findings are specific to Mexico but have something to say to North Americans considering moves to retirement destinations worldwide.

There are three types of expats, says Truly.

1. Negatively selected: They feel they had to leave the U.S. for social, political, or cultural reasons. They reject American values and have an affinity for the Mexican lifestyle. Many of them tend to shy away from gringos and instead integrate into Mexican society. These would be the least likely to return to the U.S. or Canada at any time in their life. "They're the ones who say, 'America's broken.' 'Something's missing up there that you can find down here.' They like the way kids are looked after, how grandparents are respected, how life is enjoyed in the slow lane."

2. Positively selected: They're not dissatisfied with the United States, but they *love* the Mexican lifestyle. They want an adventure, a better quality of life. "There's something there that's going to make me better," they say.

379

3. The importers: They love the U.S., and don't care much for the Mexican lifestyle, so they import their U.S. lifestyle down here. They're here because it's cheaper, warmer, and whatever American amenities they don't import, they can buy at Big Shops that have appeared after NAFTA. They point out all the imperfections, but some do change. NAFTA basically created this group.

Truly says there are two other trends, not yet concrete enough to make it onto the matrix, but clearly observable:

1. The disenfranchised: They don't like *anything*. They came down here, have no money, got stuck, don't go anywhere. Some can be found at the American Legion posts, grumbling about everything. They never change.

2. The moving-on expat, the kind who arrives seeking the safety of other Americans—becoming active at the Lake Chapala Society, for instance—but then pulls back, fleeing to smaller, more isolated villages to get away from all the other gringos.

Chapala has a history of welcoming U.S. expatriates, Truly says, which began in the 1940s, when Americans moved down here on their GI bills. It therefore has a more established infrastructure than some of the boomtowns that Americans are moving to now.

Chapala's initial gringo population consisted of educated, mobile, open-minded people who were willing to give up some of the modern conveniences for the more traditional Mexican lifestyle. Studying migration records going back ten years, Truly found that the people who stayed, who met their expectations, were those who had visited the area repeatedly before moving there, who didn't try to buy and flip a property, who contributed, who were unafraid to put down roots. The rest moved back or moved along.

Today it's the boomers. "Boomers redefined everything," Truly says, "and they'll redefine retirement." By this he means that expats settling in *Lake Chapala* may not be settling down for good. "Many boomers aren't traditional: they are more active and more willing to try new things; they aren't tied to tradition. They say, 'We'll do this for a while and then . . .'" The pattern Dr. Truly says he is seeing is expats who move to an established retirement venue like **Chapala,** but use it as a gateway—before scattering someplace else, someplace new.

He says this kind of flexible retirement pattern isn't entirely new with the boomers. He knows a woman who lived in **Ajijic** for twenty-five years, and at ninety-one, her children moved her back to be with them in Savannah, Georgia. After a year, at ninety-two, the woman moved back to **Ajijic** with her children's blessing. Why? "Because my kids loved me and knew I was happier here."

Truly reflects on what he thinks motivates this newest wave of American migrants. "I'm getting the sense that it's not just about the lower costs . . . or about the climate," he says. "It's about the potential for a second life, for reinvention, for the opportunities available at fifty-five and sixty. It's a chance to make a new 'career' of living somewhere else. Some come down for the first year or so, it's like a vacation. Then they wake up and say, 'What am I going to do for the rest of my life?' Here, any kind of new start is possible—become an artist, become a writer."

With the increased numbers, there are certainly Americans who can "spoil" it for the old-timers—the arrogant, the ones who expect to live like lords on a pittance. "I saw one the other day," says Truly. "An American guy walks into the local bank and becomes outraged and abusive because there's no one around who speaks English." He says these people will not be happy, and will probably move. "The ones who will make it are those who want to *learn* something."

Truly says he is finding evidence of "tensions" between expats and locals. He says he sees it less in **Chapala,** with its long history of living side by side, than in villages and towns where the economy shifted overnight from fishing and farming to tourism or servicing retirees. "It's been too sudden," he says. "In the old days—ten years ago—gringos would become patrons of Mexican families. They would employ them in their households, yes, but they'd send their kids to school, pay their doctors' bills, teach them to bartend, help them open their own restaurant. Now it's more about cheap labor."

Still, he agrees with the expats we interviewed elsewhere in Latin America (and in Europe), who spoke of finding "greater freedoms" abroad. "There are fewer rules outside the U.S., it's less restricted," says Truly. "If there's any place where there's free-market capitalism going on, it's Mexico. The challenge will be to figure out how to avoid destroying the intangibles people came down here for—the beauty of nature, the pace of life. This could all change very quickly unless we're careful."

Resources

Introduction

This is your homework. We've broken down resources into a general section, applicable to expatriates anywhere, and specific country resources. The general includes U.S. State Department sites, nonofficial sites, search engines, and books and magazines both informational and inspirational. The specific are individual country resources, which cover their websites, embassies, books, and newspapers.

This is by no means exhaustive, but it can serve to distinguish some of the genuinely useful sites from the thousands of sites whose main purpose is to promote real estate or tourist activities. (Where real-estate-oriented sites also provide helpful information, we say so.)

What we *don't* cover:

- Local tourist sites, for the most part.
- Specific newspapers, for the most part. But we urge you to search for publications in your country because they are among the most recent sources of information for local rents, activities, etc. Happily, you can find all of them gathered on two sites listed below.
- Online forums such as Yahoo Groups. They can be very useful, but are subject to frequent change and, if you're not careful, can be sources of unfounded rumors. Generally speaking, search for groups under titles such as "Living in Panama," and so on.
- Any book, publication, or website whose content was produced earlier than 2005.

GENERAL RESOURCES

Introductions to the Expat Universe

Government Sources

U.S. Department of State Home Page
www.state.gov

"Country Background Notes" on the land, people, history, government, political conditions, and foreign relations of each country.

INTERNATIONAL TRAVEL SECTION OF BUREAU OF CONSULAR AFFAIRS
www.travel.state.gov
"A–Z Country Index" contains country-specific information on locations of U.S. embassies/consulates, health conditions, crime and security issues, and travel advisories.

"A–Z Index of Topics" lists rules and regulations on every aspect of living abroad from pets to pandemics—including sobering topics such as marriage, divorce, and death while residing overseas.

INTERNAL REVENUE SERVICE
www.IRS.gov
Consult for general tax information, including countries that have treaties with the U.S. regarding income earned abroad. (See "United States Income Tax Treaties A to Z.")

Books

Buying a Property Abroad by Ben West and John Howell
Soup-to-nuts information on the best in-country locations to buy and build houses and ways to deal with the red tape.

The Expert Expat by Melissa Brayer Hess and Patricia Linderman
Best for how to manage the relocation process and cope with your new environment.

The Grown-up's Guide to Running Away from Home by Rosanne Knorr
Knorr's follow-up book to *The Grown Ups Guide to Retiring Abroad* (published in 2001). Full of "dare to dream" inspiration and hands-on instruction.

How to Retire Abroad by Roger Jones
Checklists and advice for all phases of moving and living overseas.

Leaving America: The New Expatriate Generation
by John R. Wennersten
A thoughtful examination of the philosophical and practical reasons for changing countries.

Patients Beyond Borders by Josef Woodman
Guide for overseas health care choices with detailed information on hospitals worldwide and data on U.S. and regional accreditation. Includes recommended centers for specific medical/surgical procedures and hospital accommodations.

Retiring Abroad by Ben West
Country profiles, practicalities of daily living, and property information from renting to buying. British-oriented.

Working Abroad: The Complete Guide to Overseas Employment
by Jonathan Reuvid
   Centered around job relocation for non-retirees, but useful financial, banking, and tax advice for any expat.

General Websites

AARP INTERNATIONAL
www.aarp.org/intl
   This section deals with the political and social issues and initiatives related to older populations worldwide.

ASA, INC.
www.asaincor.com
   Offers short-term travel insurance and expat-geared long-term health insurance.

BUPA INTERNATIONAL
www.bupainternational.com
   One of the world's largest providers of medical and health insurance for expats.

ESCAPE ARTIST
www.escapeartist.com
   You have to wade through relentless real estate promotions, but this site is considered one of the most comprehensive resource portals.

EXPAT AND CHANGE
www.expatechange.com
   A large online community for English-speaking expats.

EXPAT FORUM
www.expatforum.com
   Features chat rooms, message boards, and a useful "Cost of Living" section for twenty countries.

EXPAT STUFF
www.expatstuff.com
   Lists countries worldwide with links to expat communities, general daily life advice, real estate, forums, etc. Spotty coverage: some countries have extensive, useful, and current sites; others just have sparse menus.

INTERNATIONAL LIVING
www.internationalliving.com
   International Living is both a magazine (subscription only) and a website (some free access), covering all aspects of worldwide retirement possibilities. Caveat: it also promotes its own real estate in popular destinations. But yearly

features "Global Retirement Index" and "Quality of Life Index" are the best one-stop shopping for comparing countries you're considering. They also hold conferences in countries they cover, offering lectures by local lawyers, developers, and so on. We attended a conference in Mexico and, although there was a lot of soft sell in the air, the information provided was practical and useful.

LIVING ABROAD
www.livingabroad.com
   A site with extensive listings of forums and expat-centered links. Registration (free) is necessary.

NEWSPAPERS WORLDWIDE
www.onlinenewspapers.com
   Links to newspapers abroad, including those published in English.

OVERSEAS DIGEST
www.overseasdigest.com
   Good sources for working, entrepreneurship, and financial strategies. Links to more than one thousand newspapers. Good up-to-date resources for the range of real estate prices, both for buying and renting.

TALES FROM A SMALL PLANET
www.talesmag.com
   Personal accounts from expats and extensive links to forums, financial, health insurance, and job websites.

TRANSITIONS ABROAD
www.transitionsabroad.com
   Well organized with easy navigation to extensive websites on living, working, studying, and volunteering abroad, including links to rental listings in all countries.

WORLD NEWSPAPERS
www.world-newspapers.com
   Comprehensive links to newspapers, magazines, newsletters, and news websites around the globe, including those published in English.

Language Instruction

A constant theme in conversations with compatriots is "I wish I'd learned to speak the local language." Audio and videotapes are one answer. These make our cut:

THE PIMSLEUR LANGUAGE PROGRAM
www.pimsleurapproach.com
   The best for absolute beginners. Easily digestible, thirty-minute audio lessons. No books, written exercises, or drills. You listen to phrases and repeat them. Through repetition you build up simple, but satisfying, conversation.

RosettaStone
www.rosettastone.com
    This system is "intuitive," using image and word associations. The computer "recognizes" what you say and corrects any mistakes. Interactive, without memorization or grammar drills, moves along at a quicker pace than the Pimsleur method.

COUNTRY-SPECIFIC RESOURCES

Belize

Official Resources

Embassy of Belize in the U.S.
www.embassyofbelize.org

Consulate General of Belize in the U.S.
www.belizeconsulatela.org

Embassy of the United States of America in Belize
http://belize.usembassy.gov

Canadian Embassy/Belize Representative
www.guatemala.gc.ca

Consulate of Belize in Quebec, Canada
Email: dbellemare@cmmtl.com

Belize Tourist Board
www.travelbelize.org

Books

Living Abroad in Belize by Lan Sluder
    Comprehensive information on every aspect of daily life with surveys of prime living locations and an extensive contact/resources section.

Moon Handbooks: Belize by Josh Berman
    Specifically a Belize travel guide, but valuable for what to do there and how to do it.

Online

Belize First
www.belizefirst.com
    Online magazine with news and articles on travel and daily life.

Websites for Popular Expat Locations

Ambergris Caye
www.ambergriscaye.com

Corozal District
www.belizenorth.com

Placencia
www.placencia.com

FORUMS
www.belizeforum.com
www.ambergriscaye.com/forum

Costa Rica

OFFICIAL RESOURCES

Embassy of Costa Rica in U.S.
www.costarica-embassy.org

Consulate of Costa Rica in Washington, D.C.
www.costarica-embassy.org/consular/consulates/default.htm

U.S. Embassy in Costa Rica (also consulates)
www.usembassy.or.cr

Embassy of Costa Rica in Canada (also consulates)
www.costaricaembassy.com

Government Tourist Board
www.visitcostarica.com

BOOKS

Living Abroad in Costa Rica by Erin Van Rheenan
    Comprehensive information on every aspect of daily life with descriptions of prime expat locations and an extensive contacts/resources section.

The New Golden Door to Retirement and Living in Costa Rica
by Christopher Howard
    Perennial bestseller from expat author who also conducts well-regarded tours of favorite residential areas.

ONLINE

Association of Residents of Costa Rica
www.arcr.net/
    Nonprofit service organization with voluminous information on relocating and daily living, real estate, retirement, health care, and links to expat forums.

Casa Canada Group
www.casacanada.net
    A financial and legal services business. But also posts valuable, current

information on the laws, rules, and regulations on banking, real estate transactions, income tax, insurance, and other topics.

Costa Rica Pages
www.costaricapages.com

Portal for information on real estate, jobs, investments, retirement, community affairs. Includes informative descriptions of major expat communities and areas.

The Tico Times
www.ticotimes.net

The most influential English-language newspaper, covering everything from tourism to politics with special emphasis on expat readers' interests and activities.

Vacation City
www.vacationcity.com

The framework is a soft-sell real estate and tourist site. But the "General Information" section is well organized, with detailed reporting on dozens of daily life topics, local news, activities, and the cultural scene.

Women's Club of Costa Rica
www.wccr.org

Very active group of expats and locals that raises funds for scholarships, social service programs, and volunteer projects.

Croatia

Official Sources

Embassy of Croatia in the U.S. (including Consular Affairs section)
www.croatiaemb.org

Embassy of U.S. in Croatia (including Consular Affairs information)
http://zagreb.usembassy.gov

Embassy of Croatia in Canada (including Consule General section)
www.croatia.visahq.com/embassy/canada

Embassy of Canada in Croatia (including Consular Affairs section)
www.geo.international.gc.ca/canada-europa/croatia/menu-en.asp

Government of the Republic of Croatia
www.vlada.hr

Government website covering political and economic news, with historical, cultural, and tourist information and links to associated sites.

Croatian National Tourist Board
www.croatia.hr/english

Well-organized, expansive site covering destinations, events, accommodations, travel logistics, and many other tourist interests. An extremely useful source with many applications to living in, as well as traveling to, Croatia.

Books

Croatia by Jeanne Oliver
Reliable guide from the Lonely Planet series. Bonus: buyers can access the author's Croatia blog for queries and advice.

Let's Go Eastern Europe 13th Edition by Let's Go Publications
Practical, but knapsacky guide for your first visit to Croatia and its neighbors.

Rick Steves' Croatia and Slovenia by Rick Steves and Cameron Hewitt
Excellent all-around information from the popular travel guru. Includes itineraries useful for scouting out possible retirement locations.

Online

Croatia Estate
www.croestate.com
A real estate site, but useful for comparing locations and property/rental costs on the mainland and the outlying islands.

Ideal Croatia
www.idealcroatia.com
Combination of information on travel, tourism, moving to, and living in the country. Also has real estate classifieds and links to other services.

Visit Croatia
www.visit-croatia.co.uk
General tourist information with good descriptions of the various better-traveled areas.

France

Official Resources

Embassy of the U.S. in France (also consulates)
http://france.usembassy.gov

Embassy of France in Canada (also consulates)
www.ambafrance-ca.org

Embassy of Canada in France (also consulates)
www.dfait-maeci.gc.ca/canada-europa/france

France Guide (French Government Tourist Office)
www.franceguide.com
Anything you want to do, anywhere in France.

Books

Chasing Matisse by James Morgan
U.S. expat encounters France by following the artist's trail.

Living Abroad in France by Terry Link
  Comprehensive information on every aspect of daily living with descriptions of prime expat locations and extensive contacts/resources section.

Living in France by Patricia Mansfield-Devine
  British-oriented and authored; full of insider advice with a stiff upper lip.

Retiring in France: A Survival Handbook by David Hampshire
  Plainspoken guide to the pleasures and pitfalls of how to retire full- or part-time in France.

Working and Living: France by Monica Larner
  Comprehensive guide organized with in-depth information for each of the different regions.

ONLINE

AngloINFO
www.angloinfo.com
  Combination business/organization directory, online market/meeting place, and daily living guide. Organized by sections for individual country "departments."

Bonjour Paris
www.bonjourparis.com
  Well-established insiders guide to the usual and unusual attractions in Paris.

Expatica Communications
www.expatica.com
  Online survival guide for moving to and living in France. Includes news, features, forums, and blogs.

France USA Communications
www.fusac.fr
  A bimonthly magazine (and website) listing classified ads and services: a "yellow pages" for English speakers in Paris.

Hot Retirement Spots
www.hotretirementspots.com/france
  Use this site to get more information on the various departments of France you are checking out. Has good links to tourist boards and other resources.

Parler Paris
www.parlerparis.com
  Gateway information to living, working, and investing in France with good sources for property rentals.

Resources

Italy

OFFICIAL RESOURCES

Embassy of Italy in the U.S. (also consular services)
www.ambwashingtondc.esteri.it/

Embassy of the U.S. in Italy (also consular services)
http://rome.usembassy.gov

Embassy of Italy in Canada (also consular services)
www.ambottawa.esteri.it

Embassy of Canada in Italy (also consular services)
www.dfait-maeci.gc.ca/canada-europa/italy

Italia
The Italian Government Tourist Board
www.italiantourism.com

BOOKS

Living Abroad in Italy by John Moretti
All the usual how-to information, with special emphasis on navigating the infamous Italian bureaucratic red tape and scoping out favorite retirement areas.

Living and Working in Italy (3rd Edition): A Survival Handbook by Graeme Chesters
Practical advice for newcomers of any age including all the nuts and bolts on essentials of daily life.

Working and Living Italy (2nd Edition) by Kate Carlisle
While oriented to families, transferred employees, and so on, the basics covered apply to any expat. Useful section describing the varied regions of the country.

ONLINE

AngloINFO
www.angloinfo.com
Combination business/organization directory, online market/meeting place, and daily living guide. Organized by sections for individual countries.

Boomer Stuff
www.boomerstuff.com
Links to expat communities, profiles of popular communities, assorted daily living advice.

Dream of Italy
www.dreamofitaly.com
A travel newsletter focusing on tourism not living, but a good resource for finding the pleasures of Italy rather than just the logistics of residence.

Expats in Italy
www.expatsinitaly.com
   Info center and forums written by expats. Emphasizes consulting your Italian consulate to get a grip on the formidable paperwork necessary for extended stays.

Italy House Scout
www.italyhousescout.com
   Established source for buying and renting houses in recommended areas throughout Italy.

See You in Italy
www.seeyouinitaly.com
   If you decide to buy a property (after you rent there, of course), this is a reliable source for favorite expat locations in Tuscany and Umbria.

Wanted in Europe
www.wantedineurope.com
   Best for guides to residential areas, cultural news, and ads for extended-stay accommodations in Rome and Milan.

Mexico

OFFICIAL SOURCES

Embassy of Mexico in the U.S.
www.embassyofmexico.org

Embassy of U.S. in Mexico
www.usembassy-mexico.gov

Embassy of Mexico in Canada
www.mexico.gc.ca

Embassy of Canada in Mexico
www.vec.ca/english/10/embassy-ottawa.cfm

Official Government Site for Tourism
www.visitmexico.com

BOOKS

Choose Mexico for Retirement (10th Edition) by John Howells and Don Merwin
   A guide for retirement, travel, investment, and affordable living.

Falling . . . in Love with San Miguel by Carol Schmidt and Norma Hair
   Not a how-to procedural: a personal exploration (the positives and negatives) about adapting to and enjoying a new culture.

Gringos in Paradise: An American Couple Builds Their Dream House in a Seaside Village in Mexico by Barry Golson
   Ahem. May we immodestly recommend it?

Head for Mexico: The Renegade Guide by Don Adams
A complete manual for every aspect of daily life. Intensely personal, anecdotal, and funny, but doesn't skimp on the how-tos and what-ifs.

How to Cash In on a Second Home in Mexico by Tom Kelly and
Mitch Creekmore
How to buy, rent, and profit from property south of the border. Plus locations (old standbys and up-and-coming) which the authors think will appreciate over time.

Living Abroad in Mexico by Ken Luboff
A good first book for an overview of Mexico. Very readable with comprehensive practical advice and a feel for the lifestyle in big cities and small towns.

Midlife Mavericks: Women Reinventing Their Lives in Mexico
by Karen Blue
Single women's accounts of uprooting their lives and rebuilding them south of the border. These stories are inspirational and cautionary, joyful and rueful—and always candid about the pleasures and the pitfalls of re-creating yourself.

The People's Guide to Mexico by Carl Franz and Lorena Havens
www.thepeoplesguidetomexico.com
Widely regarded as the best guidebook to Mexico, valuable for retirees as well. Its website is a wealth of information and a breezy guide to other expat sites.

Online

Adventures in Mexico
www.mexico-newsletter.com
Advertiser free, subscription newsletter on information about budget travel and affordable retirement. One of the earliest and still one of the best.

Canadians Resident Abroad
www.canadiansresidentabroad.com
Information on the financial (taxes, banking, investments, etc.) implications of living in Mexico, Central America, and other countries.

Inside Mexico
www.insidemex.com
A valuable exception to the typical, tourist-centered site. "Inside Mexico" (free online) covers meaningful issues (cultural, political, economic, etc.) relevant to expats or locals. A weekly newsletter alerts you to the best of what to do and where to go.

Mexico Connect
www.mexconnnect.com
Arguably the best internet resource dedicated to Mexico. Covers (or has links) to every topic you'll need, with expats and locals who contribute regular columns. Free stuff, but the best is by subscription.

Mexico Online
www.mexonline.com

All things Mexican from consular alerts to cooking classes to customs regulations. Also chat rooms to reach out for specific advice from expats on-the-ground.

Mexperience
www.mexperience.com

Good site for new and old residents, with general overviews and more in-depth reports than most about travel, daily life, real estate, working, etc.

Mexico Guru
www.mexicoguru.com

In the case of this site, "opinionated" is a good thing. The "Best of" list is a great place to start to explore the country, as are profiles of retirement areas and a quiz to see where you'd fit in and enjoy the lifestyle.

Websites for Popular Areas to Live In

Baja Insider
www.bajainsider.com

Not necessarily aimed at retirees, a rich, well-organized resource site on everything Baja.

Los Cabos Guide
www.loscabosguide.com

Informative guide to **Cabo San Lucas, San Jose del Cabo,** and **Todos Santos,** with many links to area resource links.

Baja Expo
www.bajaexpo.com

Good resource covering all the states in Baja with hundreds of associated links.

Café Cancun
www.cafecancun.com

Smart reporting and a good resource guide to the area.

Focus on Mexico
www.focusonmexico.com

The *Lake Chapala*/Ajijic area is the most gringo populated in Mexico. This site explains all the reasons why and (surprise!) even offers an eight-day tour of the area.

Guadalajara Reporter
www.guadalajarareporter.com

Local news with classifieds and rental listings.

Living at Lake Chapala
www.mexico-insights.com

Like having your smartest friend show you the ropes about moving to and enjoying life in the **Ajijic** and **Guadalajara** areas. A subscription site, worth it.

Sayulita Life
www.sayulitalife.com
  The authors' personal favorite, with news, views, and real estate in a small village on Mexico's Pacific coast.

Portal San Miguel
www.portalsanmiguel.com
  Useful information (art, restaurants, etc.), maps, photos, contacts, and links to this perennially popular charmer.

Vallarta Today
www.vallartatoday.com
  Puerto Vallarta news, features, and real estate properties.

Yucatan Living
www.yucatanliving.com
  Expats living, working, and playing in **Mérida** and the **Yucatán**. Good combination of news, features, and classifieds.

Nicaragua

OFFICIAL SOURCES

Embassy of Nicaragua in U.S.
www.consuladodenicaragua.com

Embassy of U.S. in Nicaragua
http://nicaragua.usembassy.gov

Embassy of Nicaragua in Canada
www.nicaragua.embassyincanada.com

Embassy of Canada in Nicaragua
www.dfait-maeci.gc.ca/sanjose/mngua-en.asp

BOOKS

Christopher Howard's Living and Investing in the New Nicaragua
by Tim Rogers
  Information and advice, as well as investing tips, though you'll need to update yourself online as to the current political scene.

Moon: Living Abroad in Nicaragua by Randall Wood and Joshua Berman
  The best places to live and worthwhile information from expats on the ground. Includes a detailed list of resources and contacts.

ONLINE

Expat Communities and Forums
www.expatcommunities.com/nicaragua-expatriates.html
  Collection of useful links to chat rooms and message boards.

Discover Real Estate in Nicaragua
www.discovernica.com
    A starting point for rentals and property in Managua and other regions.

Nicaragua.com
www.nicaragua.com
    Huge, all-purpose site covering everything you need to know about tourism, travel, culture, forums, etc. Lots of information and well organized.

Nicaragua Living
www.nicaliving.com
    Site with general information, forums, blogs, book reviews, and some frank reporting on the actualities of life in an emerging third world country. Can be time-consuming to search for the useful entries.

Sojourn in Nicaragua
www.nicaraguasojourn.com
    Small but useful site to check out the Granada area. Good section on volunteering opportunities.

ProNicaragua
www.pronicaragua.com
    A not-for-profit site promoting the economics of investing in and doing business with Nicaragua.

San Juan del Sur
www.sanjuandelsur.org.ni
    Decent area guide with accommodations and real estate listings.

Panama

OFFICIAL SOURCES

Embassy of Panama in the U.S.
www.embassyofpanama.org

Embassy of the U.S. in Panama
http://panama.usembassy.gov

Embassy of Panama in Canada
www.vec.ca/english/7/embassy-panama.cfm

Embassy of Canada in Panama
www.dfait-maeci.gc.ca/panama

Official Tourist Office
www.ipat.gob.pa/?id

BOOKS

Choose Panama . . . the Perfect Retirement Haven (2nd Edition)
by William Hutchings
    A good retirement-planning tool with all the usual information. Includes personal reflections on the sometimes ambivalent position of expats outside their own culture.

Living in Panama (2nd Edition) **by Sandra T. Snyder**
    The "bible" for living in Panama. Covers every phase from relocation and daily life concerns to a sensitive introduction to the people and their culture. Excellent resource lists at the end of every chapter.

Living and Investing in Panama **by Christopher Howard**
    While not as comprehensive as other, similar books, you can round out your research with this book and its take on investment potential in Panama.

Moon Handbooks: Panama (2nd Edition) **by William Friar**
    This is a travel guide, but many expats now favor the more rural areas of the country and the author gives readers a real feel for nonurban communities.

RADIO BROADCASTS

Window 2 Panama
www.window2panama.com
    English-language programs on living in Panama from Boquete on 103.5 FM to the U.S. and Canada.

Panama Broadcasting Corporation, S.A. Radio Metropolis
www.pbcpanama.com
    English-language broadcasts including Sunday night show hosted by *Living in Panama* author, Sandra Snyder.

ONLINE

American Chamber of Commerce & Industry in Panama
www.panamcham.com
    A coalition of business and civic groups that promotes economic and financial development.

The American Society of Panama
www.amsoc.org
    A charitable organization of U.S. and Panamanian businesspeople, retirees, and others who work for and fund volunteer activities countrywide.

Century 21 Semusa Realty
www.semusarealty.com
    Under the umbrella of a real estate website, well-organized and objective information is provided: from cost of living charts, to lists of organizations and societies, to a summary of retiree benefits.

Expat Women
www.expatwomen.com
   A bit hit-and-miss, but search through for some useful links to organizations, forums, and various women's groups.

Gateway to Panama
www.gatewaytopanama.com
   Information for the first-time visitor with an eye toward retirement. Gives general tourist sites and links to professional service providers.

Welcome to Who's New of Panama
www.wnpan.org
   A not-for-profit group that "provides orientation assistance, and promotes friendship and culture among women of all nationalities."

Panama Guide
www.panama-guide.com
   The most trafficked news and resource site covering Panama from every angle. It has more than six thousand articles and a steady stream of current events. If there is a controversy affecting expats, this site is all over it.

Panamainfo
www.panamainfo.com
   More than a tourist resource, this site also features facts on business structure, retiree benefits, the cultural scene, and living areas.

Portugal

OFFICIAL SOURCES

Embassy of Portugal in the U.S. (also consular services)
www.portugal.com/portugal/embassies

Embassy of U.S.in Portugal
http://lisbon.usembassy.gov

Embassy of Portugal in Canada (also consular services)
www.embportugal-ottawa.org

Embassy of Canada in Portugal (also consular services)
www.geo.international.gc.ca/canada-europa/portugal/embassy/ambassador-en.asp

Official Government Site for Travel and Tourism
www.portugalemb.org

BOOKS

The Complete Guide to Buying Property in Portugal by Colin Barrow
   This guide has a chapter on renting with general and legal advice. Interesting topic: buying a home in a retirement village for the fifty-five-plus set; an option worth checking out.

Living in Portugal by Anne de Stoop

Logistics and lifestyles arranged under each of the major regions of the country, a convenient system for would-be expats to compare various living areas.

Working and Living: Portugal by Harvey Holtom

Practical information and in-depth knowledge by an expat with a welcome sense of humor.

ONLINE

AngloINFO

www.angloinfo.com

Combination business/organization directory, online market/meeting place, and daily living guide. Organized by sections for individual country regions.

Expats Portugal

www.expatsportugal.com

Forums, blogs, classifieds, rentals, and general info for newcomers and old-comers.

Portugal Info

www.portugal-info.net

Mainly a tourist site, but has a forum section where expats from all the popular areas weigh in with advice and information.

Welcome to Expat

www.expat.silvert.org

Very "ear to the ground" site with links vetted by a veteran expat guru.

Spain

OFFICIAL SOURCES

Embassy of Spain in the U.S. (also consular services)
www.spainemb.org

Embassy of the U.S. in Spain
www.embusa.es

Embassy of Spain in Canada (also consular services)
www.embaspain.ca

Embassy of Canada in Spain (also consular services)
www.canada-es.org

Official Government Site for Tourism
www.spanish-fiestas.com

Books

Living and Working in Spain, 7th Edition: A Survival Handbook
by David Hampshire
Read this for current information in the Living section. The Working section fairly represents the difficulties of employment or entrepreneurship.

Moon: Living Abroad in Spain by Nikki Weinstein
Spain has gotten more crowded and more expensive. This follow-up to the author's previous *Living Abroad in Spain* updates information on the prime locations and the costs of living and housing.

Retiring in Spain: A Survival Handbook by Joanna Styles
Practical, step-by-step guide to making the move and creating the lifestyle as a retiree. Good advice on renting in the prime areas.

Working and Living: Spain (2nd Edition) by Harvey Holtom
A frank look at the delights and dilemmas confronting a newcomer. The verdict: if Spain is your cup of sangria, the hurdles can be overcome.

Online

AngloINFO
www.angloinfo.com
Combination business/organization directory, online market/meeting place, and daily living guide. Organized by sections for individual country region.

Easy Expat
www.easyexpat.com
General information on relocation and settling in with more emphasis on families than retirees, but has useful all-purpose links to daily living topics.

Expat Stuff
www.expatstuff.com
Links and information on all aspects of daily life, expat communities, and profiles of popular areas with real estate listings.

Spanish Living
www.spanish-living.com
Mix of tourist, cultural, and daily living information. Real estate section has listings for fifty-plus retirement complexes, which are an understandably attractive option for many expats who want "turn-key" housing.

Index